MW01702749

MONIQUE WAGNER

ENERGY HEALING

345 Techniques & Strategies
to Unlock Cosmic Energies for Spiritual Transformation

ACHIEVE HOLISTIC HEALING WITH

NUMEROLOGY · ASTROLOGY · REIKI · CRYSTALS · CHAKRA BALANCING

ALL IN 1

Table of Contents

THE 7 PILLARS OF NUMEROLOGY

57 Techniques to Decode How Numbers Like Your **Birthday** Affect Your Life and Destiny. A Beginner's Ultimate Guide to **Spiritual Meaning** of Numbers for Everyday Living

MONIQUE WAGNER

Table of Contents

Introduction

There is so much mystery surrounding the origin of numerology, but the most famous myth suggests that the practice began in Pasargadae, an ancient Persian city. Pasargadae was built by the Greek demigod Perseus and his wife, Andromeda, queen of Ethiopia. Their first son Perses was born in 706 B.C.E. *(The History of Numerology, 2022)*. When he turned six, he began complaining about his name. Perses' parents did not take his complaints seriously until a stranger heard the boy muttering along the palace grounds one day. The stranger, cloaked and dirty, asked if he could speak to the boy's parents. Unconvinced of what such a beggar could do for him, Perses thought he would humor the stranger's request and invited him inside the palace to meet his parents. Upon meeting Perses' parents, the stranger unveiled himself. He was Poseidon, the god of the sea. He claimed that from then on, the boy would be called Kourosh Jahangir Hakhamanesh, or Achaemenes, and he would one day form the Achaemenid dynasty.

The parents accepted the change but laughed at the thought of their overbearing son forming such a strong dynasty. To them, it was impossible. Yet, they did not know that Achaemenes' soul, body, and personality were numerically reprogrammed according to his new name.

Achaemenes became intelligent and charismatic. He was thoughtful in his words and wise in his world philosophy. His body changed, and he grew a handsome face and muscular physique. Perseus was astounded and awed by his son's change of character, making his 10-year-old son co-ruler of Pasargadae. Achaemenes did not disappoint. He was a great leader. He gave inspiring speeches and found ways to make and keep his people wealthy, happy, and well-fed. He gave his people freedom of speech and religion. At age 16, Achaemenes was crowned king of Pasargadae *(The History of Numerology, 2022)*.

Rumors of Achaemenes' kindness spread throughout the world. Various kingdoms longed to join him, feel his protection, and witness his greatness. Thousands of people also aspired to lead the same lifestyle he offered.

With his growing dynasty, Achaemenes met again with Poseidon. Astounded by the changes within him, Achaemenes asked Poseidon what spells he had cast to help him obtain such greatness and so many loving followers. Poseidon then shared a sacred secret with Achaemenes—the secret of numerology.

Everything in the universe has a vibrational frequency. This resonance of certain numbers with our vibrational patterns is then studied by numerology.

Numerology can help you find meaning and direction. It can help you understand your past and reflect on why your path in life has been complex. And through numerology, you can look ahead and change your future.

We all have a destiny dictated by vibration patterns. These vibration patterns coincide with the vibrations of the numbers zero to nine. Once you know what number coincides with your particular vibrations and what this number means, you can change it. When you change your personal, unique set of numbers, you change your vibrations and your future.

After Achaemenes, other great leaders came into power, all equipped to use numerology to control their lives and the fates of those around them. In 549 B.C.E., a king called Darius rose to power. He formed the largest empire in the world, stretching over 35 countries from Egypt to China. Then in 520, he renamed his kingdom and changed the vibrations surrounding his empire's destiny *(The History of Numerology, 2022).* His kingdom became one of the most innovative, wealthy, and peaceful empires the world had ever seen. Seeing the benefits of numerology for himself, he chose to share the sacred secret with his empire and educated thousands of people.

As the years went on, Poseidon watched the growth of these cities with love and adoration. However, not all the gods felt this way. In 380 B.C.E., a god intending to end the human race visited Darius. He convinced him the Achaemenid Empire would grow if he changed his name *(The History of Numerology, 2022).*

The god showed Darius a sequence of numbers far more complex than Darius could understand. Trusting the god, he chose to change his name, and less than a year later, Alexander of Macedonia invaded and overthrew the Achaemenid Empire. During the invasion, temples and universities were destroyed, and the numerology books they housed were lost.

Survivors of the once-great empire fled to India, where they became known as Parsis. Today, they have tales of numerology that would captivate even the biggest skeptics. And although they no longer have access to the expanded details of numerology, they have enough wisdom to change a life.

Numerology looks into the connections between numbers and the cosmos, shedding insight into our journeys. Ergo, everything in life has an essence of predictability. The rain on your head and the chance to meet the love of your life are all events you can control. You were destined to be here and have an impactful purpose: you are not a spontaneous cosmic creation. This is your journey, and it is full of potential.

Life has many challenges. Numerology can guide your understanding of these challenges and your expectations in life. But if you are still unconvinced that numbers mean anything at all besides the value they hold, there is one thing that this book can offer you: hope.

I will admit, when I first started learning about numerology, I thought, "Really? How can I foresee my life before it is even started? Why would a higher power even allow this? If he did allow this, how could I possibly understand the meaning of any of it? All this must be a sham. Every calculated answer is simply a vague suggestion of something a million people could go through." I might have been doubtful at first, but it did not take long before I came to believe in the potency of numerology. Perhaps it is true; then again, perhaps not. However, it would seem that one can create the reality that one chooses, particularly in numbers.

In my early years, I was desperately seeking answers to understand the suffering I had endured. At the time, I was reading about numerology in the hope that it could give me some explanation. I did not find the answers I wanted, not in the beginning anyway, because I was not yet a believer. But as I continued to read about numerology, I gained ideas and hope for my future. My chart told me I should be doing something creative, traveling, and helping people. These were not things I had thought of before, but the more I looked into these ideas, the more that I consider them. I was unaware I had been passing up on opportunities that could have made a difference. Unbeknownst to me, there are opportunities out there that could have been a game-changer.

As I grappled with the implications of all this, it slowly dawned on me that numerology had provided me with numerous possibilities for the future; it had been an invaluable source of inspiration. From there, I left my previous job where my hard work and dedication went unappreciated and unrecognized— no more toiling away in obscurity. Instead, I looked forward to other opportunities that are personally stimulating and motivating. And with these realizations, I felt like I had been given a new lease on life. In the following weeks, I was astounded by how content I was while undertaking activities I never expected to do. This had nothing to do with my faith in numerology but the pure joy of doing something new.

I believe that numerology is designed to help you, similar to how it had helped me, and through this book, I'd like to share with you what I've learned about this practice. You will find 57 techniques, tips, and strategies on how the numbers in your life can help guide you to success, decode the spiritual meaning of each number, and reveal how they influence your life and destiny. These techniques, tips, and strategies are peppered throughout the entire book. And it's intentionally designed this way to serve as your guide along each step of the process.

This book will guide you through the pillars of numerology and explain how they shape your understanding and interpretation of numbers. You will find the science behind the theories and practical advice that you can readily apply to your life and relationships. In these pages, you will find a vivid history of the ancient past merged with whimsical ideas and mathematical sequences.

Moreover, as we dive into the power of numerology, you will learn to interpret numbers, create charts, understand the meaning of your given name and birth date, and discover the vibrations that impact your relationships and decisions. The first pillar will cover the fundamentals, while subsequent chapters will focus on teaching different theories and techniques to get incredible results. Know about powerful vibrations that can shape the energy of your relationships. By employing different theories and techniques in each chapter taught in this book, you can sharpen your intuition, understand the motivations of others, and increase your confidence in making important life decisions.

You will likely see incredible results in better understanding yourself and those around you.

With the help of this book, you'll learn how to tap into your inner power, get in touch with your higher self, discover your divine purpose, and put yourself on the pathway of spiritual awakening. It has the information you need to get started.

Our lives are often full of stress and adversity, something I know all too well, as I once suffered from terrible burnout myself. As an empath that came from a Scandinavian background with neo-pagan roots, I have learned how to face these struggles without relying on medication. In my devotion to understanding alternative healing practices, I have collected knowledge from both metaphysical methods and occult traditions. Sharing the expertise gained over a lifetime of experience is now my way of helping those who are in need of healing.

Numerology can guide you with any difficulties or decisions you may face. The answers are already within your grasp. Begin your spiritual journey with this book and let its teachings help you find them.

Pillar 1:
Fundamentals

Chapter 1:
Origins

Pythagoras

Do you remember learning about triangles in your high school mathematics class? If so, you will recognize the name, Pythagoras. You would have spent hours analyzing triangles and trying to allocate their measurements to letters using a formula known as the Pythagorean theorem. Perhaps at the time, you thought there was no need to measure the angles of triangles. What purpose did this mathematical formula have in your everyday life?

In fact, triangles and Pythagoras have great importance in our lives. One spiritual meaning that a triangle symbolizes is the three intricately linked systems of the past, present, and future. In the practice of numerology, understanding these systems give us insights into the reasons behind our behaviors and identities, show us how to become something entirely different if we choose to, and why we may decide against it.

But how did Pythagoras discover numerology? Where did his concept of using the triangle to understand our lives originate? We can muse over the myth that gods and goddesses were the primary providers of numerology, but how true is it? Is there more to the story?

Pythagoras believed that there was more to life than simple coincidental existence. He believed that, with the precision of the universe, coincidence could not exist. And that every single thing on this earth had an underlying purpose. Nothing was existential, and everything that played out is part of destiny.

According to ancient sources, Pythagoras was born in 570 B.C.E. to a well-off family of merchants in Samos, Greece *(Joanna, 2022)*. His father was a jewel carver, and his mother was a native of Samos island. Pythagoras lived in a well-educated and creative family setting. Throughout his life, even in early childhood, Pythagoras traveled extensively. He spent much time in Egypt, where he learned from various philosophers, religious people, and great leaders. Pythagoras devoted his life to pursuing knowledge, fascinated by possibility and reality. This fascination is a driving force behind his life that he supported with philosophy and mathematics. The tale of the Achaemenid Empire also influenced Pythagoras, prompting him to develop an entirely novel approach to numerology. However, his system was never created with humans in mind. Instead, it was designed to analyze patterns of the universe and the Earth's constant changes due to the interference of the cosmos. Pushing the boundaries of knowledge and understanding, Pythagoras endeavored to gain insight into the behaviors and dispositions of Earth. His systems had a sole focus, not to study humanity's reason for existing but to predict and comprehend our environment more accurately.

It was speculated that around 480 B.C.E., Pythagoras and his followers fled to Metapontum following persecution *(Blakeley, 2022)*. It was unclear how he died, but following his death, his work was seized and hidden due to its politically threatening content. Even so, this did not stop renowned philosophers from referring to his teachings in an attempt to escalate their ideas.

Plato and Aristotle

A Greek philosopher called Plato started the first academy, where he used many of Pythagoras' teachings within the scholarly content. Similarly, Aristotle used Pythagoras' ideas on numerology, metaphysics, and math to better understand the universe and the earth as a geocentric model, a center-lying planet in a constantly moving universe.

More students converted to the Pythagorean way of life and attempted to share his work with the world. Their ravings created a power conflict between Pagans, Catholics, and Christians. The ruling Christian church believed that the practices of numerology, astrology, and divination were forms of magic and proof of the devil's existence. As a result, they destroyed numerology books, schools, and teachings.

The Middle Ages

Building on the ideas of Pythagoras, belief in destiny was a powerful concept during the Middle Ages, and numerology was seen as a way of deciphering its secrets. And despite the many decades that have gone by since then, numerology has managed to stay relevant and continue to stand the test of time.

In the years since its destruction, Pythagoras' teachings moved to Byzantium and formed a large portion of the growing Islamic faith. Those educated in numerology, or Kabbalah, were held in high regard because they housed the knowledge of destiny, divination, and how to change one's life course. Kabbalists were like Pythagoreans because they believed that all life was a manifestation of the numbers one to nine and that each letter of the Hebrew alphabet corresponded to a number *(Abbot, 2021)*. Therefore, every letter in a person's name and every number associated with their life has significance. This significance is in the form of a vibration which matches a specific trait or experience. By determining this likeness, one can understand who they are and their reason for existing.

Numerology became heartily accepted by magicians, occultists, and even some religious leaders during the Middle Ages.

The First Mother of Numerology

In 1847, Mrs. L. Dow Balliett was born. She was a student of both the Bible and Pythagoras *(Drayer, 2003)*. Accordingly, she took it upon herself to add further depth and understanding to the Westernized approach to numerology. As alluded to by Pythagoras, each number between one and nine has an intrinsic vibration or tone, much like musical notes, that form the building blocks of life itself. Throughout her life, she worked to enlighten people and help them improve their lives by making choices associated with their number systems. Her system became known as the Balliett system.

The Second Mother of Numerology

Mrs. L. Dow Balliett was renowned for her work and teaching many philosophers who adopted and developed her ideas. At the young age of 14, Dr. Juno Jordan had the privilege of studying under Mrs. Balliett, with whom she went on to modernize numerology. Her innovative work made it clear that numbers have souls and attribute akin to humans, ultimately bringing this branch of science to life in the Western world.

Dr. Juno Jordan and Mrs. L. Dow Balliett were two of the most influential figures in the history of numerology. Their contributions to the field were connected in several ways.

Numerology Today

Numerology has been modernized to fit our more contemporary lifestyle. We live in a different time than those before us, one in which we possess individual traits and destinies that are uniquely ours. Pythagoras believed in reincarnation, suggesting that we have repeatedly returned to fulfill the same purpose. In this current life, however, we have new goals that only we can achieve in our lifetime. Together, these experiences allow us to embrace our destiny like never before so we may shape a unique and tangible purpose for ourselves.

Discovering who you are in this life, your connection with the divine, and learning lessons from previous experiences can help pave the way to changing your destiny and finding your purpose. By understanding the larger picture, you can take charge of your life and create a future that aligns with your visions.

Chapter 2:
Science

Perhaps, you are curious about finding proof beyond mere tales and uncertain accounts.

Numerology is not an exact science but draws from scientific theories and beliefs. At its core, the concept proposes that everything in the universe has a numerical value, a personality, and a purpose. Though scientists may be unable to use statistical evidence to support numerology's predictions, descriptive data from those who have used the practice are a testament to its power and potential. Faith in the spiritual connection between all things is at the heart of numerology's philosophy.

From how much money is in our bank accounts to the number of children we have, numbers touch all aspects of life. Our finances can dictate where we live and how much we spend when shopping. Additionally, the hours worked contribute to our income and the state of our relationships. Even something seemingly inconsequential as our birth date, impacts us since it correlates with astrological signs that can affect personality. All in all, we constantly interact with numbers, and they help shape the scope of our lives.

In life, our names conceal a number that defines who we are and our purpose. Yet, if fate has already decided the course of our lives, where does free will come in? It may be hard to believe that something as simple as numbers can have such an immense impact on us. Whereas if everything is predetermined, how can we make any changes?

According to some numerologists, life is just like a game of Monopoly. We are born after consulting with our advisors and deciding the timing and location of our birth. Our characters, residences, potential allies, and enemies are all chosen in advance. Ultimately, we determine who we might team up with or leave behind. But once the game has kicked off, it is up to us to choose when we invest in a property, embark on an adventure, or decide if we would rather shell out cash to be set free or take our chances with a get-out-of-jail-free card. When the game is over, we must move beyond simply passing "Go." That is how things are. But arriving there involves a mixture of predetermined elements and decisions that are up to us.

Numerology cannot tell you what small choices you will make; it would not anticipate if you will do something clumsy or turn down an opportunity. Nonetheless, it can give you insights into where you belong, your true self, and your dreams for life. Grasping your identity and understanding the why behind it can be incredibly liberating. And acceptance of that is an even greater power, unlocking many doors. Once you know where you are supposed to be, you can get there quickly. However, life without numerology is like playing Monopoly without knowing the rules. Navigating through it can be disorienting, even maddening. It may seem like you are just going around in circles and wasting time. But with knowledge of numerology, you can take action and make decisions that are meaningful, well-reasoned, and part of a larger design.

How It Works

Numerology is the practice of assigning numerical values to letters in order to analyze and understand the meaning behind a person's name or birthdate. Each letter of the alphabet is assigned a numerical value, and these values are added together to create a single digit number that represents a person's personality traits, life path, and more.

To calculate a person's name number, the numerical values of the letters in their name are added together and reduced to a single digit. For example, if someone's name is John Smith, their name number would be calculated by adding together the values of each letter in their name: J (1) + O (6) + H (8) + N (5) + S (1) + M (4) + I (1) + T (2) + H (8) = 36. Then, 3 + 6 = 9. Therefore, John Smith's name number is 9.

To calculate a person's birthdate number, their birthdate is broken down into individual digits and added together. For example, if someone was born on July 3, 1990, their birthdate number would be calculated as follows: 7 + 3 + 1 + 9 + 9 + 0 = 29. Then, 2 + 9 = 11. If the number is a master number, such as 11 or 22, it is not reduced further.

Numerology also involves the use of personal year cycles, which are calculated by adding the individual digits of a person's birthdate and the current year. For example, if someone was born on August 1, 1990 and the current year is 2022, their personal year cycle for 2022 would be calculated as follows: 8 + 1 + 2 + 0 + 2 + 2 = 15. Then, 1 + 5 = 6. Therefore, the person's personal year cycle for 2022 is 6.

Numerologists have created formulas for calculating the value of specific dates, events, and ideas. The theory suggests all numbers can be reduced to a single digit between one and nine. While the calculations themselves may be simple, the interpretation of these numbers requires knowledge and expertise.

Numbers Have Personalities

All numbers have specific properties, traits, genders, and meanings. A double-digit number containing two of the same digits is known as a "master number." Master numbers evoke spiritual powers in their owners. Numbers can be good, evil, masculine, feminine, light, or dark. They exist in the same space and have some differences. Look at them like a newborn baby who likely receives traits from both parents. Even an adopted child will share some characteristics with their caretakers. It was not possible to live for 20 years with someone and not take on similar ideas and attributes as theirs. Hence, numbers, inventions, thoughts, and ideas all have as much energy and potential for meaning as we do.

Meanwhile, the names of people, places, businesses, and countries can be transformed into numerical values, regardless of how many letters are in the alphabet or what language is used to speak. For example: "C" is three in English, while "B", "西", and "bh" are all three when spoken in Hungarian, Chinese, or Zulu, respectively *(Learn Languages, 2019)*. From that, it makes it possible to analyze these names without language-related barriers.

Likewise, birthdays and birth names are the most critical factors in predicting your destiny. Your life path number is the result of breaking down your date of birth into its last value. Furthermore, your soul, personality, maturity, and karmic numbers can be calculated from a similar equation, which we will discuss later.

Chapter 3:
Experiences

Kimberly

Kimberly lived a particularly unlucky life until she discovered numerology. She was lonely, had no money, no friends, and could not keep a job. After graduating from university, her father passed away. With her mother ill and unable to provide financial support, Kimberly was left with no choice in her career path. Out of gratitude for having a job, she accepted what came her way; however, three years of being unappreciated had worn her down and made her realize she needed to find something to make her happy.

One day while browsing the internet, she discovered a numerology forum and paid for a reading that changed her life forever. Desperately seeking something to believe in, she immersed herself in practice. After scrutinizing her number, she realized that certain scenarios were not coincidences. Her observations showed that when her numbers interacted with the environment, the results were destined to occur.

After exploring numerology, Kimberly uncovered a guide to her true self. This allowed her to discover the skills she possessed, what truly inspired her, and where she was headed in life. Once she knew, she made decisions to enable her to move forward toward her destiny.

She took part in and passed a course in software design. Her final results were outstanding and led to dozens of companies outsourcing her for her ideas and ethics. With her head held high, she attended several interviews over short months. While attending the interviews, she fell in love with the owner of a software company. The two were married a short while later and now have two sons. Both are extremely happy, confident, and passionate about their lives. It was all possible because of the growth she managed with numerology.

Taylor

Taylor was disappointed that her life was not going as she had envisioned. She felt lost and miserable in every aspect of her life, from work to home. Uselessly searching for something that could make her genuinely happy, she realized only emptiness would follow. Her days were mundane and foreseeable—a feeling she could not bear. Yet, when a friend visited one weekend, Taylor's perspective shifted when they discovered numerology. After calculating their numbers together, it seemed as if Taylor could truly understand herself from a deeper level than ever before.

Each of her traits, ideas, and experiences was there. The same occurred for her friend. Both had calculated profiles that matched who they were eerily. After the visit, Taylor borrowed her friend's books and started reading further into the practice. Taylor discovered that she was not suited to a repetitive environment but was meant to travel and dabble in the arts. She had always wanted to explore the world but never thought she could. Numerology pushed her toward following her dreams and artistic endeavors. It woke her up and helped her discover who she was.

The world tells us things, and our friends and family can sometimes instill something we are not. When we repeatedly tell ourselves this something, it eventually becomes an unshakeable truth in our minds. We can start to feel that what we have been saying to ourselves is true, even when it is not. Once we begin thinking a certain thought, it can become difficult to convince ourselves otherwise. But there is always that part of us that says, *"Is this really what I want? Is this really who I am?"* And that tiny part complains day and night, telling us we are unhappy. We get so used to being sad that we think it is a part of us. How often have you told yourself, *"That is how it is."*? Yet, these are lies. Life is not supposed to be too hard. Some people are happy and love their lives; you can be like them.

With numerology, you may discover your true self. It brings to mind our childhood aspirations and reminds us of who we once were. Through the practice of numerology, we can recall our hopes and dreams for the future.

Emma

At age five, Emma dreamt of performing like Bruce Springsteen as a dancer, actress, and role model for children. She would invite youngsters into a room and sing them her heart out, though it yielded few results. The kids were not interested in her festivities. It made her happy to try anyhow. But, as she grew older, the world told her that having a small audience was silly. Her voice was all right, but the dancing was a no-go. Unfortunately, strutting your stuff and constantly moving around on stage did not fit the idea of being "ladylike."

Struggling with ADHD and autism, she cocooned herself within a shell of protection. She strove to make her small teaching business thrive. Practicing humility, she never patted herself on the back despite her accomplishments. Eventually, her business made a hefty profit allowing her to buy a fantastic house and meet an incredible guy who could see through all the masks she had built up until then. He would ask her, *"Why do not you sing for me? Why do not you play the piano anymore?"* Her response was often a shrug and an excuse:

"No one wants to hear me play. It is too much effort for no reward." But deep inside, she knew that was merely a lie; she had been deceiving herself for years.

One day, a student came to her lesson and left behind a book. She picked it up and read the title, *"Numerology."* Emma browsed through every page and worked through every calculation in the book.

For Emma, it was like she was looking into a mirror painted with numbers. Gazing at her numbers, she realized she was destined to be an icon. But living in a bustling and affluent city, it seemed that no one could recognize her true identity. The numbers she embraced were at odds with those around her, and nothing could change that. It was clear that happiness would remain out of grasp for her there.

Before, Emma had always wanted to leave the city, but she had never been able to think of a valid reason to. Besides, who would like to move out of a big city where you make lots of money? However, as soon as she realized who she was, she knew what had to be done. She told her husband that her dream was to become a singer and could not be achieved in the city. Without hesitation, he got into the car, and they headed out to start anew in a small town in England.

Emma's destiny was to find herself cornered and then to find the courage to leave. It was her life's plan. She never knew that until she discovered numerology. Today, she has signed with a small record label in the UK and performs regularly at private events. She and her husband are happier than ever, and it is because of numerology.

Everyone's journey is unique and special; there must have been a reason you were brought into this world. This book can guide you on your quest to discover the true purpose of your existence. No matter who you are, you belong in this world. Trust yourself and find out what destiny has in store for you.

Pillar 2:
Systems

Chapter 4:
The Pythagorean Approach

Ever wondered what the future holds? Unlock your power to know everything about yourself and others with numerology. Create a chart and gain insight into what lies ahead. With this capability at your fingertips, you are capable of so much.

To become an expert in numerology and use its power, you first need to understand how to draw a chart. Start by drawing a triangle upside-down, then cut it into thirds horizontally. Next, you should draw a vertical line that cuts through the top two spaces, then two more vertical lines in each of the top boxes. In the end, your inverted pyramid should have seven sections. This inverted pyramid represents your Pythagorean numerology chart. In this chart, you will calculate your character and destiny *(Richard, 2020).*

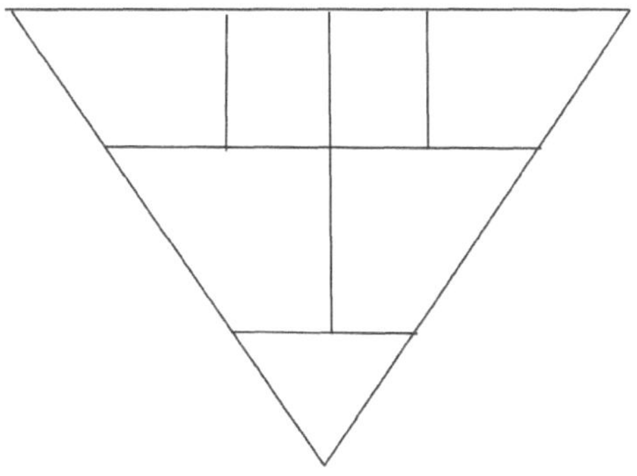

Root Number

Now that you have your chart, you need to calculate your Pythagorean numbers. Begin by noting your date of birth in the order of the day, month, and year. Make sure to write this value on the topmost point of the triangle.

For example, Michelle LaVaughn Robinson Obama was born on the 17th of January, 1964 *(Michelle Obama Biography, 2018).* This is how that date should be written:

17, 01, 1964

First, add her birthday digits and reduce them to their most basic value between one and nine.

1 + 7 = 8

Subsequently, write the number eight in the top far-left corner of your triangle. Following this, add her birth month numbers and reduce them. You can write this number to the right of her birthday number.

0 + 1 = 1

To start, the two digits of her birth year must be added and reduced. The outcome can then be written in the third box on the top row. Repeat this same procedure with the last two digits of her birth year, writing down the answer at the far-right corner of the top row.

1 + 9 = 10 = 1 + 0 = 1
6 + 4 = 10 = 1 + 0 = 1

The top of your triangle should read as follows:

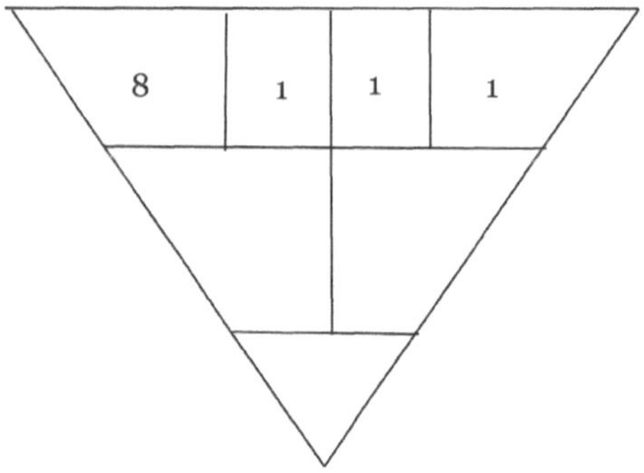

To reduce the right and left numbers, add eight and one together, then write the reduced number in the position below. Likewise, do the same for the other numerical values on the right.

8 + 1 = 9 and,
1 + 1 = 2

The second line of your triangle should read as follows:

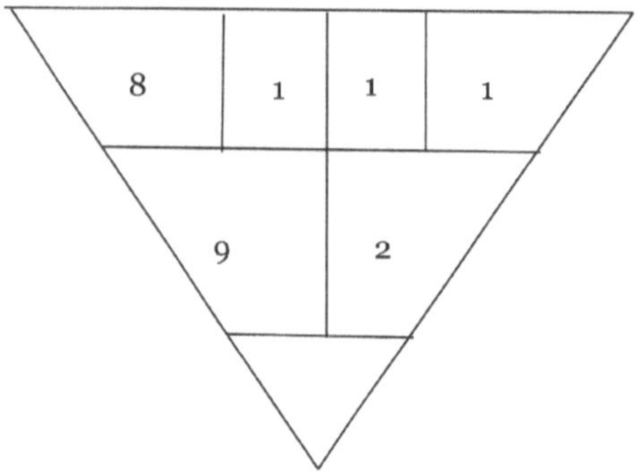

Lastly, you must add the two central digits and reduce them. You can write this value at the bottom of your triangle.

9 + 2 = 11 = 1 + 1 = 2

Your triangle should read as follows:

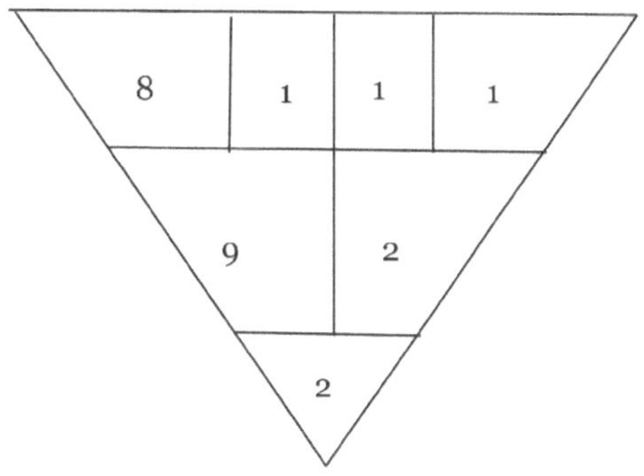

The last number you obtain is your root number. It plays a vital role in determining your destiny, the opportunities that come to you, and the obstacles you face. Moreover, it uncovers your unique identity and character. Thus, its impact on shaping our future is significant.

In numerology, the number two is a supreme feminine force. I do not know Michelle Obama personally, but that description sums up her media presence well. This number represents grace and power, peace and balance, and cooperation. The number two is one of the most intrinsically feeling numbers. If you are number two, you connect well with others.

Michelle Obama's numerology chart has already demonstrated truthfulness, which many people can connect with.

Have you ever wanted to learn how to calculate your external characteristics based on a triangular diagram? Look at Taylor Swift's birth chart for further insight and identify the numbers along the sides of the triangle. Let us dig in deeper and explore!

Taylor Swift was born on the 13th of December, 1989 *(Taylor Swift Biography, n.d.)*. We will begin by writing her birthday at the top of the triangle to ensure we make everything right.

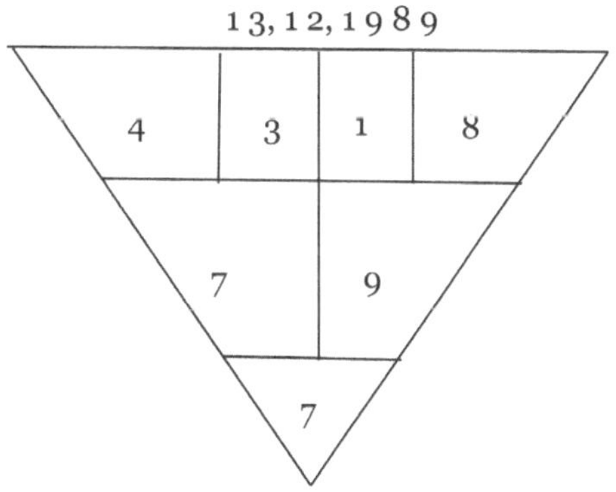

From here, we can go about calculating Taylor's root number. Add the numbers associated with her birthday and place them in the first space on the left:

1 + 3 = 4

After that, enter the digits associated with her birth month and write them in the second space:

1 + 2 = 3

Afterward, fill in the third slot using the first two digits of her birth year:

1 + 9 = 10 = 1 + 0 = 1

Lastly, you should add the last two digits and write them in the last space on the far right:

8 + 9 = 17 = 1 + 7 = 8

Add the value of the two left and right fields and write it in the field below. Then add these two fields together so that you end up with a final digit at the very bottom.

4 + 3 = 7
1 + 8 = 9
7 + 9 = 16 = 1 + 6 = 7

Taylor Swift has a root value of seven.

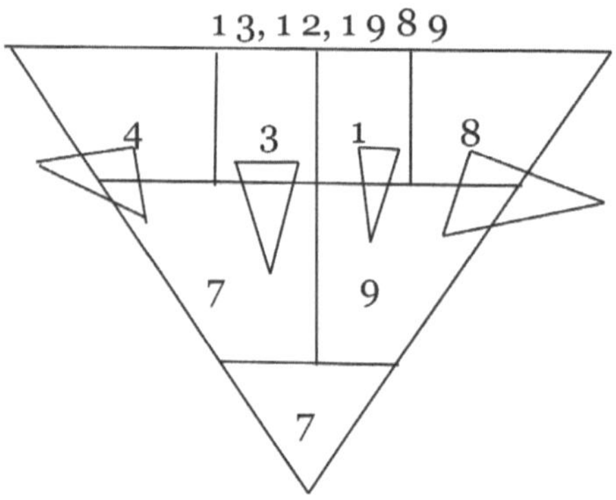

Now that you have determined Taylor's root number, envision mini upside-down triangles joining the numbers from the top row to those in the middle. First, take the number in the upper-left corner and sum it up with the one to its middle-left number:

4 + 7 = 11 = 1 + 1 = 2

Do the same process on the right side:

9 + 8 = 17 = 1+ 7 = 8

The next step is to take the number from the second box from the left and add it to the one in the middle-left section:

3 + 7 = 10 = 1 + 0 = 1

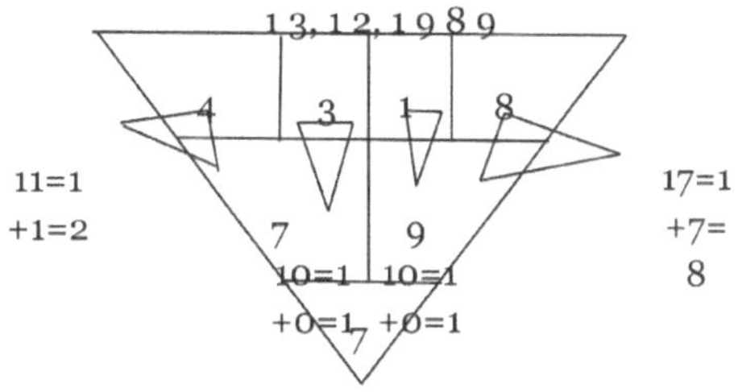

After that, carry out the same process on the right side:

1 + 9 = 10 = 1 + 0 = 1

When you have your numbers, add the ones on the left-hand side and reduce them to their simplest form. The same goes for the right-hand side, reducing them to their most basic value.

2 + 1 = 3 on the left and 8 + 1 = 9 on the right.

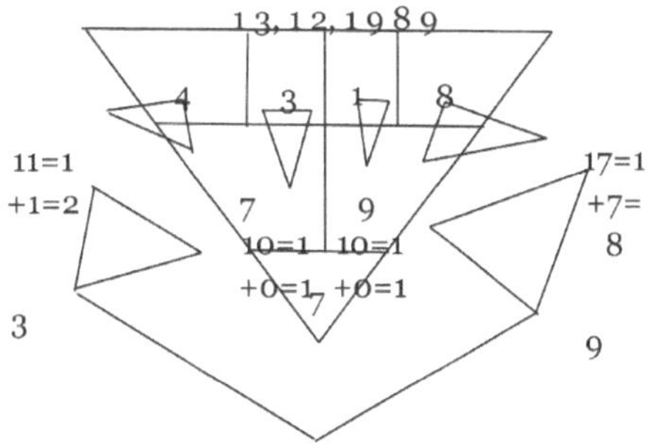

Finally, add these two numbers and reduce the result to its most basic form.

3 + 9 = 12 = 1 + 2 = 3

Taylor Swift has an expectancy number of three.

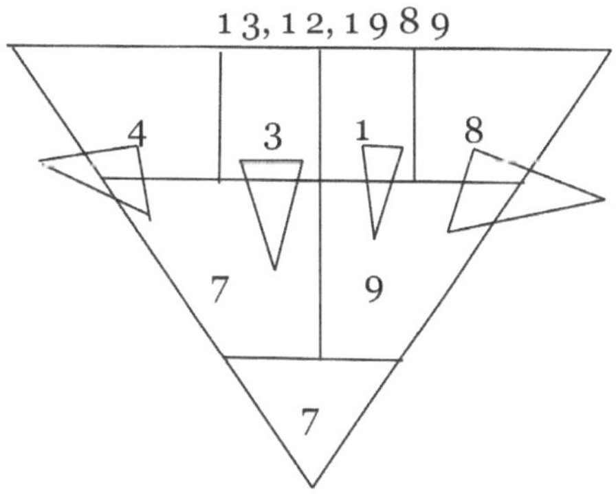

This number symbolizes who you are to others and what they expect from you. A number three is a vibrant, engaging, and amusing number that jumps joyfully and enthusiastically connects with other people. This number is so exhilarating that it has the potential to draw together romantic partners, friends, and those with the same interests. Judging from the behavior of Swift fans and media representations, the world views Taylor Swift as an iconic figure devoted to her music and fans.

Birth Number

The talents and potential that you hold can be uncovered with the help of your birth number. This number is so easy to figure out. All you need to do is add the digits corresponding to the day you were born. Having this number can help you to reach your destiny, as it encompasses the pieces of you that are essential for you to get there.

Let us take a look at Vincent van Gogh's birth chart. He was born on the 30th of March, 1853 *(Biography of Vincent van Gogh, 2009)*. The day of his birth is the 30th. To calculate his birth number, we will add these two values and reduce them to a root value:

$3 + 0 = 3$

The number three in numerology is often associated with creativity, self-expression, and the power of manifestation. It embodies enthusiasm, optimism, and the ability to communicate and express ideas. The number three resonates with the energies of the ascended masters and is considered the number of divine manifestation. Looking at Vincent's extraordinary flair for artistic expression, his innovative techniques, and his fervor for life, one might speculate if the vibrational energies of the number three influenced his journey. While there's no certainty that he was aware of his numerological significance, the universe, in its mysterious ways, often aligns numbers and destinies in synchronicity.

First Impression Number

Your first impression number is the number on the left in the middle row of your upside-down triangle. If you still remember, you can find this number by adding your day and month of birth together. Let us look at Ted Bundy's birth chart. He was born on November 24th, 1946 *(Lopez, 2021)*.

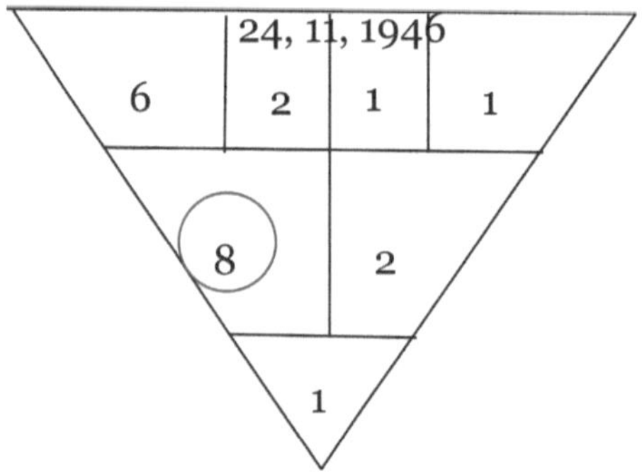

The number eight on the left is Bundy's first impression and portrays them in a successful light. With a keen eye for business and a Karmic sense, eight will pay back whatever he put into the universe. This number also speaks of how they see themselves and interact with the world. Ted Bundy believed that what he was doing was okay. For years, he was able to portray a "perfect boyfriend" image due to his charming looks. After his capture, Ted even took on his case for many trials. During this time, he played the role of a successful, balanced individual with perfect Karmic reasons for doing what he had done.

If his parents knew numerology, could they have stopped him? Could they have put a stop to the atrocities before they even began? Nowhere on any numerology scale does it say your career path will be a murderer, a singer, the wife of a president, or an artist. Our lives are predetermined to a certain extent, but the rest is free choice. Ted Bundy was destined to be a businessman, an independent, intellectual force. He was always going to do something charismatic. But Ted chose to be a killer even though he could have become the greatest president the world has ever known.

There is no way of knowing what decisions you will make. Yet, understanding yourself and how you relate to others can help you avoid destructive and hazardous scenarios, enabling you to live the life of your dreams. For such, numerology can give you insight which is somehow similar to you keeping away from a place because you know the potential destruction that the area can face. However, numerology would not provide you with specifics, like your little brother potentially being the one to cause the destruction. These details are beyond its capabilities, at least in Pythagorean numerology.

Soul Number

This number reveals your heart's greatest desires, the things you have always wanted, and the path that will lead you to your ultimate happiness. To calculate this number, you will need to find the numerical value of each vowel in your full name. Then, add them together and reduce that final number to its ultimate value between one and nine.

For instance, my name is Monique Wagner. The vowels in my name are O, I, U, E, A, and E. So, in Pythagorean numerology, every letter in the Latin alphabet is assigned a number from one to nine. To get the numerical value of each letter, count from one through nine and repeat the sequence:

1	2	3	4	5	6	7	8	9
A	B	C	D	E	F	G	H	I
J	K	L	M	N	O	P	Q	R
S	T	U	V	W	X	Y	Z	

Hence,

O = 6
I = 9
U = 3
E = 5
A = 1
E = 5

Let us put these together and discover my soul number:

$$6 + 9 + 3 + 5 + 1 + 5 = 29 = 2 + 9 = 11 = 1 + 1 = 2$$

Being an individual with a soul number two, I am fulfilled when connecting and helping others. And I am astounded by how accurately this mirrors me. Socializing and interacting with others also brings joy to me, as does making new friends and discovering different perspectives on life. From that, the sole purpose of this book is to help people find their way in life and connect with them on a deeper level. *What is your soul number? Does it accurately reflect who you are and what your true passions are?*

Character Number

People often look at your character number as an indicator of who you are and how you will be perceived. It is like a first impression, determined by the values of all the consonants in your name. Adding up the consonants and reducing them to their simplest form gives you your character number.

Let us use jazz singer Nina Simone's name in this example.

In February 1923, Eunice Kathleen Waymon was born (Nina Simone, n.d.) and later became an icon of the burgeoning Western jazz scene. Taking on the stage name Nina Simone, she flourished as a musician; only her friends knew her as Eunice. But in her daily life, *who was Eunice Kathleen Waymon to others? And who was she as Nina Simone?*

Eunice Kathleen Waymon has the consonants N, C, K, T, H, L, N, W, Y, and M. Now, let us use the chart to calculate the worth of each letter.

Thus,

$N = 5$
$C = 3$
$K = 2$
$T = 2$
$H = 8$
$L = 3$
$N = 5$
$W = 5$
$Y = 7$
$M = 4$
$N = 5$

Then,

$$5 + 3 + 2 + 2 + 8 + 3 + 5 + 5 + 7 + 4 + 5 = 49 = 4 + 9 = 13 = 1 + 3 = 4$$

As Eunice, she was rigid and decisive in all matters of morality, had a steadfast dedication to her work, and was not one to be diverted by the luxuries of life. She approached every task with great seriousness and commitment yet remained exceptionally composed and structured.

Considering if Nina Simone was different while performing, let us look at her name. While looking at the name of iconic artist Nina Simone, we see five consonants: N-N-S-M-N.

Accordingly,

N = 5
N = 5
S = 1
M = 4
N = 5

Lastly,

5 + 5 + 1 + 4 + 5 = 20 = 2 + 0 = 2

On stage, Nina Simone was a beacon of feminine power and beauty. She cared about her fans and wanted to have a connection with them. Her voice was not just an instrument of sound but a bridge that could bring together people, races, and communities.

When Nina took on a stage name, she modified how people viewed her and her destiny. Who she was on the stage was only sometimes who she was at home. By doing this, she allowed herself to be open to other individuals.

Expression Number

Uncovering your expression number can be an insightful experience. It reveals the talents, strengths, and abilities that are already inside of you. Knowing the value of each letter in your name, adding them together, and then reducing them to their most basic form is how this figure is achieved.

Now, let us embrace the knowledge and learn more about it by looking at a fictional character, Winnie the Pooh. We will see the uncanny parallel nature of Pythagorean numerology to characters invented by us.

Using the alphabet chart on the previous page, we will let it guide us.

P = 7
O = 6
O = 6
H = 8

Then,

7 + 6 + 6 + 8 = 27 + 2 + 7 = 9

Nine is characterized by completeness, unity, compassion, and usefulness. It yearns to spread joy and lend a helping hand to others. This number is perfect, holy, and spiritual and supports Karma. Reminiscent of Winnie-the-Pooh's values, nine stands for all these qualities.

Chapter 5:
Chaldean Methodology

The Chaldean numerology system is believed to have originated in ancient Babylon, around 4,000 years ago. The Chaldeans were a group of people who lived in southern Mesopotamia, in what is now modern-day Iraq. They were known for their advanced knowledge of astronomy, mathematics, and other sciences, and were instrumental in the development of the Babylonian civilization.

Their system is based on the vibrations and energies of the numbers 1 through 8, which are associated with specific letters of the alphabet. The Chaldeans used this system to predict the future, make important decisions, and gain insight into the personalities and characteristics of individuals.

Over time, the Chaldean numerology system spread throughout the Middle East and Asia, where it was used by various cultures and civilizations. It was later introduced to the Western world by the Greek mathematician Pythagoras, who is also credited with developing the Pythagorean numerology system.

This is how an Ancient Chaldean alphabet chart would be assigned numerical values *(The Surprising Ways, 2022)*:

1	2	3	4	5	6	7	8
A	B	C	D	E	U	O	F
I	K	G	M	H	V	Z	
J	R	L	T	N	W		
Q		S		P			
Y				X			

The Chaldean number system assigns them based on the sound when the letter is spoken (also called its vibration), instead of the position it has in the alphabet.

Today, Chaldean numerology is still widely used by practitioners and individuals seeking spiritual insight and guidance. Its unique approach to numerology, which takes into account the energies and vibrations of individual letters, sets it apart from other numerology systems and makes it a valuable tool for personal growth and self-awareness.

First, Second, and Third Names

Your first name can often give clues about your interests and habits. Then, your middle name holds your soul's energy, talents, and heartfelt desires. The last name may suggest how our friends and family influence us. Each element of your name carries a unique value linked to you and your destiny *(The Surprising Ways, 2022).*

Let's take the example of the full name "Michael Jordan" to demonstrate how to calculate and interpret the Chaldean numerology value:

M = 4
I = 1
C = 3
H = 5
A = 1
E = 5
L = 3

J = 1
O = 7
R = 2
D = 4
A = 1
N = 5

Adding these values together gives us:

4 + 1 + 3 + 5 + 1 + 5 + 3 = 22 (Master number)
1 + 7 + 2 + 4 + 1 + 5 = 20 (Reduced to 2)

Therefore, the Chaldean numerology value of the full name "Michael Jordan" is 22/2 (depending on whether or not we reduce the master number).

According to Chaldean numerology, individuals with a name number of 22 are believed to be powerful manifestors and visionaries who can achieve great things on a global scale. They are often natural leaders with a deep desire to make a positive impact in the world. Individuals with a name number of 2 are seen as intuitive and diplomatic, with a strong desire for harmony and balance in their relationships; characteristics that Michael Jordan exude.

The Rearranged Birth Number

The Chaldean system focuses specifically on the day of birth rather than on the month and year *(The Surprising Ways, 2022)*. Now, let us look at Albert Einstein's birth number in this example.

Einstein was born on the 14th of March, 1879 *(Albert Einstein Biography, n.d.)*. The significant number here is 14, which can be reduced to 5. Both numbers 14 and 5 give us an accurate reading of Einstein's destiny and character. In fact, having the number 14 can bring luck in finances. Those blessed with this figure can expect wealth and riches to follow.

Based on that, Albert Einstein was a German theoretical physicist who had accumulated $65,000 by the end of his life. Today, that money is worth $634,000 *(Albert Einstein Net Worth, n.d.)*. To compare that, the average American between 60 to 70 years of age has about $266,000 *(Wang, 2022)*. Einstein had almost three times that. He was not Elon Musk with $222 billion, but he was better off than most *(Jin & Oguh, 2022)*.

Meanwhile, number five suggests that Einstein was a creative man who loved to travel. By analyzing Einstein's travel diaries, one can see that he was a man who traveled a lot and enjoyed doing so. He was also known as a creative genius. From there, without a doubt, the Chaldean method of numerology is one of the most detailed and accurate systems to use. However, there may be limitations to its usage.

Chapter 6:
Kabbalah Numerology

It was believed that before the beginning of time, God gave ancient knowledge to the angels. This ancient knowledge was known as the Kabbalah. The angels first delivered it to Adam, the first man. When God told Adam and Eve to leave the Garden of Eden, Archangel Raziel gave Adam a second chance. This second chance allowed him to acknowledge his reason for existing. With the knowledge of his strengths and weaknesses, God empowered Adam to craft a competent and instinctive race. However, they became more intrigued by what the Earth had to offer and how they could benefit from it than by the ways of the Lord.

Around 1700 B.C.E., Archangel Melchizedek gifted Abraham with the Kabbalah *(Slick, 2008)*. With this ancient knowledge, Abraham spoke with God and made a covenant with Him. God asked Abraham to find the Hebrew people. In return, God promised to make the Hebrews and Abraham great and blessed peoples. As promised, the Hebrews became a great nation. Meanwhile, Abraham had the power of the Kabbalah and God on his side when he fulfilled his covenant with Him. Unfortunately, after Abraham's descendants were enslaved in Egypt, the Kabbalah was again lost.

Finally, years later, Moses went to Mount Sinai to meet God and receive the Ten Commandments. God gifted Moses with the Kabbalah. This time, God had placed the Kabbalah in the right hands. Moses protected the Kabbalah and its teachings but paid the price for it. Many of Moses' followers who participated in Kabbalah practices were persecuted and tortured. Due to that, the Kabbalah was practiced and taught through whispers in the dark. The practice was originally a male oral tradition and later changed to incorporate a wide range of people *(Slick, 2008)*.

According to the writings, Rabbi Akiva discovered the first book containing Kabbalah teachings in a cave believed to be God-given. To make these teachings accessible to more people, he rewrote them into a work called the *Sepher Yetzirah*. Centuries later, Moses de León wrote another book based on scrolls purportedly belonging to Abraham. He reinterpreted and rearranged the original practice into an alternative interpretation *(Slick, 2008)*.

For centuries, books have explored Hebrew Kabbalah numerology with the help of mathematicians, philosophers, and religious leaders. This practice encourages us to "receive" to consider our true meanings, strengths, and weaknesses, how to improve ourselves, and our purpose on earth. By doing so, we can live a more fulfilling and joyful life.

Kabbalah Energies

Kabbalah numerology places great importance on the names of people and living things rather than their numerical value alone. By decoding the value of someone's birth name, they can unlock their future, solve existing challenges and even prevent them from occurring. Understanding Kabbalah Numerology involves ten distinct energies: Kether, Chokhmah, Binah, Chesed, Geburah, Tiphareth, Netzach, Hod, Yesod, and Malkuth. These energies are best represented in a Tree of Life diagram, which reveals insights into the true nature of each energy type.

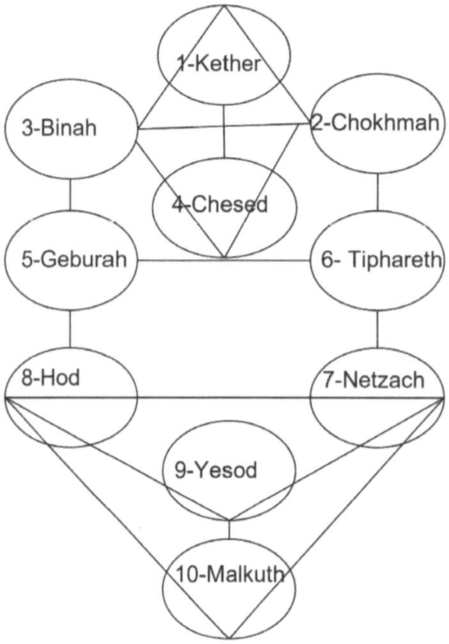

Each of the ten energies is associated with a numerical value *(Kabbalah Numerology, n.d.)*:

Kether = 1
Chokhmah = 2
Binah = 3
Chesed = 4
Geburah = 5
Tiphareth = 6
Netzach = 7
Hod = 8
Yesod = 9
Malkuth = 10 = 1 + 0 = 1

Knowing where your energy is in comparison to other energies is essential. Location can provide insight into the collective and individual effects of the energy and its related energies on a person.

Along the center lies a spiritual divinity focused on interpersonal conflict and wholeness. Kether, Tiphareth, Yesod, and Malkuth represent it. In the right column, we find Chokhmah, Chesed, and Netzach, energies centered around their actions and how they affect others. Meanwhile, Binah, Geburah, and Hod are located in the left column; these energies focus more on how other people see them.

Everyone's destiny is shaped by these energies *(Kabbalah Numerology, n.d.)*:

- The energy Kether is linked to Chokhmah, Binah, Yesod, and Malkuth *(1, 2, 3, 9, 10).*
- Chokhmah has ties to Kether, Binah, and Chesed *(2, 1, 3, 4).*
- Binah is connected to Chokhmah and Geburah *(3, 2, 1, 5).*
- Chesed is linked to Binah, Geburah, Tiphareth, and Netzach *(4, 3, 5, 6, 7).*
- Geburah has ties to Binah, Chesed, Tiphareth, and Hod *(5, 3, 4, 6, 8).*
- Tiphareth is linked to Chesed, Geburah, Netzach, and Hod *(6, 4, 5, 7, 8).*
- Netzach is connected to Chesed, Tiphareth, Hod, Yesod, and Malkuth *(7, 4, 6, 8, 9, 1).*
- Hod has ties to Geburah, Tiphareth, Netzach, Yesod, and Malkuth *(8, 5, 6, 7, 9, 1).*
- Yesod is linked to Netzach, Hod, and Malkuth *(9, 7, 8, 1).*

Kabbalah Alphabet

The Kabbalah numerology alphabet chart is the same as the Pythagorean chart, allocating each letter in the Latin alphabet to a number within the repeated sequence of one to nine *(Kabbalah Numerology, n.d.)*:

1	2	3	4	5	6	7	8	9
A	B	C	D	E	F	G	H	I
J	K	L	M	N	O	P	Q	R
S	T	U	V	W	X	Y	Z	

Your Ultimate Kabbalah Number

To uncover your ultimate Kabbalah number, all the letters in your full name must be associated with their corresponding figures. Add them together, divide the sum by nine, and take the remainder plus one to arrive at the number *(Kabbalah Numerology, n.d.).*

For example, Amy Winehouse. Born on September 14th, 1983, Amy Jade Winehouse was a gifted British singer whose blues and pop tracks like *"Rehab"* and *"Back to Black"* quickly captured the hearts of many.

The values associated with the letters of her name can be noted as follows:

A = 1
M = 4
Y = 7
J = 1
A = 1
D = 4
E = 5
W = 5
I = 9
N = 5
E = 5
H = 8
O = 6
U = 3
S = 1
E = 5

So,

Amy Jade Winehouse = 1 + 4 + 7 + 1 + 1 + 4 + 5 + 5 + 9 + 5 + 5 + 8 + 6 + 3 + 1 + 5 = 70
70 divided by 9 = 7.77

After the decimal, the remaining value is seven.

7 + 1 = 8

Amy Winehouse had a Kabbalah value of eight, which stands for recklessness. From the moment of her birth, she was destined to live a life of glory, beauty, and creation, thanks to the energy of Hod connecting Tiphareth, Netzach, and Yesod. This destiny seemed all too clear, considering she was notorious for taking drugs, having turbulent relationships, and frequently being in challenging situations. Incontestably, anyone who has seen her perform or attentively listened to her music would confirm this. Her openness was demonstrated through live shows, studio sessions, and even on the streets with the paparazzi. Likewise, Amy achieved great success; she won awards, and her music received widespread acclaim. Fans admired her, and the production agencies adored her. But most of all, she was a creator; just like magicians put on their suits, she pulled songs out of thin air. However, Amy was undoubtedly a risk-taker to achieve all that she had. And with a lifetime value of eight, it is obvious she would frequently get involved in precarious situations.

Pillar 3:
Numbers

Chapter 7:
Pythagorean

Below is a detailed list of the meaning of each of the most basic numbers in the universe, how they apply to your personality, and what they imply about your destiny *(Number Meanings 1–9, 2022)*.

- *One*

  The number one is a natural-born leader, eager to invent new things and pave the way for others. It is as inspiring as it is motivated, pushing others to fulfill their wildest goals and ambitions. Proactive and independent, it needs no permission to be creative, ambitious, and innovative. Movement and momentum surround this pioneer; its goal-oriented attitude can be both a force and a beacon of creativity. Although powerful, the number one can also be manipulative, doubtful, uninhibited, self-centered, and reckless.

  Becoming an executive, entrepreneur, contractor, manager, law enforcement officer, lawyer, engineer, sailor, producer, writer, designer, or inventor may be the paths many take. Notable persons with life path number one include Martin Luther King Jr., Bill Gates, Steve Jobs, and Mother Teresa. Others like Lady Gaga, Kate Winslet, and Gwyneth Paltrow have followed this same pattern.

- *Two*

  Number two is characterized as a supremely empathetic and feminine power, which stands for gratitude and strength. Those under its influence are generally cooperative, giving, respectful, and balanced. As a peacemaker with an intuitive spirit, this number can forge partnerships to make it even more powerful. It also has a greater ability to connect and communicate on a deep soul level. Then, its mediation skills help it see things from different perspectives in any given situation. This number is also influential, unifying, discreet, supportive, protective, and inclusive, but it can be indecisive due to its many options. Likewise, it may be unassertive or apprehensive about stepping up as a leader when needed and can easily be hurt by others.

People with a destiny value of two are often drawn to jobs that allow them to make an impact in the lives of others, from teaching and counseling to architecture, law, and medical science. Caregiving and beauty are also popular professions for those with destiny number two. Prominent figures with this same destiny value are Madonna, Jennifer Aniston, Diana Ross, Jennifer Lopez, Kanye West, and Jackie Kennedy.

- ***Three***

Number three brings positive vibes, enthusiasm, and vibrant energy. Life is always exciting when you are with someone who is a three. They have an exuberant youthfulness and optimism that is contagious. Being around them is daring and friendly, they make friends quickly as they love talking to people, recognizing their unique qualities, and learning from them. This zest for life makes them communicative, artistic, charming, curious, and ever-optimistic. Yet, threes can also be naive, unfocused, and shallow. Hard times never appeal to them, as threes like to be in situations that allow their joyful personalities to shine through.

Creative minds with a life path number three often find themselves in careers such as artistry, writing, production, speaking, design, journalism, politics, law, philosophy, psychology, and counseling. Public relations managers and athletes are also known to be part of the group. Some people with a life path number three include David Bowie, Christina Aguilera, Hillary Clinton, John Travolta, Jamie Foxx, and Shania Twain.

- ***Four***

Individuals who bear the number four are no-nonsense folks in their approach to life. Pragmatic, levelheaded thinkers are also dependable, steady, and conservative. Rather than attempting to be inventive, they take part in tried-and-trusted practices of how things operate. The four's wise energy assists them in providing reasonable explanations, with everything being seen as black or white and nothing in between. These practical people are loyal and willing to help, although they may come across as rigid, unbending, dogmatic, and hard-lined.

Ideal career fields for four are financial planning, economics, managerial sciences, engineering, law, software design, architecture, landscaping, mechanics, and banking. Some fours you might know are Drake, Nicki Minaj, Oprah Winfrey, Brad Pitt, Jimmy Fallon, Usher, and Elton John.

- ***Five***

Those born under the number five are endlessly curious, pushing themselves to explore new experiences and lead adventurous lives. With a big-picture outlook, they try to make the best out of any situation. As for their adaptability, nothing fazes them. This number is ready for anything. Despite their flexibility and determination, fives could have some negative traits, such as being untrustworthy, inconsistent, or directionless. But these people would not let that stop them from living life to its fullest.

People who identify as fives often thrive in professions like art, writing, acting, design, travel, photography, public relations, negotiation, law, sailing, architecture, flight attending, management, and stunt work. They also include some of the world's most renowned personalities, including Vincent van Gogh, Steven Spielberg, and Angelina Jolie; famous singers such as Beyoncé, Jon Bon Jovi, and Mick Jagger.

- *Six*

The number six cherishes its ability to give and receive love more than anything else. It stands for nurturing, lending support, unconditional understanding, and tenderness. Partnerships are where the number six truly shines when it is a close emotional bond. Empathy helps those around them drop their guard and welcome love into their lives. They are excellent parents as well as gentle teachers. Sixes tend to be supportive, protective, intuitive, romantic, and compassionate but can also be idealistic, self-sacrificing, and overly sensitive.

Sixes often work as entrepreneurs, musicians, designers, diplomats, lawyers, coaches, contractors, doctors, teachers, athletes, and chefs. People with sixes include Jessica Alba, Michael Caine, Michael Jackson, and Francis Ford Coppola.

- *Seven*

Sevens seeks to uncover the truth, believing everything is significant and holds a purpose. They are intellectual but also have an intuition cultivated by their constant search for answers. In-depth information is required to satisfy their curiosity and needs to be settled with a shallow explanation. Not only are sevens persistent questioners, often probing into deeper spiritual realms, but they can also be reclusive and guarded due to their skepticism, secrecy, and harshness.

Someone who identifies with the number seven is often in occupations such as counseling, law, medicine, education, designing, writing, freelancing, photography, science, research, or philosophy. Famous sevens you may recognize include Paula Abdul, Muhammad Ali, Kristen Bell, Queen Elizabeth, and Princess Diana.

- *Eight*

This digit is the ultimate achiever and measures success by the goals it accomplishes and the awards it earns. The number eight is lucky, ambitious, and enduring. However, it can also be materialistic, authoritative, and entitled. At the same time, it is balanced and treats Karma respectfully, positioning itself as a friend. With all these attributes, number eight has excellent power to succeed.

Careers for eight are often in entrepreneurship, photography, journalism, law, accounting, architeccture, pharmaceuticals, research, and real estate. From Hollywood to the business world, people with life path eight include Sandra Bullock, Penélope Cruz, Martha Stewart, Amy Schumer, and Jessica Simpson.

- *Nine*

The most complete, balanced, and spiritual digit is nine. With this in mind, number nine strives to understand the greater purpose behind all events in life. Performing good deeds brings a sense of joy and happiness while they are also kind, compassionate, and devoted to helping others. Even though it sometimes endures hardship, these moments are captured within to bring about positivity elsewhere ultimately. Number nine is tolerant, patient, supportive, wise, accepting, and kindhearted. Nevertheless, it can be resentful or even overly sacrificial.

Nines are typically sociologists, psychologists, lawyers, designers, diplomats, politicians, researchers, and teachers. Some people with nine life paths includes Jim Carrey, Morgan Freeman, Bob Marley, Prince Charles, Andrew Lloyd Webber, Mozart, Houdini, and Prince.

Chapter 8:
Chaldean

In Chaldean numerology, your root number and compound number are definitive in understanding who you are and what you can expect from your life. Below you will find a long list of symbols and meanings attached to numbers one through 50 *(Olivia, 2022).*

- *One*

  The number one signifies power, strong leadership skills, and passion. It is highly ambitious and motivated with an inspiring influence. Yet, it can also be associated with dictatorship due to its overbearing and strict nature.

- *Two*

  People associated with this number are well regarded for their cooperative and communicative nature, balanced by a sense of harmony. They tend to form stable connections with others but can be vulnerable to being taken advantage of due to their selflessness. Those born under this numeral are emotionally intelligent, compassionate, and able to work well as part of a team.

- *Three*

  Those possessing the number three are renowned for their willingness to lead and guide others and their creative and vibrant spirit. Unfortunately, this can lead to an impulsive way of life and irrational behavior, often resulting in burnout.

- *Four*

  Folks tied to the number four are reasoned, independent, and securely grounded. They are welcome during complex scenarios as they carefully process incidents and handle strain well. Though faithfully reliable, they can be obstinate and have little interest in taking risks. Generally preferring stability, they do not care for modifications.

- *Five*

The five elements of earth, water, wind, fire, and spirit are represented by this number. People with this number adapt to change quickly and go with the flow of life, often understanding that everything has a larger purpose. They are usually flexible and multitalented and can naturally adapt to any situation. However, people with this number may need help to focus and become skilled in many activities or none.

- *Six*

Six is a gentle figure, representing tranquility, and is often seen in the natural world. Those who identify with this numerical value are peacemakers gifted with the ability to observe all aspects of a problem. They have wisdom that comes from experience, allowing them to provide wise counsel. Despite their insight, they may find difficulty in actively resolving issues due to a nature that avoids confrontation.

- *Seven*

Individuals with the number seven tend to be introspective and spiritual. Associated with inner wisdom, solitude, and search for truth, they are typically curious about mysticism and are always believing that there is a deeper truth within everything they encounter.

- *Eight*

Represented by the infinity symbol and the concept of eternal life, number 8 means balance and harmony. People associated with this number are encouraged to strive for excellence while finding a healthy balance between the material and spiritual aspects of life.

- *Nine*

This digit represents a sense of humanitarianism, empathy, and selflessness. People with this number are compassionate and generous that stems from the desire to serve others. They favor creativity and emotions above everything else. They lean away from logic and passionately follow their hearts. Yet, they often grapple with tunnel vision and can lose sight of what is most important.

- *Ten*

Anyone with the number 10 can achieve much success and honor. These people are usually lucky and have a loyal group of friends.

- *Eleven*

This number represents intuition, inspiration, and enlightenment. It also represents creativity, self-expression, and individuality. Those with this number may have a heightened sense of intuition and spiritual awareness, and may be drawn to spiritual practices and pursuits.

- *Twelve*

  This number is associated with harmony, balance, and partnership because it represents a blending of the energies of the numbers 1 and 2. Those with this number may have a natural ability to bring people together and create a sense of unity and cooperation.

- *Thirteen*

  Having this number has no bearing on luck. Instead, it is associated with transformation and change. This number represents a period of transition and may indicate a time of upheaval or challenge. However, it also represents the potential for growth and evolution, and they may emerge from this period stronger and more resilient than before.

- *Fourteen*

  This number favors financial well-being above all else. Fourteens are logical, ambitious, and financially aware. They can also be evasive and unreliable, especially when they have to participate in activities they deem unworthy of their time.

- *Fifteen*

  Individuals with this number are generally well regarded. Yet, they can struggle with forming and sustaining relationships when their personality is rigid and unyielding. This attitude may lead to feelings of isolation, bitterness, and exasperation.

- *Sixteen*

  This number is associated with spiritual growth and evolution, and may indicate a time of deepening spiritual awareness and understanding. They may be called to explore their spirituality and to deepen their connection to the divine.

- *Seventeen*

  The power of this lucky number is enduring, spreading its blessings across loved ones and acquaintances alike.

- *Eighteen*

  This number represents a time of transformation and spiritual awakening. It is associated with spiritual rebirth and may indicate a period of spiritual growth and transformation.

- *Nineteen*

  The number 19 is associated with completion and endings and may indicate the end of a cycle or the completion of a project or goal. They may be called to let go of what no longer serves them and to embrace new beginnings and opportunities.

- *Twenty*

  People with this numerical identity may be called to pursue further education or to deepen their understanding of a particular subject or area of interest. 20 represents a time of learning and growth and is related to education and knowledge. 20s are more likely to be asked to share their expertise with others and to use their skills and talents to make a positive impact in the world.

- *Twenty-one*

  Life for this number is filled with creativity and self-expression. They could explore their artistic side and use their talent to create something meaningful and beautiful.

- *Twenty-two*

  Twenty twos are about balance and harmony as well as power and leadership. They can use their influence to create positive change in the world.

- *Twenty-three*

  These angelic helping hands of the universe come without expectations. Regardless of the circumstance, they are always available to assist others. They put aside their wants and needs without grappling with their repercussions. Instead, they lead a life empowered by the happiness of others.

- *Twenty-four*

  This number enjoys a strong bond with family and friends, who offer unwavering love and emotional support. Lucky in affection, this digit is also blessed with many trusted relationships filled with warmth and understanding.

- *Twenty-five*

  Hard-working individuals are represented by this number. Seeing their future clearly and prepared to give everything they have, they always strive once they reach their goals.

- *Twenty-six*

  Those with this number are inherently compassionate and devoted to relationships. Despite this, they often find themselves in complicated situations due to their tendency to enter into relationships without thought. Fortunately, resilience is a trait that serves them well in these moments. However, too many missteps can lead to an overload of stress on their shoulders which could cause them to become distrustful, unfaithful, and aggressive.

- *Twenty-seven*

  People blessed with the number 27 are knowledgeable and guided by sound logic. As long as they trust in their brilliance, these people will find great success and power.

- *Twenty-eight*

  Those with this number are practical and efficient. Their responsibilities and duties are important to them, and they always strive to find a balance between their work and personal life.

- *Twenty-nine*

  Having this particular number means that you could find yourself in complex and risky scenarios. Those with these digits tend to be highly trusting and naive, a mix that can make for dangerous situations.

- *Thirty*

  Love and affection are likely to be found in this number.

- *Thirty-one*

  Number 31 represents artistic talent, inspiration, and success. People with this number should strive for balance between their creative and practical responsibilities.

- *Thirty-two*

  This number is also associated with success and prosperity. It could mean that they need to focus on their financial and material well-being.

- *Thirty-three*

  Someone with this number is lucky, imparting support and showing love. They are believed to be natural healers and counselors who can inspire others through their example.

- *Thirty-four*

  Thirty fours put focus on love and relationships. This could indicate a need for harmony and balance in someone's romantic life.

- *Thirty-five*

  Folks numbered 35 are often free thinkers who value their individuality and possess a great deal of creativity. They have a great thirst for knowledge stemming from their desire for personal growth and learning.

- *Thirty-six*

  Those with this number are thought to be blessed with luck, power, and optimism.

- *Thirty-seven*

  For anyone associated with the number 37, life is filled with luck in relationships, friendships, and finances. A blessed life awaits them, full of joyous companionship.

- *Thirty-eight*

  This figure is associated with abundance and success.

- *Thirty-nine*

  People possessing this number are usually hardworking. Though they can be stern and unwelcoming at times, they are just as capable of showing joy and appreciation.

- *Forty*

  As the digits representing hard work, discipline, and success through effort, people with this number are often ambitious and driven towards their goals. They are driven with achievement, success, and abundance, but may also require balance and self-awareness to avoid neglecting other areas of life.

- *Forty-one*

  These people under number 41 have keen instincts. They have a trustworthy gut and should always trust themselves above others.

- *Forty-two*

  Individuals born with this number are destined for a life filled with love, support, success, and joy.

- *Forty-three*

  The number 43 represents a combination of the energies of the numbers 4 and 3. It signifies success, creativity, and self-expression. Those with this number in their chart are often natural leaders with a practical and grounded approach to life. They have excellent communication skills and trust their intuition to manifest their goals.

- *Forty-four*

  People with a strong influence of the number 44 are often highly ambitious and driven, with a natural ability to lead and inspire others. They are known to work hard to achieve their goals and dreams.

- *Forty-five*

  Individuals with this number are often successful in their careers and personal lives due to their ability to adapt to changing situations and their determination to overcome obstacles. They have a strong sense of responsibility and a practical approach to life, making them dependable and reliable.

- *Forty-six*

  These people are generally very successful in relationships.

- *Forty-seven*

  This number is considered auspicious and fortunate. People with this number tend to be natural-born leaders with an ability to inspire others to follow them. They have a strong sense of self and are often self-reliant. They are creative and innovative thinkers who possess the ability to turn their ideas into reality. This number indicates success in all aspects of life, including career, relationships, and personal growth. However, individuals with this number should be careful not to let their ego get in the way of their success. This number can bring negative energy caused by grief.

- *Forty-eight*

  The number 48 signifies material success and financial abundance. It is a number associated with leadership, authority, and power. People with this number are often successful in business, finance, and management. They have the ability to make sound decisions and achieve their goals through hard work and determination. They are practical and efficient in their approach, which helps them in achieving their desired results.

- *Forty-nine*

  49 people have a strong sense of responsibility and desire to make a positive impact in the world. They symbolize someone who's here to bring spiritual wisdom and knowledge to the world. This number is associated with great leadership abilities, intuition, and a deep understanding of human nature. Individuals with this number are often seen as wise, compassionate, and highly intuitive. They have a natural ability to connect with others on a deeper level and may be drawn to careers in teaching, counseling, or spirituality.

- *Fifty*

  It is a combination of the energies and attributes of the numbers 5 and 0. The number 5 symbolizes freedom, versatility, and progress, while the number 0 represents potential, wholeness, and infinity. Together, they create a harmonious blend of energies that signify growth, abundance, and success. Those who are associated with this digits has the potential to achieve great things in life, both materially and spiritually. It is a number of personal transformations and growth, and it may indicate that they're ready to embark on a new journey or chapter in their life. Those influenced by this number are likely to be innovative, resourceful, and confident, and they have the ability to manifest their desires into reality.

Chapter 9:
Kabbalah

One cannot simply appeal only to their calculated value. They should also analyze their representative energy, number, and energy collection when identifying their future *(Kabbalah Numerology, n.d.)*.

- *One (Kether or Malkuth)*

  One symbolizes progress, spirit, momentum, and leadership. This digit wants to change the world. Linked intricately to Kether, this digit has a divine connection with the spirit world. People with this digit have a talent for connecting with others and seeing their potential. Kether's ties with Malkuth and Yesod can grant a person skill in speech, art, writing, and music. It believes invention and creativity are the foundation of solving all issues. Likewise, it is connected with Binah on its left, meaning that this digit is also very nurturing and positive. On its right, it is linked with Chokhmah, meaning it is wise, imaginative, and insightful.

- *Two (Chokhmah)*

  Those connected with Chokhmah have an innate sensitivity, feeling things profoundly and having a sharp instinct. Helping others is something they take pleasure in, but their ambition can sometimes overpower them. Twos have ties to Binah, Kether, and Chesed. These energies make them excellent and understanding leaders.

- *Three (Binah)*

  A figure of affection, people linked with Binah are compassionate and wise, bringing understanding, nurturing, and optimism. Further associated with Chokhmah, Kether, and Geburah, this force is disciplined, intuitive, and a brilliant leader, able to resolve issues quickly and confidently while remaining determined.

- *Four (Chesed)*

This number represents futility and charity. Nothing else matters to these people except helping others. Activities and energy are futile unless they benefit someone. Also linked to Chokhmah, Geburah, and Tiphareth, this energy is nurturing, creative, good at resolving conflict, balanced, and harmonious.

- *Five (Geburah)*

Five represents newness, innovation, establishment, and travel. These digits can make a home anywhere, find friends in the most unlikely places, and make even the sternest of people kind-hearted. Geburah can set boundaries, be disciplined, and get down to business when resolving a dispute. They are honest and have patience but will always get straight to the point. People with Geburah energy do not back down easily and stand their ground and remain frank no matter what. On top of that, it is closely linked with Tiphareth, Chesed, and Binah, resulting in an equilibrium between harmony, balance, loving-kindness, compassion, and true understanding and wisdom.

- *Six (Tiphareth)*

Symbolizing implementation, strategizing, setting goals, and achieving tasks, people with six built on a foundation of logic and hard labor. Those drawn to Tiphareth strive for harmony and equilibrium, taking what life offers in exchange for what they provide, achieving contentment. Tiphareth also lies in the center of the tree of life. People who associate strongly with this energy get along well with others. They are resilient peacemakers who can think, act, and understand the inner workings of people.

- *Seven (Netzach)*

Those with the number seven are believed to have a magical power that grants them luck. They can remain unshaken and persevere through difficult times while watching out for the safety of others. Connected to Tiphareth and ultimately linked to the Earth, these individuals possess a solid connection to Chesed, Hod, and Yesod, three divine spiritual powers. As such, they can find balance in life and demonstrate great kindness and charity. Their creativity, positivity, and energy make them resilient even when their lives are in danger.

- *Eight (Hod)*

People associated with this number have the power to push through tough times. Nevertheless, their frequent engagement in strenuous scenarios affects their resilience. To stay out of trouble and make the best of the situation, they must be more conscious and stay away from naivety at any cost. The energies of Hod, Yesod, Netzach, Tiphareth, and Geburah converge within them, making them kind-hearted, selfless, balanced, and great at setting limits.

- *Nine (Yesod)*

  The luckiest of all symbols is closely connected to Yesod, allowing for a direct connection to the divine. With Yesod being held in harmony with Malkuth, Kether, Netzach, and Hod, this digit carries an innate creativity. It can be relied on for writing, art, and musical excellence while being a fearless leader. Despite any recklessness it may demonstrate, successes will always follow due to its ability to overcome all obstacles.

Chapter 10:
Master Numbers

The values, larger-than-life and double-digit, carry immense power and responsibility. When these numbers are observed, claimed, analyzed, or sensed, the people associated with their presence feel a heightened awareness. These senses may be related to intelligence, intuition, potential, finances, opportunities, or even love. Master numbers include the placement of two like numbers beside each other.

Analyzing these master numbers involves viewing them as they stand and with their reduced value *(Reed, 2020)*. Some master numbers include, but are not limited to:

- *11*

  Instinctive, influential, and cooperative, the number 11 is often called the Mother of numbers. A feminine energy that is understanding, supportive, and attentive draws people in and can accurately read their energies and intentions. Those with this path are highly perceptive, often serving as seers, clairvoyants, or psychics. However, walking this life path takes work; the strength of their power can lead them to overwhelming dread and a sensation of carrying the weight of the world on their shoulders. This can bring paranoia, depression, fearfulness, distrustfulness, and even unkindness.

- *22*

  People with these digits represent a class of master builders; they are practical visionaries. They can execute all grand ideas with ease through their confidence. Yet, despite helping others achieve their dreams, they remain unfulfilled in life. Always striving for betterment, they seek knowledge and expansion while being ungrateful for what they already have. Success is never enough, as they can never seem to feel its truth, no matter how much it has realized. Thus, these digits signify intense masculinity and logicality, providing a pathway for dreams to become a reality.

- *33*

    This rare number, known as the Master Teacher, has the power to aid and transform people, helping them reach their highest potential. As a result, the person holding this number is destined to show others the path to inner healing and enlightenment, even if they face more pain. Despite constantly searching for themselves, they must accept their plight and act as a positive example by advocating mercy and love. Finding compassion within themselves, trusting their intuition, and forgiving previous mistakes will help them achieve their ultimate destiny.

These individuals possess an extraordinary capacity for expression. From acting to art, singing to scriptwriting, they can impersonate anyone and everyone around them. They are not duplicitous; instead, their creativity skill allows them to appear as someone entirely different. Their calling is to encourage others to develop their capabilities, captivating those in need of assistance. Alas, only a select few of this group can realize their power and utilize it to its fullest potential. Despite its strength, many may never learn to depend on themselves, erase the past, or let love lead the way.

Seeing your master number in everyday life suggests that you are heading in the right direction. When this happens, take a moment to consider what you are thinking and doing, where you are, and what the future holds.

Pillar 4:
Karmic Influence

Chapter 11:
What is Karma

Karma is an ancient concept rooted in the Sanskrit word for action *(Believe, 2021)*. It is a Hindu belief that speaks to the cause-and-effect cycle of the universe. When we do something, someone else reacts, influencing our following action. This cycle continues indefinitely since we are all prone to act and have reactions ourselves, even after death. Whatever wrongs or rights you have committed will follow you through this life and even past lives, as the theory of reincarnation suggests. Our actions and mistakes often come back to haunt us; Karma is like divine justice, rewarding us for our good deeds while punishing us for our bad ones.

Life may deal you a great hand of fortune or misfortune. Your attached Karma may be the reason for such. Karma acts like a naughty sibling, always playing tricks on you. It may paint an invisible door in your path and make you believe you have a fantastic opportunity when it does not want that for you. Instead, it shocks you when you realize the door is fake. Likewise, if Karma is happy with you and wishes to reward you, it can align events to ensure you get the opportunities you deserve.

Moreover, what goes around comes around. Your thoughts and energy can affect those around you, so it is best to put out good vibes. Poor choices or negative behavior can come back to haunt you; be mindful of how your actions may affect others. To lead a successful life, try your best to stay positive and act responsibly.

Can you stop or prevent Karma? No, Karma is inevitable. But you can limit its wrath by focusing on living a happy and peaceful life, regardless of the cards you are dealt. In addition, you can calculate your Karmic lessons and debt to help you navigate the challenges that Karma may throw in your path. It can also help you know when to expect good years.

Chapter 12:
Karmic Debt

Throughout our lives, we develop a great deal of wisdom. We can show much kindness and also make many mistakes. Our mistakes need to be corrected. These mistakes accumulate in Karmic debt. To correct our past errors, Karma throws us into situations wherein we are forced to make things right or to live, feel, or behave the way we have moved on others.

Karmic debt is represented by the numbers 13, 14, 16, and 19 *(Believe, 2021)*. These numbers may appear to you when interpreting calculations associated with Pythagorean, Chaldean, or Kabbalah numerology approaches. For example, you may attempt to discover your character number but realize your full name is related to the number 14. This is a sign that you have a Karmic debt to pay. Karmic debt numbers work like master numbers. When you discover them, you should analyze the value and the reduced value.

Each of these numbers has a significant meaning which can be interpreted to help you pay for your mistakes in this life and avoid further Karma in the future. Those with these numbers embedded in their numerology chart are likely to have a harder life than others. They are also more likely to be involved in charitable work.

Assigning Debt to Numbers

Below you will find a detailed list explaining each of the Karmic debt numbers, what challenges they evoke, the reasons for their existence in your life, and how you can overcome them *(Believe, 2021)*.

- *13*

  Having a Karmic debt number 13 can be a source of immense frustration. Tasks that should naturally be achievable become arduous and seemingly never-ending, as if there is no end because of the constant interruptions. All this tends to follow from poor decisions, selfishness, and taking advantage of those around you. However, it is necessary to remember that success is not something unattainable. Instead is hard-won through perseverance, even in the most challenging times. The key is not to give up and keep pushing despite adversity. Many successful people have gone through an experience similar to this Karmic debt number 13.

- *14*

  Those with this Karmic debt may struggle to find freedom, becoming trapped in relationships, enslaved by their minds, drugs, companies, or even the whim of nature. As a result of past transgressions and enslavement of others' freedoms, they are required to learn how to master themselves emotionally and be ready for any unexpected twists life might throw at them. The only way out is a dedication to their goals, never giving up no matter what. By maintaining control and staying resilient, they can break free from this Karmic debt.

- *16*

  People with this Karmic debt number are fated to start new projects and be optimistic, only for their dreams to come crashing down around them again and again. All new ventures will never be successful, and every incident will fail. These people will feel a massive ego boost just before the venture fails. When the experience fails, they will find themselves humbled. Likewise, individuals with this number can be very understanding and empathetic. Those with this number must be wary of being selfish and bitter, for that will only stoke the fire. They need to learn to see failure as a blessing and grow more modest as they age. Such a painful price is the result of destroying the faith, belief, and success of others.

- *19*

  Possessing a Karmic debt number 19 comes with many challenges. Independence and power must be used for the greater good, and you must learn to stand your ground and lead others toward freedom. Even those closest to you can hurt and challenge you, making inner peace and forgiveness essential. However, the core lesson of this Karmic debt is the need to ask for help. Not doing so will only bring pain. Ultimately, the cost of such debt is sacrificing your well-being.

Karma might seem like something you cannot escape, but it does not need to be your master. Instead, think of it as a game; Karma has presented you with a challenge and given you the tools to succeed. Sure, you could be angry and ignore the advantages right in front of you. Or you could take the initiative and find more creative ways to progress toward a happy life and reduce any Karmic debt hanging over your head.

Chapter 13:
Karmic Lessons

The choices you have made and the mistakes you have committed in the past can come with a price. This cost is known as "Karmic Debt." Often related to your personal growth and evolution, these lessons may be required for your soul's journey. Such Karmic lessons arise from past actions and thoughts, guiding your path forward. Everything about humanity invokes something to be learned and internalized. How we treat each other reminds us to be kind, courteous, patient, gentle, and cooperative. Mastering these attributes is bound to take time, years, or even a lifetime.

According to some biblical texts, seven archangels, Michael, Raphael, Gabriel, Jophiel, Ariel, Azrael, and Chamuel, deliver messages from God to us humans. As our souls evolve over millennia of life experiences, they learn and gain wisdom that brings them closer to God. Souls who have experienced enough in their journey may become honored as angels. Those who have gone even further and achieved much can receive the greatest honor of becoming archangels and direct messengers of divine power. Guiding us with their wisdom on our path to enlightenment, these unique souls help us progress through our life journeys.

Our Karmic lessons are integral to our spiritual journey, leading us ever closer to God. By learning from these lessons, we become better people, which in turn helps bring peace and strength to those around us. These Karmic lessons can be found by looking at the numbers missing from your full name *(Karmic Numbers, 2020)*. To understand this concept further, let us look at Aileen Wuornos as an example. Born on February 29th, 1956 *(Gomez, 2022)*, Wuornos was a notorious killer who also happened to be a prostitute, robbing and shooting her clients.

1	2	3	4	5	6	7	8	9
A	B	C	D	E	F	G	H	I
J	K	L	M	N	O	P	Q	R
S	T	U	V	W	X	Y	Z	

First, we need to understand what numbers are associated with Aileen's name to establish the ones that are not.

A = 1
I = 9
L = 3
E = 5
E = 5
N = 5
C = 3
A = 1
R = 9
O = 6
L = 3
W = 5
U = 3
O = 6
R = 9
N = 5
O = 6
S = 1

Aileen had a name with the numbers one, three, five, six, and nine; missing were two, seven, and eight. Based on the Karmic lessons of these numbers, she was warned of the potential consequences if she did not heed its advice. Number two cautions against thoughtless action, letting one end up hurting others, while slow steadiness should be employed to enjoy life. Seven suggests carelessness and lack of intuition, often leading to situations that could have been sidestepped with some thoughtfulness. On the other hand, eight implores one not to remain isolated but instead share the love, which is not a sign of weakness despite feeling like it is. In Aileen's case, impulsive behavior combined with reticence indicated that she never learned those Karmic lessons, something evidenced in the events and outcomes of her life.

Assigning Numbers to Lessons

Below, you can find a comprehensive list of numbers and the associated Karmic lessons that may help you discover what life intended for your soul's growth. Not all are obliged to accept these lessons. Some are here to show others the way, some to settle debts, and some just to be here *(Karmic Numbers, 2020)*.

- ***One***

  A procrastinator of note, this number channels a character who suffers from an abundance of ideas but cannot start any of them. Your thoughts and projects accumulate in your head without being able to put them into action. This leads to frequent self-criticism and low self-esteem, further undermining your efforts. To be truly fulfilled, you must push yourself and find the courage to devise techniques to get going.

- *Two*

Your actions may often be inconsiderate and self-focused, but it is time to sit back and watch how things unfold before jumping in. Reacting too quickly can come at a cost, so sometimes it pays to wait before moving. There could be unforeseen benefits that you had not anticipated.

- *Three*

This number reveals someone who can be too easily hurt by their self-criticism. Constantly putting yourself down and being too hard on yourself will only lead to discouragement. Acknowledge and give credit for your efforts, no matter how small the achievement may be. Appreciating yourself is a must; it will help you move forward and continue striving for greatness.

- *Four*

Feeling aimless and stuck, you may struggle to focus on one thing. Even when you try, it is like trudging through mud. But there are ways to move forward by finding a balance between your professional and personal lives. Learning tactics to concentrate can help you progress and discover a sense of direction again.

- *Five*

Staying within your comfort zone can lead to a life of missed opportunities. It is essential to remember that there is a whole universe out there for you, and it may pass you by if you do not take the initiative. Instead of retreating into isolation, look for an adventure, challenge yourself, and come out of your shell, as this will open up exciting new possibilities.

- *Six*

Working on numerous tasks at once can be overwhelming and challenging to complete. When multiple projects remain unfinished, it is essential to learn to focus on one and cross it off the list before moving on to the next. Finishing something is much more satisfying than having five things in progress.

- *Seven*

Reckless behavior puts your safety and the safety of those around you at risk. Acting without thinking can lead to troubling situations, so it is essential to consider all aspects before acting. Taking the time for thoughtful planning is necessary for success.

- *Eight*

Someone who tends to be proud and independent might find it challenging to ask for help. But learning to do so can bring peace that cannot be seen by struggling alone. Life will inevitably throw battles our way, but rather than facing them as individuals, you should not be afraid to reach out for support. The results will undoubtedly be better than trying to handle everything alone.

- *Nine*

  When you talk to others, you have difficulty understanding their perspectives. Being unsure of how to respond or act in certain situations can lead to feeling confused about the behavior of those around you. Following your intuition and being open-minded can help you form better relationships and start engaging with life. Striving to ask questions and gain insight into why people act the way they do is crucial for living a full, meaningful life.

Knowing your Karmic lessons helps in understanding what role you have to play in this life. It gives our suffering and experiences meaning and reminds us that there is more to life than simply existing. Enjoyment and learning go hand in hand. To live a fulfilled life, we need to know where our skills are lacking. When we practice and refine those skills, they become stronger, and life becomes easier.

Furthermore, finishing off the lessons we need to learn in this life puts us in good stead to learn new lessons in future lives. We can open ourselves up to a peaceful existence for years to come, but we have to start now. Take little daily steps to improve yourself, and you will find happiness along the way.

Pillar 5:
Angel Numbers

Have you ever noticed the same digits repeating over and over? It could be the numbers on your clock reading 5:55, 4:44, 3:33, 2:22, 1:11, or even 12:22. Or you were on holiday and found yourself walking up a certain road and seeing the number 777 on every street you crossed. On their own, these numbers are simply coincidences. But when witnessed three or four times in a day, week, or even hour, the numbers can be associated with angelic messages. When you encounter angelic messages, pay attention as something important is happening.

Angel numbers are spiritual messages in numerology that can guide us, confirm our actions, or redirect us to safer paths. People who have a strong intuition and sense of spirituality will notice these messages quickly. Skeptics and disbelievers will need some help receiving and interpreting angelic messages. But although the numbers may be present, some people either do not pay attention to them or do not care.

For such, imagine that you are going to a school concert for your child. As you look for your kid, you spot them happily smiling on stage. Because your focus was on finding your child, you had missed a little preschooler shoving their teacher off the bleachers and into the audience. You would have seen it if you were fully looking at the entire stage. Such is the power of having a broad view and understanding of situations.

So, to truly understand the greater picture, you must be willing to open yourself up to a power larger than you. You must believe someone is seeking your best interests and guiding your life toward a predetermined purpose. This purpose is not simply about raising a family or achieving the perfect job, it is something much bigger. Once you recognize this, you will be presented with more possibilities than ever and an entirely different way of viewing the world.

But why do you see angelic numbers? Why now and not yesterday? Why this year and not three years ago? Everyone develops at their own pace, and the ability to open up to the possibility that life is larger than what it seems takes time. Before we can even imagine how big the world is, certain events need to occur. The events that lead us to believe may be predetermined or happen coincidentally.

Imagine that you are destined to end a relationship of seven years. Suppose the decisive moment is at seven o'clock at a house on the seventh street, yet you do not make it. As a result, you miss your chance for a life-changing event and never progress further in life. On top of everything, it takes another eight years before you make the breakup. Unbeknownst to you, the love of your life has been waiting around the corner during that time. Unfortunately, your shot had already passed because you were not paying attention, leaving you unaware of what could have been yours within just a few months.

Once you spot these numbers, it is almost as if you invited them into your life. You anticipate what knowledge they may bring, and the value of this message can be seen in its ability to save you eight invaluable years. Pay close attention; this could be the key to unlocking something extraordinary.

To open yourself up to angelic messages, you must first be aware of their presence and potential. You can start by analyzing your surroundings and taking in the presence of numerals within them. Look around you now. *Are there any numbers in the space you are in?* Maybe it is an alarm, a watch, a thermometer, a bill, or an account number. You do not need to write these numbers down; you just need to make yourself aware of them. Every day, take some time to look around you and take note of the numbers in your vicinity. Perhaps set the alarm to go off at different intervals throughout your week. When your alarm goes off, look around where you are and take note of what you are doing. Look for numbers in the room and see if they are familiar. At first glance, nothing may appear out of the ordinary, but as time passes, you will sense something like déjà vu. Though the link may not be obvious, it will cause your memories to awaken. But when you feel that touch of déjà vu in your mind, you will know that you are finally open to receiving angelic guidance.

Chapter 14:
The Power of Three

When you first see a series of digits, you should ask yourself if this is a message or a coincidence. The general rule is that seeing a number once is as coincidental as seeing it twice. These are merely numbers within a space. There is still a limited possibility that they mean anything at all—until they appear a third time, you can interpret them as messages *(5 Powerful Ways, 2022).*

Take, for instance, that you are reading this book. You have discovered your root number is three. Then you calculate the value of your name using the Chaldean techniques and learn your name has a value of 33. These are still coincidental. The numbers have been found purposefully, but they are merely coincidental calculations. Yes, they have a purpose, but they are not necessarily messages from the angels. An hour later, you are walking down your street when you notice a house with the number 33 on it. At this point, you should become more aware of your surroundings, but do not gravitate to the presence of angels yet. Focusing on the number three is plausible, considering you addressed that number in your numerology studies. Now let us say a few hours later, you get a water bill for $330. Then an hour after, the electricity meter reads 33 units left. Your partner comes home at 6:30 while you set a timer on the oven for 30 minutes. Now, the number three has meaning. It was repeated too many times to be coincidental. You have to find the line between what is an everyday occurrence and what is not. This is hard to do. But the rule is, if you see this number three times or more, it means something.

So, what can you do when you believe that angels are messaging you?

Before anything else, analyze your current situation. *Are you at home or out and about? What activities have been occupying your mind?* Write these details down in the corresponding entry in your numerology journal. Then, reflect on a previous time when you encountered the same number. *Where were you then? Have you gone out somewhere or had some other plans for that day?*

This number may occur when you pass a particular street. For whatever reason, that number might be pulling your focus. Perhaps the message the angels are trying to give you has to do with the direction you have been going. Maybe you have been investing your time in a new career path, and they want you to know that you are on the right track.

Or possibly they want you to know you are taking a wrong turn and you should stop investing time and effort. There is only one way to know for sure—write the number down and find out what it means. And to gain deeper insight into this number's significance, compare your past experiences with this one.

Number Combinations and Patterns

Number combinations refer to sequences of numbers that appear repeatedly and carry specific meanings in numerology. These combinations may include single-digit numbers, double-digit numbers, or even triple-digit numbers. They can be seen in various aspects of our lives, such as birthdates, phone numbers, addresses, and even license plates.

One of the most common number combinations in numerology is 11:11. It is believed to be a powerful spiritual sign indicating that you are on the right path and in tune with the universe. Other number combinations that are considered significant in numerology include 222, 333, 444, and 555. These combinations are thought to represent different messages and guidance from the divine or spiritual realm.

The meaning of number combinations can also vary based on the individual numbers within the sequence. For instance, the combination of 123 is often associated with creativity, growth, and self-improvement, while the combination of 666 is often associated with negativity or dark energy.

Numerologists believe that number combinations can provide insight into one's life purpose, strengths, and weaknesses. By analyzing the frequency and meaning of number combinations in one's life, a numerologist can offer guidance and advice on how to navigate life's challenges and opportunities.

Overall, number combinations in numerology can be a powerful tool for self-discovery and spiritual growth. They offer a unique perspective on the patterns and energies that govern our lives and can help us better understand our purpose and potential.

Below is a list of all the potential combinations and patterns you may interact with daily. You must learn the affiliated meanings for each so that when you encounter them, you can interpret their meaning and follow through on the right course of action that will land you in happier stead *(5 Powerful Ways, 2022)*.

- *111*

  This number is associated with God. When you see this number, it means that you are isolating yourself and need to fall back under His hand, the warmth of friends, and the support of loved ones. It reminds you that nothing was built on one sole promise, person, or covenant.

  Even God needed the help of Jesus to clear humanity of sin. Jesus needed the guidance and support of His followers to help Him find courage in His journey. God made the angels to assist Him in creating the earth and protecting humankind. Wherever you are and whatever you are doing, you cannot do it alone.

- *222*

  When you see the number two, it could remind you to bring balance into your life. Maybe you are allowing yourself too much indulgence and missing out on your true purpose or not giving in enough and prohibiting natural events from taking place. If this number appears, look at your actions and then go in the opposite direction.

- *333*

  Having this number appearing in your life over and over can state a solid creative force bubbling within you. Embrace this power and create something meaningful like a book, poem, movie, or song. Transform your imaginative vision into a lasting art form or take that leap of faith and attend the audition you have been pondering.

- *444*

  An angel will appear to you with this special number, letting you know they are there for your support and comfort. This number reminds them that they are by your side and will help guide you as needed. They do not want you to feel alone. Furthermore, it is a sign for you to put careful planning into everything you do. For whatever reason, the angels need you to think through your choices. The angels know that if you think through things, you will make the right choice. However, you need to be more careful with your actions.

- *555*

  Embrace the new opportunities in front of you when this number appears. Take that walk you have been thinking about, call up someone and ask them to dinner, or head to that gathering at the restaurant. The angels tell you everything will be alright; only good is on the horizon. So, step out of your comfort zone and see what blessings await.

- *666*

  Noticing the number six might signify that you are about to experience some loss to yourself or someone you care for. To avoid this, take advantage of this time to surround yourself with friends and family and make the most of it. Gathering those close to you can help provide a good source of comfort and joy.

- *777*

  Seeing the number seven means that your angels are very pleased with the decisions you have been making, and they want you to know that you are on the right path. Hence, your destiny lies ahead of you down the path you have been taking. You are in perfect harmony with the universe, and it wants to show you that all is as it should be. Keep making the choices you have been and stay open to what comes your way; all will continue to be right. When the time comes, you will discover your true purpose in life and feel whole, knowing that everything that has happened up until now has true meaning. Everything will continue to make sense and bring you joy along the way.

- *888*

The angels have heard your distress and have sent eight angelic acknowledgments to reaffirm your strength. Lending their love and light, they are showing you the way forward, as some doors will be opened for you, so stay motivated by selecting the right ones. Keep yourself in balance by trusting these divine energies to guide you through times of pain. However, when you repeatedly see this number and do not feel very hopeful, it makes opening the right doors hard. But if you can find the strength to stay positive in times of crisis and know that someone is looking out for you, you will discover those doors quickly, and your pain will be alleviated.

- *999*

Something in your life may end, and this number is a sign of that. It could be the end of a project, a relationship, or even a milestone. Whatever it is, you must acknowledge that something will end and let it. This is the angels' way of asking you to let something go and, at the same time, telling you it will be okay.

- *000*

New beginnings are coming your way when you see this number over and over. It is crucial to remain focused and positive because something unique is about to happen to you. Let it.

- *Triple-digit patterns*

Witnessing numbers repeating in threes signifies that angels are with you and influencing your life. Listen carefully to your thoughts, analyze your dreams, and explore your spiritual gifts because the line to the spirit world is ringing, and someone on the other side wants to talk to you.

Chapter 15:
Angels and Their Messages

From the moment you were set to embark upon your journey here on Earth, God blessed you with the persistent presence of angels. They guided your soul through the passage into your mother's womb and were there as you entered the world. Even today, they remain steadfastly by your side, understanding and knowing you more deeply than perhaps even yourself. You can feel their assurance in the unexplainable yet resonating part of yourself you often forget when trying to make sense of this world. A piece that contains the truth about who you are, what drives you, and where your destiny lies.

But who are the angels exactly? Are we surrounded by multiple angels or just one? How do we know who is watching over us? Will they ever reach out? If they do, how do we interpret this? How do we respond?

Firstly, multiple angels and spiritual beings are watching over each of us. These spirits may be close friends or family members who have passed away, souls we encountered in past lives, or angelic spirits God has asked to watch over us. But we all have one particularly powerful angelic being watching over us and assisting in our journey—an archangel. Archangels play essential roles in our lives. They guide, protect, and support us along our journey. Furthermore, they were created to fulfill specific missions, protect humans against evil, and help God's ultimate plan come to light. There are hundreds of archangels, but only seven are originals, as they were the first archangels created by God: *Michael, Raphael, Gabriel, Jophiel, Ariel, Azrael,* and *Chamuel.*

Finding Your Guardian Angel

Knowing who your specific guardian angel is will help you understand your life's journey. If you know who your guardian angel is, you can talk to them and ask for advice regularly. You can receive angelic messages daily and ensure you are on the path to a happy and fulfilled life. *But how can you find out who your archangel is?*

Finding your guardian angel is as easy as adding up the numbers in your birth date and reducing them to a single-digit number from one to nine. As such, let us see if we can identify Princess Diana's guardian angel.

Diana Frances Spencer was born on the 1st of July, 1961 *(Diana, Princess of Wales, n.d.)*. Her guardian angel equation is as follows:

$1 + 7 + 1 + 9 + 6 + 1 = 25 = 2 + 5 = 7$

The archangel Raphael is the guardian angel associated with seven, symbolizing comfort and health. Diana embodied all these same qualities that her guardian angel stands for. Meanwhile, when you know who your archangel is, you can seek out its guidance.

The Archangels

Below you will find a list of the archangels and their numbers:

- *Raguel (One)*

  Being associated with number one is all about invention and pioneering. This can be an intimidating force to reckon with. However, those who have Raguel close by can call on him and harness his courage when starting new endeavors. With a name that means "friend of God," he is the embodiment of harmony. He is not just the source of miracles; he can also give you the strength to do anything. Not only does he provide knowledge but also energy for all types of undertakings.

- *Uriel (Two)*

  Uriel is considered a heavenly emissary, a source of solace during hard times. Being associated with him allows one to summon his power and make sound decisions in the face of difficulty. With Uriel by your side, you will always be guided and make wise choices.

- *Jophiel (Three)*

  Like the number three, Jophiel is enthusiastic, creative, and happy. His power can help you create visionary music, art, and plays. He will motivate and inspire you to work hard, overcome obstacles, and complete unfinished work. If you are connected with this angel, you are undoubtedly on a creative mission. And so, Jophiel can enhance your creative abilities when needed.

- *Haniel (Four)*

  This archangel can bring about significant changes to your character, ideas, relationships, and life. Drawing from his formidable skills in building solid foundations, he is an ideal companion if you aim for stable relationships. He also helps maintain precarious careers and can keep your spirits up even during trying times. You can call on Haniel to fill you with joy and to help those around you find it too. Ergo, if you see messages from this angel, listen—they are trying to make you happier.

- ***Jeremiel (Five)***

  Jeremiel is a confident rebel who is unafraid to tackle the dangerous, the impossible, and the challenging. When you see messages from this angel, know that he is encouraging you to go into battle unafraid. Some battles are destined to happen, some fights are meant to be had, and some losses are meant to be lost. Call on Jeremiel when you need the strength to face your problems. With unyielding kindness and tempered bravery, he will shepherd you toward understanding. He will also provide you with mercy when you cannot bring even an ounce of it to yourself and guide you to justice in any situation.

- ***Michael (Six)***

  This angel is the closest to God, the embodiment of justice, mercy, and righteousness. He strives for peace in all circumstances and does his utmost to prevent violence. When you are afraid, you should call on St. Michael with the following affirmation: *"Help me, help me, help me, St. Michael."* If you say it three times, he will come. You will feel his energy enter the room, and you won't be scared anymore.

- ***Raphael (Seven)***

  Offering help and understanding, he will give you comfort and guidance. Raphael has an innate knowledge of your body; he knows when it is time to nourish yourself with food, take that much-needed rest, and provide it with extra care. Not only did he witness your heart's initial beat and your lungs' first breath, but he was also aware when something was not quite right. If you see messages from him, know that he is trying to keep you healthy. You might need to go for a checkup at the doctor, eat, or take the day off from work. Strong ties to this angel give you the power to feel your needs better. Call on Raphael when you want to sense your destiny and desires more clearly.

- ***Raziel (Eight)***

  The angel of mysteries receives messages from God to relay to others. If you are receiving messages from him, know that you have reached a deeper relationship with a higher power and are on the right path toward enlightenment. Your senses may become heightened. You may feel light-headed and be able to understand your reason for existing better. To be connected with Raziel allows you to harness an intuitive power that lets you sense your choices and opportunities more clearly.

- ***Ariel (Nine)***

  Receiving messages from this angel is a sign that you need to embrace a more peaceful life. Ariel is a beacon of hope within the celestial realm as she helps all living things live in harmony. *Why does the antelope not avenge the lion?* This is because God has sent Ariel to help them coexist. Her role is to ensure that the environment and humanity live harmoniously. Acquiring messages from her could be a sign to protect your environment further, to let go of past frustrations, and to live in peace. You can call on her to tap into her power of greenery and connection. She might be helpful when starting a garden, beginning new projects, and making new friends.

Manifesting with Angels

Once you understand archangels' different properties and associated numbers, you can use them and call on them whenever you need. And you do not need to wait for angels to send you a message before communicating with them, as you can share with them at this very moment. Moreover, everything in the universe vibrates, including our desires. By attaching the number associated with your needs to an angelic number, you can connect with angels and fulfill your deepest desires and needs.

Luck	Happiness	Job	Love	Success
5	2	1	2	1
7	3	3	3	3
9	8	4	6	4
	9		8	

Let us use Princess Kate in this example. Catherine Middleton was born on the 9th of January, 1982 *(Catherine Princess of Wales, n.d.).* Her guardian angel equation reads as follows:

$$9 + 1 + 1 + 9 + 8 + 2 = 30 = 3 + 0 = 3$$

The archangel associated with Kate Middleton is Jophiel, the angel of new beginnings and creativity. Kate could call on any angel to guide her. Yet, she is likely to get faster answers that will make more sense to her when they have come from the angel who knows her most intimately. As such, imagine that before meeting Prince William, she prayed to Jophiel for love. One way she could do this is to place Jophiel's number at the beginning and end of her sequence: *3x3.*

Numbers represent the essence of love and connection: *two, three, six, and eight.* Kate can use any of those digits as the center point, from *323, 363, 333,* or *383*, and it will all be accepted just the same. The threes, in particular, symbolize who will answer and receive the call, emphasizing that paramount importance lies within the number right in the middle. Likewise, if she wrote this number sequence multiple times, she could send a message to the angels asking them for guidance in her love life.

However, you do not need to restrict your contact with the archangels to only your own; you can call on any angel you like. You can reach out directly to other angels too. Yet, know that the lines of communication are always strongest when talking to the one that knows you best.

Pillar 6:
Numerological Cycles

Numerological cycles studies the mystical relationship between numbers and events in your life. These cycles refer to the idea that your time here on earth is divided into different periods, each of which is associated with a particular number and has its own unique energy and characteristics. Understanding these cycles can help you make more informed decisions about your future.

The three primary cycles in numerology are personal year cycles, pinnacles, and challenges, each of which is determined by calculations based on your birth date and name.

Chapter 16:
The Pinnacles

In numerology, Pinnacles refer to four long-term cycles in your life that represent specific challenges, lessons, and opportunities you might encounter.

The four Pinnacle cycles cover your entire lifespan. Each one begins after the previous one ends, and they are all of different lengths.

The First Pinnacle

First Pinnacle: This cycle begins at birth and lasts until the age of 36 minus your Life Path number.

This pinnacle is associated with the number 1 and represents the start of a new cycle, the beginning of a journey of self-discovery and self-expression.

During this stage, you're likely to experience a sense of newfound independence and confidence. You may feel a strong desire to assert yourself and make your mark on the world. This is a time of exploration and experimentation, as you begin to develop your unique identity and find your purpose.

The energy of the first pinnacle is characterized by initiative, leadership, and individuality. In this stage, you're encouraged to take risks and pursue your passions, even if it means going against the norm or facing criticism from others. This is a time to build a strong foundation for future success, and to cultivate the courage and determination needed to achieve your goals.

The Second Pinnacle

The second cycle starts after the first ends and lasts for 9 years.

During this cycle, you try hard to cooperate, share, and work with others. Relationships take priority in your life, and you strive to form close, supportive bonds while keeping your values intact. Fostering meaningful partnerships is at the top of your list as you endeavor to make connections that matter. No matter what comes your way, your values will remain unscathed. *(Pinnacles and Challenge Numbers, 2017).*

You may also experience a shift in focus and perspective that can lead to significant personal and spiritual growth. This cycle is often associated with career changes, new relationships, and other major life events that can have a lasting impact on your trajectory.

The Third Pinnacle

The third cycle starts after the second cycle ends and also lasts for 9 years. During this cycle, one becomes intimately familiar with one's habits and character. As a result, one will test the boundaries of their knowledge. Self-expression, taxing patience and trying new things are all events one may experience during this course *(Pinnacles and Challenge Numbers, 2017).*

This is the time of spiritual growth and self-discovery. You may begin to question your beliefs and values, find the need to speak your truths, and seek out new sources of inspiration and guidance. You may also feel drawn to social and humanitarian causes, and may seek out opportunities to make a difference.

The Fourth Pinnacle

The fourth cycle starts after the third cycle ends and continues for the rest of your life. It is associated with hard work, stability, and achievement. It's a time when you're likely to reap the rewards of your previous efforts and may find yourself in a position of authority or leadership. This can be a very productive and fulfilling time, as long as you remain focused and dedicated to your goals.

One of the key themes of the fourth pinnacle is responsibility. This is a time when you're called to take ownership of your actions and decisions, and to be accountable for your impact on others. You will be tested on everything you have learned. To be successful during this cycle, you will need unwavering beliefs, strong friendships, and a stable career. Without these aspects, you will wear yourself thin by doing too much with minimal support *(Pinnacles and Challenge Numbers, 2017).* So, you must pour in the foundation for your future, manifest the right opportunities, and immerse yourself in supportive, positive, and realistic energies. It would not help to anticipate larger-than-life events coming your way. Think practically and rationally, and do not be hasty.

Understanding what you need to learn will give you a sense of instant gratification. Having an idea of what you should achieve makes reaching that goal far easier and quicker, allowing you to anticipate any roadblocks before they even present themselves. By being aware of the transformation ahead and taking the right steps in preparation, your transition will be effortless, gentle, and stress-free. This way, you will have very few friends lost along the way and readily accept new changes. *Does not that sound comforting?*

Chapter 17:
Numbers and Their Challenges

Each pinnacle period or cycle is associated with a pinnacle number. These numbers represent the specific energy or influence that will dominate during a particular pinnacle cycle of your life.

Each pinnacle number carries a specific vibrational energy that is understood through the numerological meaning of the numbers 1-9, and potentially the master numbers 11, 22, and 33.

Below, you will find a detailed list of the numbers one to nine and their associated meanings concerning the four cycles. In this case, these numbers do not have a universal understanding. Instead, their purposes and intensities are subject to your cycle *(Pinnacles and Challenge Numbers, 2017).*

- *One*

  The number one concerns finding courage in facing an adversary, learning to stand up for yourself, and becoming self-reliant. This number calls for one to step up and learn fast. With this number in your destiny, you will have to perform and learn simultaneously. As such, you will act like a musician trying to keep up with the -band while still learning to play the instrument. It will be an intense and challenging time, but if you keep your focus and stick to your values, you can avoid being overpowered by those more mature than you. Ergo, your challenge is to find the courage to realize when you are becoming overwhelmed and refocus your energies on your sense of self.

  - *Pinnacle One*

    To experience number one in your first pinnacle means you will spend much of your initial development trying to form original ideas and find your identity. You will be called to lead without knowing what you are getting into and without being able to rely on yourself. It will be a challenging time. All eyes will be on you, waiting for you to make a wrong step. Likewise, you will make mistakes because you are learning as you go. Mistakes are inevitable, especially when you do not know what you are doing. Learn to embrace them to avoid looking back on yourself negatively later in life. Remain positive, and do not let your ego get in your way.

- *Pinnacles Two and Three*

  Focusing on your courage, drive, and vision during this cycle will prime you for leadership. Knowing and holding unwaveringly to your values is necessary. Hence, taking on a sterner outlook may be critical. Determination and integrity will also come into play, but only if you can discern your values and strive to keep them.

- *Pinnacle Four*

  With number one as the driving force in your fourth pinnacle, you are not likely to retire soon. Instead, you are destined to work harder than ever and accomplish great things in your leadership positions. You will be challenged to find new creative ways to enhance harmony and independence in your life.

- *Two*

This number encourages partnerships, cooperation, sharing, balance, and patience. You are likely to encounter many teamwork opportunities. Your challenge is to learn how to relate to and understand others while maintaining your values. Furthermore, you will need to find creative ways to compromise comfortably. While this number encourages you to look to others, it does not suggest a parallel. Likewise, you will sense that others cannot be bothered to do for you what you would do for them. This could make you bitter and resentful. Yet, try not to let the behavior of others get you down. Focus on what you can control, who you are, and the good you can do, and then you will be happy.

- *Pinnacle One*

  If you experience the number two within your first pinnacle, you can expect to be overly sensitive, easily hurt, and empathic. You will feel many emotions and not understand what to do with them. And so, your challenge is to make yourself comfortable by inviting others to help you assess these emotions and learn to cope with them.

- *Pinnacles Two and Three*

  During these stages, you will feel the effects of working with others in a balanced and harmonious setting. This wonderful and peaceful experience should encourage you to find ways to enjoy this kind of cooperation more frequently. The work you engage in during this time will be challenging, detailed, and plentiful. Thus, you will need to work well with others to help you get through.

- *Pinnacle Four*

  Having two energies influencing your fourth pinnacle will bring harmony and opportunity. Then, you can retire or continue to work a balanced and fulfilling career. The wonderful news is that you get to choose. However, you will need to watch your growing sensitivity. If you can get your emotions in control, you can live happily and cooperatively with those you care for most.

- *Three*

Number three proposes an opportunity to get to know yourself better. Your challenge is to dig deep and locate your emotions, their causes, and methods you can use to cope with them. This number forecasts your learning to share your feelings openly.

- *Pinnacle One*

Number three revealing itself during your first pinnacle is a sign that you will have to learn how to navigate a creative path. Likely, you will participate in something requiring creative vision, understanding, and skill. Chances are, you will not have the wisdom or the ability to see your dreams through, but you will have many pleasures in creating them. Focus your energy on creation rather than follow through, lest you become bitter and resentful at a young age.

- *Pinnacles Two and Three*

In the second and third pinnacles, the number three brings good friends, stable relationships, joy, and creative self-expression. With the number three, accomplishments are limited to how well you get along with others. Ever heard the saying, *"It is who you know, not what you know?"* That applies to you now more than ever.

- *Pinnacle Four*

The number three in the fourth pinnacle presents a good chance of travel and social activity rather than hard work.

- *Four*

As number four draws in, it signifies a need for family and stability. Yet, it will be challenging because you are learning to set good foundations, think with caution, and work sequentially. Overall, four encourages you to work hard to enjoy a blissful future.

- *Pinnacle One*

Four in the first pinnacle represents a demanding childhood with economic challenges, hard work, and lots of effort. It is a stage of life where you will be devoted to your education and future career. There is also a little frivolity and lots of stress and high-pressure settings.

- *Pinnacles Two and Three*

A four in your second and third pinnacles promotes a chance to achieve and get ahead in your industry. You will develop a competitive drive that will propel you toward success. But you must have courage in the foundations you have set, as there will be setbacks.

- *Pinnacle Four*

    The four energies in the fourth stage of life leaves one unlikely to slow down or retire. And while working hard, you will find plenty of joy. Besides that, you will know your limitations and be able to control and balance your career and social life optimally.

- *Five*

This number signifies a call for transformation. As such, it encourages us to open up and explore, allowing us to release our previous limitations. It also represents freedom, liberation, and exciting opportunities. Adapting to our ever-changing environment requires us to be flexible and prepared for the unknown.

- *Pinnacle One*

    Establishing stability and discovering your identity can be tough when the number five comes up during your first life stage. This could cause frequent travel, relationship break-ups, and career changes. You may also get into trouble often, with intense cravings and desires that are hard to resist. Setting beneficial intentions and maintaining healthy limits will help you make sensible choices without taking too much risk.

- *Pinnacles Two and Three*

    The vibrational influence of five brings progress and high achievement in your second and third pinnacles. Your desire for freedom will be quite powerful during this stage, but you must be careful not to let go of too many relationships and friendships.

- *Pinnacle Four*

    A five in the last stage of your life limits your ability to slow down. Instead, you will be in a fast-paced setting, startled by change and variety. You will overreach financially and domestically. To get through, you will have to build resilience. Remember, the mistakes you make do not define you. Errors only form part of your evolution, not the end product.

- *Six*

The number six draws family, relationships, service, and love into one's life. With a six in the works, you will need to find a balance between the amount you receive and the amount you give. Moreover, you will have to learn to pull away when your actions are not reciprocated. Similarly, you will learn to give back when required. Yet, the challenge is fighting your sense of responsibility. Reminding yourself that you are not the answer to everyone's problems is also essential. Hence, you do not have to try and fix their issues, only your own. Likewise, letting go when you are 'drowning' in pressure is okay. Focusing on yourself can also help those around you in the long run.

- *Pinnacle One*

  If you have number six involved in the first stage of your life, you will likely feel much pressure around caring for your family. The challenge is to find ways to remain a child while quickly growing into a mature and concerned adult. Life will deal you rough cards, but you need to remind yourself that none of it is your fault, and you are not responsible for the actions of adults, only your own.

- *Pinnacles Two and Three*

  The vibrations on a six within your second and third pinnacles influence your focus on your family. So, concentrate more on those you care for than your work. Likewise, you will be happiest when developing yourself as an individual.

- *Pinnacle Four*

  A fourth pinnacle, combined with the number six, adds a sense of philanthropy to your existence. Hence, you will find you are happiest in giving rather than receiving.

- *Seven*

Learning and studying are the major influences a seven can bring into your life. Thus, isolating yourself from others as you further your career is natural, but striking a balance between work and social life is a challenge that should be embraced. Working alone may bring the most satisfaction, though finding pleasure in other aspects of life is equally important. That said, you should push yourself to be among others to avoid isolating yourself completely.

- *Pinnacle One*

  If you experience a seven in your first few years of life, you will often feel isolated and alone. You may choose to suffer in silence and focus your pain on understanding the meaning behind your life. This will gain you much intellect and intuition, but you will be lonely. Remember to ask for help when you need it. Emotions are normal, so you should not be embarrassed to feel sad. Everyone feels that way sometimes.

- *Pinnacles Two and Three*

  The presence of seven within the second and third pinnacles offers a chance to specialize in the spiritual realm. Unless you actively use your intuitive and philosophical skills, progress at this stage can feel taxing, mundane, and slow. Practice your skills readily, and you will find success easily. Aside from that, you will find the most happiness in spiritual and charitable activities during this cycle.

- *Pinnacle Four*

  Understanding the depths of knowledge you possess can make it challenging to connect with those around you. So, it is wise to seek out individuals with similar interests and perspectives on life. Likewise, be open and brave, and let others hear your words, as it will help you find like-minded friends. Overall, experiencing the number seven during this pinnacle prepares you to become a spiritual teacher.

- *Eight*

Power, money, business, and abundance are associated with this number. If you are endowed with an eight, you have been blessed with opportunities to have power, make money, and succeed. Under its influence, you will have to keep control of your judgment, virtues, and sense of right and wrong because you will likely lose yourself and make hasty decisions with so many offerings. Therefore, you need to find the courage to stick to your values.

- *Pinnacle One*

  With the number eight associated with your first few years of life, you will become interested in business activity. You can help your family run their business or start your own. Your focus and drive in creating and running a business will be unyielding. But at such a young age, you will likely fumble over many obstacles. However, with patience and grace, you will become satisfied and energized.

- *Pinnacles Two and Three*

  The number eight within these life periods invites a more rational way of thinking. Subsequently, you will have to limit your emotions and try to think as often as possible. Meanwhile, your focus will be on your ambitions and achievements. With a clear head and straight values, you can gain much honorable success and power.

- *Pinnacle Four*

  In your last stage of life, eight pulls you to develop your wealth and power further. Likewise, giving back your knowledge and passion to others will make you feel best. However, you will have to ration with your years of success to give back and find happiness. Thinking charitably will be difficult at first, but it will help you gain a long-lasting legacy in the long run.

- *Nine*

Number nine promotes the development of a true humanitarian. It allows you to develop charitable attributes like compassion, love, ethics, and patience. Whenever you go, strive to spread encouragement and wisdom and foster peace. Meanwhile, nine can also lead to intense moments of vulnerability when desperately trying to voice your feelings. Through it, remember the power of maintaining emotional balance. Furthermore, you must commit to the concept of the right place and right time when it comes to personal feelings and questions.

- *Pinnacle One*

  A child with the number nine influencing their life is a silent hero on the path of everyday life. They stand up for those who are bullied, do not fear retribution, and do what their hearts and teachers have taught them is right and just.

- *Pinnacles Two and Three*

  The vibrational pattern of the number nine in these pinnacles pulls forth emotional expression and humanitarian views. You will be happiest doing charitable work, fighting for change, and engaging in political action. Hence, your purpose is to effect change and promote compassion.

- *Pinnacle Four*

  Having nine in your fourth pinnacle favors charity above all else. Consequently, you will be given many opportunities to give of yourself. Likewise, you may retire or invest time in helping others find harmony and balance.

- *Master Number 11*

This number represents the intuitive visionary. It is associated with spiritual insight, enlightenment, and a strong connection with the subconscious mind. With this influence, you may find yourself drawn to seek a deeper understanding of the world around you and the spiritual realms.

- *Pinnacle One*

  A person with Master number 11 influencing their first Pinnacle is likely to experience a heightened sense of intuition and spiritual awareness early in life. This can lead to a strong desire for self-discovery and a fascination with the metaphysical world. They may find themselves naturally drawn to situations that require insight, empathy, and understanding.

- *Pinnacles Two and Three*

  During these Pinnacles, the vibrational energy of the Master number 11 may lead to a deepening of spiritual understanding and the development of psychic abilities. There may also be an increased interest in humanitarian causes, and a desire to contribute to the greater good. These are periods for introspection, growth, and personal transformation.

- *Pinnacle Four*

  Having 11 in the fourth Pinnacle suggests a time of spiritual enlightenment and profound insights. This period may bring opportunities for leadership roles in spiritual or humanitarian fields. The challenges faced during this period will test the person's faith and inner strength, pushing them towards their highest potential.

- *Master Number 22*

This number is known as the Master Builder. It represents practical idealism and the power to turn dreams into reality.

- *Pinnacle One*

A person influenced by the Master number 22 in their first Pinnacle is likely to demonstrate a unique blend of intuition and practicality. They may exhibit remarkable potential for leadership and a strong ability to manifest their dreams into reality from an early age.

- *Pinnacles Two and Three*

During these Pinnacles, the vibrational pattern of the Master number 22 can result in a period of considerable productivity and the achievement of significant life goals. There may be opportunities to lead and inspire others and to make a lasting impact on a large scale.

- *Pinnacle Four*

Having 22 in the fourth Pinnacle suggests a time of significant achievement and the realization of long-term goals. This is a period of life where the person's leadership skills and ability to manifest will be at its peak, potentially bringing great success and fulfillment.

- *Master Number 33*

This number, known as the Master Teacher, symbolizes selfless service, love, and the spiritual uplifting of mankind.

- *Pinnacle One*

A person influenced by the Master number 33 in their first Pinnacle is likely to show a strong tendency towards selflessness and a desire to serve from an early age. They may demonstrate an unusual level of maturity and a deep concern for others.

- *Pinnacles Two and Three*

During these Pinnacles, the vibrational pattern of the Master number 33 might lead to a deepening of compassion and a desire to help others. There may be opportunities for teaching, healing, and service, and these are periods for profound personal and spiritual growth.

- *Pinnacle Four*

Having 33 in the fourth Pinnacle suggests a time of great spiritual understanding and the potential to make a significant impact on the lives of others. This is a period when the person's capacity for love, healing, and teaching will be at its highest.

How to Calculate

To be able to map out your Pinnacle chart, you need to calculate three general things. They are your:

1. Life path number
2. Pinnacle numbers
3. Pinnacle cycle periods

Let's use the birthdate of Martin Luther King Jr., a well-known civil rights leader, as an example. He was born on January 15, 1929.

1. **Calculate the life path number:** You calculate the life path number by reducing the numbers of the birth date to a single digit or master number (11, 22, 33). Here it would be 1 (Jan) + 15 (day) + 1929 (year) = 1945, then 1+9+4+5 = 19, and finally 1+9 = 10, then 1+0 = 1. Thus, the Life Path number is 1.
2. **Calculate the pinnacle numbers:** Your pinnacle numbers are derived from calculations based on your birth date.
    - First Pinnacle: Add the day and month of birth and reduce to a single digit or master number. For instance, using the above date, 1 (Jan) + 15 = 16, then 1+6 = 7. So, the first Pinnacle number is 7.
    - Second Pinnacle: Add the day of birth and the year of birth and reduce to a single digit or master number. In this case, 15 (day) + 1929 (year) = 1944, then 1+9+4+4 = 18, then 1+8 = 9. So, the second Pinnacle number is 9.
    - Third Pinnacle: Add the first and second Pinnacle numbers and reduce to a single digit or master number. For this example, 7 (first Pinnacle) + 9 (second Pinnacle) = 16, then 1+6 = 7. So, the third Pinnacle number is 7.
    - Fourth Pinnacle: Add the month and year of birth and reduce to a single digit or master number. For this case, 1 (Jan) + 1929 = 1930, then 1+9+3+0 = 13, then 1+3 = 4. So, the fourth Pinnacle number is 4.
4. **Calculate the pinnacle cycle periods:** The Pinnacle cycles have different durations and are determined by subtracting the Life Path number from 36.
    - First Pinnacle: This cycle starts from birth and continues until the day before your 36th birthday, minus the Life Path Number. In this example, it would be 36 - 1 = 35 years.
    - Second Pinnacle: This cycle starts from your 36th birthday, minus the Life Path Number, and lasts 9 years. In this example, it starts from age 35 and continues until age 44.
    - Third Pinnacle: This cycle starts after the second Pinnacle and also lasts 9 years. So, in this case, it begins at age 44 and goes on until age 53.

- Fourth Pinnacle: This cycle starts after the third Pinnacle and lasts for the rest of your life. In this case, it starts from age 53 onwards.

Martin Luther King Jr.'s Pinnacle numbers are 7, 9, 7, and 4, and these cycles span from birth to age 35, 35 to 44, 44 to 53, and 53 onwards, respectively. It's interesting to look at the meanings of these numbers and how they might correlate with the major phases of his life.

It is so important to understand the value of calculating the four pinnacles. Doing so allows you to understand what you went through, why your experiences were what they were, and how you can move on without regret.

Here's a general chart showing the different Pinnacle periods based on the Life Path number. Use this to map your own chart. Remember, the age ranges for each pinnacle cycle are calculated by subtracting the life path number from 36.

Life Path Number	1st Pinnacle (Birth - X)	2nd Pinnacle (X - Y)	3rd Pinnacle (Y - Z)	4th Pinnacle (Z onwards)
1	Birth - 35	35 - 44	44 - 53	53 onwards
2	Birth - 34	34 - 43	43 - 52	52 onwards
3	Birth - 33	33 - 42	42 - 51	51 onwards
4	Birth - 32	32 - 41	41 - 50	50 onwards
5	Birth - 31	31 - 40	40 - 49	49 onwards
6	Birth - 30	30 - 39	39 - 48	48 onwards
7	Birth - 29	29 - 38	38 - 47	47 onwards
8	Birth - 28	28 - 37	37 - 46	46 onwards
9	Birth - 27	27 - 36	36 - 45	45 onwards

If your life path number is a master number (11, 22, and 33), reduce them to a single digit (2, 4, and 6 respectively) for the purposes of determining the pinnacle periods. However, you should still consider the Master number interpretations when evaluating your Pinnacle numbers.

Pillar 7:
Year Planning

Calculating what you are supposed to learn in each period of your life is helpful if you are trying to understand what it is you need to achieve and when you need to achieve it. Once you know this, you can learn major life lessons and enjoy a fulfilled and exciting life. Likewise, along the way, you are going to experience many challenges. And likely, you will have many questions about these challenges, such as when they will happen and what you can do to resolve them quickly. Fortunately, numerology has the potential to provide exceptional detail.

Have you ever wondered what the year has in store for you? Have you thought of when you will finally achieve that promotion? Have you been praying to meet the love of your life? Are you begging to know when you will quit your horrible job?

Numerology can give you the answers to all these questions. It can provide detailed accounts of what to expect throughout your year. You can use these details to guide your decision-making and planning.

Chapter 18:
Personal Year Numbers

Is this even possible? Can you predict the events of the upcoming year? Has your life been predetermined to a greater extent than you initially thought? Calculating your personal year numbers may help you do that.

Personal year numbers refer to the yearly cycle that an individual goes through. It is calculated by adding the numerology of the current year with the numerology of the individual's birth month and day.

It is said to influence one's experiences and opportunities throughout the year. It can help give you an idea on what to expect during the year and guide your decisions and actions accordingly.

For example, if your personal year number is 5, it may indicate a year of change, adventure, and growth. Understanding personal year numbers can be a helpful tool in gaining self-awareness and making the most of each year.

Let's say someone was born on May 15, 1990, and they want to calculate their personal year number for the year 2023. Here's how they would do it:

First, they would reduce the month and day of their birth to a single digit. May is the fifth month, so 5. The 15th day reduces to 1 + 5 = 6.

5 + 6 = 11, which is a master number, so it is not reduced further.

Next, they would reduce the year they want to calculate to a single digit: 2 + 0 + 2 + 3 = 7.

Finally, they would add their birth number to the current year number: 11 + 7 = 18.

If the resulting number is a double digit, it is reduced to a single digit by adding the two digits together: 1 + 8 = 9.

So for someone born on May 15, 1990, their personal year number for 2023 would be 9.

Chapter 19:
Universal Numbers

Another way that you can glimpse of what the future holds is by calculating your universal number. A universal number is a means of predicting what the world can expect in future years. It's derived from the date of birth, by adding the digits of the birthdate and reducing them to a single digit. Each universal number has its unique characteristics that you can feel throughout your lifetime, most especially during major life events. By understanding the characteristics of each number, you'll be able to play to your strengths, make more informed choices, and achieve your goals more effectively.

Numbers and Meanings

Universal numbers range from 1 to 9, with each number holding its own vibrational energy. Below you will find a list of numbers and their associated meanings concerning universal numbers. These meanings can help you know what to expect in future years *(Universal Year Numbers, 2022)*.

- *One*

  This number suggests the start of new things, new beginnings, and foundations. The general theme is confidence. A year with this number requires you to have the courage to step up to the plate, take the initiative, and follow your dreams. You must also acknowledge that only your fear is holding you back. Ergo, be optimistic and have faith in your future, now more than ever.

  If you have goals, now is the time to work toward achieving them. Do not hold back. Likewise, while chasing your dreams, ensure your responsibilities have been taken care of to avoid getting sucked into your new project. You must act with a hint of caution. Think through your decisions carefully, and do not be too hasty.

  Moreover, it is an exciting time, but be wary of taking risks. You must be cautious of doing too much. This may lead you to exhaustion. You should pick one project and stick to it until it is finished, then move on to the next. Be sure to separate your time evenly. Also, do your best to live a balanced life filled with friends and worthwhile work. Finally, your energy this year will likely attract red and mineral ruby.

- *Two*

The number two favors relationships, feelings, compassion, and partnerships. A year with the number two suggests preparing for teamwork and group settings. You will find working with others will bring you much happiness. You will have better results in terms of achieving your goals if you communicate and work cooperatively with others.

This year, your energy will attract the colors white and light blue and the minerals moonstone and pearl.

- *Three*

A year influenced by the number three is likely to hold potential for a creative flood, initiative, and imagination. Enjoyment and creativity are the main themes for this number. You will have many opportunities to have fun. However, your responsibilities will likely fall out of reach, allowing you the space to make new friends and develop stable relationships. Push yourself to be more expressive and sociable. Talk about your feelings and open your heart up to those around you.

Your energy this year will attract the color yellow and the mineral topaz.

- *Four*

This number suggests a year of hard work, little frivolity, and much self-improvement. There will be endless opportunities to expand your career.

Four is calling you to make commitments to your work and personal life. This year is all about putting in the effort.

Tackle things slowly and avoid impulsive decisions at all costs. This is a great time for you to practice and master various skills. Set up a neat calendar and make time to improve your career and friendships

This year your energy will attract the color green and minerals emerald and jade.

- *Five*

Such a number suggests uncertainty, change, and freedom. This is a time of transformation and bountiful opportunities are waiting to spring at you. Look closely at your choices and apply the right amount of consideration to all your options.

You must think big and more creatively. Find a solution that will solve four or five central problems instead of searching for multiple fixes. Be adaptable and embrace new experiences and you'll find this time of change in your life as an adventure. Your energy will attract the color blue and the mineral aquamarine.

- *Six*

This number suggests that home relationships and family duties should be the primary focus this year. Now is the time to make adjustments in your home life. You are allowed to change duties in your home and family relationships. You can also find joy within them again. This is a good time to bring closure to your partnerships and stability to your financial troubles and to ask for advice from loved ones.

The challenge is keeping promises to ensure your home's stability. You must be disciplined, loyal, and dedicated to making changes. It would not be easy, but you will have to endure it for the security of your family. Furthermore, take the year to work on your empathy and compassion. Hence, allow yourself to understand and work better with those you care for most.

Likely, your energy this year will attract the color purple and the mineral sapphire.

- *Seven*

The seven bring forth spiritual ideas, meditation, and inner peace. That said, it is a great time to focus on yourself, your patience, your sense of self-worth, and your empathy. Likewise, ask spiritual questions and search for answers. Other than that, take things slowly, make decisions cautiously, meditate, and learn to go with the flow. You may feel the need to take control, but try to resist; learn how to follow others and act as a team player. Let yourself be emotional, creative, and happy.

This year, you can expect your intuition to enhance. As a result, your relationships and social life will improve. So, you should try to relax this year and let your gut guide you toward success. You may not have all the answers, but be confident that you have enough experience to know what paths to take. Now is a great time to remind yourself of how amazing you are. By learning to believe in yourself, you will find your career and relationships work out better.

Your energy will attract the color violet this year and the mineral amethyst.

- *Eight*

An eight symbolizes a year of praise, rewards, and great success. This year you will be flooded with career, material, and financial achievements. As the year brings you abundance, it is the time to focus on your professional goals. It is also a good time to start building your investments.

Meanwhile, you will desire control above all else and become skeptical of life's pleasures. If you let mistrust rule you, your well-being will be affected. So, you have to stay levelheaded and tackle each task as they come. Let go of people who do not support you. They are not worth fighting for right now. You and what you have worked for are worth your energy and focus. That said, do not purposefully burn out any relationships. Let those who have supported you for years help and appreciate you when you need it most. You will need them to make your achievements feel worthwhile.

This year, your color is brown, and your mineral is a diamond.

- *Nine*

This number often signifies a period of giving back and making a positive impact on the world. You may have strong feelings of empathy and compassion for the less fortunate, those who suffer or those in need.

This is the year to focus less on yourself and more on helping others. Volunteer your time, talent, or treasures for causes that you believe in.

Your color this year is white, and your minerals are opal and gold.

Conclusion

Numerology was developed over many years to appeal to and predict the lives of people of all backgrounds and cultures. Its long history in the hands of Romans, Greeks, Israelites, scientists, and religious leaders has accumulated masses of cultural and philosophical value in the art, which can be enjoyed, understood, and respected by people globally today. Even skeptics will find the ideologies around numerology interesting even if they do not believe it can predict anything.

Aside from its rich history, numerology is fun to practice. There is something so soothing about sitting down with a piece of paper and solving a complex equation. Numerology is a rewarding practice because it forces us to use those spaces in our minds that not everybody uses and because the calculations themselves can be challenging. But the real puller is when we come across a value that intrinsically outlines our personality, character, or fault.

Furthermore, numerology helps people in making safe and worthwhile decisions. Even if numerology does not help immediately or provide you with a complete understanding of your experiences, in the long run, it does. Likewise, numerology helped me know where I wanted to go with my life. It gave me alternative options for career paths. In a way, numerology acted like a career counselor, except cheaper and more knowledgeable about my character. It gave me ideas, which gave me hope.

Perhaps, numerology makes you think. Maybe your calculations suggest that you struggle with something but you do not believe you do, or your associated number means you prefer to be alone when you are happiest around other people. Regardless, the next time you hear a friend does not want to be around others, you might understand why. You will also begin to understand your choices better. Likewise, you do not need to pinpoint that understanding to a value you found in this book.

Likely, numerology may have helped you open up to more possibilities and reason with your behavior and attitude, or it might help you accept who you are. Nevertheless, it can help in many ways without giving hard, accurate facts. Plus, it allows us to imagine and see potential in our lives. For such, *how often have you sat back and wished you could dream like a kid again?* Fortunately, numerology gives you that chance. However, it does not happen overnight. Regardless, somewhere along the line, you will find yourself different from the person you once were, except with little accreditations to this book and the study of numerology.

This book has delved into Pythagorean, Chaldean, and Kabbalah approaches to numerology. Although these practices are inherently different and not, one can give you an accurate reading on their own; collectively, the game changes. If you want to develop a detailed reading of yourself or someone else, you should use all three and explore the fundamental questions and calculations of each. Your root number is just as valuable as your matching Kabbalah energies. The Chaldean rearranged birth number is as pivotal in understanding your destiny as your Pythagorean birth number. Your understanding of yourself within these subcategories is as valuable as collective descriptions of you. These tests will collectively give you a deep, complex, and profound characterization of yourself, your life, and your destiny.

People are not one-dimensional pictures. We are not this or that. We are not always doing things, and we are not doing something. We are made up of multiple layers from many experiences. Our understanding of ourselves has to match that. When reading and calculating your destiny and character, you need to use many techniques. Only then can you truly understand how rare and complex you are.

We have discussed the importance of Karma and finding balance within the universe. Whether Karma is just or unjust is beside the point. It is natural and inevitable.

Have you ever heard the tale of the Mpondo king? The Mpondos was a clan in Africa during the 18th century when Shaka Zulu, king of the Zulu people, was conquering all the lands (*King Faku ka Ngqungqushe*, 2022). There were many battles fought over power. Lives were lost, tricks played, foes destroyed, and friends brought to a bloody end. It was an intense time. The Mpondo king knew that if he tried to defeat Shaka Zulu and his band of fierce warriors, the Mpondo kingdom would be lost forever. The Mpondo king was thoughtful, always thinking and never acting. The favoring of thought over action was something his people frowned upon. They wanted him to act as bravely as Shaka. They wanted their kingdom to take over Africa. They did not want a king who thought and thought and thought. But that was who the Mpondo king was. He thought, and after thinking, he would think some more. The cycle continued until he had found an answer he could cherish. He decided he had to allow Shaka Zulu to pass through his kingdom to fight battles on the other side. However, he did not choose to befriend the king but to assist him.

The other clans witnessed this alliance and became angry. They asked the Mpondo king for the same assistance given to Shaka. The Mpondo king thought some more before turning to Shaka and explaining that he shall not pick sides but allow his kingdom to be marched through by all clans expecting to fight battles on the other side. Although the Mpondo kingdom was not lost, it became dense with travelers, vengeful men, and hungry warriors. As the indigenous clans marched through, many locals were injured, attacked, and humiliated. The locals were very cross and began to abandon their king, moving in with more powerful clans that could protect them better. Still, the Mpondo king chose to let peace thrive in his lands instead of violence. Years passed, and the Mpondo king's wife finally gave him a son.

As the years went by, the Mpondo kingdom lost much of its regard. The Mpondo prince watched the warriors as they passed. He had a keen eye for detail and an even greater skill for fighting. The Mpondo prince quickly grew into the greatest warrior Africa had ever seen. His destiny was to become the warrior that would kill Shaka Zulu and restore the Mpondo kingdom to even greater regard.

Do you think this is interesting? I love this story because it shows how miraculous this world is. Stories like this should not be real, but some are, and Karma is undoubtedly as real as any story.

The miraculousness of tales like this makes one wonder if there exists a higher being that watches over us all. Angels are everywhere. They exist to help us on our path toward God's plan. You can communicate with them. You do not need to wait for them to call you. Just write out the relevant numbers and see what happens. Let the activity of speaking to angels bring you peace of mind, even if it is only when you are afraid. Let the angels help you.

While talking with angels, you can start planning the rest of your life. You know now how to calculate the approximate dates of particular events. You know how to calculate when your character will begin to evolve. Now you can plan and ask for help when you need it most. If your pinnacle charts are not detailed enough, phrase specific questions and find when exactly certain events will happen. You can find out when you will get married, meet the love of your life, have your first child, and when your life may end. You can determine these things in approximations, and your calculation may be unexplainably accurate if you are lucky.

Remember, some things are meant to be. Your life path was constructed before your birth. You have a destiny you need to reach. But you also have some free will, and how you get to where you need to go is up to you. Perhaps you have been going through life unguided. Maybe you have been unsure where you are supposed to be and when you are supposed to be there. You do not need to be uncertain anymore. You now can find the inevitable and can distinguish destiny from choice. You have a superpower that you can use quickly and effectively. Use this power, teach it, and practice it as often as you desire. Your happiness is now in your hands, as it was in Moses', , Adam's, and Archimenes,' who were once Perses.

Glossary

Birth number: This number reveals your talents and potential, the pieces of you that you will need to reach your destiny.

Chaldea: A kingdom that existed in what is now Iraq within ancient Southern Babylonian society around 940 B.C.E.

Character number: This number represents the first trait people notice about you, how they perceive you, and how they will interact with you.

Expectancy number: This number symbolizes who you are to others and what others expect from you.

Expression number: This number symbolizes your talents, strengths, and powers.

First impression number: This number determines how you view yourself and your goals.

Guardian angels: Divine messengers sent by God to help us in our life's journey.

Kabbalah: This is an ancient Hebrew knowledge and lifestyle.

Karma: A cosmic system of judgment that bestows punishment and reward on every living creature.

Karmic debt: The punishments we are exposed to as a result of our negative actions toward others.

Master number: Powerful double-digit numbers that guide your understanding of reality.

Numerology: The study of numbers and how they cosmically relate to people and their past, present, and future.

Personal year number: This number can help determine what is in store for you during a particular year.

Pillar: A foundation of knowledge.

Pinnacles: These are cycles that are time frames within one's life where one evolves in different areas.

Pythagoras: A Greek mathematician, astronomer, and philosopher.

Root number: Your root number reveals your true life path, ultimate destiny, and inner character.

Soul number: This number reveals your heart's greatest desires, the things you have always wanted, and the path that will lead you to your ultimate happiness.

Universal number: This number can be used to predict what can be expected within a specific year.

References

Abbot, R. (2021, June 19). Origin stories: Numerology. *Isbourne.* https://www.isbourne.org/blog/origin-of-numerology-isbourne-wellbeing-centre-cheltenham

Adele biography. (n.d.). The Famous People. https://www.thefamouspeople.com/profiles/adele-6088.php

Albert Einstein biography. (n.d.). Vendantu. https://www.vedantu.com/biography/albert-einstein-biography

Albert Einstein net worth. (n.d.). Celebrity Net Worth. https://www.celebritynetworth.com/richest-businessmen/richest-designers/albert-einstein-net-worth/

Amy Jade Winehouse biography. (n.d.). The Famous People. https://www.thefamouspeople.com/profiles/amy-jade-winehouse-691.php

Believe. (2021, May 18). *Karma debt.* Arcbali. https://arcbali.com/en/numerology-concept-of-karmic-debt-cause-and-effect/

Biography of Vincent van Gogh. (2009). Vincent van Gogh. https://www.vincentvangogh.org/biography.jsp

Blakeley, S. (2022, April 9). *Pythagoras biography and accomplishments.* Study. https://study.com/learn/lesson/pythagoras-history-facts.html

Buchanan, M. (2013). *The numerology guidebook: Uncover your destiny and the blueprint of your life.* Hay House, Inc.

Catherine Princess of Wales. (n.d.). Biography. https://www.biography.com/royalty/kate-middleton

Chaldea Al Fusaic. (2022). Al Fusaic. https://www.alfusaic.net/civilizations-101/chaldea

Chaldean numerology vs Pythagorean numerology. (2011, April 14). Astronlogia. https://astronlogia.com/numerology/chaldean-numerology-vs-pythagorean-numerology/

Chinese alphabet. (2019). My Languages. https://mylanguages.org/chinese_alphabet.php

Clevinger, N. (2021, November 14). *One and only: How did Adele get famous?* The Sun. https://www.thesun.co.uk/tvandshowbiz/celebrities/16734901/how-did-adele-get-famous-one-night-only/

Delhi, R. (2020, August 30). *Is numerology a science or a myth.* Raag Delhi. https://www.raagdelhi.com/numerology-science-or-myth/

Diana, Princess of Wales. (n.d.). Royal. https://www.royal.uk/diana-princess-wales

Drayer, R. (2003). *Numerology: The power in numbers.* Square One Publishers, Inc.

Ellen DeGeneres biography. (n.d.). Notable biographies. https://www.notablebiographies.com/news/Ca-Ge/DeGeneres-Ellen.html

Everything about Chaldean numerology. (n.d.). Sylbu. https://slybu.com/chaldean-numerology/

Field, S. (2020). *May 2020 weather history of Indiana.* Weather Spark. https://weatherspark.com/h/m/19729/2020/5/Historical-Weather-in-May-2020-in-Indiana-Pennsylvania-United-States

5 powerful ways to manifest with angel numbers (rituals). (2022, May 14). Manifest Like Whoa. https://manifestlikewhoa.com/manifest-with-angel-numbers

Gomez, J. (2022, 24th August). *Aileen Wuornos.* Metro Biography. https://metrobiography.com/aileen-wuornos/

Haim, J. (2018, August 3). *The energy centers of Kabbalah.* Wellbeing. https://www.wellbeing.com.au/mind-spirit/spirituality/energy-centres-kabbalah.html

Handel biography—History of George Frideric Handel. (2018, April 17). C Muse. https://www.cmuse.org/handel-biography-george-frideric-handel-composer-history/

The history of numerology. (2022). Numerology Toolbox. https://numerologytoolbox.com/numerology/history-of-numerology/

How to predict timing of events. (2022). Affinity Numerology. https://affinitynumerology.com/using-numerology/predict-timing-of-events.php#maincontentcontinue

Hungarian alphabet. (2019). My Languages. https://mylanguages.org/hungarian_alphabet.php

Jeffrey Dahmer biography. (2022, September 26). Biography. https://www.biography.com/crime-figure/jeffrey-dahmer

Jin, H., and Oguh, C. (2022, October 28). *Explainer: How Elon Musk funded the $44 billion Twitter deal.* Reuters. https://www.reuters.com/markets/us/how-will-elon-musk-pay-twitter-2022-10-07

Joanna, E. (2022, March 23). *Pythagoras: Life, work, and achievements.* Live Science. https://www.livescience.com/pythagoras

Kabbalah numerology. (2022). My Pandit. https://www.mypandit.com/numerology/types/kabbalah/#kabbalah-numerology-reading

Kabbalah numerology: Meanings with numbers and reading chart. (n.d.). Slybu. https://slybu.com/kabbalah-numerology/

Karmic numbers. (2020). Numerology Savvy. https://numerologysavvy.com/karmic-numbers/

King Faku ka Ngqungqushe. (2022, June 29). SA History. https://www.sahistory.org.za/people/king-faku-ka-ngqungqushe

Learn languages. (2019). My Languages. https://mylanguages.org/

Let numerology answer your question. (2022). Truthstar. https://www.truthstar.com/let-numerology-answer-your-question/

Lock, S. (2020, September 11). *When did the Twin Towers fall and what does the World Trade Center look like now?* The Sun. https://www.the-sun.com/news/1455693/when-twin-towers-fall-world-trade-center-9-11-terror-attack/

Lopez, C. (2021, June 20). *Ted Bundy: Biography of a serial killer.* Warbleton Council. https://warbletoncouncil.org/ted-bundy-7767

McKoy, J. (2021, October 7). *Depression rates in US tripled when the pandemic first hit—Now, they're even worse.* The Brink. https://www.bu.edu/articles/2021/depression-rates-tripled-when-pandemic-first-hit

Michelle Obama biography. (2018, February 26). Biography. https://www.biography.com/us-first-lady/michelle-obama

Nathan, S. (2022, May 14). *Ellen DeGeneres preps for her TV farewell: She's 'been crying a lot'.* Page six. https://pagesix.com/2022/05/14/ellen-degeneres-preps-for-last-show-shes-been-crying

Nina Simone. (n.d.). Ninasimone.com. https://www.ninasimone.com/biography/

Number meanings 1–9. (2022). Numerology. https://www.numerology.com/articles/about-numerology/single-digit-numbers-in-numerology/

Numerology—The meaning of natural numbers. (2022). Number Academy. https://number.academy/numerology/

Olivia. (2022). *Everything you need to know about Chaldean numerology.* Just Numerology. https://justnumerology.com/chaldean-numerology

Pinnacles and challenge numbers. (2017, March 17). Felicia Bender. https://feliciabender.com/pinnacles-and-challenge-numbers

Queen Elizabeth II. (2022, September 26). Biography. https://www.biography.com/royalty/queen-elizabeth-ii

Reed, L. (2020). *What are master numbers and what do they mean.* Simply New Age. https://simplynewage.com/what-are-master-numbers-and-what-do-they-mean

Richard. (2020, May 2). *Numerology calculation—The Pythagorean method.* Character Numerology. https://characternumerology.com/numerology-calculation-the-pythagorean-method/

Selene. (2022, August 4). *Using manifestation numbers.* Psychicsource. https://www.psychicsource.com/article/other-psychic-topics/manifesting-with-numbers-by-psychic-selene/24104

Slick, M. (2008, December 5). *The origins and history of Kabbalah.* Carm. https://www.carm.org/kabbalah/the-origins-and-history-of-kabbalah/

Taylor Swift biography. (n.d.). Famous People. https://www.thefamouspeople.com/profiles/taylor-swift-13896.php

The surprising ways that Chaldean numerology will unlock your destiny! (2022). Numerologist. https://numerologist.com/numerology/4-things-you-need-to-know-about-chaldean-numerology/#chaldean11

Universal year numbers—What they are and how to calculate them! (2022). Numerologist. https://numerologist.com/numerology/universal-year-number-calculate

Wang, J. (2022, September 16). *What is the average net worth by age in America?* Best Wallet Hacks. https://wallethacks.com/average-net-worth-by-age-americans/

What is Kabbalah. (2022). The Kabbalah Center. https://www.kabbalah.com/en/pages/what-is-kabbalah/

Zulu alphabet. (2019). My Languages. https://mylanguages.org/zulu_alphabet.php

THE 5 PILLARS OF ASTROLOGY

71 Beginner Techniques & Tips to **Self-Discovery** and **Transformation.** Know Your Higher Purpose by **Decoding** the **Secrets** of Your **Zodiac**. Predict Your Future With Horoscopes

MONIQUE WAGNER

Table of Contents

Introduction

There are more things in heaven and earth [...] than are dreamt of in your philosophy.

–William Shakespeare, *Hamlet*

Have you ever felt like there was more to life than what you have been taught? Or that there were more forces at play than what you can see in the physical world? Or that maybe your life and feelings were being shaped by things beyond your comprehension? Well, you're not alone. Spiritual thinkers and healers have spent thousands of years studying these forces, coming up with ways of describing their influences on the world. They have identified several such things, many to do with the stars and planets above our heads, that can explain how these forces affect us. This study is called astrology. By learning about astrology and all its branches, we can understand the world more clearly, finally beginning to comprehend all those mysterious influences that lie beneath the surface.

In this book, I will be teaching you about the five main pillars of astrology. These five pillars describe some of the most fundamental forces at play in our universe. You will learn all about how things like the planets, the constellations, and their movements impact your life and the people around you. I will explain important concepts like the zodiac, birth charts, and houses, all of which have a profound impact on you. You will also find 71 techniques, tips, and strategies on how you can decode the secrets of your zodiac. These techniques, tips, and strategies are peppered throughout the entire book. And it's intentionally designed this way to serve as your guide along each step of the process.

Once you really start understanding how these stars work and your relationship with them, you will be able to better understand your life as a whole. It is only by identifying root causes that we can begin to make the journey toward solutions.

I know more than anyone what it's like to feel lost and burned out. I have experienced so many of the hardships that all of us face today—never-ending work hours with seemingly no payoff, a lack of belonging and understanding of the world, and difficulty with relationships. I knew I had to make a change. So, I connected with my Scandinavian roots, tracing my lineage back to a succession of neo-pagan spiritual leaders, and I began to find answers. These answers helped me construct a clearer narrative about my life and stabilized me, allowing me to chart a stronger course toward the future. I have since devoted myself to the study of many different occult and alternative medicine practices from around the world. As an empath, I now want to share those teachings with the rest of the world in the hope that the wisdom I have gained from my journey might help you.

This book is designed for those with little to no background in astrology. It is meant to guide you through those initial learning curves with the goal of eventually making you an expert in the subject! To help ease you into this rich and complex world, I have structured the book around the five pillars of astrology. We will start with the first pillar, which deals with the fundamental aspects of astrology itself. Then, we will move on to the second pillar, which is the zodiac. After that, we will begin our discussion about the planets, which are the third pillar. Subsequently, you will learn all about the fourth pillar, the houses. Then, finally, you will read about the fifth and final pillar: birth charts. Putting together all these pillars of astrology will help you to start making sense of the universe and your place inside it.

Pillar 1:
Fundamentals

Before we get into all of the complex aspects of astrology, we should cover the fundamentals. In this pillar, we will look at all the foundational aspects of astrology, learning the history of the practice of astrology and the differences between different practices. By the end of this pillar, you should have a good understanding of the definition and basic practice of astrology.

Chapter 1:
The Basics of Astrology

On your astrology journey, you will be learning about many different specifics of the discipline. For now, we need to get the very basics out of the way. We need to define the very fundamental aspects of the discipline and help you understand where it all started. We also need to make some critical distinctions between different sects of astrology that cannot be confused. Let's get started!

What Is Astrology?

First and foremost, how do we formally define astrology? Well, astrology is the belief that celestial bodies in outer space (planets, moons, stars, etc.) have a definite influence over life on earth. One of the most popular and well-known subsections of this belief is the idea that the position of the stars, moon, and planets at the time of your birth will have an influence over your personality and life outcome. You have probably heard people say they are a "Libra" or a "Sagittarius," or maybe even a "Leo moon" or a "Capricorn rising," for some of the more advanced astrology enthusiasts. These are all categories to do with the position of the celestial bodies at the time of that person's birth. These categories are the signs of the zodiac and correspond to 12 dominant constellations in the night sky, each represented by an animal or a character. Your "sun" sign, or your dominant sign, corresponds to the time of year during which you were born. Astrologers use a combination of the current astrological map (i.e., where the stars, moon, and planets are at that moment) with your birth chart (i.e., where the stars, moon, and planets were at the time of your birth) to calculate certain things about your life. You can ascribe astrology to any aspect of life. If you struggle with relationships, money, self-esteem, your career, family, or any number of things, astrology can help you both make sense of these problems as well as work toward solutions.

The History of Astrology

Many cultures throughout human history have practiced some form of astrology. For this reason, it is hard to pin down a strict lineage of where it originated. For example, China has had an independent form of astrology unrelated to the "Libra" and "Capricorn" terms above. In the Chinese zodiac, there are 12 signs that all correspond to a different animal, but your sign is based on the year in which you were born, not the month. So, this tradition is a little different from the tradition we are talking about.

The dominant astrological tradition in the West today is based on something developed in Ancient Greece. More specifically, it came about during the Greek Hellenistic period. The Hellenistic period was a great time for Ancient Greece, a time of brilliant innovation and prolific artistry. The beginning of the period was marked by the death of Alexander the Great, whose rapidly grown empire spanned all the way from Greece to China. The aftermath of this period meant that Greece had much more contact with the rest of the world than ever before, especially Asia and the Middle East. As a result, they began expanding their minds with art, philosophy, and literature brought from thousands of miles away. Many new religions and philosophies of life began to emerge in Greece during the Hellenistic period, including astrology. It was especially influenced by Egyptian theology, which drew a strong connection between mankind and the heavens. The constellations, such as Pisces and Cancer, were already Greek inventions based on their existing mythologies. Astrology took this a step further and assigned these constellations to certain times of the year and to the ruling of the world around us. Thus, the origins of modern astrology were born.

From there, astrology as a concept only expanded. Greece was colonized by Rome at the end of the Hellenistic period, but the Romans did not let astrology die out. The Romans were enamored by all things Greek and adopted many of their traditions, particularly religious ones, and astrology was no exception. It reigned powerfully throughout the heyday of Ancient Rome. Due to Greece's and Rome's extensive contact with the Middle East, Hellenistic astrology also became popular there. However, astrology in Europe significantly declined after the introduction of Christianity to the Roman Empire in the 4th century C.E. Astrology contradicted the Christian order of the universe and therefore fell out of fashion in Europe during this period. In the Middle East, though, it was still thriving. In fact, it kept up even after the Islamization of Saudi Arabia and North Africa in the 7th and 8th centuries. But, for a time, it seemed like astrology was never to be practiced in Europe again.

Europe did not see a significant incline in astrological interest until the early Renaissance in the 12th century. Spain and Italy were under significant influence from the still-powerful Islamic Empire, due partially to Mediterranean trade and the colonization of Spain by the Western Islamic Empire. Through these connections, Europe began to have a renewed interest in the Islamic culture as well as the Ancient Greek and Roman cultures. By the 14th and 15th centuries, the stories of the zodiac were making the rounds all the way up to England. Chaucer, an English poet from the late 14th century, included many Ancient Greek and Roman stories in his famous epic, *The Canterbury Tales*, demonstrating that this history was on the upswing everywhere in Europe.

The next major boom astrology would enjoy would be the rise of neo-paganism and spiritualism in the 19th century, particularly in England and the United States. The Victorians were fascinated by all things ancient and mystical. Famous figures like Harry Houdini exploited this belief in the paranormal with his magic shows while many other similar figures held public séances and fortune tellings. Tarot cards and crystals also began to gain significant interest, showing how much Victorians were willing to adopt metaphysical traditions. This period of neo-paganism formed the basis of our modern practice of astrology today. Things like birth charts were refined and calculated more precisely, and the discipline of astrology turned into a bona fide science. The prevalence of astrology in the West only grew throughout the 20th century, especially during the new age movements of the 1960s and '70s, culminating in the immensely popular and widespread tradition we know today.

Modern vs. Traditional Astrology

Now, even though there is this clear line from the Hellenistic tradition of astrology to our current practice of it, there are still some important distinctions we should make between them. Making the mistake of conflating these two philosophies might result in you getting mixed readings or even possibly offending someone. You want to make sure that you aren't claiming any tradition as your own when you are really practicing something else. To clarify, almost all Western practices of astrology, including the traditions laid out in this book, are classified as modern astrology. There may be some similarities or overlaps between modern and traditional astrology, but the two are not the same. Traditional astrology is rooted in times and places different from our own, and modern astrology has been adapted to fit the way we currently live our lives. Here, we will explain in more detail the difference between these two versions of astrology.

Traditional Astrology

Traditional astrology is astrology as it was practiced by the Ancient Greeks, Romans, Muslims, and even South and East Asians. These are all the premodern interpretations of astrology, the foundation on which all astrology is based. Even within this classification of "traditional" astrology, there were many different traditions. This is why it's important not to claim to be practicing traditional astrology: Every practice from this era is slightly different. They have all merged, with varying degrees of importance, to create our current version of astrology, but no one today can claim to be practicing astrology in exactly the same way as the ancients. For one, many astrological traditions would merge with the local religion. Thus, those practicing astrology in Ancient Rome would have had a different spin on the mythology than those practicing in early medieval Egypt given their differing local philosophies and religions. Traditional astrology had not yet been standardized and thus lacked the cohesion we have today. It was a necessary stage in astrology's development and had its own inherent value, but for the purposes of modern astrologers, it is significant only as a stepping stone toward the current version of astrology.

Modern Astrology

"Modern" can mean anything from the Renaissance to the 21st century, depending on who you ask. For our purposes, "modern astrology" means the practice of astrology as it first appeared in the early 20th century and, more accurately, as it was more refined in the 1960s and '70s. This is the version that almost all Western astrologers practice today and likely the version that you have come in contact with the most throughout your life. Some practical things have influenced the shift in a more concrete way. For one, new planets have been discovered since ancient times (namely, the outer planets Uranus, Neptune, and Pluto) which have changed the calculations. Additionally, increased communication around the world has allowed astrology, along with languages, time zones, and mathematics, to be standardized and streamlined. Now, much larger groups of people can practice the exact same type of astrology at the same time thanks to things like the internet and even mass literacy. But besides these practical changes, there have been ideological changes too.

Modern astrology's defining ideological feature is that it is primarily focused on the individual. Back at the beginning of the chapter, when I gave you a brief overview of what astrology is, I described it as having a bearing on your life and personality. While the Ancient Greeks did discuss astrological signs as they corresponded to behavior, the idea that your personality is fundamentally a certain way because of your astrological sign is primarily a modern idea. Modern astrologers focus on life journeys and personality profiles. They discuss how the planets might have influenced a person since their birth and how they will help guide them through their future relationships. Modern astrologers can help people to navigate their astrological system, leading them to a future where they are working with, not against, their astrological signs. They might also consult on things like a person's compatibility with other signs and thus future successes or failures in relationships with others. It might also help you understand your natural aptitudes and passions, leading you toward a particular career or calling. In short, modern astrology is more about individuals' relationships with the universe at large, helping to explain their own behaviors, motivations, and skills as well as those of the people and world around them.

The reasons behind this ideological shift vary, but there are two main value changes between the ancient world and our world that have influenced it. First of all, individualism is the dominant ideology in modern Western culture, whereas the Ancient Greeks leaned toward collectivism. We are now more interested in the nature of specific individuals as unique beings rather than the nature of humanity as a whole. Astrology that explains humans' collective relationship with the stars does not speak to our cultural values of individual personalities and consciousness. Second of all, modern Western culture values free will over fatalism. The Ancient Greeks were famously fatalistic, believing that human beings' life courses were fixed and could not be changed, even if the individual consciously tried. Plays like Sophocles' *Oedipus Rex* explored this theme, with Oedipus walking directly into his tragic fate in the pursuit of escaping it. Modern Westerners, on the other hand, believe in the idea of shaping our own destinies and being masters of our own fate. Thus, our version of astrology focuses on how an individual can shape their own identity using knowledge of the stars. They are not huge differences, but they can influence a culture's relationship with astrology and spiritual readings.

Vedic vs. Western Astrology

Another distinction to make within astrology is between Vedic (or South Asian, or Eastern) and Western astrology. This is not a distinction of time, like the above, but a distinction of place. In places like India, astrology is practiced very differently than in the West. We already talked about Chinese astrology and how it differs, but India also has its own version of astrology. Vedic astrology is similar to Western astrology but follows a distinctly different lineage. It is derived from Ancient Indian texts called the *Vedas*. The Vedas are a collection of Sanskrit-language texts that date back thousands of years on the Subcontinent. They form the basis of the Hindu religion as well as many other aspects of Indian culture. It is disputed when the first mention of astrology is made in these texts, but some estimates date it as far back as 12,000 years. It is unclear whether Ancient Greek astrology was originally influenced by Vedic astrology since there was contact between the two and Vedic astrology clearly predates Greek. Some historians might claim that this is true, but it is unknown. Regardless of the relationship, Vedic astrology has some clear similarities to and differences from modern Western astrology.

The Similarities

Despite their very different origins, the two are actually quite similar. For one, they share a monthly calendar that determines the relative personality of the individual born in that month. These monthly signs are also based on animal characters that have distinct personalities. They even retain some of the same characteristics month to month, meaning that your sign and its attributes might actually be the same in Vedic and Western astrology. Furthermore, Vedic astrology is also focused on individual destiny and relationships. You will find a lot of spiritual and personal guidance within the teachings of Vedic astrology. So, as you can see, there are a lot of parallels between Vedic and Western astrology.

The Differences

However, there are also some attributes the two don't share. In terms of practical differences, the main one is that the dates don't line up. Even though there are 12 signs per year that tend to match up neatly with the Western signs, the date ranges for the months that each sign covers are different. While modern astrology goes by the 19th–22nd of the month, Vedic astrology goes by the 12th–15th of the month, so you might actually be a different sign in each of the two calendars. In terms of spiritual or ideological variation, the Vedic texts tend to be more karmically focused. This is because of the Vedas' close relationship with Hinduism, which invented the ideas of reincarnation and karma. So, though both versions of astrology focus on how an individual acts, the Vedas will focus more on how the individual's actions correspond to their karma and reincarnation, whereas Western astrology will focus more on how their actions influence personal happiness and growth. This is not to say, though, that Vedic astrology doesn't provide personal guidance. It still offers insight into things like relationships, personal aptitudes, and other individual-based concerns, just with a slightly different religious spin. And finally, Vedic astrology ranks the types of signs differently, placing the rising sign as the most important, while Western astrology places the sun sign at the apex. Chances are if you ask a Vedic astrologer what their sign is, they will most likely give you their rising sign first, not their sun sign. Therefore, while the two practices are very linked, they are also not identical and have some sharp contrasts.

Pillar 2:
The Zodiac

Now that you understand the basics of astrology, as well as the specific type of astrology we are studying in this book, you are ready to look more deeply into the pillars. In the second pillar, we will be talking all about the zodiac. The zodiac is the chart of constellations that correspond to each astrological sign. It is a very complex diagram that charts the movement of the earth, sun, and moon all on the same image. Essentially, it creates a ring around the earth, mapping out the night sky in a 360° view. This sky view is then divided into 12 sections to represent the 12 essential zodiac signs: Capricorn, Aquarius, Pisces, Aries, Taurus, Gemini, Cancer, Leo, Virgo, Libra, Scorpio, and Sagittarius. The zodiac is the mathematical basis for all astrological sign interpretation. The zodiac signs can also be categorized in multiple ways. There are elements, modalities, and polarities of the zodiac that all interact with each sign's original meaning. In this section, comprised of Chapters 2–5, we will examine each aspect, sign, and categorization of the zodiac to pursue its true meanings.

Chapter 2: The Signs and Their Meanings

Every sign on the zodiac has a particular meaning. When people talk about their zodiac signs, they are talking about the archetype that defines who they are. These signs are calculated based on the position of certain celestial bodies in relation to the constellations. The sun sign is determined by the constellation through which the sun passes each month of the year. When the sun is passing through a constellation, that sign is in sun. The same goes for the moon, which is instead on a 28-day cycle with the constellations. Rising signs are determined by what constellation was over the horizon at the time of your birth and is determined by your birth location. In this chapter, we will look at the importance of sun, moon, and rising signs as they determine personality types as well as the specific meanings of each sign when they are in sun, moon, and rising. By the end of this chapter, you should have a solid grip on all three of your signs as well as the ability to see how they interact with each other on your chart.

The Difference Between Sun, Moon, and Rising

We have already mentioned throughout the last chapter the existence of sun signs, moon signs, and rising signs, but here we will explain in a little more detail what these things actually mean.

Sun Signs

Sun signs follow the conventional monthly zodiac calendar. In other words, your sun sign depends on the month you were born in. Sun signs are the core of your being, the base personality traits with which you conduct most of your life. As the sun rules the sky, so too does your sun sign rule your life. This is why many people focus on their sun sign as being their "main" astrological sign, calling themselves a "Pisces" or a "Taurus" without mentioning their moon or rising. When it comes to Western astrology, the sun is dominant.

Moon Signs

Your moon sign, on the other hand, represents your inner self. This is the person you are when you are alone or with only close friends. It is a vulnerable part of yourself, something you might want to hide or even be ashamed of. It is calculated based on what constellation the moon was in during your birth, which corresponds to the day of the month. Because there are 28 days in the moon's cycle, it will rotate to the next zodiac sign roughly every 2.3 days.

Rising Signs

Finally, rising signs are the constellation that was rising at the time of your birth. Your rising sign represents your public self, the main personality you project into the world. If you notice a trait in someone else that only really comes out when they are in public or trying to impress others, this is their rising sign at work. It might sound like the rising is the most superficial of the signs—and the moon the deepest—but this is not so. In fact, rising characteristics can run very deep. Rather than representing someone's "fake" side, the rising sign represents someone's social side or their relationship with the social world, which is extremely important. When discussing relationships, be they business, platonic, or romantic, astrologers often look very deeply at the rising sign as it can tell us a lot about how we interact with others.

Combining Them

All three signs are important to understanding a person's astrological profile. Even more significant is how these three signs interact with one another. Everyone will have a unique combination of the three which influences how they present with each of their signs. This is one of the most convincing cases against people who are skeptical of astrology and who argue that it isn't possible that *everyone* born in the same month has the same personality. This is a simplified and erroneous assumption about astrology on the part of the detractors since astrologers know the moon and rising signs play a huge role in a person's disposition both on their own and interacting with their other signs. So, for example, a Gemini sun with a Leo moon will be very different from a Gemini sun with a Cancer moon. Even two Gemini suns with Leo moons might differ because of their rising sign. Even if someone has all three the same, they might have different readings for the planets and houses, which we will explore more in later chapters. For now, we will be focusing on the main 12 astrological signs, looking at how they manifest in all three versions: sun, moon, and rising.

Aries

(Figure 1, Aries's symbol)

Animal/Symbol:
The ram

Element:
Fire

Dates:
March 21–April 19

As Sun:
Aries are known to be an intense sign. Related to the Greek god of war, they are fiercely competitive and passionate individuals who know how to win in a fight but also how to protect those they love. They might be intense, but they are also fiercely loyal. Another interesting quality of Aries is that they are very open to new things, so you will often find that they are more welcoming to new ideas and inventions than the average person.

As Moon:
Aries moons will often surprise you with their intensity. Their competitive streak might be something that only comes out in certain contexts, such as while playing a game or even a romantic rivalry. The competitiveness of the Aries moon will be related more to the deeper things in them, such as love, self-esteem, and family. They will also be more willing to quickly accept new things or people on a deeper level.

As Rising:
Aries risings might seem like Aries suns on steroids. Since their competitive side is brought to the forefront of the social world, they will seem like the stereotypical "frat boy" seeking out any opportunity to prove their worth. Just know that this is how they show a connection. They don't seek to destroy others, merely to connect through competition. They may also be sexually promiscuous.

Taurus

♉

(Figure 2, Taurus's symbol)

Animal/Symbol:
The bull

Element:
Earth

Dates:
April 20–May 20

As Sun:
Often known for being a more chilled-out Aries, Tauruses have the fierce loyalty and headstrongness of the Aries but none of the intensity. You will often not see the big personality of the Taurus until they show it to you.

They're the kind of person who doesn't get angry… until they do. It's hard to set off their fuse, but once you do, it can be crazy! Tauruses also have a luxurious and sophisticated side. A Taurus's idea of a perfect day would be to visit an art gallery before being pampered at an exotic spa. Mixing this love for the high life with a keen interest in the intellectual world makes Tauruses some of the most complex and intriguing types.

As Moon:
Taurus and the moon are perfectly compatible. Taurus's sweetness and emotional intensity are perfect when put in the moon position. Taurus moons are sometimes slow to accept new people in their life, but once they do, they will experience some of the most profound connections possible. Taurus moons particularly shine in one-on-one relationships where they can get to know people at their core.

As Rising:
Taurus risings can come off as a little strange. They won't be the life of the party but rather the cool person who sits in the corner while everyone wonders about their mysterious qualities. You might feel drawn to approach a Taurus rising in a social situation as they will exude allure, but they will rarely come to you first.

Gemini

(Figure 3, Gemini's symbol)

Animal/Symbol:
The twins

Element:
Air

Dates:
May 21–June 20

As Sun:
Geminis often get a bad rap, but they are really one of the most delightful signs out there. Geminis are social butterflies, valuing the building of relationships within large groups of people. They are amazing communicators which makes them great leaders. However, they do have a tendency to overshare, possibly saying things that can be considered inappropriate or brash. But don't let this put you off—Geminis can be delightfully cheeky in this regard and make excellent comedians.

As Moon:
Gemini moons are interesting since Gemini has such a reputation for being social. Depending on the combinations with other signs in sun and rising, a Gemini moon will likely be more reserved but might be something of a covert social butterfly. They might be able to juggle many close relationships at once, something

many people struggle to do. A Gemini moon will also have remarkable honesty when it comes to those deep, heart-to-heart conversations.

As Rising:
Gemini risings are able to put their outgoingness at the forefront. Their social circles are considerably more widespread than Gemini suns, and they will be able to start parties and relate to anyone they meet. Gemini risings have an amazing ability to find a point of connection with everyone and will certainly make you feel special.

Cancer

♋

(Figure 4, Cancer's symbol)

Animal/Symbol:
The crab

Element:
Water

Dates:
June 21–July 22

As Sun:
Cancers are the most caring and loving of the signs. They are known for being particularly connected with home and hearth. Cancers will be strongly connected to their families, whether their born or found family. They will not only be loyal to these people but prioritize nurturing them as well. Despite being somewhat reserved outwardly, they have a rich inner life and often are quite connected to their dreamer or spiritual sides.

As Moon:
With Cancer moons, this rich inner life is dialed up. Those with a Cancer moon will focus mostly on the deep care and inner spirituality of Cancer. They might be poets, driven to investigate the mysteries of life through their bright creativity. These Cancer moons might have a little bit harder of a time outwardly expressing how intensely they care about others, perhaps demonstrating it in more indirect or nonverbal ways.

As Rising:
Cancer risings thrive in care positions. They have the ability to extend their familial circle to a wider range of people, allowing them to ascribe the same degrees of importance to more people in their life. Cancer risings make great nurses, childcare workers, and even social workers.

Leo

♌

(Figure 5, Leo's symbol)

Animal/Symbol:
The lion

Element:
Fire

Dates:
July 23–August 22

As Sun:
Leos are the most confident of the signs. They radiate a leader's energy wherever they go. Leos will be able to accomplish their dreams with sheer determination and charm. Sometimes, that makes people feel that Leos are extraordinarily lucky, but it isn't luck—it's their ability to seek out what they want at all costs. But don't let this make you think that Leos are selfish. They can be fierce defenders of their friends and some of the most passionately loving people in the world.

As Moon:
Leo moons are strange. They might be able to mask this inner confidence with a more modest place of work or smaller circle of influence, but they will still rule this with the inner charm and confidence. A Leo moon might not seem confident unless they are with their inner circle, where their more primary Leo traits are more apt to appear.

As Rising:
Leo risings are sometimes actually less confident than Leo moons. This is because all that charisma they exude is limited to the social world. They might feel like kings or queens with their friends but return home feeling less confident. Leo risings should learn to extend some of that confidence to their inner selves.

Virgo

♍

(Figure 6, Virgo's symbol)

Animal/Symbol:
The maiden

Element:
Earth

Dates:
August 23–September 22

As Sun:
Virgos are sometimes considered the left-brainers of the zodiac. This means that they love all things organization, from spreadsheets to lists to schedules. But Virgos more than love organization, they crave it. An unstructured Virgo is an unhappy Virgo. At their worst, Virgos can be bossy and controlling, but at their best, they can be amazingly conscientious leaders. Put them in the right position, and they will run things as neatly and smoothly as a well-oiled machine.

As Moon:
Virgo moons often have their cravings for organization relegated to their personal routines. They might come across as an easygoing person out in public, but they are in desperate need of routine in their personal life. So, while they might be fine going to an unstructured event, they would be devastated if their morning rituals were disturbed. You might meet a Virgo moon thinking they are laid back only to realize that their inner world is tightly regimented. Virgo moons often need help coming out of their shell and allowing themselves or their personal lives to be messy.

As Rising:
Rising Virgos will almost always seem like they have it all together. They're the ones immaculately dressed at the party who show up ten minutes early and help everyone clean up at the end. Depending on their sun and moon signs, they might actually have a messier interior life that they mask with extreme organization. Sometimes they need to learn to bring their sharp minds into the more emotional aspects of life.

Libra

♎

(Figure 7, Libra's symbol)

Animal/Symbol:
The scales of justice

Element:
Air

Dates:
September 23–October 22

As Sun:
Libras are sometimes considered the quintessential air signs since their qualities are so identifiably airy. Libras are sometimes considered to be the flakiest of the signs. This is because they tend to be dreamy and indecisive, easily swayed by others' opinions. But look closer and you will realize this is a strength, not a weakness. Their indecisiveness isn't necessarily an inability to commit to opinions but rather an extreme openness and willingness to consider all sides of an issue. For this reason, Libras are amazing mediators, working very well as judges or marriage counselors. They are able to genuinely understand where everyone is coming from and thus make a decision that is actually more objective and informed than some of the more fierce or emotional signs. However, this flakiness can easily veer into weakness, especially when in the presence of someone very forceful or persuasive. Libras should be careful not to allow more willful signs to take advantage of their easily swayed natures.

As Moon:
Libra moons are some of the most romantic people you will ever meet. They prioritize love and relationships in their life, so if you are in a relationship with a Libra, you will always be their number one. However, Libra moons are especially at risk of being taken advantage of in relationships. They might downplay necessary conflicts or avoid confrontation. Libra moons should take some of their mediation abilities and ascribe them to their own lives, helping them to help themselves.

As Rising:
Libra risings make amazing leaders. Though they may lack the natural charisma of a Leo or the competitiveness of an Aries, they more than make up for it with their intelligence. Libra risings are deep thinkers and careful considerers. They would do well to apply these innate skills in the world of politics or even art.

Scorpio

(Figure 8, Scorpio's symbol)

Animal/Symbol:
The scorpion

Element:
Water

Dates:
October 23–November 21

As Sun:
Scorpios are some of the most misunderstood signs out there. They can very easily come across as standoffish because they are a very private sign. Scorpios have a very hard time letting people in, especially on a deeper

level. They hesitate to share their deepest secrets and often don't let even their close loved ones know their next moves. This might come across as suspicious or paranoid, but it's just their way of guarding themselves. If they are able to fully trust someone, then they will let them in on everything and have a hard time letting that person go if the relationship comes to an end. One of the most intense signs, Scorpios really know how to commit when they decide something is right.

As Moon:
Scorpio moons are often even tougher to crack than Scorpio suns. Even though they might have a very outgoing sign in their sun, letting many people in on a superficial level, their Scorpio moon means that breaking through to their deeper layers will be all the more difficult. The Scorpio moon will need a lot of coaxing to allow someone to break through to their inner shell. But again, once you do so, they will be bonded to you for life.

As Rising:
Scorpio risings are very interesting since they are known for being deeply reserved. Thus, Scorpio risings might project an air of unattainability when they are really soft and gooey underneath. You might meet a Scorpio rising and assume they are a very private person only to have them spill all their deepest secrets after a few months of friendship—or even a few drinks!

Sagittarius

(Figure 9, Sagittarius's symbol)

Animal/Symbol:
The archer

Element:
Fire

Dates:
November 22–December 21

As Sun:
You will never miss a Sagittarius. No shrinking violets, Sagittariuses have some of the biggest personalities you will encounter. They are all about living life in the moment and seeking out all the amazing thrills and experiences this world has to offer. For this reason, Sagittariuses love things like travel, adventure, and meeting new people. Any chance to learn and explore is never a waste of time in a Sagittarius's book. They are also known for being the life of the party. You can always find a Sagittarius at the center of a table at the pub, telling jokes and making the whole room shake with laughter.

As Moon:

Sagittarius moons will often break out these qualities only when they are with their closer circles. They might explore their love of travel and experiences through more subtle means, like enjoying reading interesting books or watching foreign films. A Sagittarius moon with their sun in, say, Virgo might come across as organized at first only to bust out their more passionate and fun-loving side once you get to know them better.

As Rising:

Sagittarius risings might seem like the life of the party all while housing some mysterious secrets. You might find them looking pensive at the end of the night, retreating back into that more private inner life they have for themselves. They might like traveling or partying with others but enjoy a more stable and calm life when they are by themselves. Often, Sagittarius risings with more emotional moons or suns will need a lot of downtime in between their socializing stints.

Capricorn

(Figure 10, Capricorn's symbol)

Animal/Symbol:

The goat

Element:

Earth

Dates:

December 22–January 19

As Sun:

Capricorns are the high achievers of the zodiac. They are similar to Aries and Leo in their thirst for recognition, but the earth in their sign helps them to stay grounded and work toward achievement for their own personal fulfillment, not just fame or glory. In fact, Capricorns can actually be very introverted compared to the more bombastic Aries and Leos. They will hold their noses to the grindstone while they are working on a project and won't remove them until they feel their work is done. They can become workaholics, but they will also always be certain to get amazing results.

As Moon:

Capricorn moons are more subtle about their ambition than Capricorn suns and risings. They might not be workaholics or out for recognition, but this doesn't mean they don't still strive for achievement. Instead, Capricorn moons' hunger for accomplishment will run deeper. They might find satisfaction in more personal and private projects, such as writing a novel or even learning a hobby or language. As long as they feel that they are accomplishing their goals and moving forward, Capricorn moons are happy people!

As Rising:
Capricorn risings are stars in the professional sphere. This is the version of Capricorn that is most at risk of becoming a workaholic. They will certainly go far, but they also run the risk of losing the motivation for their high achievement. Unlike the Capricorn moons, who get a lot of personal fulfillment out of their accomplishments, Capricorn risings might start to feel that their achievements are empty if they only do them for the sake of recognition from others. Capricorn risings should emphasize connection with others in their achievements to continue to give them meaning.

Aquarius

(Figure 11, Aquarius's symbol)

Animal/Symbol:
The water-bearer

Element:
Air

Dates:
January 20–February 18

As Sun:
Aquarians are unconventional and open-minded. They are freethinkers, intending to push boundaries and forge their own unique path through life. They are unburdened by any sense of traditionality and won't think any less of themselves if they don't meet the standard measures of success like marriage or homeownership. Aquarians are less fiercely loyal in relationships and tend to value communities over one-on-one relationships. This means that they can lean toward interesting arrangements like open marriages but are dead serious when it comes to volunteering for good causes. All in all, an Aquarian is a unique and stunning individual you will never forget.

As Moon:
Aquarius moons might not wear their unconventionality on their sleeves. Instead, they might emphasize the more publicly acceptable aspects of their personality while keeping the more unorthodox ones quiet. You might find an Aquarius moon very ordinary at first glance only to learn that they have a different kind of lifestyle or don't really care on a deeper level if you think they're weird.

As Rising:
Aquarius risings absolutely do wear their unconventionality on their sleeves, sometimes to a fault. They might dress in a very provocative or artsy way, have an interesting job, or talk very openly about taboo subjects in public. If they have very different signs for their sun and moon, you might find that this "wacky" outward appearance does not translate to their inner life, which might be more conventional. An Aquarius rising with a Virgo moon might be unusual on the surface, but hiding inside is a deeply regimented person.

Pisces

(Figure 12, Pisces's symbol)

Animal/Symbol:
The fish

Element:
Water

Dates:
February 19–March 20

As Sun:
Pisces have a reputation for being the "emotional" sign, but this is only partially true. Pisces are very interesting because they are outwardly extremely emotionally intelligent but actually lack a lot of emotional awareness when it comes to themselves. This is not to say that they don't feel deeply. Often, Pisces will find themselves in the throes of an emotional breakdown that they can't explain. One reason they are like this is their extreme empathy. Pisces pick up on and feel the emotions of others very deeply and are also very easily hurt. They have very thin skin, which can either be a weakness (for example, if they are unable to take criticism or have difficulty watching intense films) or a strength (when they are deeply empathetic and passionate about helping others, for instance). For this reason, Pisces actually do better in less emotionally stimulating environments so that they don't become overwhelmed.

As Moon:
Pisces moons can be one of the more difficult moons to have on your chart. This is because your emotional intensity runs deep but isn't immediately obvious to people, meaning that others might take liberties or offer criticism that they don't realize the Pisces moon can't handle. Pisces moons need to learn to understand and communicate their emotional sensitivities to others to avoid these kinds of situations.

As Rising:
Pisces risings are very interesting since their emotional reactions are more tied to others than ever. You might even say that their emotional selves are rooted in others' emotions. If a Pisces rising lacks a Pisces moon or sun, then they may not have as strong a sensitivity to things like emotional intensity or criticism. Thus, Pisces risings do very well in careers that require a lot of emotional labor, like therapists or even actors. They can engage in emotional work without really risking their inner selves too much.

Chapter 3: Elements of the Zodiac

Throughout the last chapter, we included a heading indicating the "element" of each zodiac sign. There are four elements: fire, earth, water, and air. This is another aspect of the zodiac that runs parallel to the signs. You might have noticed some similarities between some of the signs. If you look closely, some of the signs where you noticed crossover likely had the same element attached to them. This is no accident. The elements each have an important role to play in the system of the zodiac and each has distinctive qualities in and of itself. In this chapter, we will look closely at the four elements and how they create their own subsystem of the 12 zodiac signs.

Origins of the Four Elements

You might be a little confused if this is the first you are hearing of the four elements. Maybe you're wondering how they correspond to the periodic table of the elements, which you probably learned about in high school chemistry class. The periodic table has more than a hundred of elements like iron, hydrogen, magnesium, and so on, so why does the zodiac only have four? Well, it all originates from the birthplace of astrology itself: Ancient Greece. You can think of these four elements as a kind of ancient version of the periodic table. The paradigm served essentially the same purpose: to explain the forces at play in the world around us.

Because the Ancient Greeks didn't have microscopes with which to observe the minutiae of the natural world, they used their naked senses to discern what elements were controlling the world. They came up with four forces that they believed described the world around them. The first was earth, encompassing everything from dirt to rocks to plants and animals, even humans themselves. The second was water, appearing as seas or rivers or rainstorms. The third was fire, a force of warmth and life but also of destruction. And finally, there was air, representing the space between everything up to the heavens as well as wind and breath.

By categorizing the elements into these four simple forces, the Greeks were able to describe some very fundamental aspects of human life. To this day, you can still categorize many of the periodic table's elements into earthen elements (minerals and rocks), fiery elements (such as gases), aquatic or liquid elements, and those which evaporate into the air. This system of elements was also closely related to the Greek gods, mythology, and of course astrology as well. Today, we observe the element system as a central aspect of both the zodiac and other spiritual practices, such as tarot cards. In tarot, the elements each rule over a suit in the deck, also corresponding to four aspects of life discussed in tarot readings. So, even thousands of years later, the four Greek elements still play an important role in helping us understand the universe.

The Four Elements in Relation to the Zodiac

When the Greeks developed their system of the four elements, they wove them into many of their spiritual practices. They assigned meanings to these elements, which all related to constellations, planets, and gods. You may have heard of earth goddesses like Demeter or water gods like Poseiden. The idea that the wind, sea, fire, and land were all ruled by fanciful gods was central to Greek theology and helped them make sense of things like extreme weather, plagues, and even personal tragedy. They were also a lens through which people could be viewed, corresponding certain behaviors to "fieriness" or "airiness," which formed the basis of the personality-centric sign system.

The elements relate to the zodiac calendar in a very mathematical way. Because 12 divides neatly by four, you get a clean three signs for each element. The elements also alternate in perfect sequence through thc calendar. If you go back and read the last chapter, you will see that the elements play out in a particular pattern. The elements that are mapped onto each zodiac sign relate to the symbol that the sign represents. Some have more obvious connections than others. Pisces, the fish, is a water sign, while Capricorn, the goat, is earth. Some are difficult to connect at first, such as Libra, the scales, being an air sign, or Sagittarius, the archer, being a fire sign. However, if you look at the mythological significance of these constellations, their meanings will line up more thematically with the element in question. By being mapped onto the 12-sign zodiac system, the elements run parallel to the signs, creating another layer of meaning behind them.

Qualities of the Four Elements

As we mentioned above, each element has its own distinct qualities. You can see how signs of the same element echo one another, suggesting that though they have some different superficial qualities, they share a deeper connection. Some people value their sign's element very highly, proclaiming that they are an "air sign" or an "earth sign" as confidently as they would assert that they were a Taurus or a Scorpio. In this section, we will look at the deeper archetypal meanings behind each element and how they connect the three astrological signs that they rule.

Air

Presiding over Aquarius, Gemini, and Libra, air signs share a penchant for two essential things: logic and sociability. All three of these signs are unemotional thinkers who have the ability to look past emotions and think rationally. They are also, in a way that might seem contradictory, lovers of communication and socializing. The worst quality of the air signs is their flightiness. They have a tendency to be somewhat flippant or nonchalant about the deeper connections in life. They might end up abandoning relationships without much thought or struggle to stick to their opinions, values, or even personality traits. Air signs are great people to have on your side, though. Immensely intelligent and brave, they will always be interesting. In the Tarot, air signs are represented by the suit of swords, which denotes truth and intellectual pursuits.

Earth

Considered to be the polar opposite of the air signs, earth is the—you guessed it—down-to-earth element. Virgos, Tauruses, and Capricorns all share earth as their ruler. An earth sign will be a strong force in any situation, although not as an aggressor but rather as a quiet strength that stays true through thick and thin. It takes a lot to sway an earth sign, and they will likely be skeptical of anyone they perceive as fake or manipulative. Because they are so grounded in reality, earth signs are very hard to fool and might even bring out an authenticity you didn't know you had. That being said, earth signs can lean toward the boring side. They are quick to judge and therefore quick to dismiss, often being the last to adopt a new idea or social movement. Despite this extreme caution, you will never find someone as steadfast as an earth sign. In the Tarot, earth is represented by the pentacle suit, which focuses on money, practical concerns, and material prosperity.

Water

Connected to Cancer, Scorpio, and Pisces, water signs are considered to be the emotional signs. Water signs feel emotions very deeply and are also very caring toward others. We can see in each of these three signs how this manifests slightly differently. For Cancers, it's all about taking care of those they love and pursuing happiness through nurturing. For Scorpios, it's about shielding themselves from the extremity of the emotions they keep so deep inside. And for Pisces, it's about feeling as deeply and intensely as possible at every opportunity. As is probably obvious, water signs can be the most sensitive of the signs, which can be a good and a bad thing. At their worst, water signs can be needy and easily hurt, requiring others to walk on eggshells around them. At their best, water signs turn their emotions outward and use that intelligence to heal those around them. If you're in need of a deeply loving partner, look no further than a water sign. In the Tarot, water corresponds to the cup suit, which predicts events relating to family and relationships.

Fire

Finally, we get to the most intense of the elements. Fire rules Leo, Aries, and Sagittarius. It is obviously the most intense and passionate of the elements, bearing striking similarities to the physical form of fire. Besides intensity and passion, what fire signs really share is confidence and charisma. As with all the other elements, there are good and bad sides to this. At their worst, fire signs can be vain, a love of themselves turning into disinterest in others. A fire sign who has given in to their worst qualities might come across as conceited or even narcissistic. At their best, though, fire signs can be the life of the party, amazing leaders, and brilliant artists. Many famous actors and rock stars are fire signs, letting their confidence propel them to greatness without letting it get to their heads. In Tarot, fire corresponds to the wand suit and deals with creative inspiration and execution.

Chapter 4:
Modalities of the Zodiac

Besides the elements, there are other ways of dividing up the zodiac signs. One of these is called modalities, and it represents the way that the signs pursue activities. While the elements more have to do with the core values and personality traits of the signs, the modalities are more connected to behavior and choices. Like the elements, the modalities map very neatly onto the 12 zodiac signs. However, instead of four groups of three, the modalities have three groups of four. The three modalities are cardinal signs, fixed signs, and mutable signs. Each modality has four signs it rules over. As with the elements, signs that share the same modality will all have certain similar characteristics, though they are different from the shared qualities of the elements. Because of the perfect mathematics of the zodiac, each modality will have one sign that represents each element, allowing us to see how the elements can be broken up and recategorized along a different framework. In this chapter, we will explore the three modalities and their relationships to the zodiac signs they rule over.

Cardinal

The cardinal signs are Aries, Cancer, Libra, and Capricorn. The quality that distinguishes cardinal signs most of all is their energy. Cardinal signs are considered the go-getters of the zodiac. If you look back at some of their descriptions, you will see that a forward drive, whether that's in pursuit of competition, emotional depth, truth, or professional success, cardinal signs are always moving forward toward their goals. Cardinals are also known for being "idea" people, always innovating and thinking of new ways to improve the world. They are visionaries, living off inspiration and drive.

What's interesting about these different methods of categorizing is that they bring out different aspects of each sign and demonstrate how intersecting value systems can highlight one trait or another. For example, Aries is both a fire sign and a cardinal sign. This means that its fellow fire sign, Leo, might share the core trait of confidence but does not share the action trait of constant pursuit. Thus, these fire signs are connected in one regard but not in another, showing how multifaceted each sign truly is. The fact that Aries, Cancer, Libra, and Capricorn are all fairly superficially different also demonstrates that modalities are not as close to the surface as the elements. While you might be able to spot an air sign from a mile away, it might take you a little bit more time to spot someone's modality in the same way. Modalities really demonstrate how someone's behavior can cut through personality lines and form bonds between unlikely types.

Fixed

In the fixed category, you will find Taurus, Leo, Scorpio, and Aquarius. Fixed signs are the doers, the practical implementers that take the spearheading cardinal ideas and turn them into reality. The defining characteristic of fixed signs is perseverance. While cardinal signs might struggle with losing interest or burnout because of their intense bursts of energy, fixed signs are able to keep going even when the road ahead seems tough or boring. Finding joy in the accomplishment of each step is how fixed signs keep their interest afloat. You won't find a fixed sign giving up easily. In fact, it takes a lot for them to genuinely abandon a task. The other secret weapon that fixed signs have in their back pockets is inherent confidence. Where cardinal signs gain confidence from their amazing ideas, fixed signs gain confidence from proof of their undeniable success. They are able to point to the things they have accomplished and say, "I know I can do that again." Finally, fixed signs also share remarkable patience. They are not swayed when a project takes longer than they think it will. In fact, they are sometimes encouraged by this because they adore the methodology so much.

Mutable

Gemini, Virgo, Sagittarius, and Pisces are the lineup for the mutable signs. Mutable signs, as their name suggests, are looser than the other signs and able to adapt to any situation very easily. They are not usually the signs that spearhead huge movements, nor the ones that slog through the long process to get them done. They are, however, the ones who see to it that the finer details always fall into place. These are the very malleable signs, the ones that will go with whatever the majority wants. However, this doesn't mean that mutable signs are mindless sheep. Mutable signs are actually very intelligent, it's just that they don't tend toward strong convictions or leadership. They prefer to make use of what they have, putting their exceptional resourcefulness to good use. If the mutable signs had a motto, it would be "You get what you get, and you don't get upset," or rather, "You get what you get, and you do something amazing with it!"

Relationship to the Sun and Moon System

So, how does the modality system relate to the concepts we talked about in Chapter 2 regarding the specific signs and their qualities? More precisely, how do these signs and qualities relate to your sun, moon, and rising positions? You may have been asking yourself, "What does it mean if I have a mutable rising? Or a cardinal moon? What if all my signs are in the same modality? What if I have all three in my chart?" These are all amazing questions that have very definitive answers in astrological philosophy. In the earlier chapters, I said that the modalities represented your behavior or choices more so than your personality, but even this distinction can be broken down further. In fact, the modalities have very clear purposes when put into the context of sun, moon, and rising, representing three very different sides of this behavioral approach.

Sun Modalities

The sun sign, as we have already discussed, represents the core of your identity. Thus, the way your sun sign affects your modality has to do very clearly with your general behavioral patterns. This is the overarching way that you behave in most contexts, particularly those that are very neutral. Your sun modality is fundamental enough that it will meaningfully affect the rest of the modalities, representing a sort of base framework for the moon and rising modality.

Moon Modalities

The moon in the general zodiac represents your inner self, but its meaning changes slightly when brought into the world of the modalities. Instead of your general inner self, the moon modality represents your emotional life and your relationships with others. When we look at the modalities from this perspective, their meaning changes a little bit. Cardinal moons are usually the initiators in relationships. They are usually the first to ask others out, plan dates with their significant others, and come out with big gestures for their friends or partners. In other words, cardinal moons are amazing at reaching out and forging connections with new people and reconnecting with those already in their life. Fixed moons are amazing at emotional maintenance. Once you have established a relationship with a fixed moon, you know they will never neglect that relationship. They keep a close watch on the people in their lives. When it comes to mutable moons, they are usually the more accommodating members of a relationship. They want to keep their partner happy at all costs and will ensure that nothing happens to make the other upset. This might seem like walking on eggshells, but it is actually a careful kind of consideration. So, we can see how the moon position will affect how your modality is read.

Chapter 5: Polarities of the Zodiac

The third way in which the signs of the zodiac are sectioned off is through something called polarities. The term "polarities" usually refers to a binary or spectrum system. In the case of the zodiac, polarity refers to two groups of signs. In Chapters 3 and 4, we looked at different groupings of the zodiac signs, the first being four groups of three and the second being three groups of four. Now, with the polarities, we will be looking at two groups of six as well as six groups of two, classifying the zodiac signs into two categories as well as into pairs of opposites that complement and challenge each other. The polarities of the zodiac are based on the system of yin and yang, or positive and negative energies. Don't be intimidated by what seems like a value judgment. Even if your sign is "negative," it doesn't necessarily mean that you are a negative person. These things are simply archetypes and complex categorizations we can use to better understand the zodiac. In this chapter, we will look at the relationship between yin and yang and the zodiac.

History of Yin-Yang Polarity

As you might already know, the concepts of yin and yang are an ancient Chinese idea born in the 3rd century B.C.E. You are probably most familiar with it through its iconic symbol of the black and white sections making up a single circle. Each section has a smaller section with its opposing color inside, illustrating some of the complexity of yin and yang, suggesting that each has a part of the other inside of them. In Chinese mythology, yin and yang are the origin forces of the universe. Back before all the complex matter we have today, there were only two forces: chaos and control, masculine and feminine, dark and light. The world existed only in opposite but complementary forces. As the universe grew in complexity, the base of these opposite forces remained. Today, according to this philosophy, everything can be categorized into yin and yang forces, allowing us to see and interpret the world as being a part of these base concepts from the beginning of time. In relation to the zodiac, both the Chinese and Western zodiacs employ polarity as a method of grouping the signs as archetypes. Not only this, but they have also paired the opposing signs with specific ones that are considered to be connected. Using the concept of yin and yang, we can observe how opposing forces interact with and mold each other, whether in the zodiac or outside of it.

The Negative or Yin Signs

First, we are going to look at the way polarity appears on the yin side of the zodiac. This half of the system is ruled by many concepts that have corresponding yang opposites. As an overview, yin is the feminine side, represented by things like the moon, darkness, passivity, water, transformation, and the spirit world. Yin is thus shrouded in mystery, embodying the dark and unseen forces that underpin all life on earth. It is not a force of evil. In fact, yin is a force that digs deeper into the inner meaning of things, weighing people down with the knowledge of their spiritual truths. If you are looking for guidance at the deepest layer of yourself, you should look toward yin forces. Yin does have a bad side though. It can become misguided to dwell only on these mysterious philosophical and spiritual forces, losing track of your real life. When dwelling in yin, remember not to become stuck in the spirit world, and make sure you have that little bit of yang left to guide you out when you need it.

The yin zodiac signs are Cancer, Scorpio, Pisces, Capricorn, Taurus, and Virgo. The first thing you will probably notice about this list is that these are all water and earth signs. Water and earth are the yin elements because they are the "heavier" elements. Water and earth are both bound to the core of the planet, never flying up to the heavens. They are also life-sustaining elements, providing hydration and nutrients for life on earth. Finally, earth and water are also where mysterious forces lie. Deep oceans and thick forests house mysterious creatures. Most mythologies include these kinds of settings as places of dark mystery but also deep spirituality. If you are a yin sign, you probably feel a strong connection to the spirit world, to the higher questions in life, and to your deepest feelings. It is an essential element of anyone's chart, helping them through life's metaphysical side.

The Positive or Yang Signs

On the other side of the spectrum, we have yang. Yang represents all the things that yin lacks. As the masculine pole, yang presides over forces like light, the sun, youth, activity, and mountains. Yang is the doing pole; it is all about movement and taking action in the real world. You will notice that rationality and irrationality do not appear in this binary. This is because both sides have elements of rationality and irrationality to them. While yang is certainly more functional in the real world than yin, it also is an important force in creativity and imagination. Rather than being grounded by yin's strong earthen energy, yang is able to fly up and dream of new possibilities for change. Progress and innovation are yang's bread and butter.

The rest of the signs on the zodiac are the yang signs: Aries, Leo, Sagittarius, Libra, Aquarius, and Gemini. To complement the yin signs, these are all air and fire signs. Air and fire are both free elements, flowing in the wind or crackling toward the sky. Unlike earth and water, which are weighed down, air and fire are light and, therefore, unburdened. If you are a yang sign, you are probably a very energetic person who doesn't bother too much with the "why" of it all—you're just interested in the "how." The negative side of yang is forgetting to investigate those deeper questions in life in order to give all that activity more profound meaning. Make sure that you dip your toe in the waters of yin once in a while to make sure you really understand the purpose behind your life and actions.

The Complementary Signs

As I said at the beginning of the chapter, the other aspect of the yin-yang categorization of the zodiac is complementary signs. This polarity works somewhat separately from the yin-yang dichotomy since all the opposites are actually within their respective yin-yang categories. The fact that the complementary signs can even exist within an overarching category shows the diversity of yin and yang as well as the multifaceted nature of the zodiac signs. This complementary system does not necessarily have to do with compatibility. There are many factors that go into whether two sides are compatible with each other or not. However, these two signs will certainly bring about something in each other. Because of their opposing nature, they will often ignite a deep connection of opposites but also possibly a clashing of philosophies and values. It's the kind of relationship which might begin with contention and seeming incompatibility but will ultimately end with much learning on both sides. In this section, we will look at each pair of complementary signs to examine their relationship with one another.

Virgo and Pisces

Given the extremely logical nature of earthly Virgo and the emotional nature of watery Pisces, these signs seem diametrically opposed. On the surface, it seems as if they would have absolutely nothing to say to one another. However, since these are both extreme signs, each extreme can actually lend some much-needed balance to the pair. This is not a relationship born out of extreme love and passion but rather mutual respect. For this reason, Virgo and Pisces make a good pair in many different contexts, usually consisting of institutions. As work colleagues, friends, and even artistic collaborators, Virgo and Pisces are able to bring their polarized qualities together to make something truly magical. In terms of marriage, you will find a very steady relationship between Virgo and Pisces. They might not have the passionate ups and downs that can make a marriage exciting, but they will have the commitment and drive to make it work no matter what. As we can see, the balance of Virgo and Pisces makes for a very well-rounded pair.

Leo and Aquarius

Moving on to a fire and an air sign, Leo and Aquarius also have some very contradictory traits. For one, Leos feel the need to be well-liked while Aquarians very much march to the beat of their own drums. Thus, it can be easy for Leos to look at Aquarians as weird or even deviant, while Aquarians might tend to think of Leos as show-offs or conformists. Their extreme difference in social values can very easily lead to some strong clashes. However, if Leos and Aquarians are able to look deeper into themselves and each other to see the hidden qualities underneath, they will be able to find some common ground. They are both fiercely loyal signs who also share a strong ambition. If they are able to fuse these things, they will become full of dynamism. What results is a passionate relationship that might not have the staying power of Virgo and Pisces, but which more than makes up for it with intensity.

Cancer and Capricorn

One of the most compatible pairs in this group of signs, Cancer and Capricorn have sometimes been called perfect lovers. The reason for this compatibility comes from an ideal combination of perfect values and differing personalities. Where Capricorns are extremely forceful, Cancers are easygoing. Where Cancers are perceptive and nurturing, Capricorns are iron-skinned and strong. These dichotomies fit together like puzzle pieces, feeding off one another in a harmony of reciprocal care. They seem to have every quality that the other lacks, making any relationship between them very fruitful. The main danger between these two is that Capricorn's coldness can harm Cancer's soft interior. Cancers might also struggle to get Capricorns to come out of their relatively tough emotional shell, possibly causing friction over a lack of open communication between the two. But as long as they both establish proper boundaries and know what each others' touchy points are, especially Cancer's, then they will get along famously.

Gemini and Sagittarius

Another fire and air pair, Gemini will fan Sagittarius's flames beautifully. These signs are actually fairly similar, despite being opposite on the zodiac wheel. Because they are both mutable, they are incredibly easygoing and work hard to accommodate the other when needed. Thus, you will find few conflicts between them for a complementary pair. They will be a very passionate couple who seem attached at the hip, both best friends and lovers at the same time. This can be a blessing and a curse. On one hand, they will have a deeply engaging and fulfilling relationship that can push them both past the boundaries of what they thought was possible. Yet, at the same time, it can also cause them to lose track of the real world, preferring to stay in their own little invented world together. The notable lack of earth in this pairing means that flying off into the sky is always a possibility. If one or both have some strong earth elsewhere in their chart, especially in their moon, then they will be able to keep their adventurous escapades grounded in reality. All in all, these signs have amazing compatibility.

Taurus and Scorpio

Taurus and Scorpio are one of the most spark-inducing compatibilities out there, and also one of the most volatile. When it comes to these two, it's really all about cycles of intense attraction and repulsion, sometimes at the same time! When they meet, they will instantly notice each other, establishing an electricity that will define the rest of their relationship. Unfortunately, this extremely intense relationship often struggles to get past the honeymoon phase. Contention and unrest await Tauruses and Scorpios when the initial excitement has worn off. They are often found fighting intensely very shortly into a relationship which, if the commitment is missing, might cause them to give up on each other altogether. If they intend to make their relationship last, they will have to learn to work through the disagreements they will inevitably have.

Aries and Libra

Two passionate signs at their core, Aries and Libra can be a great match. They will have high compatibility in the passion department, but they will also have enough levelheadedness to get through the messier side of the relationship. The main issue Aries and Libras might run into is an incompatibility of wills. Unlike a lot of the other sign pairs on this list, Aries and Libra have very mismatched wills as Aries is very forceful and Libra is comparatively meek. They might find themselves falling into an uneven power dynamic, with Aries always taking the lead and Libra always following. When it comes to trivial things like taste in music, this needn't be an issue, but when it comes to bigger things, Libra needs to learn to use their voice in the relationship, making sure that they don't get walked all over.

Pillar 3:
The Planets

So far, we have talked exclusively about the sun, moon, and constellations. These are some of the more important parts of the zodiac system, but they are only pieces of the whole. Even though the zodiac might already seem very complex, with many different forms and categories of signs, it is still more complex. Astrologers are also very interested in the planets and how they interact with the sky and subsequently influence human behavior. The word "planet" is actually derived from the Greek word meaning "wanderer." This was because planets appeared like stars but behaved differently from them. To the Ancient Greeks, it seemed like the night sky consisted of five (at the time there were only five observable planets) stars which did not stick to the constellation forms at all but rather appeared in a different place in the sky every night.

Thus, the Greeks attached special importance to these celestial bodies, which seemed to have minds and personalities of their own. In fact, they even named these planets after their gods, thereby attaching all the mythology and meaning of that particular god to the planet. Today, we use the Romanization of the planet names but retain the meanings. Mercury, the closest planet to the sun, is based on the Greek god Hermes, the messenger of the gods who can run very fast, just like Mercury's quick orbit. Venus, Mercury's neighbor, is named for Aphrodite, the goddess of love. Mars, also known as Aries, is the god of war, matching the bloodred intensity of Mars's surface. Jupiter, the Roman version of Zeus, is so named for being the biggest of the planets and thus the ruler. And finally, the furthest observable planet at the time was named Saturn, called Cronos in Greek, who is the oldest and father of all the gods, famous for devouring his children. These five planets make up the basis of Greek planetary astrology.

The zodiac, however, acknowledges ten planets. So, where do the other five come from? Well, three more came during the Renaissance when, thanks to inventors and astronomers like Galileo, the first astronomical telescopes were created and allowed for the observation of three more planetary bodies: Uranus, Neptune, and Pluto. When they made these discoveries, they continued with the Greek/Roman god theme, assigning the planets their names in relation to this ancient mythology. They named their innermost new discovery, the new seventh planet from the sun, Uranus, unchanged from the Greek, one of the original two gods, alongside Gaia, the earth goddess. Uranus is very similar to the archetypal concept of yang, being the prototypical male energy. Neptune, a blue planet, was named for the Greek god Poseidon, ruler of the seas. And finally, the outermost planet in the solar system was named for the ruler of the underworld, Hades. With this simple discovery, our perception of the skies, and astrology, were changed forever, now consisting of eight planetary bodies (nine if you count the earth) instead of five.

The other way in which this list was expanded to ten instead of eight was by including the sun and moon in the list of planetary bodies. Even though they are not planets in the astronomical sense of the word, they are considered so in astrology. So, with the discovery of three new planets, astrology changed forever, now having three more bodies to observe and derive meaning from. For context, we can see the inclusion of the sun and moon in the seven days of the week, which were named after the seven acknowledged planetary bodies. The names have been changed in English, altered by the influence of Norse mythology, but their rough outline is

- Sunday (sun - day)
- Monday (moon - day)
- Tuesday (Mars - day)
- Wednesday (Mercury - day)
- Thursday (Jupiter - day)
- Friday (Venus - day)
- Saturday (Saturn - day)

This is just another example of the importance of the planets in Ancient Greek culture.

Including the planets in our astrological methodology helps us to expand on the facets of ourselves that are influenced by the celestial world. We have already touched on this a bit with sun, moon, and rising signs. As we talked about, a sign being in your sun is very different from a sign being in your moon. The sign will manifest differently given the planetary body that was in that sign. The planets are an extension of this system. Just as the sun and moon pass through certain constellations on their planetary journeys, so too do the planets, albeit in different patterns. Each planet is ruled by a certain emotion or facet of life. On your birth chart, you will also get a description of where all the planets were at the time of your birth. So, beyond your sun, moon, and rising, you will also have what sign your Venus, Mercury, Jupiter, and so on, were in. This can help you add further complexity to your astrological profile, being able to assign the sign you were born under to different planetary categories and compartmentalizing the way you think about your position within the zodiac. In this pillar, we will be examining all ten of these planetary bodies in great detail, explaining their relationship to astrology and the zodiac.

Chapter 6:
Inner Planets

In our exploration of how the planets work in astrology, we will be starting with the first five planets on the list, or the "inner planets." These are the planets that are closest to the earth and thus are the brightest when we look at the night sky. These inner planets are the sun, the moon, Mercury, Venus, and Mars. The main difference between the inner and outer planets is their degree of influence and the type of influence that they have. Inner planets have a more immediate effect on your individual life, pertaining to personal issues like your relationships, career, and even personality. This distinction between the levels of planets has more to do with their degree of orbit than their distance from earth. The further out a planet is, the longer its orbit, and thus the slower it will move through the zodiac. For example, Mercury has an 88-day orbit, meaning that it moves through the zodiac at around four times the speed of the earth. This means that the week of the year you were born will define your Mercury position, and therefore everyone's will be quite varied. Pluto, on the other hand, takes 248 years to orbit the sun, meaning that it only enters a different zodiac sign every 20 years. This means that each generation will have its own distinct Pluto sign. So, you see how the inner and outer planets have more connection to the individual versus the collective. While inner planets have the ability to influence individual lives, outer planets can influence generations. Here is a list of all the inner planets and their significance in the zodiac.

The Sun

The sun needs no introduction. It is the center of the solar system—although not in the Greek geocentric model—and the force that dominates our skies. It creates day and night and nourishes crops so we have food to eat. As we have discussed in earlier sections, the sun of your zodiac sign is the most important and overarching. It is usually the sign people identify themselves as when asked, constructing their base zodiacal identity around their sun sign. Almost every other sign on your chart will be filtered through your sun sign. If you tell an astrologer your moon or any other planet, they will likely also need your sun in order to give you a proper interpretation. As in the real world, the sun rules all.

The Moon

As we also talked about back in Chapter 2, the moon on your chart represents the inner self, the person you are under the facade you show to the world. It is characterized by emotions, instinct, and inner reasoning. Your moon sign will reflect not only who you are on the inside but also how you see yourself. For this reason, the moon is very important for inner work, even in relation to other people.

Mercury

Now we start on the planets, the ones we have not talked about previously. Each of these planets will have a specific area in which they influence your life. In Mercury's case, it's the intellectual world. The sign that is in Mercury for you will heavily influence the way you speak, write, and, above all, pursue knowledge. Because everyone will have a Mercury sign, and all signs will behave differently when in Mercury, you need not be an intellectual person in the conventional sense of the word to have a Mercury value. Everyone communicates and pursues knowledge, just not necessarily in the same ways. You might pursue knowledge through reading, talking to others, or even moving your body. Everyone has a unique intelligence that can be seen in different ways. The constellation that Mercury was passing through will influence these things in you no matter the pursuit you choose in life.

As with any other aspect of the zodiac, Mercury has its good sides and bad sides. Negative relationships with Mercury involve the corruption of intellectual facilities or using intelligence to hurt or deceive others. These involve trickery, conning people, or simply outsmarting others for personal gain. Those who have more aggressive or ambitious signs in Mercury should watch out that they don't fall prey to these kinds of temptations. When manifested positively, Mercury can be the sign of great intellectual power. Those who have strong relationships with Mercury, or more empathetic signs in Mercury, will instead use their powers to help others, such as through teaching or artistic accomplishments. Manifesting a positive relationship with Mercury will help you harness this planet's amazing powers for good.

So, what are some examples of how different zodiac signs might manifest in the Mercury position? Regardless of your sun or moon signs, the sign that Mercury falls under will rule your intellectual side. So, you might be one sign in your sun, moon, and rising, but if you have your Mercury in another sign, that sign will rule your academic pursuits. For example, say you have your Mercury in Leo. Regardless of your other signs, you will probably be a pretty ambitious thinker. You might take a lot of pride in your intelligence and seek out recognition from others even though you might be shy in other areas. Mercury Leos make amazing innovators because they will stop at nothing to make a name for themselves in the intellectual world. If your Mercury is in Aquarius, however, you might have a really avant-garde approach to intelligence. You might seek out new or experimental literature or music. Mercury Aquarians are born artists. They are able to present as totally weird with the intelligence to back it all up. You'll likely find a Mercury Aquarius setting up their latest art installation or trying to make their way through *Finnegan's Wake*. These are just a few examples of how the signs might manifest in Mercury.

Venus

Venus, the planet of love, unsurprisingly dictates your approach to romantic relationships and even passion in general. The sign that Venus is in will indicate powerful things about your love life. What is interesting about your Venus position is that it doesn't just describe you, but the people you are attracted to as well. As much as Venus indicates what you are like in love, it can also be a strong indicator of what you are looking for in a partner. Another interesting thing about Venus is that, because of the orbital nature of the planet and its relationship to the earth, it does not stray far from the sun. Therefore, your Venus will always be either the same as your sun sign or one immediately beside your sun sign. Those with both their sun and Venus in the same sign will likely experience smoother love lives where they are able to understand their romantic self more easily since it runs so similarly to their core self. Those with differing Venuses and suns might have a little trouble in the early days of their romantic life, figuring out the different side of themselves that comes out when they are in a relationship. A smaller side of Venus is your general hedonistic or materialistic side—the things that bring you comfort or material fulfillment.

The positive and negative sides of Venus can be somewhat polarizing. On one hand, Venus can be a lackadaisical planet if it's interacting with the wrong sign. Venus is pliant and therefore very easily swayed. If it is mixed with a mutable sign, then you can run the risk of becoming excessively passive, especially in love. You might also risk becoming too hedonistic or excessive, consuming too much good food or luxury items for your own good. Venuses in more passive or excessive signs need to learn to control themselves in order to resist always giving in to their desires. On the good side, Venus can manifest as wonderfully decadent and passionate. Having a more giving sign in the Venus position can allow you to share your excesses with others, turning hedonism into a party! More loving signs in Venus will create some of the best lovers possible as their Venus energies are perfectly aligned. For the Venus position, it's all about controlling and outwardly projecting your desires.

Let's look at some examples of how certain signs might manifest under Venus. To start, if you have your Venus in Aries, you will be one of the most intense lovers imaginable. You might be drawn to competition in love, perhaps preferring to pursue people who are already in relationships or are playing hard to get. You see love as a conquest, but be careful not to see your lover as a prize. Remembering that there is still a relationship to be nurtured after it is achieved will help the Aries Venus stay in control of their intense fantasies. If you have your Venus in Libra, then you are especially vulnerable to the passive side of Venus. You might be prone to letting your partner make all the decisions, never really making any for yourself. Libra Venuses should find ways to harness their inner desires in order to have a voice for themselves. These are just a few ways in which your Venus position could be manifested under some signs.

Mars

While Venus represents passive energy, Mars represents all action. Your Mars sign will therefore represent your relationship to activity, competition, and ambition. How you act when faced with a rival will be dictated by your Mars position. How you plan your career goals might also correspond to your Mars sign. And finally, the way in which you pursue daily action versus passivity has a strong relationship to Mars. Since everyone has a

Mars position, even the meekest among us, it does not necessarily indicate that you *are* a competitive person, but rather the degree of your competitiveness and how you go about it. Having a less competitive sign in Mars will indicate that you approach competition from a more laid-back perspective or even avoid it altogether. These planet positions indicate that everyone has a relationship with all facets of life and that even trying not to have a relationship with something is still some kind of a relationship after all.

The positive and negative aspects of Mars are strongly related to the positive and negative aspects of the Aries sign. If you have too fiery or strong of a sign in Mars, you will likely struggle with your competitiveness. You might become a chronic game player or a sore loser. You might overexert yourself, prioritizing constant action over taking a break. Having a more toned-down sign in Mars will indicate that you have a more passive, or potentially healthier, relationship with competition and action. Those with more mutable or even fixed signs in Mars will be able to strike a balance, possibly enjoying a mildly active life or some friendly competition once in a while but never taking it too far.

Mars is an interesting planet in the zodiac because it has a clear sign equivalent: Aries, which is derived from the same Greek god of war. Having your Mars in Aries obviously indicates a harmony where your competitive side can reach its full potential. For this reason, it might seem hard to picture how other signs can interact, but it actually works quite smoothly. If you have your Mars in Cancer, this might mean that your active or competitive side is very focused on your loved ones. You might be the kind of person who would drive three hours to help a friend whose car broke down or spend hundreds of dollars at a carnival game to win your significant other a prize. Cancer Marses are lovers who go all the way. On the flip side, you might have your Mars in Virgo, which can manifest as being extremely controlling or even overworking yourself at the expense of other important aspects of life. If you have your Virgo in Mars, you really need to make sure that you keep your work ethic in check, otherwise, you might end up sacrificing other important aspects of your life for the sake of ambition. From these examples, we can see how Mars often takes certain aspects of a sign to the extreme.

Chapter 7:
Outer Planets

As we move outward in the solar system, we are moving toward more big-picture ideas. Thinking back to our explanation of the inner and outer planet dichotomy, we can remember that the farther away from the sun a planet is, the wider its scope becomes, and the longer the orbit of the planet is, the more people that sign has influence over and the more it can define eras. In this chapter, we will discuss the qualities of the outer planets, demonstrating their most important qualities and how they interact with the signs.

Jupiter

The largest planet in the solar system, Jupiter occupies a transitional position in the planet zodiac. Although it is categorized as an outer planet, it is still related to the individual. However, it occupies an interesting position pertaining to an individual's relationship with the higher world at large. Jupiter is all about higher causes, spiritual and charitable pursuits, and honesty. Your sign in Jupiter represents how you connect to the world as a whole and enact these personal philosophies. Where your Jupiter falls will dictate your feelings about things like religion—organized or not—and altruism. This planet bridges the gap between the individual and the collective. Your Jupiter sign will indicate your degree of solemnity about life and your level of obligation toward others.

Though Jupiter might sound like a sign that is all good, there is bad in it too. Signs who tend too much toward traditionalism or judgment might end up becoming religious extremists under Jupiter. Signs with a lot of pride might end up being smug or self-righteous about their charity, whether it is religious or not. Remember to connect with *why* you are helping others or pursuing spiritual questions and try to keep your ego out of it as best you can. On the other hand, signs that lean toward caring deeply will be greatly exaggerated under Jupiter. They might be able to finally break out of their shells and create something beautiful or help lots of people in a meaningful way. If Jupiter and its sign are aligned, these people make amazing philosophers, nuns or monks, and poets. Able to devote themselves fully to exploring the mysteries beyond, they can go very far.

Jupiter will manifest very differently within different signs. In Sagittarius, Jupiter might create an outgoing version of charity in a person's life. They might pursue giving charity and altruism by connecting with others.

They will be the kind of person to start a food drive or yoga class, searching for ways to bring people together toward higher and noble causes. With their social butterfly skills, they will be more than capable of banding people together and reminding them of the true meaning of caring. In Taurus, however, some of the values of Jupiter might get lost. Jupiter Tauruses might find themselves caught up in bureaucracy, forgetting that true meaning is found in the little things. They might find themselves delaying their goals in life in favor of things like stability, perhaps continually putting off traveling, having children, or even creative pursuits until they feel they have gained enough traction in their careers. Taurus Jupiters should remind themselves that the best things in life are free and true fulfillment doesn't necessarily come from hard work, just love. Clearly, Jupiter is a highly variable planet, with every sign taking its own interpretations of its vague values of truth and benevolence.

Saturn

Previously considered the "evil" planet of the chart, Saturn is connected to limitation and rigidity. But these things aren't always bad. In fact, everyone needs some limitations in order to succeed in life. You can think of Saturn's limitations like the structure of a sonnet. Instead of limiting the sonneteer with its strict 14 lines and iambic pentameter, it opens up a wide variety of possibilities for the poet to create endless art through a very structured medium. The sign that is in Saturn for you will represent your approach to limitations and planning. It might reflect how you schedule yourself or whether you are more methodical or free-spirited. As with all the planets, Saturn deals in degrees, helping you to see where you fall on the scale in relation to a certain category. Depending on what sign your Saturn is in, or even what your sun or moon signs are, you will have a different approach to planning.

As we said above, the qualities of Saturn can be very good in some regards. Planning is needed to have a fruitful life. You can't always just wing everything. Similarly, you have to limit yourself sometimes, otherwise, you can become too hedonistic or carefree. The qualities of Saturn keep you grounded. Of course, too much limitation can bog you down as well, closing doors on exciting possibilities that might have been within your grasp. You don't want too strict of a sign in Saturn or you might find yourself living a repressed and rigid lifestyle. Striking a balance is the most important thing about Saturn.

The sign that is most obvious to place in Saturn is Capricorn. Because of their hardworking and driven nature, Capricorns are given to depriving themselves of things they don't see as relevant to their goals. They limit and streamline their lives. If your Saturn is in Capricorn, you must make sure not to become too regimented and learn to stop and smell the roses once in a while. On the other hand, if your Saturn is in Pisces, this might mean that you are mainly regimented about your emotions. You might have a certain kind of relationship that you think you "should" have and, consequently, avoid all others because they might not fit your mold. You might even become emotionally repressed, refusing to feel certain things that you don't deem acceptable. Like Saturn in Capricorn, Pisces Saturns should learn to loosen up a little bit and allow themselves to feel whatever they are feeling.

Uranus

Uranus symbolizes truth and renewal, even revolution. The sign that Uranus is in will reflect the area of your life or yourself that you feel is most subject to radicalism or change. This might mean that this facet of your life will undergo some massive upheaval at some point during your life, or it may even be an area where you are particularly honest or rebellious. This can be good or bad. On one hand, this could mean something catastrophic like a devastating breakup or divorce, the death of a loved one, or a major job loss. On the other hand, it could mean an international move, finding love later in life, or changing your career path to something that brings you more fulfillment and joy. The possibilities are endless, but you can be assured that wherever Uranus falls, this will never be a stable or boring part of your life!

Obviously, destruction can be a force for good and bad. In Hinduism, there is a very important god devoted to this concept. Shiva, the god of destruction and renewal, is symbolized by fire and denotes that though destruction may be painful or difficult on the surface, it is necessary for new things to form. Just like death is necessary to make way for new life, winter is necessary to make way for spring, and night is necessary to make way for day, the world is made up of cycles of death and rebirth. This concept is also important in Tarot. The common sitcom joke of the Death card actually being good is based on truth. Cards like Death, the Tower, or the Hanged Man all symbolize how destruction, death, and even seeing things from a new perspective are all necessary for experiencing renewal in life. You might get the Tower card before a major career change, symbolizing the death of your routines and relationships with colleagues at your old workplace to make way for a new routine, new friends, a new place, and even a new personality. You can think of Uranus as being similar to these tarot cards or the god Shiva—a force of destruction that can bring about growth.

If your Uranus is in, say, Cancer, then the upheavals you might experience will be connected to family and friends, those close, homey relationships. This might be a precarious position to be in. It could symbolize a rocky home life but also one that values authenticity above all else. Even though you might not have the most stable relationships, you will never be in an inauthentic one. You will always value living your truth with others and won't suffer any fools who try to change you. If your Uranus is in Scorpio, then the massive changes to your life might be internal. You might change political affiliations or religions at some point in your life. You will also always be true to yourself in terms of your internal life. You might have a hard time lying to yourself and will always put in the hard work of evaluating whether you truly believe something. Denial is not a familiar state for those with their Uranus in Scorpio. So you see, whatever area you have in Uranus will be rife with change but also realness.

Neptune

Neptune exists exclusively in the realm of the ideal. Neptune represents your dreams and the things you want to explore in your life. Because Neptune is the Roman god of the sea (the equivalent to the Greek god of the sea, Poseidon), the planet Neptune's qualities are related to the flowing, mysterious sea. If you are familiar with the concept of Platonic ideals, then you will have an idea of how the sign Neptune works. The sign that your Neptune is in will have a strong connection to your ideals and deepest wishes for your life. It will cover both the sphere to which you attach the most romanticism or idealism as well as the way you go about pursuing these ideals. Depending on what sign your Neptune falls in, you might be more or less of a romantic or idealistic person, or your idealism may just manifest in a different way.

There are of course pros and cons to the Neptune sign. On one hand, people who are too strong in their Neptune might fall prey to too much idealism. This can manifest in one of two ways. It can either make you excessively dreamy, too distracted by your made-up world to focus on what's actually happening, or it can cause you frustration, believing in your ideals so much that the real world never measures up and you are forever unsatisfied. However, a lot of good can still come from having a strong Neptune in your chart. For one, those with particularly creative or industrious signs in Neptune are apt to be amazing artists or writers. They have strong connections to their imaginations and have a remarkable ability to bring what they see in their mind's eye onto the page. This is the visionary planet, the one that allows us to see past the physical world and into those unfathomable things beyond.

Different signs will have a huge impact on how Neptune manifests, some more positive than others. Having your Neptune in Gemini, for example, might create an excessively dreamy personality. Because Gemini is an air sign and prone to some shallowness, Neptune in Gemini can easily create a person who comes across as too flaky or too caught up in their dreams. Gemini Neptunes have to be very careful how they conduct themselves and would do well to have some strong earth signs elsewhere in their chart to help ground them. Having your Neptune in Virgo, however, will create a very interesting person. Combining idealism and creativity with a methodological disposition will form a very industrious artist. You might find a Virgo Neptune planning out an elaborate fantasy book series with complex worlds or making huge oil paintings with meticulous detail. Virgo in Neptune forms the perfect balance to create a visionary, but productive, thinker.

Pluto

In charge of more grand archetypes, Pluto is the planet of change and the relationship between the ego and the collective. It represents grand transformation in one or another facet of life. It can also be related to sexuality and power, even money. The sign that is in Pluto will shape the way in which these things manifest. If there is a particularly unorthodox or restless sign in Pluto, then this signifies a life or period of time of significant change. However, if there is a meek or subtle sign in Pluto, then these changes might be more internal or underground in the person or culture. The sign also might signify how you react to change or how change is enacted by you. It all depends on the level of confidence of the sign.

The planet with the most widespread influence will be Pluto since entire generations share the same Pluto sign. If you look back on Pluto's schedule, you can see how it could possibly have had an influence on that generation's sensibilities. For example, Pluto was in Leo from 1937 to roughly 1958, which are generally the defining years of the "Baby Boomer" generation. This generation was known for confidence, pride, and paving their own path. They were sometimes referred to as the "me" generation by their parents, possibly reflecting their intense individualism. All having their Pluto in Leo suggests that that generation was given to more bold, individualistic, and passionate thinking, which reflects in the sexual revolution, the large number of social movements during the time, and the general prosperity they experienced. It seems like the Baby Boomers achieved a lot of their goals, still to this day remaining the wealthiest and most successful generation in history.

Those born from 1958 to 1972, on the other hand, all had their Plutos in Virgo. The intense hard work and often disappointing success levels of their generation ("Generation X") are reflected in this. Gen Xers are known for being unlucky economically, graduating into depression, and having less professional prosperity than their parents. We can see how Virgo's more frugal nature is reflected in this. Finally, those born from 1995 to 2008, or "Generation Z," have their Plutos in Sagittarius. Given the more charitable and equitable nature of Sagittarius, we can see how the deep devotion to social movements and inclusivity, along with extreme anger toward inequality, are reflected in Gen Z's Pluto-Sagittarius position. As we can see, Pluto has clearly influenced some defining aspects of certain generations throughout the 20th and 21st centuries. Who knows what those born in the current stage, Pluto in Capricorn, will bring to the world?

Chapter 8: Chiron Planet

Another astronomical phenomenon that has an important place in astrology is the newly discovered Chiron. Chiron was first spotted in 1977 and has since undergone many reclassifications. First, it was classified as an outer planet, then an asteroid, and now a comet. It exists among the outer planets of the solar system, just between Saturn and Uranus. It has since been introduced as an important player among the celestial bodies in astrology, especially since its discovery coincided with the height of the new age movement when astrology was being profoundly redefined. Its location right in between Saturn and Uranus, two completely opposite planets, positions Chiron as a kind of mediator between the two. Since Saturn is the planet of restriction and Uranus the planet of breaking free, Chiron lies somewhat in the middle, helping to bridge the full spectrum of emotions.

What Does Chiron Symbolize?

Chiron is, simply put, the celestial body of healing. Its name comes from a famous Ancient Greek healer with a tragic story. He had immense powers to heal other people yet was sick himself and could not heal his own ailments. His story represents that, while many people have the ability to recognize flaws in others and even help them heal, it can be much more difficult to recognize your own faults and begin to heal yourself. The planet Chiron represents this contradiction. Thus, it works toward the process of using our own pain to heal others, of recognizing in ourselves what might be wrong and then sharing those findings so others can learn from them. Among these things, Chiron also stands for your own healing as well, if you choose to meet it. Periods of Chiron healing are opportunities to truly investigate the depths of your pain psyche, paving the way for transformative change. If you allow your Chiron sign and cycle to fully enter you, then you will be able to heal from many of the things that have brought you pain throughout your life. The process won't be easy, but the results will be beyond amazing.

The Chiron Cycle

As with the ten planetary bodies, Chiron has its own schedule for how it moves through the zodiac. First of all, its complete rotation takes roughly 50 years. This is the amount of time it takes to go all the way around the sun and return to its original position. This means that Chiron is in a different sign every four years. The complete cycle is very important to your life cycle. The phase Chiron is in during your birth will shape the rest of your life. When it comes around again, roughly at your 50th birthday, this is a time of profound change. Sometimes this is called a "midlife crisis," but it doesn't have to be a crisis. It can be a period of learning and growth.

When your Chiron returns, you will be able to confront many of your core qualities. You will be under the influence of its original sign, and thus it will feel like a full circle or a homecoming to you. Many people use this time to make serious reevaluations of major things in their lives, like marriages, careers, friendships, personal style, and more. You might notice your 50th birthday as a turning point where you either start to feel more lost and disconnected or begin to shed the excesses and live a more authentic life. Those who choose to ignore the insights of their Chiron return might double down on their illusions and continue on their existing path, purposefully blinding themselves to the inauthenticity or discomfort of some aspects of their life. Those who choose to embrace it, though, will find themselves in a state of destruction and renewal. You might have to end relationships or career paths, but what you will be left with is a more honest way forward, a new life that will allow you to shed all the excess you have accumulated over the years and truly start to be your authentic self.

One way you can help yourself harness the power of the Chiron cycle is to take a close look at all aspects of your life and really ask yourself whether these are the things you want to be doing. A small way to start is by decluttering. Many people have far too many things in their homes, so taking some time to throw out or give away some of those extra things you don't need can leave you feeling renewed and refreshed. Another way is to make a list of the goals you have for the rest of your life and to ask yourself whether the path you are currently on is one where you will be able to accomplish those goals. You might also want to see a counselor or open up to a close friend to start having some of these deep conversations with another person. If you are able to navigate this transitional period, then you will be able to live out the rest of your life feeling more honest and authentic.

Chiron and the Signs

So, how does your sign manifest in Chiron? The way the signs are typically talked about in relation to Chiron is through wounds and healing strategies. Every sign will have both a pain point (something with which they will struggle throughout their lives) and a healing point (their way of sharing their wisdom with others). Depending on the sign your Chiron is in, you will have a very different relationship to emotional pain and suffering as well as a totally different method of dealing with it. Here, we will look at the ways the 12 zodiac signs interact with the Chiron.

Aries

Those born under the sign of Aries are born with the implicit pain of always channeling their emotions into anger. Almost every feeling an Aries experiences is turned into anger. This means they will have a big problem harnessing their anger because so much of what they experience turns into it. Anger management is thus one of the biggest issues for the Aries Chiron. Aries Chirons might also struggle with self-worth, unable to see what is so great about themselves even though other people might be able to see it easily. Finally, their cutthroat approach to competition is likely to make them feel lonely. They might cut people out of their lives in pursuit of being the best. If they do this, though, they will soon realize that it can be very lonely at the top.

However, Aries Chirons can show other people some amazing things. The best gift that Aries Chirons can give those around them is showing them how amazing they are and building their confidence. If an Aries's energy is channeled properly, they can be the ultimate cheerleaders. They will especially empower others to embrace their unique qualities and be unashamedly themselves. They might also be able to channel their anger more creatively, using all that energy to make something extraordinary. If you have a well-adjusted Chiron Aries in your life, they will help you make many amazing discoveries about yourself.

Taurus

Chiron in Taurus will struggle primarily with stubbornness and rigidity. They will likely fear change to the point of avoiding important transitions in life, possibly entering a state of arrested development at some point. They might struggle to move out of their parents' house when they are young or to request a promotion at work when they are older. Taurus Chirons also might fall into the trap of going with the crowd rather than forming their own distinct opinions. They might find themselves joining organized religion or politics more easily without really considering whether it is what they actually believe. They might also be given to materialism, potentially squandering their skills in pursuit of money alone and losing sight of meaning in their lives. All these faults and points of pain are very common among Taurus Chirons.

There are also very important gifts associated with Taurus Chirons. For one, they are exceptional at creating comforting environments for those around them. They always know what makes someone feel good, so they will almost magically be able to provide that exact thing you didn't even know you were lacking. They will also be the ones to keep their cool in a crisis. You will never see a Taurus Chiron panicking—they always find a way to stay calm in any circumstance. For this reason, they make great emergency service people since they aren't easily shaken. Finally, they are also excellent planners, especially when it comes to money. You can learn a lot from the way this sign deals with their finances. Therefore, despite the flaws listed above, Taurus Chirons also have many important things going for them.

Gemini

Because Gemini is the sign of twinship and companionship, their main point of pain will be fear of abandonment or loneliness. Geminis may become extremely distressed or volatile if they fear that someone might be leaving them or that they might end up alone. They might resort to groveling or people-pleasing behavior where they sacrifice their own comfort for the placation of someone else. Because of this, Gemini Chirons often end up suppressing their true selves because of their intense fear of not being liked. Another major difficulty Gemini Chirons might struggle with is a tendency toward flakiness and being unable to finish what they started. Unfinished projects will often litter the homes of Gemini Chirons, who tend to be able to muster the energy to start things only to lose interest halfway through. This is the wispiness of the air infiltrating the minds of these Gemini Chirons.

Yet, when channeled in the right way, Gemini Chirons can be some of the most amazing people in the world. They will particularly shine in the social world, dominating teaching and inclusivity initiatives. Where Gemini Chirons really excel is in learning through play. They are able to make learning even the driest information a great time because they approach it with a playful curiosity. If you have a Gemini Chiron as your teacher, you will likely not even realize you are learning because you will be having so much fun. They are also amazing at making outsiders feel at ease in social situations. They're the kind of people who will notice the wallflower and make sure they feel included and welcome. At a party with a Gemini Chiron, you can bet that nobody is going to feel left out.

Cancer

Those with Chiron in Cancer will usually have anxieties and pain centered around security. Cancer Chirons often have heavily fortified homes, possibly with multiple locks on the door or even a guard dog. They might struggle to ever feel like they are secure, piling on security blanket after security blanket to no avail. Due to this borderline paranoia, they might have a particular mistrust of strangers. People they don't know, foreigners, or even people with different belief systems from them might seem suspect in their eyes. Because of their nesting compulsion, Cancer Chirons are also wont to hoard things, such as money or possessions. They might become misers, gluttons, or even full-on hoarders. If they aren't careful, these tendencies can cause their inner space to become even more unstable, leading to family dysfunction.

If the Cancer Chiron is able to turn their "nesting" and security tendencies outward, broadening the circle of those they trust, then they can become amazing community organizers. Cancer Chirons have a wonderful ability to mobilize people in a community toward positive change. They will usually focus on the most vulnerable in the community, possibly people lacking homes or who struggle with mental illness or addiction. The crux is that they are able to see these people as insiders who share their community, which will allow the Cancer Chiron to see this community aid as an extension of their own home. They will also use food as a love language, often making huge batches of recipes and giving out their warm and hearty sustenance to anyone who asks. Finally, Cancer Chirons are incredibly good with money and will budget very well, taking all the people in their life into account.

Leo

Chiron Leos will struggle with all the main flaws of Leo and more. The pain points of the Leo Chiron are very similar to those of the Aries. They are terrified of not being well-liked or succeeding in their endeavors. Chiron Leos will become very easily frustrated with themselves. Because Leo is known for, and therefore used to, succeeding at things without much effort, failure is devastating. If a Chiron Leo finds that something does not come easily to them, they will either blame themselves and have an identity crisis over their abilities or they will shun the thing they tried and deem it not worth doing. Both situations are bad since they don't involve the necessary growth failure can bring. Leo Chirons might also struggle with an addiction to intense relationships, forgoing commitment in favor of a string of short, overstimulating flings. This might be fun at first, but it can cause them to start feeling empty over time.

Where Leo Chirons really shine in their healing is through the arts. Using their talents for good, Leo Chirons can do great things with creativity. This might mean using their skills to spread an important political message, or it might mean moving a lot of people by creating something beautiful. Either way, they will be able to greatly touch people and even heal them. Their other healing qualities are similar to those of Aries and Gemini. They are amazing at uplifting others and building others' self-confidence. If they are in a team setting, they will be able to work exceptionally well with their teammates, satisfied enough with their collective goals to avoid showing off.

Virgo

When Chiron is in Virgo, anxiety will rule. The type of anxiety will depend on the person and their other signs, but some of the most common are perfectionism, body dysmorphia, social anxiety, and hypochondria. In terms of perfectionism, this is common for Virgos, but with the Chiron pain point, it can be debilitating. Excessive perfectionism often leads to withdrawal from the world and an unwillingness to submit things or engage with people unless you are "perfect." Perfectionism can also appear through body dysmorphia, obsessing about appearances to the point of delusion. Social anxiety might also plague the Virgo Chiron, being paralyzed by the idea of being judged by others. Finally, Virgo Chirons might also struggle with an obsession with health, leading either to excessive doctor visits or extreme "healthy" lifestyle practices that can border on dangerous if unchecked. Conversely, Chiron Virgos might turn these anxieties outward and become excessively critical of people, causing them to possibly lose friends.

At their best, Chiron Virgos can be amazing guides. They can provide others with extremely useful structures for living their lives. For this reason, they thrive particularly in advice positions, such as counselors, financial advisors, wedding planners, and any other organizational care position. If you're making plans for your life or an important event, you'll want no one but a Chiron Virgo helping you. They also can be very wise when it comes to helping others. You might be surprised that a Chiron Virgo who seems a bit neurotic could give you such clear-headed advice. Finally, Chiron Virgos are great communicators and thus can create pieces of writing, media campaigns, and other types of communications that can truly move and inspire people. They are undoubtedly the communicators of the signs.

Libra

The core of all Libra Chirons' struggles is indecisiveness. When Libra Chirons are in pain, it's almost always because they are unable to confront something or make a clear decision. This creates a real rock-and-a-hard-place situation for the Libra Chiron. On one hand, they are incredibly afraid of commitment. They might not be willing to definitively choose a partner until it's too late and the person has gotten fed up. This indecisiveness might end up losing them many relationship opportunities because they failed to choose when the time came. However, on the other hand, Libras are terrified of conflict and thus often get stuck in unfulfilling relationships because they are unwilling to deal with the confrontation of breaking up. Relationships are where Libra Chirons really feel the brutality of their confrontation anxieties and indecisive natures.

But when they are able to look outward to others, Libra Chirons can truly foster harmony and community wherever they go. For this reason, they are amazing diplomats. They have a remarkable ability to mediate even the most difficult of conflicts, helping people who might be completely opposed eventually see eye to eye. This helpfulness and mediation might also manifest in a romantic way. Libra Chirons are known for carrying messages between lovers, like Friar Lawrence in *Romeo and Juliet*. They find joy in bringing people together, whether in politics, love, or even friendship.

Scorpio

The dark sign of Scorpio might find some truly difficult anxieties with Chiron. At their worst, Scorpio Chirons are given to nihilism. They might struggle to find meaning in life and end up plain giving up. This is especially common among younger Scorpio Chirons, but it can also happen to older people, especially after a destabilizing life change. The other problem Scorpio Chirons tend to struggle with is jealousy over love or power. They might be particularly jealous partners and can even become possessive if they don't keep it in check. Like Libra suns, they might also have trouble getting out of unfulfilling relationships.

On the flip side, Scorpio Chirons can do a lot for others in terms of deep soul-searching because they are all about the deepest parts of the human soul. If you are contemplating deep questions about yourself, your close relationships, or even your place in the world, no one will be able to guide you through those things better than a Scorpio Chiron. They are especially good at helping people through difficult or transitional times. Scorpio Chirons might, for this reason, seem like "foul-weather friends," or people who seem to always be around when the going gets tough. Births, deaths, major moves—you can bet your Scorpio Chiron friend will be right there with you. For this reason, they are excellent as grief counselors or divorce lawyers, dedicating their lives to the messier parts of other people.

Sagittarius

In their more negative states, Sagittariuses are very prone to dogmatic or even cult-like thinking. They might be particularly vulnerable to joining cults or making big dramatic changes in their ideology at the drop of a hat. They are the kind of people who can go from being an extreme atheist to a devout believer in a matter of months. Pair this with their extreme wanderlust and tendency toward a nomadic lifestyle, and they are very vulnerable to a cultish lifestyle. They will leave their homes on a whim in search of their next thrill, possibly sacrificing important relationships or good situations. They might also be flippant with others, not really acknowledging the deeper implications of the things they are saying or downplaying the significance of certain relationships. A tendency to abandon or shirk responsibility will always follow them.

But turn them outward, and a Saggitarius Chiron will be a magnetic and electric personality. They will always be able to crack the right joke to lighten even the most somber of circumstances. They are also able to impart wisdom to others with genuine compassion. If they're the ones to tell you about something major in your life, then you can be assured that they will use all the care and consideration in their heart to try to make it acceptable to you. Sagittarius Chirons are also known for producing great creative works, excelling particularly in the field of socially conscious art.

Capricorn

Capricorn Chirons can't help but be obsessed with their careers. On the most negative side, the Capricorn Chiron is pursuing professional success with the goal of attaining money, completely disregarding the ideas of personal fulfillment or contribution to society. They can easily fall into high-power, high-status positions that might be morally dubious or lack anything creative or personally satisfying. The Capricorn Chiron is thus at risk for deep dissatisfaction with their professional life, failing to understand why they feel discontented since their values are misaligned with their happiness. Usually, this will ricochet into the family, causing strife or even dysfunction in the home.

If the Capricorn Chiron is able to use their talents to help others, they will find themselves to be much more fulfilled. Instead of using status to better themselves, they will instead turn their hard work into something that benefits the community. They will particularly shine as leaders with their go-getter attitudes, making strides and ensuring that everyone gets what they need. Capricorn Chirons can also demonstrate an intense environmental consciousness.

Aquarius

The rebellious nature of the Aquarius is only made more destructive under Chiron. While their unconventional natures can be a positive thing, even sparking social change, Aquarius Chirons can become rebellious for the mere sake of being so. These rebels without a cause might bring about undue damage to others by refusing to think about consequences. Somewhat contradictorily, Aquarius Chirons also have a tendency to try to fit in with the crowd, especially if they perceive that crowd as unique or exciting. For these two reasons in tandem, Aquarius Chirons are most at risk during their youth when peer pressure around doing drugs, skipping school, or committing petty crimes is at its highest. In adulthood, this desire to fit in with the cool crowd might manifest in them shirking major responsibilities until a mature age or refusing to settle down. They might also be somewhat emotionally detached.

Because of their disregard for the status quo, Aquarius Chirons can do a lot to help others through social justice. They have a strong sense of fairness and right and wrong, so they will never let a group of people be silenced, offering themselves up as spokespeople for the disenfranchised. Whether or not they belong to the group they are protecting, they will fight just as fiercely. Their idealistic natures will help them shine a light on many issues and help people in need.

Pisces

The emotional and imaginative nature of the Pisces means that the main issue they will face in life will be a divergence from reality. The Pisces Chiron tends to experience difficulty with hard or adult situations, preferring to shy away from the darker parts of the world and live in a more dreamlike state. They might experience intense denial or distress when anything difficult happens to them as they lack the emotional skills to process it adequately. They will often seek out escapism, creating a life in which they don't have to think about unpleasant things. They might also have trouble setting boundaries with other people, becoming stuck in negative cycles they are too timid to break.

On the other hand, they possess strong spiritual skills when it comes to other people. They are the best people to go to for advice on metaphysical or emotional problems. They will still live in fantasy, but because of this, they are amazing at helping you access the core of what you really want. If you're a particularly repressed person, a Pisces Chiron will be the best person to help you unravel those repressed feelings and unlock what your true desires are. Pisces Chirons are so good at these things that they can sometimes veer into the psychic. Many fortune tellers or psychics are Pisces Chirons because of their acute perceptive abilities and their alignment with the spiritual world.

Chapter 9:
Retrograde Planets

Besides the individual planets themselves, there are also specific states a planet can be in that will affect its meaning. The most common one of these states is retrograde. Retrograde is when a planet is moving backward through the night sky, opposite to its usual course. Whether or not a planet in your chart is in retrograde greatly affects its meaning. In fact, a planet in retrograde might completely change that planet's meaning, and in turn, its effect on you. Retrograde in astrology is somewhat similar to reversed cards in the Tarot. If a card is in the upside-down position in a Tarot reading, then its meaning will be the opposite. Retrograde, however, is somewhat more complicated than Tarot reversals, creating a very specific change in meaning. In this chapter, we will talk all about retrograde and how it can have an effect on your chart.

How Does Retrograde Happen?

Retrograde is a well-documented astrological phenomenon. Astrologers have charted retrogrades since the dawn of time. Before the heliocentric model (i.e., the sun as the center of the solar system instead of the earth), retrogrades appeared merely as the planets acting up. Thus, astronomers began to think of these retrogrades as the planets "acting out of character," or contradicting their natures. As a result, the concept of astrological retrograde was born.

Once scientists were able to more closely chart the planets as they revolve around the sun, they discovered the true reason that planets retrograde. It is a complex optical illusion caused by the earth and another planet passing each other's orbit. Remember back in the section on the inner planets how I explained that all planets have different orbiting speeds and times? We talked about how Mercury spins the fastest and has the shortest journey while Neptune and Pluto spin the slowest and have the longest journeys. Well, that is important to the concept of retrograde. Because all the planets have different orbiting speeds, they will have to pass each other at some point. When the earth passes another planet, which it does with every single one at some point, that planet momentarily appears to be going much slower, even backward! When you chart the planet's position in the sky, it will appear to not be moving at all, or even moving briefly backward, before regaining its original course and moving forward again. Similar to the orbits, each planet's retrograde will depend on its speed. Mercury has the shortest period of being in retrograde, while Pluto has the longest.

What Does Retrograde Mean?

So, what does retrograde do to the meaning of the planets? Let's think back for a second to how the planets function in astrology. Each planet has a different meaning or facet of life over which it presides. Its interaction with a particular zodiac sign will determine the person's personality type in relation to that facet. If, however, a planet happens to be in retrograde at the time of your birth, then that meaning will be changed. Therefore, a Mars Gemini will be significantly different from a Mars Gemini retrograde.

The specific way in which retrogrades affect planets is by blocking or obscuring their meaning. It transforms the meaning of the planet from the outside or core world to the inner world. In a way, planets are to their retrogrades as the sun is to the moon. You will experience the same personality profiles as the sign, just on an inner or more hidden level. So, while a Leo Venus might have a very bold and show-offy attitude toward romance, a Leo Venus retrograde will still have that attitude but will hide it from the world. They might only want to do big romantic gestures in the privacy of their home or only show their deeply romantic side after they've really gotten to know someone. You can think of retrogrades as sort of putting the planet's meaning in shadow, relegating it to a more private or deeply felt arena.

Which Planets Are in Retrograde?

All of the planets orbiting the sun have the potential to be in retrograde and go through a scheduled retrograde period at their appointed times. However, I did say that the term "planets" in astrology technically referred to the sun and moon as well. This is not the case for retrogrades. Since the sun and moon are on distinct orbiting paths, they cannot experience retrograde. They each have their own internal cycles of things such as lunar and solar eclipses which affect their meanings, but retrograde isn't something that applies to them. For the purposes of retrograde, "planet" is used with the conventional meaning: the eight (or nine, if you count the earth) celestial bodies that orbit the sun.

How Retrograde Affects Each Planet

Because every planet has a different meaning, retrograde will affect them all differently. Some planets involve a very fundamental part of life, making their retrogrades particularly tricky. Other planets might already deal with a very internal or private area of life, which can cause them to become excessively insular. The other thing that will affect the planets is their retrograde schedule. Planets like Mercury and Venus go through very rapid and frequent retrogrades, while the outer planets can be in retrograde for months. Thus, the inner planets' retrogrades will be more randomly dispersed, while there can be whole half-years worth of people who have the same Pluto in retrograde, leading to more significant numbers of people. Here, we will look at how retrograde affects the meaning of each planet in the solar system.

Mercury

So, I have actually lied to you so far. Technically, Mars and Venus don't go through a conventional retrograde. Because these planets are both closer to the sun than the earth, they experience a slightly different version of retrograde. They pass the earth, but the earth does not pass them, so it won't look the same as a Mars or Jupiter retrograde. However, the effect on astrological charting is still the same, so they are important to consider.

Mercury is the most common planet to be in retrograde. For this reason, a lot of people have Mercury retrograde in their charts. Because Mercury is related to intellectual pursuits, having your Mercury in retrograde means that you will have a much deeper, more internal intellectual life. You might not be an amazing public speaker, but you will be a voracious reader and have the ability to ponder questions at a deeper level than the average person. You will likely relate everything in your life to something philosophical and might find that you can't help always looking at things through the lens of their deeper meanings.

Venus

Again, Venus technically does not go through a true retrograde, but the retrograde rules still apply. The planet of love being in retrograde means that your romantic affairs will be much closer to your heart than most. You might have trouble even telling your friends when you have a crush on someone, let alone the person themselves. This can lead to being extremely guarded and having a difficult time really showing love unless you feel incredibly secure. However, this is all made up for by the level of intensity that Venus retrogrades experience in relationships. They often seek a higher level of intimacy than other people and will have some of the closest bonds possible with friends and lovers.

Mars

Mars is one of the more interesting and difficult to pin down retrogrades. It can manifest in one of two ways. Either the Mars retrograde internalizes their competitive desire to be the best so deeply that they end up trying much harder and becoming aggressive as a result, or the Mars retrograde becomes ashamed of this competitive side and attempts to hide it. Thus, they might come across as the opposite of competitive, comparatively meek and shy. You can think of this side of the retrograde as being somewhat similar to an Aries moon where these competitive desires only come out in specific or private situations. Either way, Mars retrogrades will struggle with their desires, possibly not recognizing them or taking longer than usual to acknowledge them.

Jupiter

Jupiter retrogrades have the advantage of being both genuinely imaginative and very good planners. What results is a fascinating person who is able to put even the most far-fetched of goals into action. They will often have a very strong work ethic, believing that hard work is the only thing that can truly lead to a person's success. If they follow these beliefs, then they will certainly go far in life, creating some of the most beautiful and well-planned things ever.

Saturn

Saturn retrogrades will often have difficulty trusting others. They will struggle with vulnerability, taking a long time before they are able to truly open up to someone else. They might also struggle with guilt, feeling far too much responsibility for their own good and often being severely bothered by things they may feel culpable for but that were outside of their control. And finally, Saturn retrogrades have a very hard time with structure. For them, this goes both ways. They will at once hate anyone trying to impose structure on their lives while also struggling to do so themselves. What results is a highly unstructured life, leading to possible misdirection and feelings of being lost. Saturn retrogrades will need to go through a lot of internal work to overcome these struggles.

Uranus

As Uranus is the planet of revolution, its retrograde will want to avoid these things while being preoccupied with them at the same time. Uranus retrogrades struggle deeply with the idea of change as it seems to strike a chord deep inside them. They will likely suppress any of their unconventional qualities, which from the outside might make them appear boring or square. But don't be fooled by appearances. Once Uranus retrogrades are comfortable, either alone or with close friends and family, they will let all their wacky energy flow and finally show the world the eccentrics they really are on the inside. They will likely spend their lives in constant strife between order and chaos, convention and rebellion, or repression and release.

Neptune

Those with the deeply spiritual planet of Neptune in retrograde can be covertly religious. They keep their intense philosophical natures to themselves, preferring to play it cool around other people while housing a strong conviction deep inside. For this reason, Neptune retrogrades might steer away from organized religion, preferring a quiet spirituality that might even be atheistic. If they are involved in organized religion, they will keep this very separate from the rest of their life, perhaps even attending church in a different town to avoid having to worship around people they know. The trademark of a Neptune retrograde is someone who comes across as very laid-back and unserious only to reveal a deeply pious interior.

Pluto

Those with Pluto in retrograde will probably experience pretty extreme unrest. They will have a lot of contradictions running through them, and because they are in shadow, they will have a hard time unraveling them. Pluto retrogrades will crave yet also fear control and power. They will also hate when someone else has power over them. They will desire power yet also be unaware of this desire and experience frustration around this unnamed craving. And finally, Pluto retrogrades will lack introspection, making them one of the most lost and confused retrogrades out there.

Pillar 4:
The Houses

Moving on to the fourth pillar of astrology, we have the houses. Houses in astrology are an entirely different system, separate from the zodiac and the planets. They do, however, bear some distinct similarities. First of all, there are 12 houses, which matches up with the 12 signs in the zodiac. This is purely a superficial similarity since the zodiac is based on the 12 moon cycles and the houses are based on earth's daily rotation, 12 being one-half of the day's 24-hour cycle. They are also similar to the planets in that they preside over different facets of life. So, each house will represent a different part of your life that is also influenced by other astrological factors. In this section on pillar four, we will look at two important elements of the houses. First, in Chapter 10, we will look at each house and give a description of the influence it has over your life. Then, in Chapter 11, we will look at house positions and the impact they have on your birth chart as well.

Chapter 10: Individual Houses

Just as the signs and planets all have their individual meanings, each house has its own unique meaning as well. There are 12 houses in the zodiac and thus 12 meanings. But how do we calculate these houses? Well, you can think of a house in astrology as being like a slice of the sky. If the entire three-dimensional dome of sky surrounding the earth was divided into 12 slices like an orange, you would get 12 triangular pieces. As the day progresses, we move through all 12 of these houses. Because there are 12 and not 24, the house actually changes every two hours instead of every hour. For this reason, it's necessary to know the exact hour of your birth in order to be able to calculate all your houses. The houses start at the horizon and go up incrementally from there, tied to the location and hour of your birth. When you are born, the constellation (and planet) that is passing through each house will indicate something about it. Though we said that the 12 houses are separate from the zodiac signs astronomically, they are each linked with a corresponding zodiac sign that relates closely to their themes. In this section, we will focus on descriptions of the individual houses.

First House

Luckily, we already know something about the first house because it is the same as the rising! This house, known as either the first house, the rising, or the ascendant, is the house immediately over the horizon. As we talked about way back in Chapter 2, the rising sign presides over your outward or public self. It is your "mask," or the image you project into the world. Sometimes, this image runs deep, influencing important parts of yourself, and sometimes this image is something you shed the moment you are out of the public sphere. It all depends on the signs and their relation to the first house. The first house is ruled by Aries, reflecting that sign's appearance-based ethos.

Second House

The second house is all about a person's financial life. Like it or not, everyone has a relationship with the material world. The kinds of bodies occupying the second house will dictate your lifelong relationship with material possessions and wealth. Having a lot of planets in the second house doesn't necessarily indicate that you will be wealthy, though. Rather, they will dictate things like your feelings about money, your luck with money, and the importance monetary success will have to your life. The second house is ruled by Taurus, influenced by that sign's earthiness and staunch practicality.

Third House

The third house is primarily concerned with communication. Things like talking, writing, traveling, and forming communities will all be covered in the third house. The bodies in your third house will likely dictate your particular communication style, whether it is honest and direct or coy and distant. This house might also dictate your feelings about travel and movement, possibly indicating whether you will be a homebody or full of wanderlust. It will also denote whether you are destined to live in the same place all your life or inclined to move around and see more of the world. Because communication is so central to relationships, professional as well as personal, the third house will also have a bearing on the way you interact with the people in your life on a deeper level. The third house is ruled by Gemini, going with that sign's tendency toward companionship and social skills.

Fourth House

The fourth house of the sky rules over home and family. This is the house that will reveal answers about the way you operate in a family setting. Certain planets or signs in the fourth house might indicate your specific relationship with your home and family and whether you are someone for whom family is very important or if you are a lone wolf or a wanderer. This house doesn't necessarily have to mean blood family. It could indicate something about your blood family, whether you are involved with them or not, but it could also refer to your adopted, found, or friend family. Any relationship that is tied to your home and inner space falls under the fourth house. Cancer is this house's ruling sign, continuing with Cancer's themes of nurturing and care.

Fifth House

When you're in the fifth house, it's all about pleasure. But because pleasure has such a wide meaning, the fifth house has a huge variety of life situations over which it presides. Sometimes, philosophers divide pleasures into "high" or "low" pleasures, with low pleasures being things like food or sex and high pleasures being things like taking care of children or learning to play an instrument. However, the fifth house makes no such discrimination and deals with pleasures of all kinds. It sees drinking expensive wine as being on the same level as reading a dense Russian novel or going to a party. Anything that stimulates your senses or makes you feel fulfilled goes under the fifth house. The bodies that interact with the fifth house, however, will determine how you interact with pleasure; how much you allow yourself, how you go about seeking it out, and whether or not you value it in your life. The fifth house's corresponding sign is Leo, given its fiery, egocentric qualities.

Sixth House

The sixth house deals with health and wellness. More specifically, it refers to the more choice-based aspects of health and wellness. Besides the health qualities you are born with, you also make many choices throughout your life that impact your overall health. The amount of exercise you get, the kinds of foods you eat, and even the strength of your relationships can all contribute to your general health. The sixth house deals with these choices and how they reflect on your mind and body. Thus, whichever bodies are in the sixth house will be reflected in how you feel about and make choices related to your health. It will correspond to whether you are very health-conscious, whether you value mental health more or less than physical health, and whether you are inclined to fulfill your health-based goals. Virgo, with its systematic approach to life, is the equivalent sign to the sixth house.

Seventh House

Moving into the second half of the houses, we begin to look outward a bit more. The first six houses deal primarily with individual choices, whereas the next six houses focus more on the things that influence you throughout your life. The first of this second half, the seventh house, sits directly opposite the first house. The seventh house is often called the descendant since it is directly opposite the ascendant. The seventh house is mainly focused on transformational relationships in your life. These are the kind of intense, one-on-one relationships that will have an indispensable role in shaping who you are and what you choose to do in life. This is someone more intimate than a teacher or mentor. This kind of relationship is usually with a parent, a very close friend, or a spouse or partner. It will be someone who has seen you at your best and at your worst and seems to know you inside and out. They will feel like a soulmate and someone you can always rely on, shaping the very depths of your soul. Most people will only have a handful of these kinds of relationships throughout their life, so remember to cherish them. Libra is this house's defining sign, ready to allow themselves to be shaped by other influences in the best way possible.

Eighth House

The eighth house is one of the more intense houses. This is the house of transformation, a mysterious phenomenon that has a few branches. People with a lot of natal planets—or planets at the time of their birth—in the eighth house will be very attracted to the beyond, such as occult practices, astrology, and mysticism. They will seek a place for themselves not just in the real world, but in the order of the universe as well. Other aspects of the eighth house are sex and death, two foundational aspects of life that represent the cycles of creation. There is a reason the French call an orgasm *la petite mort*, or "the little death"—there is certainly something of a rebirth in the sexual experience, linking the two forces of the cycles. The planetary bodies in your eighth house will thus reflect your choices and feelings in regard to these significant forces. The eighth house is ruled by Scorpio's intensely pensive and private nature.

Ninth House

The ninth house also deals with one's relationship with the world but in a more grounded sense. This house presides over travel and learning. This can either mean a practical form of learning, such as interacting with new people, especially those who live in different cities or countries, or a more internal learning, such as reading challenging books or taking courses. Those with many natal planets in the ninth house will likely value education very highly and pursue many different kinds of knowledge. Of course, which planets those are will dictate the types of intelligence or exploratory pursuits you value the most. Sagittarius, with its love for exploration, rules over the ninth house.

Tenth House

Another aspect of the latter houses and their focus on the outside world is the status-focused tenth house. While the seventh house focused on intimacy, the eighth house on spiritual belonging, and the ninth house on forging new connections, the tenth house is all about your social identity and status in the world. Having a lot of natal planets in the tenth house will usually mean that you are more ambitious or a social climber. You might value your career or even fame more than some of the more internal qualities of the other houses. The specific bodies in the tenth house will indicate your direction in this socially conscious paradigm. Capricorn's staunch ambition and work ethic rule the tenth house.

Eleventh House

The eleventh house, in contrast, rules over friendship or the kinds of relationships we have in life that offer us nothing materially but everything emotionally and spiritually. The field of friendship can be broad—it can mean your work friends, your neighbors, your classmates, and of course, those close friends you keep for life. The eleventh house is all about community, surrounding yourself with a network of people who support you and make you feel accepted. For this reason, the eleventh house also has a relationship to humanitarianism and charity as well as innovation. Aquarius and its penchant for both relationships and uniqueness rule the eleventh house.

Twelfth House

The twelfth house occupies an interesting position in the sky and in the houses: It is just below the horizon and thus invisible. It represents the parts of the self and the universe that are mysterious, unseen, or even unknowable. Dreams and secrets will occupy this house, things that are never spoken aloud or that are even lost to time. If you have a lot of natal planets in the twelfth house, then you will have a strong relationship with the shadow world. You will be able to know things that are hidden from most other people. This might even result in psychic powers. Due to their deeply emotional nature, the twelfth house is ruled by Pisces.

Chapter 11: House Positions

Just as the signs fall under different categories—such as the four elements, the three modalities, or the two polarities—houses too have certain categories under which they fall. You may have noticed some similarities or patterns between certain houses that link them together closely. This isn't a coincidence. There are many houses that share a strong connection with one another. These patterns are called the house positions, and they reflect the house's relationships with one another. There are three categories of houses that group four together: angular houses, succedent houses, and cadent houses. These categories alternate throughout the zodiac wheel and have distinct relationships. Angular houses are considered the most powerful, with their neighboring succedent houses being less powerful, and their neighbor cadent houses being the least powerful of them all. These house categorizations line up with the modalities of the zodiac, with the cardinal, fixed, and mutable signs being grouped in the same way according to their house counterparts. In this chapter, we will look at how angular, succedent, and cadent houses influence their meaning.

Angular Houses

Corresponding to the cardinal signs, the angular houses are the first house (Aries), the fourth house (Cancer), the seventh house (Libra), and the tenth house (Capricorn). These are the leading houses, representing some of the most fundamental aspects of life. If you look into the meanings of each of these houses, we can see how they create important tent poles for your life. Astrologers consider these four houses to be the basic needs, the things you must have satisfied in order to live a fulfilled life. The first house deals with your base identity and will form the way that you construct your sense of self. The fourth house, symbolizing home and family, represents the second of the four integral aspects of life. The seventh house comes in with the third foundational quality, which is close, intimate relationships. Finally, the tenth house represents professional ambition and status. All four of these houses are needed to hold up the others, representing the strongest four values.

Because the angular houses are so foundational, those with at least one natal planet in all four of these houses will be incredibly balanced individuals. They will have a firm grip on life and their reality on which they can build a very solid foundation and branch out into more superficial things. Those who lack natal planets in any of these four houses will, by contrast, seem and feel more shallow in their identity and relationships. They might struggle to feel things to their full extent or to build a solid and consistent identity. They might also struggle to form truly rock-solid relationships that will propel them into their best selves.

An important aspect of these house positions is pairing. Each set of four houses has two pairs within it—two houses that have a particularly special relationship with one another. In the case of the angular houses, the pairings are the first house with the seventh and the fourth house with the tenth. These pairings are based on the houses' positions on the wheel, with signs that are positioned opposite one another being the pairs. This concept is fairly similar to the sign polarities, which pair zodiac signs with their opposites. This system shows us how certain aspects of each house contrast with and complement each other.

The first pairing within the angular houses is between the first and seventh houses. We have actually already talked about this pairing a little bit with the comparison between the ascendant and the descendant. The first house represents the beginning of the self journey of the first half of the houses, whereas the seventh house represents the beginning of the self-world journey of the other houses. In other words, they are both leaders in their respective categories. If we were to think about these houses in terms of narrative structures, the first house (and by extension, the first six houses) is man versus self, while the seventh house (and by extension, the last six houses) is man versus society.

The second pairing within the angular houses is between the fourth and tenth houses. These houses represent opposite sides of the spectrum in terms of public versus private life. The family-focused fourth house is as private as you can get, while the status-focused tenth house is as public as you can get. They do, however, share some key similarities. They are both focused on duty and relate to established institutions. They don't deal much with the realms of pleasure or desire but rather the things we owe. Still, they are opposing houses that preside over two very different facets of life.

Succedent Houses

The succedent houses correspond to the fixed signs and consist of the second house (Taurus), the fifth house (Le0), the eighth house (Scorpio), and the eleventh house (Aquarius). These signs are slightly less foundational than their angular counterparts, but they all still function in most people's lives as important forces. The succedent signs thus take up a slightly less necessary position in the houses. If you are lacking in one or even all of these areas, you can still live a fulfilling life, especially if you have a lot of angular houses. However, having all angular houses and no succedent or cadent houses can make life a little boring without all those other little aspects and twists and turns that make it interesting.

The first pairing that exists within the succedent houses is between the second and eighth houses. The second house represents the material or financial world while the eighth house represents the mysterious, nonmaterial world. You can see how these signs would be opposed, one presiding only over wealth and prosperity and the other presiding over only the higher, spiritual forces that don't consider the earthly world below. They do, however, have a point of connection in the form of upward mobility. Money and spiritual guidance alike both have an infinitely expanding goal that attempts to reach beyond what the person might have been born into. Yet, besides this, these two houses deal with two fairly oppositional parts of life.

The fifth and eleventh houses make up the other duality in the succedent houses. While the fifth house governs over pleasure, the eleventh house governs over friendship. These houses might seem similar on the surface, both dealing somewhat with interpersonal relationships and even love, but that is where the similarities end. At their core, these are very oppositional houses. The fifth house is ultimately an inherently individualistic house. Yes, it can deal with certain relationships in your life but mostly as vehicles for pleasure. There is no duty under the fifth house, nor obligation. If you are a parent, it is because your child brings you joy. In the eleventh house, however, the communities you build come with obligations and duties. You must take care of others under this house in order to be taken care of in turn. So, while they may seem similar, these two signs stand on opposite ends of individualism.

Cadent Houses

The final category within the house positions is cadent houses, which are based on the mutable signs and contain the third house (Gemini), the sixth house (Virgo), the ninth house (Sagittarius), and the twelfth house (Pisces). The cadent houses are significantly less central than the angular and succedent houses. If you have too many cadent houses, you could get stuck in the world of possibilities or options, never being able to take action. This is why those with too many cadent houses in their chart can come across as flaky and might lack a strong identity or relationships. However, this is not always completely true, since there are some valid reasons you should absolutely have cadent houses in your chart. These are considered the "abstract" houses, the ones where ideas have not yet come to fruition. You need some of these to keep a sense of possibility, variety, and mystery in your life.

The first duality within the cadent houses is between the third and ninth houses. The third house is all about communication, while the ninth house is all about learning. Like the second and eighth houses, they might on the surface seem similar, but they are opposing in a parallel way. The third house is how you present yourself and your ideas to the world, how you best articulate the thoughts in your head. The ninth house, however, is all about how you take in new information, the way you process new things and allow yourself to be shaped by them. In other words, the third house is all about output while the ninth house is all about input.

Pillar 5:
Birth Charts

All of the things we have been talking about so far in this book encompass what is called the "birth chart." This is the cumulative representation of all the zodiac, planetary, house, and other astrological principles of your birth. Essentially, the birth chart is an astrological representation of the night sky at the time (and place) of your birth that will tell you all you need to know about your natal astrology. You can find all your planets and their corresponding signs and houses as well as your sun and moon signs in your birth chart. It is the centralized location for all your astrological information. In this pillar, we will show you how to bring together all of the many facets we have discussed throughout this book. You will be able to conglomerate everything you have learned so far in the form of your birth chart. This pillar is separated into two chapters, each with a slightly different focus. The first chapter, 12, will instruct you on how to create a birth chart using information relating to your birth. The next chapter will instruct you on what to do with the sum of information on your birth chart as well as inform you of some extra stray pieces of information we have not covered elsewhere in the book. At the end of this pillar, you will be more knowledgeable about birth charts in general and yours in particular, and you'll be able to cast and interpret many important astrological events.

Chapter 12:
Creating Your Birth Chart

Before you can read your birth chart, you need to create it. Designed to put all your astrological information in one place, astrologers have been creating birth charts for thousands of years. Obviously, given the varying levels of complexity involved in astrology, casting a birth chart can range from extremely easy to very difficult. You can likely do your simpler calculations yourself as an amateur astrologer, but for the more complex calculations, you might need to consult an online calculator or a professional astrologer. In this chapter, we will give you some of the most pertinent information surrounding the calculation of your birth chart.

Getting Started

Now that you understand the birth chart and all the things that it can encompass, you will need to figure out what yours looks like. But how do you do this? It's not like you can go back in time and chart all the sun, moon, star, and planet positions at the time of your birth. Well, luckily all the planetary bodies involved in your chart move in fairly regular patterns that can be backtracked mathematically. So, no matter when you were born, you will be able to retroactively create a picture of the sky at the time of your birth. Furthermore, astronomers have records of all the planetary positions dating much further back than the birth year of anyone alive today. Whether you research these things yourself or consult the experts, you will be able to get very clear answers on all these positions at your specific date, time, and location of birth. Location is important for time zone purposes. Obviously, the most important thing is that you know your basic information yourself. The basic information you will need to know with absolute certainty is the date, the time (to the hour), and the geographical location of your birth (meaning the town or city). You will not be able to calculate your birth chart to its full accuracy if you do not have all three of these pieces of information. So, before you start casting, you will need to consult with whoever you need to, or even medical records, to ensure that you are completely accurate in your birth information. From there, you can start casting!

Online and Expert Birth Charts

Before we get into the "how," you should know that you don't necessarily have to cast your birth chart on your own. Many of the determinations you need to make will be complex as you will need to make complicated calculations about the phases of the moon, the positions of the planets, and the planet rotations at the time of your birth. All of these things can be found online but might require more digging. In the case of all aspects of your birth chart, to receive a complete and accurate picture of your astrological sign, you have the option to consult an expert or an online birth chart calculator. In terms of online calculators, there are many free versions as well as some paid versions that have more in-depth descriptions. Some even include long profiles for each of your signs and their relationships with one another. These will provide interpretations for you in addition to your birth chart, so they might be useful if you are not yet as knowledgeable as you would like to be in all of the sign meanings. For interpretive (and casting) purposes, you might also want to consult an astrologer. These people will not only be able to cast for you and give a basic description of your chart, but they will also be there for you to ask questions and possibly provide a more individually tailored profile, depending on the service. If you want the easiest, most accurately calculated version of your birth chart, you have the option to consult one of these things, even just to verify that your calculations were correct.

Calculating Sun, Moon, and Rising

For those who want to calculate your own birth chart, we will now move on to the instructional aspect. Right off the bat, you will notice that some aspects of your birth chart are easier to calculate than others. These are the things that are on very regular schedules that don't change from year to year. However, there are some things that are more complex and will require you to look at planetary records for the time you were born. In this section, we will look at how to calculate your three foundational signs: the sun, the moon, and the rising.

Calculating Your Sun

The sun is by far the easiest sign in the zodiac to calculate. You will only need your day of birth on the calendar. Dates for sun zodiac signs never change because our calendar is based around them. So, you can simply consult your date of birth, regardless of the year, and find your sun sign. In Chapter 2, we included the dates of birth associated with all the signs, so you can simply refer back to those when calculating your sun sign. Again, the time of day, year, and location of your birth have no bearing on your sun sign. No matter what is going on with the rest of your chart, everyone born on May 31st will be a Gemini and everyone born on February 10th will be an Aquarius.

Calculating Your Moon

The moon is more difficult to calculate since you will need the exact date and time, to the hour, of your birth. You will not, however, need your location. The moon's zodiac changes every 2½ days, so you will have to find out what sign your moon was in at the time of your birth. You can usually find this information through records that list the different zodiac signs of the moon. The easiest way is to search your day, month, year, and time of birth online with "moon zodiac" attached. You should be able to come up with your moon sign from this search. You might also be able to find a book of moon records from which you can calculate your moon sign, given that you were born within the book's range. One of these two ways is necessary to calculate your moon.

Calculating Your Rising

To calculate your rising, you will need to know all of your pertinent birth information, including date, year, time, and location. Your rising sign is fairly easy to calculate thanks to rising charts. Rising charts show the relationship between your sun sign and your rising sign. Even though risings are not as regular as the sun sign, they shift on a regular axis relative to the sun, which means you can use your sun to calculate your rising. The rising chart will show you a simple cross section of sun signs and birth times. For the sake of simplicity, the chart uses standardized time zones, meaning you will have to convert your birth time to the standard time zone. From there, you can simply follow the X-axis showing your sun sign to the Y-axis showing your time of birth to find the square containing your rising sign. So, for example, if you are a Leo and were born between 6 and 8 p.m., then you are a Pisces rising. Consulting one of these charts is the simplest way to calculate your rising. Of course, you can always follow the same instructions as with the moon and simply look up your date and time of birth to find your rising. Either way, you should have an easy time calculating your rising sign.

Calculating Your Planets

The planets function very similarly to the moon in that there is no regular pattern of how they move relative to our human calendars. Because the sun and the rising sign are tied to the turn or orbit of the earth, they can be calculated by standard means. However, the planets, like the moon, need to be calculated based on orbit records. When finding each of your planets' zodiac signs, you should conduct an internet search similar to finding out your moon sign. Using a search phrase such as "date/time [planet] zodiac" should suffice. Your outer planets will also be easier to calculate since they remain in the same phases for longer periods of time. However, they do sometimes tend to move into a different sign very briefly before snapping back to their original sign. Make sure to keep track of these differences so that you don't miscalculate any outer planets.

Calculating Your Houses

The houses are actually very easy to calculate simply because you have already done it! Remember that your rising sign is actually just another name for your first house. If you can calculate your rising sign, you will instantly know the rest of your houses. They should proceed in order from your first house. So, if your first house (or rising, or ascendant) is in Leo, then your second house would be in Virgo, your third in Libra, and so forth. However, it is important to note that cusps and angles might affect this clean order of your houses. If you want to ensure that you are calculating all your houses 100% correctly, then you will have to consult an online calculator. This way, you might find out about some angles that could cause two of your houses in a row to be in one sign. Better to be sure than have an inaccurate chart!

Calculating Retrogrades

When you calculate your planets, your source may or may not tell you whether a planet was in retrograde. Thinking back to our chapter on retrogrades, you will remember that this is a critical aspect of your chart, carrying a completely different meaning than a non-retrograde planet. When you look at your planets, you should check whether it was in retrograde at the time of your birth to ensure that you have the right phase of the planet.

Chapter 13:
Reading Birth Charts

Your birth chart will likely look very complicated at first, especially if you don't have a baseline knowledge of general astrology. However, once you understand the role of all the celestial bodies in your birth chart, the complicated markings will start to become clear and you will begin being able to discern important things about your relationships with the stars and planets. In this chapter, we will get into some of the specific ways you should be reading your birth chart.

What Should I Look For in My Birth Chart?

The specific areas you should be paying attention to in your birth chart are, well, all of them! But it can be hard to know where to start. For the purposes of clarity, you can follow the structure of this book as a general guide to understanding your birth chart. The first things we talked about in this book were the sun, moon, and rising signs. These are the bread and butter of your zodiac profile. They tell you some of the most important basic information about yourself and will give you a clear entry point when constructing your astrological identity. Remember to also consider the different zodiac groupings, like polarities and modalities, to get a more complete sense of your zodiac profile. Then, you can move on to the planets, which will give you deeper insight into how the zodiac signs play out in subtler and more specific aspects of your life. You might not initially connect with your sun sign only to realize that the planets underlying it influence the sun sign and make it more relatable to you. Then, you can move on to the houses, giving your planets and star signs even more clarity and nuance. This methodology will give you a near-complete view of your birth chart as well as your whole astrological identity. There are, however, a few stray things that will matter to your birth chart that we have not yet discussed. In this section, we will look at some of these extra little things that you should keep an eye out for on your birth chart and what they mean for you and your place in astrology.

House Cusps

Cusps are a very contentious issue in astrology. Many people claim to be born on the "cusp" of two different signs when they really mean that they were just born near the edge of the divide between two signs. When it comes to sun signs, most astrologers will dismiss this idea. They maintain that your sun will be firmly in one sign but concede that you might be a more difficult sun to categorize given your specific birth time or year. So, for example, if you are born at the stroke of midnight on June 20, does that make you a Gemini or a Cancer? Well, it actually depends on the specific year, which you can look up in more detail if you are unsure about your sign. It is guaranteed, however, that you will be firmly one or the other and cannot convincingly argue influence from both signs.

However, when it comes to planets and houses, this is a different story. Because houses are calculated as a matter of degrees, the house that a certain planet falls under is a little messier. Thus, some astrologers agree that being born within a certain small degree of the dividing line between two houses can be considered a cusp and can therefore cause influence from both houses. The jury is still out over the precise degree, but the cusp still stands. So, for example, if you were born when Venus was in the third house but within 10 degrees of the fourth house, then you might have your Venus traits straddling the realms of both communication as well as home and family. Pay close attention to the degrees on the planet-house section of your birth chart as you might be a cusp baby!

Quadrants

Similar to how all the aspects of astrology have categories, the birth chart has its own categories. These categories are called the quadrants, and they represent the journey of life from birth through youth to maturity. This journey is similar to the Major Arcana of the Tarot, which represents the journey of The Fool through trials culminating with enlightenment, or The World card. Starting with the horizontal radius on the left side, or your ascendant sign, these quadrants move clockwise until they reach the 12th house, just under the ascendant. The first quadrant (comprised of the first three houses) deals with your initial identity and personal foundation. The second quadrant, in the top right section, represents the behavioral patterns that form throughout your youth. This will usually determine your direction in life and your sensibilities regarding politics, values, and relationships. The third quadrant, or bottom right, represents a midlife perspective shift. This shift will come from gaining experience that might be disillusioning, enlightening, or even both. A more realized version of yourself will emerge from this stage. Finally, the fourth house represents maturity and reaping rewards. You should finally be seeing the outcomes of your life and appreciating what you have accumulated, be it wealth, family, fame, happiness, or even just beautiful memories. It is the culmination of the quadrants and the most fulfilled of all.

Lunar Nodes

Have you ever gone outside to observe a lunar or solar eclipse? Most people have. They are amazing visual feasts. However, did you know that these events are also important in astrology? These moments when the moon and sun overlap in your chart, known as lunar nodes, have a significant role to play in your life's journey. Although you might only be able to see an eclipse once every few years in one particular location, these lineups actually happen at regular intervals. In fact, the nodes go through the signs of the zodiac in perfect order, changing signs roughly every 18 months. Thus, everyone born in that period will have the same lunar nodes, much like the yearly Chinese zodiac. What is especially interesting about lunar nodes is that there will be two on everyone's chart. They are known as the North node and the South node. These two nodes will always be on opposing sides of the zodiac, creating an opposing contrast between one sign and its opposite. Thus, if your North node is in Aquarius, your South node will have to be in Leo, or if your North node is in Taurus, your South node will have to be in Scorpio, and so on. Here, we will look a little deeper into the North and South nodes and what they mean for you and your life's journey.

North Node

Your North node represents your destiny or the events that will transpire throughout your life that you might not have control over. This is a call to action that will take all the effort inside of you, but it will be worth it. If you feel the need to create great art, climb a mountain, give to others, or any other great life goal, that is your North node talking. No doubt this North node journey will take you far out of your comfort zone, but it will be a journey absolutely worth taking.

South Node

The South node, on the other hand, represents the abilities and interests innate within you. These might not come with a strong calling, but they will be things that are very easy for you. This innate ability does not always align with your North node calling. In fact, they are often misaligned to create important challenges for you in life. You might find that doing math problems comes as second nature, but it is really writing that calls you to action, even if it is not an innately easy task. Your South node qualities will always be there for you, though, even if you choose not to pursue them in your life journey. These help us build a sense of identity early in life and can give us the earned confidence to pursue what really drives us.

Reading Combinations

One of the most complex aspects of your chart is how all your signs combine together to form something cohesive. It might be overwhelming to calculate so many different aspects of your chart. You'll probably find that you have almost every sign represented somewhere in your chart, which can be confusing to a beginner astrologer. How do you know what it means to have a Pisces sun, a Taurus moon, and a Scorpio rising? Those signs seem so different from one another, so how can you have all three of them in your chart? If you feel truly lost, you can always go to an astrologer and consult their take on the specific combinations of signs. There have also been many books written that painstakingly describe every single possible combination of the signs. For the sake of time, we will not be listing all these combinations, which would take up multiple books in and of themselves, but we will give you some useful tips on how to read your birth chart combinations.

The first important tip is to start with your sun sign. Learn all there is to know about that sign. Even if you have many other signs in your chart, your sun sign will preside over all of them, so it should always be your starting point. Use it as a springboard for combinations, looking at how all the different signs in your chart work under your sun sign. From there, another important technique is to look for patterns. All your signs add up to form your distinctive personality, so it is useful to note if there are any trends among signs. Look back on some of the early chapters of this book where we talk about sign groupings, such as modalities and elements. You might notice that you have a lot of fire in your chart, which means that your overall personality leans toward the fire element qualities. Similarly, you might notice that you have overwhelmingly negative signs in your chart, which means you lean more toward feminine energy. All these categories can help you start to grasp a sense of your birth chart as a whole and examine how your signs mingle together to create something truly unique to you!

Conclusion

Astrology is one of the most mysterious and complicated fields out there, but with the right education, you can start to get a good grasp on how it works. Throughout this book, you have learned some of the most important and foundational concepts in astrology. You have learned about the 12 signs of the zodiac and all their primary and secondary traits. You have also seen how these signs interact with others, grouping them into elements, modalities, and polarities. Next, you were given an introduction to how the planets figure into the zodiac, learning the distinctive differences between how the sun, moon, and each of the planetary bodies interact with the signs. After that, we pivoted to the houses and looked at how this system of dividing the night's sky relates to your life journey and the way you pursue your goals. Finally, we gave you some important tips and advice on how to create and read your birth chart. Through all of these aspects, you have gained a very solid foundation in astrology and are now on your way to becoming an expert!

So, what can you do with this information? How can you employ these astrological principles to better live your life and work toward a good future? The first step is to truly allow your birth chart to wash over you. Read in-depth descriptions of all your planet signs and houses to get a good profile of who you are. Look for patterns like common elements or quadrants in your chart. Allow these signs to interact in order to fill out a distinctive profile of who you are astrologically. Don't worry if you feel like some of your signs don't really describe you very well. This is normal. Sometimes signs exist only within certain contexts or your shadow self. They might also be signs that represent a direction your life will take or a future version of yourself. Truly taking in your astrological chart is the first thing you should do when beginning your astrological journey.

Then, you need to start bringing astrology into your everyday life. When meeting people, consider your signs around relationships and sociability to gain insight into your behavior. Consider signs that are compatible with your own to get a sense of what kind of people you should be trying to attract in your life. When planning your career, look at your lunar nodes to tease out the relationship between your dreams and your abilities. Your chart, if respected and interpreted properly, will be a foundational aspect of your life, showing you who you are in ways you might never have considered. If you take anything away from this book, I hope that it's that you are written in the stars. You have a beautiful connection to the sky above your head and the celestial bodies that guide your life. Astrology is about reaching out to touch them.

Glossary

Angular houses: The strongest houses in the birth chart consisting of houses 1, 4, 7, and 10.

Aries: A zodiac sign characterized by ambition and social magnetism; symbolized by the ram.

Aquarius: A zodiac sign characterized by uniqueness and social community; symbolized by the water carrier.

Ascendant house: Also known as the first house, it is the house just over the horizon.

Birth chart: A complete account of your signs, planets, and houses.

Cadent houses: The least powerful houses in the chart consisting of houses 3, 6, 9, and 12.

Cancer: A zodiac sign characterized by a focus on family and relationships; symbolized by the crab.

Capricorn: A zodiac sign characterized by fiscal ambition; symbolized by the goat.

Cardinal sign: One of the visionary signs consisting of Aries, Cancer, Libra, and Capricorn.

Chiron: A large asteroid in between Jupiter and Saturn that has an influence on astrology.

Complementary signs: Signs that are in the same modality but share an important oppositional quality.

Descendant house: Also known as the seventh house, it marks the halfway point in the house cycle.

Fixed sign: A category of sign that is characterized by hard work consisting of Taurus, Leo, Scorpio, and Aquarius.

Gemini: A zodiac sign characterized by social communication; symbolized by the twin.

House: A method of dividing the night sky in relation to the horizon consisting of 12 distinct areas.

House position: Groups of the houses that correspond to the modalities of the zodiac.

Inner planets: The first five planets in the solar system, including the sun and moon but not the earth, consisting of the sun, the moon, Mercury, Venus, and Mars.

Jupiter: The fifth planet from the sun; characterized by philosophy.

Leo: A zodiac sign characterized by pride and charm; symbolized by the lion.

Libra: A zodiac sign characterized by malleability and diplomacy; symbolized by the scales.

Lunar node: A moment in your birth chart where the sun and the moon align in a certain sign.

Mars: The fourth planet from the sun; characterized by aggression.

Mercury: The first planet from the sun; characterized by intellectualism.

Moon sign: The sign that the moon is in when you were born; influences your inner self.

Mutable sign: A more low-key sign in the zodiac consisting of Gemini, Virgo, Sagittarius, and Pisces.

Neptune: The eighth planet from the sun; characterized by the ideal world.

North node: One of the lunar nodes on the birth chart representing your life's destiny.

Outer planets: The outer five planets from the sun consisting of Jupiter, Saturn, Uranus, Neptune, and Pluto.

Pisces: A zodiac sign characterized by emotional availability; symbolized by the fish.

Pluto: The ninth planet from the sun; characterized by the relationship between the collective and the ego.

Polarities: Dualities within the signs that are characterized by yin and yang energy.

Quadrant: A quarter of the birth chart that represents one-quarter of your life's journey.

Retrograde: When a planet moves counter to its orbit, from the perspective of earth, thereby reversing the planet's meaning.

Sagittarius: A zodiac sign characterized by easygoingness; symbolized by the archer.

Saturn: The sixth planet from the sun; characterized by limitation.

Scorpio: A zodiac sign characterized by private intensity; symbolized by the scorpion.

Sign: The constellation a particular celestial body passes through in the zodiac.

South node: One of the lunar nodes representing your innate abilities.

Succedent houses: The less intense houses consisting of 2, 5, 8, and 11.

Sun sign: The constellation the sun is passing through at the time of your birth.

Tarot: A type of card deck with a strong relationship to the zodiac; used for interpretation and prediction purposes.

Taurus: A zodiac sign characterized by dependability; symbolized by the bull.

Uranus: The seventh planet from the sun; characterized by destruction and renewal.

Venus: The second planet from the sun; presides over love and relationships.

Virgo: A zodiac sign characterized by strong organization; symbolized by the maiden.

Yang: A foundational concept in Chinese philosophy; characterized by positivity, light, and masculine energy.

Yin: A foundational concept in Chinese philosophy; characterized by negativity, dark, and feminine energy.

Zodiac: The 12 constellations that make up the cycle of astrology.

References

Angles and angular houses in astrology. (n.d.). Molly's Astrology. https://www.mollysastrology.com/topic/angular-houses/

Aquarius and Leo: Love and friendship compatibility. (2020, June 19). Thought Catalog. https://thoughtcatalog.com/january-nelson/2020/06/aquarius-leo-compatibility/

Aries and Libra: Friendship, sex, and love compatibility. (2021, March 9). Thought Catalog. https://thoughtcatalog.com/january-nelson/2021/03/aries-and-libra/#:~:text=Libra%20and%20Aries%20can%20work

Beginners corner: Cusps and interceptions. (n.d.). Big Sky Astrology with April Kent. https://bigskyastrology.com/beginners-corner-cusps-and-interceptions/#:~:text=%E2%80%9CCusps%E2%80%9D%20refer%20to%20the%20division

Bejan Daruwalla, C. (n.d.). *Pisces compatibility with Virgo.* The Times of India. https://timesofindia.indiatimes.com/astrology/zodiacs-astrology/pisces/pisces-compatibility-with-virgo/articleshow/90457951.cms

Brown, M. (n.d.). *If your zodiac sign doesn't feel like a fit, look to your big 3.* Shape. https://www.shape.com/lifestyle/mind-and-body/sun-moon-rising-sign-meaning#:~:text=While%20your%20sun%20sign%20speaks

Campion, N. (2018). *Astrology in Ancient Greek and Roman culture.* In *NASA ADS.* https://ui.adsabs.harvard.edu/abs/2018oeps.book...46C/abstract

Cartwright, M. (2018, May 16). *Yin and Yang.* World History Encyclopedia. https://www.worldhistory.org/Yin_and_Yang/#:~:text=In%20Chinese%20mythology%2C%20Yin%20and

Cast your horoscope. (n.d.). Scribd. https://www.scribd.com/document/144923092/Cast-Your-Horoscope

Chiron | astronomy. (n.d.). Britannica. https://www.britannica.com/topic/Chiron-astronomy

Co-Star: Hyper-personalized, real-time horoscopes. (2020). Costarastrology. https://www.costarastrology.com/natal-chart/

Development of astrology from ancient to modern times. (n.d.). Britannica. https://www.britannica.com/summary/astrology

Faragher, A. K. (n.d.). *What each "house" represents in your birth chart.* Allure. https://www.allure.com/story/12-astrology-houses-meaning

The four quadrants in astrology: Where your main focus in this lifetime. (n.d.). Cosmic Cuts. https://cosmiccuts.com/en-ca/blogs/healing-stones-blog/quadrants-in-astrology#:~:text=Quadrant%201%20includes%20the%201st

Here's what it means if you have retrograde planets in your natal chart. (2020, May 25). Well+Good. https://www.wellandgood.com/retrograde-planets-in-natal-chart/

Horoscope obsessed? It might be time to read up on Vedic astrology too. (2020, May 29). Mindbodygreen. https://www.mindbodygreen.com/articles/vedic-astrology-101

How to create an astrological chart for free. (n.d.). WikiHow. https://www.wikihow.com/Create-an-Astrological-Chart

How to find your rising sign (with pictures). (n.d.). WikiHow. https://www.wikihow.com/Find-Your-Rising-Sign

How to interpret north nodes & south nodes to find your true purpose. (2020, December 28). Mindbodygreen. https://www.mindbodygreen.com/articles/astrology-101-north-nodes-south-nodes-reveal-your-life-purpose#:~:text=Astrologers%20use%20the%20lunar%20nodes

Inner planets in astrology: Planetary meanings and more. (n.d.). WikiHow. https://www.wikihow.com/What-Are-the-Inner-Planets-in-Astrology

Is your zodiac sign cardinal, fixed or mutable? (n.d.). Bed Threads. https://bedthreads.com.au/blogs/journal/cardinal-fixed-mutable-astrology-signs#:~:text=In%20astrology%2C%20there%20are%20three

Learn the purpose of an astrological birth chart, and how to read one. (n.d.). LiveAbout. https://www.liveabout.com/learning-to-interpret-birth-charts-207239

Mahtani, N. (n.d.). *Your astrology birth chart reveals more than you might expect.* Nylon. https://www.nylon.com/astrology-birth-chart

The meaning behind each modality in astrology. (2021, October 16). Well+Good. https://www.wellandgood.com/modality-astrology/

Modalities in astrology and their meaning. (n.d.). Astrology. https://www.astrology.com/modalities

Modalities: Cardinal. (n.d.). Astrology. https://www.astrology.com/modalities/cardinal

Modalities: Fixed. (n.d.). Astrology. https://www.astrology.com/modalities/fixed

Modalities: Mutable. (n.d.). Astrology. https://www.astrology.com/modalities/mutable

Modern astrology. (n.d.). Astrodienst Astrowiki. https://www.astro.com/astrowiki/en/Modern_Astrology

Montúfar, N. (2022, April 20). *Everything you need to know about that Taurus moon in your birth chart.* Cosmopolitan. https://www.cosmopolitan.com/lifestyle/a39777529/taurus-moon-meaning/#:~:text=Your%20Taurus%20Moon%20exudes%20sensuality

The need-to-know traits and qualities of every single zodiac sign. (n.d.). Shape. https://www.shape.com/lifestyle/mind-and-body/zodiac-signs-meanings-dates

Neptune and Pluto in the signs. (n.d.). Cafe Astrology. https://cafeastrology.com/natal/neptune-pluto-signs.html

The planets in astrology and their meaning. (n.d.). Astrology. https://www.astrology.com/planets

Planets in astrology—Lesson 5. (n.d.). Astrolibrary. https://astrolibrary.org/planets/

Retrograde: Planets in retrograde meanings. (n.d.). Astrology. https://www.astrology.com/retrograde

Robinson, K. (n.d.). *Polarity in astrology: Meaning and opposite signs.* Astrology. https://www.astrology.com/article/what-does-polarity-mean-in-astrology/

Saint Thomas, S. (2020, March 24). *Everything to know about the zodiac signs and their elements.* Allure. https://www.allure.com/story/zodiac-signs-elements-fire-earth-air-water

The seven-day week and the meanings of the names of the days. (n.d.). Crowl. https://www.crowl.org/Lawrence/time/days.html

Shakespeare, W. *Hamlet.* (c. 1600). https://www.gutenberg.org/files/1524/1524-h/1524-h.htm

Stardust, L. (2022, January 26). *Literally everything you need to know about understanding nodes in your birth chart.* Cosmopolitan. https://www.cosmopolitan.com/lifestyle/a30198931/north-south-node-meaning-placement-birth-chart/

Thomas, K. (2022, October 3). *Don't freak out, but you probably have some retrograde planets in your birth chart.* Cosmopolitan. https://www.cosmopolitan.com/lifestyle/a41389256/retrograde-planets-birth-chart/

Trentin, S., & Sneed, D. (2018, June 14). *The Hellenistic period-cultural & historical overview.* Department of Classics. https://www.colorado.edu/classics/2018/06/14/hellenistic-period-cultural-historical-overview#:~:text=The%20three%20centuries%20of%20Greek

12 astrological houses—Astrology lesson 4. (n.d.). Astrolibrary. https://astrolibrary.org/houses/

Ward, K. (2019, February 26). *Why doing your birth chart will help you figure out your life.* Cosmopolitan. https://www.cosmopolitan.com/uk/entertainment/a26085821/birth-chart/

What are the Greek classical elements? (with pictures). (n.d.). Cultural World. https://www.culturalworld.org/what-are-the-greek-classical-elements.htm

What your Chiron sign reveals about your greatest strengths & weaknesses. (2018, May 9). Mindbodygreen. https://www.mindbodygreen.com/articles/what-your-chiron-sign-says-about-you#:~:text=In%20modern%20astrology%2C%20Chiron%20represents

Why a Gemini-Sagittarius relationship proves that opposites attract. (n.d.). Bustle. https://www.bustle.com/life/gemini-sagittarius-zodiac-sign-compatibility-astrologers-love#:~:text=Are%20Gemini%20%26%20Sagittarius%20A%20Good

Why a Taurus-Scorpio relationship can be a constant struggle. (n.d.). Bustle. https://www.bustle.com/life/taurus-scorpio-zodiac-sign-compatibility-astrologers-love

Zodiac signs and their dates. (2017, July 25). Universe Today. https://www.universetoday.com/38076/zodiac-signs-and-their-dates/

Zodiac: Symbols, dates, & facts. (2018). Encyclopædia Britannica. https://www.britannica.com/topic/zodiac

Image References

Image 1: OpenClipart-Vectors (2013). https://pixabay.com/vectors/signs-of-the-zodiac-zodiacal-signs-160494/

Image 2 OpenClipart-Vectors (2013). https://pixabay.com/vectors/signs-of-the-zodiac-zodiacal-signs-160494/

Image 3: OpenClipart-Vectors (2013). https://pixabay.com/vectors/signs-of-the-zodiac-zodiacal-signs-160494/

Image 4: OpenClipart-Vectors (2013). https://pixabay.com/vectors/signs-of-the-zodiac-zodiacal-signs-160494/

Image 5: OpenClipart-Vectors (2013). https://pixabay.com/vectors/signs-of-the-zodiac-zodiacal-signs-160494/

Image 6: OpenClipart-Vectors (2013). https://pixabay.com/vectors/signs-of-the-zodiac-zodiacal-signs-160494/

Image 7: OpenClipart-Vectors (2013). https://pixabay.com/vectors/signs-of-the-zodiac-zodiacal-signs-160494/

Image 8: OpenClipart-Vectors (2013). https://pixabay.com/vectors/signs-of-the-zodiac-zodiacal-signs-160494/

Image 9: OpenClipart-Vectors (2013). https://pixabay.com/vectors/signs-of-the-zodiac-zodiacal-signs-160494/

Image 10: OpenClipart-Vectors (2013). https://pixabay.com/vectors/signs-of-the-zodiac-zodiacal-signs-160494/

Image 11: OpenClipart-Vectors (2013). https://pixabay.com/vectors/signs-of-the-zodiac-zodiacal-signs-160494/

Image 12: OpenClipart-Vectors (2013). https://pixabay.com/vectors/signs-of-the-zodiac-zodiacal-signs-160494/

THE 5 FOUNDATIONS OF REIKI

65 Energy Healing Techniques & Tips for Beginners.
Heal Yourself and Others Through the **Power** of **Your Hands.**
Discover Remedies to Improve Your Overall Health and Wellbeing

MONIQUE WAGNER

Table of Contents

Introduction

You have always believed that everything in the universe is interconnected. Perhaps you are facing a challenging chapter in your life, and you have finally come to a place where you want to understand this connection better so that you can reclaim your power, make better life choices, and get in touch with your higher self. Deep down, you know there is more to reality than what is commonly taught in many contemporary cultures. This also probably means you are interested in exploring the esoteric and spiritual realm so that you can become more empowered and enlightened. In this book, I will share the five pillars of Reiki with you. These can shape the way you understand the life-force and spiritual energy that is both within and around you. In addition to the science behind the theories of energy healing, you will also be given strategies and practical advice that you can readily apply in your own life, as well as in the lives of others.

Unfortunately, stress and illnesses are a part of our busy, everyday lives. As someone who was born and raised in a Scandinavian family with neo-pagan roots, I am well-acquainted with different ways of facing and dealing with these difficulties without the use of medication. I, too, have suffered burnout before; as a result, I have devoted myself to studying different healing methods. During my journey, I have learned a great deal of medical wisdom from metaphysical practices and occult traditions from all around the world. I am also an empath and, because of this, I have made it my lifelong mission to share my experiences and years' worth of extensive research with those in need of healing.

I wrote this book to make the information it contains accessible to anyone interested in exploring and learning more about the power of Reiki. Whatever physical, mental, or emotional stress you may be experiencing currently, I believe that Reiki has the potential to help you address and even heal it. You will find 65 techniques, tips, and strategies including symbols and mantras, to improve physical, mental, and spiritual health. These techniques, tips, and strategies are peppered throughout the entire book. And it's intentionally designed this way to serve as your guide along each step of the process.

Every person—including you—has powerful healing energy already inherent to them: You have everything at your fingertips, and *you* are capable of changing your life. This book will help you do that by guiding you on your spiritual journey. All that is required of you is to tap into the energy of the universe and allow its healing power to flow through your hands.

This book takes on a simple, yet powerful and elegant approach to Reiki. It has been divided into five pillars, each aimed at addressing a different aspect of this ancient practice. Pillar 1 discusses the fundamentals, history, and benefits of this form of energy healing, while Pillar 2 and Pillar 3 dive deeper into the different elements of Reiki healing and the process involved in becoming more attuned to the energy around you. Pillar 4 trains you in the art of self-healing; and finally, Pillar 5 gives you specific strategies and practical advice that you can use to heal yourself. By reading this book, you will come to understand the nature of the energy that serves the highest and greatest good, and how this knowledge can bring about healing. Furthermore, it is perfect for beginners because it gives you all the information you need to get started on your journey to a healthier and more fulfilled self.

Thanks to the techniques described in this book, I was able to unlock the universal power of energy healing. I learned that it can change lives, and to some extent, influence the energy of the planet and the universe in positive ways. Spiritual awakening is all about finding your divine purpose and getting in touch with your higher self, and the aim of this book is to help you on your journey. Regardless of where you are in your life or on your path, this book can serve as a blueprint in the search for empowerment, healing, and self-discovery. It allows you to explore the common principles and practices of Reiki, as well as how this knowledge can be used to correct the energetic imbalances that can cause physical, mental, and emotional stress.

The techniques and strategies described below are proven to yield incredible results for those who want to make use of the energy of Reiki. Each chapter in this book aims to teach you about different aspects, theories, and aspects that you can use in your own spiritual journey to better understand and heal yourself and those around you. You were right all along—everything in the universe is interconnected, and you can use that information to free yourself of physical, mental, and emotional pain, to lead the life you have always dreamed of.

Please note that Reiki healing should not be used as a replacement for conventional Western medicine practices, but rather as a supplement to it. If you are receiving treatment of any kind, please consult a professional healthcare practitioner before making any changes to your treatment regimen.

Pillar 1: Fundamentals

Chapter 1:
What Is Reiki?

The popularity of Reiki in the contemporary West continues to soar, and this is not without reason. Although it is an ancient practice, Reiki's increased use as a form of energy healing is a testament to its effectiveness. That being said, while more and more people are turning to Reiki to heal their ailments, many of us still do not quite understand what the practice is about. The following chapter aims to give a broad overview of what Reiki is and how it works. It is an introduction to many of the concepts that are discussed later in the book—and it is also the beginning of your journey with Reiki!

Definition

The word *Reiki* has been showing up more and more in the contemporary West, but where does it really come from? Originally a Japanese term, it combines the words *rei*—meaning "universal"—and *ki*, *qi*, or *chi*, which refers to the life-force energy that is inherent to all living beings (Anderson & Wolk-Weiss, 2008). Many Eastern philosophies hold the belief that this life-force energy is what animates all of life, and that without it, existence would not be possible. Additionally, this energy is what links all of us, not just to each other but also to the universe as a whole. Like an ecosystem, there is balance in the flow of this energy; when this flow becomes blocked, interrupted, or imbalanced in an individual, it gives rise to the various physical, mental, and emotional ailments that so many people suffer from.

The vital life-force energy that all human beings are imbued with flows through us in pathways. When these pathways become blocked, our energy flow is impeded and the ecosystem is thrown off balance. In our modern lives, it is easy for our inherent energy to become disrupted, and the result is a long list of physical, mental, and emotional ailments that cause incredible suffering for many people. Studies show that the world is currently facing a "global mental health crisis," and more people than ever are suffering from illnesses such as depression, anxiety, chronic stress, and fatigue (World Health Organization, 2022). There are many reasons why the world has come to look this way, but one of the most obvious causes is that we are facing increasing amounts of tension since our lives have become unnaturally busy and stressed. As a result, our vital, life-giving energy has become imbalanced, and this has painful consequences.

At its core, Reiki is an energy-based form of healing that works by transferring energy from one person—or place in your body—to another through gentle touch using the hands (Rosenbaum, 2020). It is therefore the practice of restoring the energetic balance in the body and unblocking any of the pathways so that energy can flow freely and harmoniously, and healing can occur. Because of its focus on the life-force energy of individuals, Reiki can be considered a form of energy healing, or *energy medicine*. Like other such practices—including *Qigong*, *Zen shiatsu*, meditation, and Pranic healing—Reiki draws on the universal energy that animates life. Unlike many contemporary Western medical practices, Reiki is considered an art form—and to fully appreciate the "art of healing," it is important to keep an open heart and mind.

How Does It Work?

In many Eastern philosophies, it is believed that the *ki*—or life-force energy—that animates the human body functions by continually taking up energy from the environment. One way of doing this is through breathing, also known as *prana*. Another way is through the *chakras*, which is a Sanskrit term meaning "wheels of life" (Judith, 2016). The aim of the chakras is to take up vital life-force energy from the universe, much like a spinning tornado sucks in air. However, the motion of these "wheels" can become slower or blocked in some way when we age or become stressed. The resulting change in our energy uptake causes the many physical, mental, and emotional imbalances many people suffer from. Understanding the chakras is an essential part of Reiki, and they are discussed in more detail in Chapter 7.

The body houses seven chakras, and they are all connected to the pathways of energy that flow through the body (Stelter, 2016). The aim of Reiki is to focus on—and rebalance—the pathways of energy that flow through an individual human being. In a traditional setting, a practitioner will place their hands on their patient's body in different places, starting from their head and moving downwards. The purpose of this is to detect where the energy flow is blocked or disrupted. At the same time, they will use the placement of their hands to draw energy from the universe and channel it directly to those places in the body where healing is required. Practitioners draw energy from the universe through their intention, and this is why they need to have an open heart and mind.

There are no predetermined time intervals that tell practitioners how long to keep their hands in a specific place. Instead, they will intuit where healing is needed, and focus on those areas specifically. This means that a practitioner can give their patient exactly what they need, and not what they believe the patient needs. Additionally, there is a mutual benefit for the practitioner and the patient in this process: While the patient experiences healing, the practitioner can enhance their own life-force energy by acting as a channel for the transfer of energy to their patient. This is why many practitioners are encouraged to practice Reiki on themselves in addition to their patients.

Research shows that there is a connection between the body, mind, and soul and that healing in one of these is inevitably related to healing in another (Bhogal, 2020). For instance, physical ailments such as headaches may have their root in an emotional or spiritual imbalance, like stress. Similarly, addressing mental imbalances such as depression often results in an individual experiencing an overall improvement in their physical health. It is for this reason that while the focus of Reiki practices is on the body, it is concerned with far more than purely physical aspects or ailments. Reiki is not only aimed at healing a variety of physical, mental, and spiritual ailments but is also an expression of the individual's spiritual connection to the rest of the world. To act as a conduit for the transfer of energy from the universe to an individual, a practitioner, therefore, has to be connected to the life-force energy of the world. Furthermore, to receive this energy, they have to be open to it in body, mind, and spirit.

Reiki is extremely powerful, and that makes it an attractive form of healing. It is also non-invasive, natural, and safe, and therefore will not do any harm to your body or mind. While it is a form of touch-based therapy, there is no massage, pressure, or physical manipulation involved in the process of healing. That being said, a patient may experience sensations such as tingling, pulsing, or warmth while they are receiving treatment. These feelings are not harmful but are merely physical manifestations of energy. Reiki can help with decreasing pain and provide some sort of emotional release. It is also possible that you will not feel any sensations at all aside from a deep sense of relaxation and peace—and it is not uncommon for people to fall asleep during a Reiki session! Despite its increasing popularity, there continues to be a lot of debate about energy-based practices such as Reiki, and there are even those who believe that these methods of healing can pose physical, mental, and spiritual danger (Locke, 2012; Sadhguru, 2015). However, to quote Theresa Gilberti (2004, p. 480): "Reiki is not a religion, dogma, or creed, nor can it create or cause anyone harm."

Despite its ancient roots, Reiki has become an increasingly popular practice in contemporary alternative medicine, and it is often used in conjunction with other medical treatments in order to heal patients of various illnesses (Bedosky, 2022). While the main focus of Reiki healing is energy transference, it is also about restoring balance to our life force and bringing healing and peace in this way. For this reason, it is also often used by people who wish to relax and recenter themselves. It is important to remember that Reiki focuses on ailments that result from energy disruptions, and not those caused by external trauma or injury, such as broken bones and tissue damage. However, in the case of the latter, Reiki can assist and speed up the healing process by strengthening the body's responses to any trauma or injury. In addition to determining the performance of your body, your *ki* is also the very thing that animates you and gives you the ability to live. If you are able to influence this energy at will, there is almost no end to the healing power you can have at your disposal.

Chapter 2:
The History of Reiki

In order to make the most effective use of something, we have to understand its origins—and that is what this chapter aims to do. If history is to be believed, Reiki is an ancient practice that became lost to the world and was then rediscovered (Anderson, 2008). Since then, the practice has undergone many adaptations and changes: The Reiki we know today is not the Reiki of old. That does not, however, impact the practice's effectiveness; if anything, Reiki's evolution over time is a sign that it was able to survive often-dramatic shifts in culture. Despite skepticism, some people have dedicated their lives to cultivating and sharing the healing power of Reiki with the world. It is to them we owe much of our gratitude for this wonderful practice we have at our very fingertips.

The Origins of Reiki Healing

Travel back in time to ancient Tibet, and you will find the birthplace of Reiki healing. Although not well-documented, it is believed that many Tibetan scripts make reference to not only the specific practice of Reiki but also the philosophies that underlie it (Deacon, 2003b). Ancient Tibetan healing practices are rooted in Buddhist thought, which claims that all living beings are imbued with an energetic lifeforce (Reshel, 2016). Furthermore, these teachings tell us that physical, mental, and spiritual illnesses are interconnected and that a mind that is free of ignorance is also free of imbalance and disease. Years of revolutions, conflicts, and cultural shifts saw the loss of many Buddhist monasteries and the imprisonment or deaths of thousands of Tibetans. As a result, some of the ancient practices of this inspiring culture became lost to the world for some time. Thankfully, many of these teachings are being unearthed and rediscovered by the world—and in this way, the magic of Reiki has found its way back to us.

The Saihoji Temple in Tokyo hosts a large memorial stone dedicated to a man named Mikao Usui, which describes him as a "gentle, humble, and prudent" person who had an unquenchable thirst for knowledge (Powell, 2012, para. 12). Among his many interests were history, psychology, medicine, astrology, divination, and theology. Usui also had a passion for profound philosophical questions about the nature of reality and life and how to go about reaching enlightenment. In addition to his studies, Usui was a teacher who imparted his knowledge of spirituality to thousands of students. He also fasted and meditated regularly in an attempt to better understand the meaning of life.

In the early 1920s, Usui evidently spent some time in meditation at the sacred Mount Kurama (Powell, 2012). It was here where he discovered—or possibly rediscovered—the powerful form of energy now known to us as Reiki. Usui first used this healing energy on himself, and later he started sharing it with his family members. After much success, he began using it to heal others, and people soon began to seek out his guidance. At the time, it was customary for many healers and martial artists to keep the particulars of their practices secret. However, Usui chose to share his insights with the world by teaching others how to use the energy of Reiki to heal themselves. After a devastating earthquake in Tokyo in 1923, Usui used Reiki to bring healing and peace to countless people affected by the disaster (Powell, 2012). This increased his fame and popularity exponentially and cemented the popularity of Reiki in the contemporary world.

Usui dedicated his life to developing his methods, and he also trained others in the art of energy healing. The more time he spent exploring the healing power of Reiki, the more he realized that spiritual health was just as important as physical health. Additionally, he found that those who were able to learn gratitude through practicing Reiki were in a better position to achieve and hold on to improved health. This led him to develop a system aimed at teaching spiritual progression using the principles of Reiki. His particular teachings became known as *Usui Reiki Ryoho*, which can roughly be translated to mean "Usui's method to cure and heal one's True Self" (Stiene, 2015b).

Usui opened his first training hall—or *dojo*—in 1922 in Tokyo (Powell, 2012). During this time, he came into contact with a naval officer named Dr. Chujiro Hayashi, who later became one of his students. Hayashi later opened his own healing center where he built on the work of his master and further developed the practice of Reiki. He gradually changed Usui's spirituality-centered approach to a method that places more emphasis on the physical healing benefits of Reiki. He also famously developed the "attunement process" of Reiki healing. Using his knowledge and his own style as a basis, Hayashi wrote a handbook known as *Reiki Ryoho Shinshin*, or "Guidelines for Reiki Healing method" (Stiene, 2015b).

It is widely believed that Usui is the only person to have introduced the modern world to Reiki. However, there are historical studies that show that at least four other styles of Reiki were practiced in Japan before Usui began developing his method (Rand, 2014b). One of these, *Reiki Ryoho*, was developed by Japanese therapist Matiji Kawakami in 1914. He outlined his method and style in the book *Reiki Ryoho to Sono Koka*, which can be translated to mean, "Reiki and Its Healing Effects". Other practitioners of Reiki during this time include Reikaku Ishinuki, who created the *Reikan Tonetsu Ryoho* method, Kogetsu Matsubara, whose method was known as *Senshinryu Reiki Ryoho,* and Reisen Oyama, who is credited with creating the *Seido Reishojutsu* method of Reiki healing (Rand, 2014). While historical sources seem to be unclear about this, it is believed that these styles of Reiki were lost during the events of the Second World War. Additionally, it is also claimed that Usui's method survived because it was spread to the world—and especially to the West—by his lineage of students (Rand, 2014b).

Reiki's Spread From the East to the West

In the mid-1930s, Japanese-born Hwayo Takata traveled from Hawaii to her country of birth to visit her family (Anderson & Wolk-Weiss, 2008). While there, she suffered from gallstones and appendicitis, and she also had a tumor. Although she was scheduled to receive surgery, a message from her husband after his death convinced her to try alternative forms of treatment. As a result, Takata went to Hayashi's healing center in the hope that his methods could provide her with some relief. Four months later, she was completely cured. This convinced her of the value of Reiki, and she decided to become Hayashi's student. She stayed in Japan until 1936, and she finally became a Reiki teacher in 1938. For the next 30 years, she taught and practiced Reiki in Hawaii. Finally, in 1937, she brought Reiki to mainland America when she began training students in the country. Takata's teachings were very similar to that of her master, Hayashi, and her students came from many different places, including North America, South America, Europe, Australia, and New Zealand. It was through them that the principles and practices of Reiki spread to the rest of the Western world. Today, there are thousands of Reiki practitioners all over the globe.

Takata brought up 22 Reiki masters. One of them, Iris Ishikuro, developed a style of Reiki known as *Raku Kei Reiki* in the 1980s (Robertson, n.d.). This project was part of a collaboration with one of her students, Arthur Robertson. *Raku Kei Reiki*—or "The Way of the Fire Dragon"—made many contributions to the style of Reiki most often practiced in the West today, some of these include *hui yin* breathing, the *Johre*—also known as "White Light"—symbol, and a specific set of hand mudras (International House of Reiki, 2010h). In addition to *Raku Kei Reiki*, there are many other styles of Reiki being practiced today, all of which can be traced back to Usui's lineage. Some of these methods include: *Hayashi Reiki Kenyukai* (Hayashi Reiki Research Group), *Jikiden Reiki* (Directly Taught Reiki), *Komyo Reiki* (Enlightenment Reiki), David Jarrell's *Reiki Plus*, *Usui Shiki Ryoho*, *Tera-Mai Reiki* as developed by Kathleen Milner, and Barbara Ray's *Radiance Technique*, which stemmed from the American Reiki Association Inc (Sunrise Reiki Centre, 2015).

Reiki in the Contemporary West

The energetic *ki*—or *prana*—that flows through all living organisms has played a central role in Eastern philosophies for thousands of years, but it is in stark contrast to Western philosophies of medicine (Mailoo, 2002). While the latter focuses on chemistry and matter to treat illnesses and imbalances, traditional Eastern healing practices such as Reiki make use of the laws of physics and energy to address our physical, mental, and emotional ailments. Previously, the notion of a life-force energy—and the energy healing practices based on this concept—was discredited by Western medical science, because it was unseen and immeasurable. However, increased research into the laws of nature has brought the West to a deeper understanding of energy healing in recent years. As a result, it has become increasingly popular with both individuals and medical practitioners in the Western world. This recognition of Reiki is further encouraged by the practice's success rate, much of which is being recorded in official scientific studies with increasing regularity (Mailoo, 2002).

Currently, the Royal College of Nursing offers an accredited course in Reiki healing; furthermore, given the practice's ability to alleviate pain and increase the healing process, free Reiki training is provided by an estimated 800 hospitals in the United States (Lotus, n.d.). According to statistics provided by the International Center for Reiki Training, an estimated four hundred thousand people worldwide have enrolled for at least the first level of Reiki healing (Rand, 2014b). For the first time ever, there are also several formal regulatory bodies for Reiki practitioners in the West, including the Reiki Federation and the Reiki Alliance in Great Britain.

There is increasing anecdotal evidence that suggests Reiki can be used effectively in conjunction with other medical practices to treat chronic illnesses, address the symptoms of stress, and improve and enhance the body's ability to heal itself (Mailoo, 2002). These studies are gaining ever more traction thanks to the work of William Lee Rand. In 2005, Rand opened the International Center for Reiki Training. He also initiated the Touchstone Process, which aims to analyze the many scientific studies done on Reiki programs in formal medical environments such as hospices, hospitals, and clinics. According to evidence published in 2008 and 2009 Reiki does indeed have a positive influence on the health and well-being of both humans and animals (Lotus, n.d.). Some of the advantages of Reiki described in these studies include reduced stress, depression, and anxiety. These studies also showed that the practice is effective in controlling pain levels and that it has a positive effect on the autonomic nervous system. The benefits of Reiki are discussed in greater detail in Chapter 3.

Chapter 3:
The Benefits of Reiki

The life-force energy that animates you extends through your entire body—which gives Reiki the potential to be extremely beneficial. One of the main purposes of this practice is to heal the body, mind, and spirit—but each of these can constitute a large number of aspects. Our physical bodies are extremely complex, as are our minds and spirits, and one of the biggest benefits of Reiki is that it can be focused to target those parts of our being that require the most attention and healing. At the same time, our body, mind, and soul are interconnected. Healing in one part of the body will inevitably have a positive impact on it as a whole. As a result, one of the biggest benefits of Reiki is that it is a holistic and integrated approach to healing that can influence all of the different aspects that make up a human being.

Contemporary society is riddled with stressors and tension, and as a result, many people suffer from a variety of physical, mental, and spiritual illnesses. While we cannot necessarily change our circumstances, the good news is that we can take measures to improve our health—and Reiki is one of the most powerful of these measures.

Why Choose Reiki Healing?

Reiki is non-invasive and harmless, and this makes it a very popular form of therapy. The practice requires no physical contact and minimal—if any—communication, and is therefore accessible to even the shyest among us. It also has no side effects and is generally a safe practice that does not rely on chemicals or potentially harmful medication. Additionally, Usui's original system has been refined to such an extent that Reiki can easily be taught to the public, in particular the contemporary West. There are many courses that can be completed in-person or online, and many of them have been made increasingly affordable. Possibly the biggest benefit of all is that Reiki is not just limited to those who suffer from imbalances: It can improve the health of already-flourishing people, and help to ensure their continued well-being in the long term. It also promotes self-healing, which makes it an ideal form of preventative medicine.

The world is facing a mental health crisis, and the United States government is spending more money than ever on health and wellness (World Health Organization, 2022). However, thanks to Reiki's potential to prevent illnesses, this practice benefits not only individuals but society at large. While it is mostly noted for its positive impact on physical, mental, and emotional health, it has a strong spiritual component that can bring many people comfort in times of great instability and uncertainty. Furthermore, Reiki can be integrated quite smoothly into the National Health System as a complementary form; in fact, this has already been done in several places (Billot et al., 2019).

Physical Healing

What Is Pain?

The human body is an incredible masterpiece consisting of a complex system of interconnected parts. Every single cell in your body has a function, and all of the different cells that you are made up of are organized in such a way that they influence each other. If you experience pain or discomfort in one part of your body, you will undoubtedly feel the effects on your body as a whole. Healing such pain or discomfort is not only useful in getting rid of the pain itself, but also in improving the overall functioning and health of the human body.

While the majority of people do not enjoy experiencing pain of any kind, it does serve an important function in the way our bodies communicate with us. Pain and discomfort is our body's way of telling us something is wrong. It is therefore important to understand that pain relief is not just about alleviating discomfort—it is also about healing the underlying problem that is causing your suffering.

Because of the stressful nature of contemporary society, many of us suffer from energetic blockages and imbalances that show up as physical pain and discomfort. The aim of Reiki is not to relieve this pain by focusing purely on the physiology of the body, but instead to alleviate discomfort by addressing the root of the problem. For example, while Reiki will help to release the back muscles that are causing your headaches, its true purpose is to relieve you of the energetic imbalance that is causing the tension in the first place. This means Reiki is beneficial for relieving pain in the short and long term because it addresses not only the pain itself but also the underlying cause of it.

The Physical Benefits of Reiki

Our bodies consist entirely of energy because every single cell that we are made up of vibrates at a certain energetic frequency. As a result, energetic imbalances can manifest in countless ways, and in almost every corner of the body. Thankfully, the power of Reiki is such that it can reach all of these places, no matter how deeply they may be buried beneath our skin. Its healing magic can also be focused on specific parts of the body in cases when there are definite issues that have to be addressed. Some of the physical benefits of Reiki include:

- healing damaged tissue
- healing damaged bones
- stimulation of the immune system
- relief of acute and chronic pain and tension

- alleviation of digestive problems and illnesses, including Irritable Bowel Syndrome, Irritable Bowel Disorder, Chrone's disease, gastritis, diarrhea, and constipation
- increased fertility and improved reproductive health
- relief from, or lessening of, the symptoms of Parkinson's disease

Because of the positive interaction with our energy, Reiki can induce a state of peace and tranquility. This has many benefits for our stress levels, as well as the many illnesses associated with anxiety and chronic stress. It calms our nervous systems and brings us to a place of peace and harmony—and ultimately, health. Some of the stress-induced illnesses that can be healed by Reiki include:

- difficulty sleeping
- digestive problems
- high blood sugar
- heart disease
- colds and flu as a result of decreased immunity
- depression
- memory impairment and difficulty concentrating
- headaches
- muscle tension
- Alzheimer's disease
- obesity and weight gain
- neck, shoulder, and back pain

While Reiki can be used to focus on healing a specific part of the body, it can also serve a more holistic purpose. For instance, people who wish to improve their immunity and their body's ability to heal itself before or after surgery can turn to energy healing as a healing method. Reiki can also aid in maintaining or improving overall health, especially if practiced regularly.

Reiki and Cancer

Cancer is one of the most serious—and most feared—diseases in the world. Studies have shown that cancer in people under the age of 50 has increased dramatically, and it is believed one of the biggest reasons for this is related to the lifestyles of those living in the contemporary West (Rapport, 2022). We are busier and more stressed than ever before, and this has dramatically impacted our ability to eat well, exercise, and get enough sleep. Many of us struggle to stay healthy in body, mind, and spirit; this severely affects our long-term health and well-being.

Reiki has become a popular complementary treatment for those suffering from cancer (Bedosky, 2022). Its practices are useful for managing stress and anxiety, as well as alleviating pain. While most healthcare practitioners will not suggest cancer patients abandon all contemporary medical interventions in favor of Reiki, the practice has many benefits for patients when used in conjunction with other medical interventions. Some of the benefits include:

- inducing a meditative state that relaxes the body and mind
- promoting a sense of peace, security, and wellness
- introducing patients to a holistic system with spiritual components that can bring them comfort in difficult times
- decreasing the psychological effects of serious, or even terminal illness, including depression and anxiety

Mental and Emotional Healing

We are busy and stressed, and this is most evident in the global mental health crisis the world is currently facing. More people than ever suffer from mental imbalances, such as depression, bipolar disorder, anxiety, chronic stress, eating disorders, chronic fatigue, sleeping disorders, neurodevelopmental problems, insomnia, post-traumatic stress disorder, and even schizophrenia and borderline personality disorder. The impact of this is severe: Employers are at a loss, families are being torn apart, and communities can no longer bear the weight of an overloaded healthcare system. Even those who do not suffer from diagnosed mental illnesses often report emotional disturbances that can be so severe that it impedes their functioning or manifests as physical ailments.

Imbalances are the result of blocked energy flow in our bodies. When our chakra wheels stop spinning, it is very easy to lose perspective and become unwell. On a purely physiological level, our parasympathetic nervous systems are also under severe strain, and this impedes many people's ability to calm themselves down in stressful times. By realigning our energetic centers and inducing a sense of calmness and relaxation, we can resolve many of these imbalances—and this is where the art of Reiki enters the picture. The mental and emotional benefits of Reiki are nearly endless, including the ability to alleviate the symptoms of many of the illnesses described above. Ridding yourself of the painful effects of mental imbalances will benefit your family and friends, as well as your work life. Following this, Reiki will also improve your overall quality of life.

Spiritual Healing

The scientific world has very little to say about spiritual illnesses, but that does not mean these diseases do not exist. We often do not realize that we need spiritual healing: You might feel worried and tense, and think this is purely a result of having little time and too much to do. The reality, however, is that there is more to many of our imbalances than meets the eye. We have become disconnected from the universe, each other, and ourselves. Many people do not believe in the power of energy, nor are they convinced that this is where their well-being lies. We have placed limitations on ourselves because we believe we are "only human;" the result is that many of us have given up on reaching our full potential, and this causes dissatisfaction, disheartenment, frustration, and despondence. Subconsciously, we all know we are capable of more—we can live bigger, better, and fuller lives—but too many of us have given up on achieving that. This is what human potential is all about; it is also the root of spiritual illnesses.

A lot of people become alarmed when they hear the word "spiritual." A common misconception is that spirituality refers to religion. This is true in many instances, but not so much in the case of Reiki. *Spiritual* is derived from the Latin *spiritus*, which means "breath of life." Our energy is most prominent in our breath: Every time we inhale or exhale, we are causing an energetic exchange with the world around us. Reiki healing is centered around the power of energy, as directed by the breath. When a healer connects to the universal *ki* and channels that energy into their patient, they are rebalancing the energetic centers of that person.

Think of how we use language to talk about our general well-being. Someone who is tired might say they are "low on energy," while a healthy person is described as "energetic" or "bursting with energy." Even if it is not widely believed in the contemporary West, we inadvertently refer to ourselves as made up of energy. This means that you do not necessarily have to believe in reiki for it to affect you. Attending a Reiki session with the intention to be healed will greatly improve the efficiency of the practice, but even skeptics can benefit from these sessions. A healer who channels energy into their patient is not basing their efforts on the patient's beliefs, but on the energy that constitutes their body—whether they believe that energy exists or not.

Reiki teaches us that we are connected to the universe, but also that we *are* the universe. That universe is infinite and limitless—and being part of its energy, so are we. This means human potential is not constrained by human limitations, because those are in reality self-imposed. By connecting to the universal *ki*, we can not only rediscover our spirituality but also our limitlessness. The world is open to anyone willing to venture into it, and health, well-being, and flourishing is possible for all.

Pillar 2:
Elements

Chapter 4:
Precepts and Principles of Reiki

The various foundational elements that make up the practice of Reiki are quite meaningful in themselves, but a true Reiki journey requires more than simply knowing what it is, where it came from, and how it works. Successful and sustainable healing comes from shifting your perspective so that you no longer engage in the thoughts that cause physical suffering—and this is where the power of words comes in. The Reiki precepts are five simple sentiments with a profound influence, and they form the essence of a journey to health and happiness.

Your mind is an important part of how you use your energy because your mind is what you use to direct your focus. The aim of the precepts is to train the mind of a Reiki practitioner, firstly, so that they no longer pay attention to the things that do not benefit them. More importantly, these precepts are there to help practitioners move their energy toward what is most meaningful and productive in the journey of life.

The Reiki Precepts

When Reiki master Usui first introduced Reiki to the rest of his community, his success in healing people convinced him that the practice was worth pursuing. However, he also noticed that many people's health problems returned soon after they had been treated. This led him to realize that a true journey of healing required more than isolated Reiki treatments. Instead, the practice requires a spiritual, emotional, and mental shift if one wishes to derive sustainable and long-lasting benefits from Reiki healing. To improve the mindset of those he had healed, he encouraged constructive thoughts. To help his students and patients keep negativity at bay, he developed the "five precepts of Reiki" (International House of Reiki, 2010d). These are known as *Gokai*—or five principles—in Japanese, and they have come to be regarded as the foundation upon which all Reiki practices should be based.

The form used by Usui to develop his precepts mimics that of many ancient Japanese practices. Japanese Buddhism, for example, is based on the precepts that one shall not steal, kill, tell lies, commit adultery, or consume intoxicants (EurekAlert!, 2022). Like these ancient *gokai*, Usui based his principles on sentiments he translated from early ninth-century Buddhist texts. Over time, they were adapted to formulate the precepts we are familiar with today.

Usui believed these five principles were an essential part of "the secret art of inviting happiness; the spiritual medicine for all diseases" (Harris, 2014, para. 2), mostly because there is such a strong connection between mental and spiritual well-being and physical health. This famous statement not only sums up Usui's firm belief in the power of the precepts but is also used as a preamble to anyone who recites these principles as part of their daily practice. They can purify thoughts, boost feelings of power and positivity, and encourage self-healing, all of which have benefits for the human body as well as the environment in which it lives. The *gokai* are therefore considered the code according to which Reiki is engaged and performed.

The original principles were as follows (Birchler, n.d.):

- Just for today, do not be angry.
- Just for today, do not worry.
- Just for today, be grateful.
- Just for today, do your duties.
- Just for today, be kind to others.

Most hypnotherapists and psychologists believe that the human brain is unable to process negative statements (Harris, 2014). Because some of the precepts contain the word "not," this posed a question to some Reiki practitioners as to whether or not the precepts are suitable in the translation presented above. After a lot of reflection, Reiki instructor and practitioner Neal Harris came to the further conclusion that reciting these principles as they were originally translated felt suffocating rather than empowering. He recalls feeling like "a stern someone was standing over him telling him what to do as well as what not to do" (Harris, 2014, para. 1). This led him on a journey to rephrase the original principles so that they hold even more power than they did before. Where the initial *gokai* sounds like commands, Harris' version implies that it is an individual's choice to follow them. They are no longer orders, but something that is *felt* rather than *followed*. While this adaptation does not affect the original Japanese, it does change how they are perceived by English-speaking Reiki practitioners, even if the phrases are still spoken in the original Japanese during practice. The modified principles are (Harris, 2014; Jayne, n.d.):

- Just for today (*kyo dake wa*), I release angry thoughts and feelings (*ikaru na*).
- Just for today (*kyo dake wa*), I release thoughts of worry (*shinpai suna*).
- Just for today (*kyo dake wa*), I am grateful for many blessings (*kansha shite*).
- Just for today (*kyo dake wa*), I practice expanding my consciousness (*gyo-o hage me*).
- Just for today (*kyo dake wa*), I am gentle with all beings including myself (*hito ni shinsetsu ni*).

On the other hand, some believe that the precepts in this adapted form sound too much like affirmations and that this contradicts their purpose. Affirmations, which are positive statements used to declare a certain fact, have become increasingly popular in the contemporary West. As far as the individual is concerned, they are used to affirm a certain mindset or goal or to help someone overcome negativity and self-sabotage. Common examples are: "I am happy" or "I believe in myself." In contrast, precepts are rules of conduct; their purpose is to tell people what to do—and as such, it is no surprise they give the impression of someone stern commanding your actions.

Regardless of your position on whether the precepts should be adapted or not, it is still believed that it is best to recite them in their original Japanese form during Reiki practices. The reason for this is the *kototoma* in them—that is, the magical power that lives inside words. Also translated as the "soul of language," the concept of *kototoma* was scientifically investigated by Dr. Masaru Emoto from 1999 onwards (Kawano, 2011). Emoto wanted to study the effect of words—if any—on water. Using several glasses of water, he exposed each of them to different words or pictures while they were in the process of being frozen. The result was that the ice crystals in each glass had vastly different structures, proving that words have an influence beyond their merely spoken meaning.

The principles were developed to help Reiki students and practitioners on their spiritual journey, but simply knowing about them is not enough. In addition to these principles, Usui also outlined how they should be used by those who have decided to embark on the spiritual journey of Reiki. Ideally, the precepts must be repeated aloud three times every morning and every evening. When doing so, it is best if they are spoken in their original Japanese—there are audio sources available to help you learn how to pronounce them correctly. They should also be accompanied by a *gassho* meditation, which is described in Chapter 5. Along with verbally repeating the *gokai* daily, it is also believed Usui's students wrote down these principles—word for word—as part of their training (International House of Reiki, 2010d). This was a further way to help them incorporate these words into their everyday thoughts and lives.

Usui recognized the enormity of the task of living according to these principles. He, therefore, developed other pillars in conjunction with the principles to help his students on their spiritual journey. These are discussed in Chapter 5.

A Guided Practice

When Harris first reflected on the principles and reworded them to give them more power, he also intuited a method that can be followed by those wishing to bring happiness into their lives by improving their mental, spiritual, and physical health (Harris, 2014):

1. Start your practice by reciting the preamble out loud.
2. Next, say the first principle: "Just for today, I release angry thoughts and feelings."
3. Take a few moments to reflect on this statement: At which point were you angry during the current day, or the day before? Acknowledge that while your anger was triggered by something external to you, the anger itself lives inside you.

4. Recall other events in the past that have triggered your anger and try to find similarities between the different instances in which you experienced angry thoughts and feelings.

5. Ask your spiritual helpers—your Reiki guides, your masters, your angels, and your higher self—to help you release your past angry energy, and transform it into something that can encourage healing and growth for all.

6. Take a few slow, deep breaths; every time you exhale, imagine you are releasing any remaining anger from your body, mind, and spirit.

7. Repeat steps 2 to 6 for the next principle: "Just for today, I release thoughts of worry." Recognize that worry is triggered by thoughts about the future, but the worry itself resides in you.

8. As before, recite the third principle out loud: "Just for today, I am grateful for many blessings." Think of the blessings in your life, whether they be people, objects, or events; name and visualize each of these blessings, and allow the feelings of gratitude to expand your heart.

9. Say the fourth principle out loud: "Just for today, I practice expanding my consciousness." Thinking back to the present or previous day, recall times when you attempted to expand your consciousness. These instances could include meditation practices, trying to understand someone's behavior from a different perspective, or doing an exercise that aims to relax you; visualize and acknowledge these moments.

10. Repeat the fifth principle out loud: "Just for today, I am gentle with all beings including myself." Think back to the previous days, and recall times when you were not gentle with yourself and others. Visualize these instances, then ask your spiritual helpers to help you release any feelings of guilt or anxiety you might have about your behavior. Take a few deep, slow breaths; every time you exhale, release any of these heavy feelings and feel your body, mind, and spirit become lighter with each breath.

Repeating these principles may sound simple enough, but the truth is, they pose a great challenge to anyone who chooses to truly engage with them. They outline the struggle faced by many of us when trying to control our emotions and manage our thoughts. Simply repeating them is not enough—you have to keep them in your mind all day long and reflect on them whenever you find yourself in moments of possible turmoil. In addition to contemplating the principles, they also ask you to cultivate a constant awareness of your thoughts and your emotions. They serve no purpose if they are forgotten, and to know when to recall them, you have to learn to stop yourself before you engage in any negative thinking or unconstructive behavior. This, of course, takes time and practice—do not be discouraged if you initially struggle to incorporate the principles into your everyday life! Changing your mindset does not happen overnight, but the benefits of doing this are endless for those who are willing to persevere in their journey.

Chapter 5:
The Three Pillars

Despite the seeming simplicity of the *gokai*, Usui knew that living according to these precepts is no small task. This is why he developed three pillars as part of his method to help his students follow the "rules" of Reiki as they get deeper into their spiritual journey (Fraley, 2017). The first pillar is *gassho*, a style of meditation that aims to help you cultivate stillness and peace in your life. The second is *reiji-ho*, and the third is *chiryo*. The ultimate purpose of these pillars is to train Reiki healers in growing and maintaining a peaceful, grounded, and focused state of mind as part of their personal "spiritual hygiene." The pillars also invite the practitioner to set their ego aside so that they can sharpen their intuition, cultivate mindfulness and self-awareness, and ultimately form a deeper connection to their patient, and to the universal *ki*.

Gassho

The Japanese term *gassho* can be directly translated to mean "two hands coming together" (Rataic, 2017). More specifically, it is the union of the Divine Mother and Divine Father by symbolically bringing your hands together in a prayer position. The left hand represents human beings as they are found in the physical world. In contrast, the right hand symbolizes the Buddha as an example of an enlightened being. Symbolically, bringing these two hands together implies that human beings are also able to achieve enlightenment.

The *gassho* hand position has several purposes: It can serve as a greeting or it can be used to show respect or gratitude. It is also used as a hand *mudra*—a "pose" or "gesture"—in *gassho* meditation practices. The purpose of this hand position is to bring awareness to the tips of the fingers or the space between the hands while meditating. In this way, the pose signifies a deeper connection to the universe so that you can clear your mind and open your heart. Simultaneously, your hands—and especially your fingertips—come to form the central focus of your meditation.

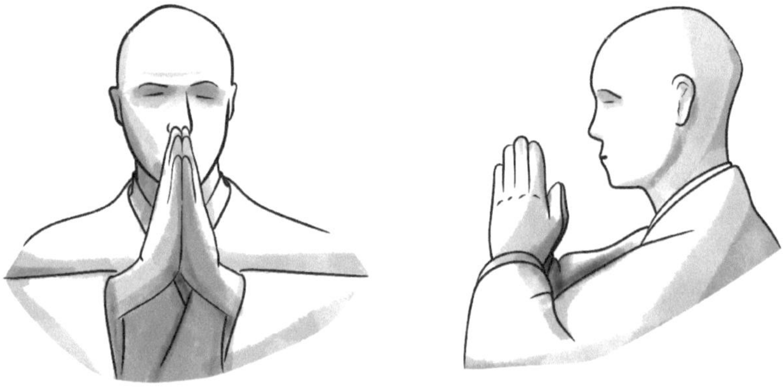

The aim of *gassho* meditation is to cultivate inner stillness as part of the spiritual journey toward enlightenment. This stillness is necessary for us to connect to our spiritual helpers and our higher selves, and to open up our intuition to their divine guidance. It is also an effective way to calm your body and mind, and expand your energy. While divine guidance is helpful in everyday life, it is especially important during a healing session, when your hands are directed by your patient's needs and the energy you are channeling.

This is a fairly simple form of meditation and is often recommended for beginners, or those wishing to delve deeper into meditation as a whole. *Gassho* meditation also forms a central part of Usui's specific style of Reiki. According to his teachings, *gassho* should be used before and after every Reiki session, as well as 15 to 30 minutes every day in the morning or at night. It should ideally be accompanied by the five precepts of Reiki.

If you want to begin with *gassho* meditation practices but have no idea how to get started, there are a few steps you can follow:

1. Sit, stand, or lie down in a comfortable position, in a place where there are no distractions. If you are sitting or standing, make sure your spine is straight so that it forms a single line from your tailbone to the top of your head. Do not strain your neck, and remember to relax your shoulders. You can also sit in a straight-backed chair or prop yourself up with pillows if sitting on the floor or standing is very uncomfortable for you.

2. Close your eyes and place your hands in the *gassho* position. Your thumbs should be aligned with your heart chakra in the space where your breastbone is located, and you must be able to feel your breath on your fingertips when you exhale. Make sure your hands are relaxed, and that you are not straining to push them together.

3. Think of the place where your two middle fingers meet, and focus your attention there. Take deep breaths in and out. With every exhale, imagine you are letting go of all the things that no longer serve you.

4. Maintain your concentration and try to let go of everything else. If thoughts come up, do not try to suppress them; rather, acknowledge them and then watch them float past you.

5. Do not become discouraged if you get distracted: Meditation is about learning to refocus your attention when thoughts come into your mind. Simply return your focus to the tips of your fingers, and remember that it gets easier the more you do it!

6. In addition to your thoughts, you might also notice energy around you in the form of different sensations. As you did with your thoughts, simply acknowledge these, then return your focus to your fingertips.

7. If you are using this meditation as a way to focus on the precepts, you can recite them out loud or in your head once you are fully immersed in your practice. Instead of concentrating solely on your fingertips, imagine the principles are in the space between your middle fingers; train your attention on them.

8. If you are new to the practice, you might find it uncomfortable to keep your hands in the *gassho* position for 15 to 30 minutes. If they get tired, let them rest in your lap while keeping them pressed together.

9. Once your meditation time has passed, take a moment to come out of it. Rest your hands in your lap and take a few deep breaths while enjoying the peacefulness of this moment. Remember: You carry this peace inside you, and you can access it whenever you need to.

10. When you are ready to move on with your day, bring your attention to your body and let your eyes slowly flutter open. You should feel more focused, relaxed, centered, productive, and even creative.

11. Depending on how intuitive you are, you can either set a gentle timer to end your practice, or you can come out of it whenever you feel you are ready. It is also your choice if you want to play music or not, as long as it does not distract you from your meditation.

12. You can return to this practice whenever you need a moment of peace—even if you only have a few minutes.

Usui suggested his students practice *gassho* ritualistically as a way to set intentions, improve their focus, cultivate mindfulness, and put aside their egos. He also thought of this meditation as a way to invite and kindle the energy that is channeled during a healing session. In addition to performing this meditation daily, he also recommended students practice *gassho* for five to ten minutes before a Reiki session.

Starting a new meditation practice can be difficult, especially if you have never done it before. It can be particularly frustrating if you have a restless mind that you cannot seem to calm down, no matter how hard you try! Give yourself time: Like anything else, meditation takes practice. Focusing your mind is a skill that cannot be learned overnight. If you feel yourself becoming distracted, acknowledge your thoughts, then watch them pass you by like clouds in the sky. It can also be helpful to start with shorter meditations and build them up over time. With patience and persistence, you will soon see improvements in your levels of peace and happiness.

Reiji-Ho

The second pillar of a Reiki session is *reiji-ho*, which refers to the intuition and divine guidance that a practitioner relies on when healing someone (Phillips, 2021). Directly translated, *rei* means "spirit" or "soul," *ji* means "indicate" or "point out," and *ho* is a "method" or a "way." Put together, the phrase can be translated to English as an "indication of the spirit." In broad terms, *reiji-ho* is therefore associated with the intuition of a healer, or the divine guidance received by a Reiki practitioner during a healing session. Various studies have found that children have a natural intuition that dims and disappears as they grow older (Delgado, 2016; McCartney, n.d.). By practicing *reiji-ho*, a healer can regain their intuitive abilities so that they can once again open themselves up to the universal *ki*.

In contemporary Reiki courses—especially in the West—many students are taught specific hand positions that they can follow during a Reiki session. Even though these positions are predetermined, the energy will still naturally flow where it is needed most. However, these hand positions were not part of Usui's original system. Instead, the Reiki master used his intuition to guide his hands to where they had to go—he became one with the energy and used this to direct the healing process (Powers, 2017). Many Reiki healers who have been practicing the art of energy healing for a long time will find they have similar capabilities. They use the pillar of *reiji-ho* to guide their hands, and to help them decide what techniques and symbols to use during a Reiki session. This is because they have learned to trust their intuition as divine guidance to show them the way forward in their healing sessions, and it means every one of their patients receives a unique treatment that is tailored specifically to their needs.

Reiji-ho is deeply intertwined with the *gassho* meditation, as this is when the practitioner sets aside their ego, cultivates a spirit of mindfulness and awareness, and allows their intuition to guide their actions. Practicing *reiji-ho* requires you to become united with the Reiki energy, and there is no better way to find guidance than through meditation. It is for this reason that *gassho* meditations are usually practiced before a Reiki session. However, whenever you feel stuck or unsure during a session or you find yourself becoming distracted, you can always return to *reiji-ho* through *gassho* to receive the divine guidance you require. To do this, stand at your patient's feet or head, place your hands together in front of your chest, and return to a meditative state until you feel your energy has once again become calm and focused. Ask for the energy to move through you freely, and for your spiritual helpers to guide you during the practice. Raise your hands to your third eye and touch your thumbs to your forehead. Once you have recentered yourself, you can resume the session by allowing your intuition to guide your hands, breath, or gaze. Try to focus on your senses rather than your mind, as this will help you to act more intuitively. Follow the flow of the energy wherever it may lead, and above all, remember to trust yourself and your spiritual helpers.

Chiryo

Chiryo, simply put, means "treatment"—and this third pillar is the active component of a Reiki session (Shirleytwofeathers, 2019). For new Reiki practitioners, this means placing their hands in specific positions; for those who are more experienced, *chiryo* happens more intuitively. Action in a Reiki treatment is often associated with hovering the hands over the areas of the body that require the most healing. Still, it can be more than that: *Chiryo* can also entail gazing, stroking, tapping, blowing, or even visualizing. Additionally, it requires using different parts of the hand, such as the palms and fingertips.

To begin a treatment, place your hands in the *gassho* position and set an intention for your treatment. Allow yourself to feel the Reiki energy around you, and let it guide you as you heal your patient. Once you have completed the session, remember to give thanks to your spiritual helpers by once again performing a *gassho* meditation. Next, release the energetic connection between yourself and your patient, and allow your energy to return to you. If you want to ground yourself, you can touch the ground or wash your hands in cold water.

Chapter 6: Energy

Reiki is the art of healing with energy—and therefore your personal energy is essential for a successful practice. The theory of entrainment is central to many fields of study—most notably physics; at the same time, it is also an essential component in the practice of Reiki healing. Understanding how energy works and how different people and objects interact with each other and the energy that surrounds us is vital for any successful Reiki session. In addition to understanding this concept, it is also important to be aware of the methods you can use to enhance your own energy so that you can open yourself up even more to the power of Reiki.

While the methods below are typically used by practitioners who are treating patients, they can easily be adapted for the purposes of self-healing. Whether you are treating yourself or somebody else, the frequency of your energy matters—and it is in your hands to make sure you get the most out of your Reiki practices.

Entrainment

In 1665, Dutch physicist and astronomer Christiaan Huygens discovered that if he placed two pendulums swinging at different rates next to each other, they would eventually sync up to swing in rhythm with each other. He used the laws of physics to further research this phenomenon and came up with the physics concept known as *entrainment* (Clayton, 2012). He also noticed that entrainment applied not only to physics, but also to the laws of chemistry, biology, pharmacology, psychology, medicine, and even sociology.

Entrainment is universal and present in nearly everything we know—but what is it? A basic definition of *entrainment* is the "process of making something have the same pattern or rhythm as something else" (Cambridge Dictionary, n.d.). For example, if a person is exposed to music, they will likely tap their foot subconsciously to the rhythm of the song; or an individual male firefly will synchronize the flashing of its light to that of other males. A leaf falls at the same rate as the breeze holding it in the air, and a stick in a river will flow at the same rate as the river's current. People who spend a lot of time together will inevitably start dressing and speaking in the same way, and when you are around other people, your brain waves will sync up with theirs so that you begin to mimic their mood and experience it as your own. In other words, the energy of one object is "entrained" by the energy of the other so that the less dominant object moves in harmony with the other. The reason why this occurs naturally is to conserve energy: When the different parts of a system work together, the overall system uses less energy than it would've done otherwise. Simultaneously, this also means that the same system can conduct more energy, making it more efficient.

Because energy is a big part of the theory of entrainment, it has important consequences for Reiki healing. When a practitioner heals someone, the universal Reiki energy around them flows into their crown chakra, down their arms, and into their hands. From here, it leaves their body and enters the body of their patient; it then travels to the places where recentering or healing is required. The Reiki energy entrains the energy of the patient to its own vibration, and in this way, the harmony of the patient's energetic vibrations is restored to that of the universal *ki*.

While there is an interaction between the energy of the universe and the energy of the individual, there is also a relationship between the energetic vibrations of two individuals. Remember that two vibrating bodies—which is what human beings are—will "lock" into each other to vibrate in harmony. More specifically, the energy of the weaker body will lock into that of the stronger body to vibrate at the same frequency as the first. In the Reiki practice, this means that the energy of the patient will vibrate at the same frequency as that of the practitioner, provided the practitioner is the more balanced and harmonious body of the two. This is why patients often feel calmer and more at peace soon after a Reiki session has started: Their energy has become synchronized with that of their healer, who should ideally be calm and centered.

Along with their patient, a Reiki healer is likely to have a physical experience of the energy around them. This may include sensations such as pulsing, vibrating, or heat in the different chakras and the hands. A practitioner may also be able to see the energy in the form of particles of golden or white light through their inner eye. Simultaneously, the healer might feel their mood becoming more joyful, peaceful, and uplifting.

The more relaxed a Reiki practitioner is, the more relaxed their patient will be. Furthermore, as long as they remain in a meditative state, their energy will be in sync with that of the universe, which means so will the energy of their patient. A patient will also entrain to the environment provided for them by their healer. If the energy in the room is balanced and tranquil, this will reflect in the energy of both the patient and the healer. Hence, it is important for a Reiki practitioner to not only take care of the space in which they perform their sessions but also to focus on their own energy and perform practices to raise their energetic vibrations.

Enhancing the Energy of Your Practice

The Energy of the Room

The air around us is made up of tiny vibrating molecules, each moving at a specific energetic frequency. When we move through a space, the vibrations of these molecules interact with the movement of the atoms our bodies are made up of, and so we become influenced by our environment. Simultaneously, these molecules influence the vibrations of our brainwaves, which is why a Reiki practitioner needs to pay very careful attention to the energy in the room during a healing session.

The first way to ensure that a room has "good" energy is to make sure the temperature is comfortable. A room that is either too hot or too cold will distract the healer and their patient, and negatively impact the energetic vibrations of both. It is also important to make sure the room is ventilated and that there is a sufficient flow of fresh air through the space. Clutter and disorder tend to collect negative energy, so make sure the room is well-ordered and free of unnecessary objects. To further enhance the energy of the space, you can smudge the room using a smudging stick or dried cuttings made of cedar, sweetgrass, lavender, or frankincense, depending on the type of energy you are trying to cultivate. For example, cedar invokes protective energy, while sweetgrass invites feminine energy into the room. Other sacred herbs that are used in smudging ceremonies include copal—which is similar to frankincense—or myrrh. To smudge a room, you need to do the following:

1. Take some time to calm your mind and spirit. You can even meditate before you start the smudging ceremony. It is important to set an intention before you begin the process and to reflect on the type of space you wish to create for your Reiki practices.

2. Light a candle—this candle should be used for smudging rituals only.

3. Using the candle, light your smudging stick; it should smolder and smoke, but not have any flames.

4. Begin at the entrance of the room. Holding your smudging stick in one hand, move around the room in a clockwise direction so that the smoke fills the entire space. Make sure the smoke drifts into every nook and cranny, including cupboards and corners. This clockwise movement is called circumambulation.

5. As you move around the room it may be useful to hold a container—such as a clay bowl or abalone shell—underneath the smudging stick to catch any embers or ashes falling from the stick. This container should only be used for smudging ceremonies.

6. You can also chant mantras as you move around the space; if you decide to do this, choose something meaningful to you and your practice. Call on your spiritual helpers and ask them to guide you through the healing process.

7. Once you have finished moving around the room and arrived back at the entrance, extinguish the smudging stick in a bowl of sand.

8. Imagine the room has been filled with a bright white light, then reflect once again on the intention you set for your ceremony. You can even speak this intention out loud into the room to make sure it fills up the vacuum that has been left by the smudging process.

Smudging should preferably take place before and after a healing session, first to prepare the room for the patient, and second to clear the room of any negative energy they might have brought into it. The energy of a space can also be enhanced by using essential oils or burning incense, or even placing flowers in the room. Objects such as crystals or pictures of Reiki healers—specifically Usui, Hayashi, and Takata—can also have a positive impact on the energy of a space. To improve the receptiveness of the patient, you can play soothing music during the session.

The Energy of the Healer

To balance your own energy, begin by performing a *gassho* meditation before your patient arrives. Next, place the master and power symbols on your palm chakras; this is discussed in more detail in Chapters 7 and 11. To protect your own energy, draw a large power symbol on the front of your body using your hands, and smaller power symbols on all of your chakras. To raise the vibrations of your client, you can send Reiki energy to them while they are still on their way to you. It is also helpful to place the symbols you have drawn on yourself into their crown chakra before you begin the healing process.

While performing a Reiki session, it is best to remain quiet and focused on the practice at hand. Treat it with reverence: You are performing a spiritual act, and the energy flowing through you deserves the necessary respect and appreciation. Try to focus your attention on the feeling of the energy moving through you to increase its flow. By meditating on this energy, your mind will begin to vibrate in harmony with it, and this can only benefit you and your patient. Prayers said either out loud or quietly to yourself can also enhance the energy of the practice; these can be aimed at any higher power, including ascended Reiki masters, Saint Germain, Jesus, Babaji, Krishna, Buddha, angels, your higher self, spirit guides, or even the source of the Reiki energy itself.

Another important aspect of energetic frequencies is your intention while performing a Reiki session. It is important to express a sincere desire to merge with the energy around you and to heal the energy of your patient. This desire should be accompanied by an open heart and mind, and the willingness to step aside and allow yourself to be guided. One way to enhance your energy is by moving deeper into your practice. For example, by receiving additional attunements and using the relevant symbols, you can merge even further with the Reiki energy around you and so bring more healing to your patients. Other enhancement methods include self-hypnosis, meditation, or listening to the "Chanting Reiki Masters" tape, which is a chant containing the names of all the Reiki symbols.

Practitioners are only human, and sometimes, their energy can become blocked or imbalanced. By receiving Reiki treatments yourself, you can ensure your energetic vibrations remain high and your connection to your spiritual helpers continues to be strong. Treating others also improves your energy, so do not be afraid of helping those who need it! There is an abundance of energy in the world and it can never be used up: The more you share, the more you will receive. Also, keep in mind that your physical health plays an important role in your energy flow. Maintaining a healthy diet, exercising regularly, and getting enough sleep are essential to enhancing the energy flow within your own body. The more you take care of yourself, the more you can take care of others.

Chapter 7:
Chakras

Imagine your body as a machine powered by energy. It is all good and well to say you absorb energy from the space around you, but how is it distributed through your body from one area to the next? The answer: Chakras. Reiki aims to heal and rebalance the energy of an individual, and the only way to do this is to go to the mechanisms by which this energy moves. Understanding chakras—what they are, where the concept comes from, and what impact they have on your body, mind, and spirit—is essential for anyone wishing to heal themselves or others using the magical powers of Reiki.

What Is a Chakra?

As mentioned in Chapter 1, *chakra* means "wheel of life." It is an ancient Sanskrit concept derived from the sacred Indian Vedas. It is unclear when the knowledge of the chakras was first documented, but it was most likely sometime between 1500 B.C.E. and 1000 B.C.E. (Stelter, 2016). This means that while chakras are a relatively new term in the contemporary West, knowledge systems in the East have been working with them for thousands of years. They are considered spiritual and sacred—and most importantly, essential for life.

The chakras are spinning disks—or wheels—located at various points along your body. Their aim is to move the energy around between the different parts of the body, including the nerves, organs, cognition, and emotional areas. These disks form an interconnected system of movement and energy channels that animates the body and gives us life. What happens to a clock when one of its gears gets stuck? Or a cart, when a wheel comes loose? That is right: The entire object stops working. The same thing happens to our bodies when one of our chakras becomes stuck or falls out of alignment. Energy is no longer transported through our system in a balanced way, and the result is the different imbalances we see as physical, mental, and emotional ailments. We are dependent on them, but at the same time, they are dependent on each other—if they are not all functioning effectively, there is bound to be an imbalance in the overall system.

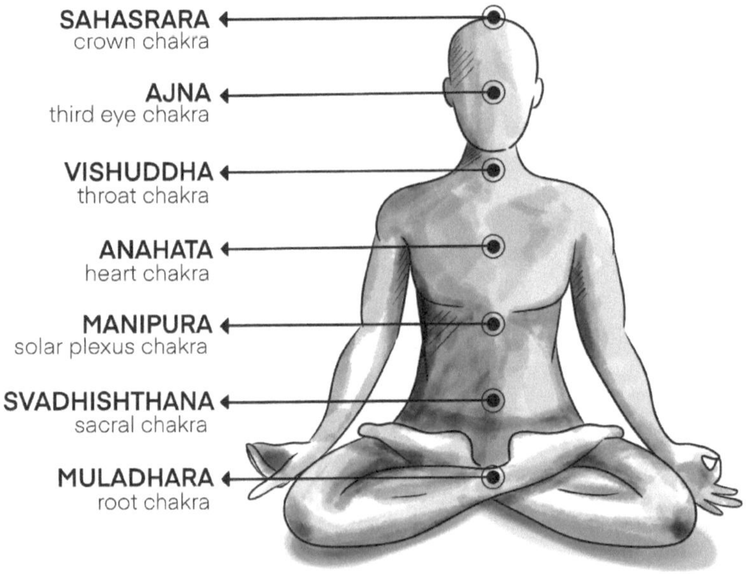

There is some dispute as to exactly how many chakras there are, but it is generally believed that every human being has seven main chakras located along the length of their spine. Starting from the top, these are the crown chakra, third eye chakra, throat chakra, heart chakra, solar plexus chakra, sacral chakra, and root chakra. Each chakra corresponds to a different part of the body and when they become stuck or out of balance they can be responsible for different imbalances and illnesses. Each has a distinct location, name, and number, and each chakra is associated with its own color, mantra, element, symbol, stone, and animal. To heal a chakra that is out of alignment, it is important to know what physical, mental, and emotional aspects the particular chakra is responsible for, as well as what the symptoms of disharmony are for that specific energy point. Additionally, knowledge about the different associations of every chakra—its element, color, animal, and symbol—can help you treat the imbalance in your body or mind. Each chakra also has a specific yoga pose and hand *mudra* assigned to it that can be used as part of the process of realigning that particular chakra.

The Seven Chakras

The Root Chakra

The first chakra is known as *chakra muladhara*, or *root chakra*. It can be found at the base of your spine in the same region as your tailbone. The color of this chakra is red and its element is earth. Its symbol is a red lotus flower with four petals, its symbolic stone is hematite, and the animal it is associated with is the elephant. The root chakra has to do with stability and groundedness, as well as our physical identity and our ability to survive. It also signifies our connection with the ground beneath our feet and the planet as a whole. This chakra is home to the human survival instinct, our potential, our ability to experience pleasure and pain, and our sexuality. On a psychological level, *muladhara* is what governs our sense of stability, our sensuality, and our spirituality; it is also what gives us a sense of security.

The root chakra is deeply associated with survival, security, and stability, and it is therefore blocked by fear. It is also the site of courage, so any feelings of anxiety or restlessness are a sure sign that the root chakra requires attention. Other signs of blockages in this region include a lack of discipline, financial instability, insecurity, laziness, lethargy, depression, greediness, a fear of change, and disorganization in your life. Physical symptoms of *muladhara* imbalance are arthritis, constipation, colon problems, bladder issues, pain in the lower back, constant tiredness, and unnaturally cold hands and feet.

One of the most effective ways to realign the root chakra is through physical exercise or by performing the warrior I yoga pose. You can also surround yourself with the color red—for instance, by eating red food or wearing red clothing—or you can attempt to analyze your fear so that you can let it go. To meditate on a root chakra imbalance, touch the tips of your thumb and index finger together and let your hands rest on your legs. Try to clear your head, and focus on the mantra of *muladhara*, "lam" (pronounced "lang"). If possible, say it out loud: Vocalizing the mantra of the root chakra—or any other chakra—can create the special frequencies needed to bring that chakra back into alignment.

The Sacral Chakra

Chakra svadhishthana—or the *sacral chakra*—is located in the space between the navel and the groin. Its color is orange, its stone is a tiger's eye, and its associated element is water. It is symbolized by a crescent moon inside a white lotus flower with six orange petals. The animal of the sacral chakra is the crocodile of Varuna, the Hindu god. The body parts it is associated with are the testes or ovaries, as well as the sex hormones produced by these organs and the reproductive cycle that they are responsible for. It also has a strong relationship with the endocrine system—especially the adrenal glands—and the urinary system.

Chakra svadhishthana is the source of our passions, ambitions, fantasies, and dreams, and it is what regulates our sexual and emotional centers. Most importantly, our ability to be creative is associated with our sacral chakra, as is our ability to experience pleasure. This chakra is blocked by feelings of guilt or shame, and this may cause us to question our self-worth, especially in matters related to pleasure, sexuality, and creativity. Disharmony in this region can also lead to emotional disassociation, poor social skills, lack of enthusiasm and passion, difficulty finding motivation and direction, and a need to deny yourself pleasure. Physical symptoms of sacral chakra blockage are urinary tract infections, impotence, and lower back pain.

The mantra of *svadhishthana* is "vam" (pronounced "vang"). To perform a meditation that is focused on this chakra, put your palms on top of each other and place them in your lap. Vocalize the mantra, and send your focus to the space below your belly button. Other ways to open this chakra include exposing yourself to the color orange or stimulating emotion or excitement in yourself by watching movies or reading books. You can also perform a bound angle pose to stimulate the lower abdominal region. Most important, however, is to understand the cause of your guilt and shame, and to relieve yourself of the blame you have placed on yourself. Only once you let go will you be able to come back to a place of peace and harmony.

The Solar Plexus Chakra

The space in the upper abdomen between the stomach area and the breastbone is the site of *chakra manipura*, or the *solar plexus chakra* or *navel chakra. Manipura* is symbolized by the color yellow, stones made of amber, the element fire, and a yellow upside-down triangle surrounded by ten yellow petals. Physically, it is associated with organs related to the digestive system and metabolism, as well as the pancreas and adrenal glands. Thus, any blockages in this area can lead to digestive issues such as heartburn, ulcers, constipation, and indigestion. The solar plexus chakra can also be responsible for eating disorders, diabetes, and even memory loss.

There is a strong connection between our feelings of self-worth, self-confidence, and self-esteem. If you struggle to accept parts of yourself—whether it be aspects of your personality or things that had happened to you in the past—*manipura* can become blocked. This, along with shame and self-doubt, can undermine your confidence and leave you feeling weak, insecure, out of control, and powerless. It can also cause you to overthink your actions and behavior, and make you overly concerned with how others perceive you. As a result, you may start to blame others for your unhappiness, or place yourself in the position and mindset of a perpetual victim. On the flip side, an overstimulated chakra can make you come across as domineering, controlling, and competitive.

The solar plexus chakra is remarkable because it is the site of our "gut feeling." Whenever you feel butterflies or heaviness in the pit of your stomach, your chakra is communicating with you through physical sensations. To harness the ability to listen to yourself and make good choices, you can stimulate *manipura* by practicing boat pose, or meditating on the mantra "ram" (pronounced "rang") with your hands placed on your stomach and your straightened fingers pointing away from you. It can also be useful to pay attention to your relationship with yourself, especially things that make you ashamed of yourself or that cause self-doubt. The solar plexus chakra can further be unblocked through physical activity or mental exertion, such as completing puzzles.

Heart Chakra

Chakra anahata—or the *heart chakra*—is located in the center of the chest, alongside the heart. As one can expect, this is the chakra of love: It is where our compassion comes from, as well as our ability to connect with others. *Anahata* is symbolized by two intersecting triangles, circumscribed by a green flower with twelve petals; the intention of its symbol is to signify the union of the male and female. The heart chakra is also the bridge between the lower chakras that symbolize materiality—the sacral chakra, the root chakra, and the solar plexus chakra—and the three upper chakras, which are associated with spirituality. Other signifiers of the heart chakra include rose quartz and the element air.

A blocked heart chakra will impede your ability to give and receive love, and you might find that you put others before yourself in a way that causes you harm. Feelings associated with disharmony in this region include loneliness, fear of rejection, fear of intimacy, shyness, insecurity, a sense of isolation, and difficulty connecting with others. It may also cause you to lack empathy, or to become jealous or possessive. Physical symptoms of a blocked heart chakra include heart problems, difficulty maintaining a healthy weight, asthma, breast cancer, muscle tension, and high blood pressure.

Anahata typically becomes blocked as a result of grief and pain. To release this blockage, it might be helpful to reach out to family or friends or to plan a romantic outing with a partner. Open communication, hugs, and time spent in nature are all ways to find your way back to your own heart, as is performing heart-opening yoga poses such as camel pose. Alternatively, you could engage with the color green by eating green food, wearing green clothing, or surrounding yourself with green objects or the symbols of the heart chakra. To perform the hand *mudra* for *anahata*, bring the tips of your right thumb and index finger together. Place this hand in front of the place where your breastbone ends, and rest your left hand on your knee. To focus on this chakra during meditation, you can also chant the mantra "yam" (pronounced "yang") while turning your attention to feelings of love and compassion. Remember that loss is an end, but it is also a new beginning, and the best path through grief is to focus on the people who love and care for you.

Throat Chakra

In addition to swallowing, your throat is most often used to talk; this is why the *throat chakra*—or *chakra vishudda*—is the chakra of communication. It can be found at the base of the throat in the center of the collarbone. The symbol of the throat chakra is a circle within a downward-pointing triangle, circumscribed by 16 blue petals. The color of *vishudda* is blue, its element is sound or music, and it is signified by aquamarine gems. It can be stimulated by performing the yogic fish pose.

The throat chakra is connected to the thyroid, voice box, and larynx. Disharmony in this area can present itself as problems with the voice and throat, thyroid, hormones, gums, teeth, or mouth. It can also cause mood swings, menopause, or fever. People with a blocked throat chakra may find themselves gossiping, speaking without thinking, or having difficulty expressing themselves well. Another way in which *vishudda* manifests is through the constriction you feel in your throat when angry, frustrated, or scared to talk in front of people.

When your throat chakra is in alignment, you will find it easy to stay true to yourself through your words and to speak with sincerity and confidence. You will also be able to listen with compassion and know how to time and phrase your responses so that they have a positive impact on the people around you. *Vishudda* is blocked by self-denial, self-doubt, and most importantly, lies. The way to unblock this chakra is to reflect on the lies in your life or the truths you keep denying: These may be things you are telling other people, or yourself. You can also perform the *vishudda* hand mudra by crossing your fingers inside the palms of your hands and touching the tips of your thumbs together above your crossed fingers to form a circle with your hands. Combine this mudra with the mantra "ham" (pronounced "ham") as you focus on the space at the base of your throat. Another way to open the throat chakra is by freely vocalizing or articulating your feelings: Singing in the shower, speaking to other people about things you are passionate about, and even writing someone else a letter can all help you better express yourself and bring your chakra back into alignment.

Third Eye Chakra

Chakra ajna: The *third eye chakra* or *brow chakra*. This energetic point can be found between your eyes, in the center of the lower part of your forehead. It is the site of intuition and imagination, and it is associated with amethysts and the color indigo. It is a sign of communion with the divine, which is why this chakra's element is light. It is symbolized by a violet, deep blue, or indigo lotus flower with two petals. To stimulate *ajna* through yoga, you can place your forehead directly on the ground while performing child's pose.

The third eye chakra is directly linked to the glands and nerves around the eyes, head, and ears. A blocked chakra can manifest as problems with memory, eyesight, hearing, concentration, disorientation, and headaches. It can also be the root of sleeping disorders and learning disabilities. An overstimulated chakra can cause hallucinations, delusions, and nightmares, as well as obsessive behavior. On a metaphysical level, disharmony in this area can lead to difficulties with intuition and our ability to see the bigger picture and visualize the future.

If *ajna* is in alignment, you will find yourself much more in tune with yourself and your environment, and you may even become privy to visions. You will also be able to read people more easily and have more insight into their intentions. To open up this chakra—and all the potential it holds—you can engage in visual art, such as drawing, painting, or coloring. Massaging your third eye with essential oils while appreciating a beautiful scene—such as the stars or a landscape—can also bring it back into alignment. Any indigo, deep purple, or dark purple food, clothing, or objects can stimulate *ajna*, as will chanting the mantra "om" during your meditation practice. To perform the hand mudra of the third eye chakra, put the tips of your middle fingers together and keep them straight while bending the other fingers toward the palm of your hand. Touch the tips of your thumbs together, and point them toward you.

The third eye is essential for insight and knowledge; it is blocked by any illusions about yourself or others. To keep *ajna* open, it is important to continually reflect on the illusions we surround ourselves with and to release ourselves from their grip. As a prospective healer, your intuition plays a big part in your Reiki practices as one of the three pillars of Usui's system. Any difficulties practicing *reiji-ho* can therefore possibly be resolved—or at least improved—by paying more attention to the alignment of your third eye chakra.

Crown Chakra

The epitome of spirituality is found on the top of your head in the form of *chakra sahasrara*, or the *crown chakra*. It is the source of connection, purpose, and enlightenment. Its characteristic color is white light—although it is often depicted as violet—and its associated element is the divine consciousness. While this energetic center is predominantly linked to your nervous system and brain, it is also connected to every other organ in your body, as well as all of your other chakras. *Sahasrara* is symbolized by clear quartz and by a lotus flower with a thousand petals of different colors.

An open crown chakra will give you a sense of heightened awareness and intelligence. It is also the site of spiritual consciousness and the place where wisdom can be found. When a Reiki practitioner communes with the universal *ki*, the Reiki energy will first flow into their crown chakra before spreading through the rest of their body. It is therefore a very important center for long-term health and an ongoing connection to the universe. The more open and balanced *sahasrara* is, the more open the other chakras will be, and the closer an individual will come to experiencing true bliss. Someone whose chakras are in complete harmony and who is fully connected to their spirituality is also said to have access to a higher consciousness.

The crown chakra is symbolic of enlightenment and consciousness, and it is therefore brought into disharmony by earthly attachment. Such a person might display a cynical attitude toward spirituality and they may have difficulty learning. Other mental and emotional symptoms of a blocked crown chakra include narrow-mindedness, stubbornness, greediness, and apathy. Physical symptoms of an imbalance in this region include headaches, rashes, and a lack of coordination. On the other hand, someone whose chakra is overstimulated might become disassociated from their physical existence—especially their bodies—and they may struggle to find focus and direction in life.

The mantra for *sahasrara* is "om" or "ha." To unblock this chakra, reflect on and verbalize this mantra while placing your hands on your belly with the ring fingers pointing away from your body. Let the tips of the ring fingers touch while crossing the rest of the fingers with your right thumb over your left. It is important to pay attention to the body, mind, and spirit when opening this chakra, so take some time to grow and explore your connection to the earth and the heavens. Think of the burdens you experience in your physical life: What is holding you back, or attaching you to this world? Allow yourself to let these attachments go, and instead reach your energy out to your higher consciousness. *Sahasrara* can also be opened by surrounding yourself with violet or white food, objects, or clothing, or by paying more attention to your dreams and ambitions. You can also access this energy by performing yoga poses such as headstands.

The most important thing to remember is that the crown chakra can only be opened once all the other chakras have been brought into harmony. Balancing your chakras is an ongoing process: As human beings, we are subject to emotions and attachments that can block our energy and stand in the way of our flourishing. That being said, with ongoing awareness and a commitment to the well-being of yourself and others, it is possible to cultivate and grow your energy and bring yourself back to a state of harmony.

Chapter 8: Tanden

The Vedic tradition teaches us that every person has seven energetic chakras distributed along the length of their spine. In a similar vein, Taoism and Buddhism talk of the "Three Diamonds:" Three energetic centers in the human body from where we share and assimilate energy. While the Three Diamonds were predominantly used in traditional Reiki practices, references to the chakras became more common as Reiki became more westernized.

The *tanden* energetic system differs slightly from the chakra system, but it is equally valid and important for anyone wishing to embark on a journey of healing. In fact, if you dig deeper into traditional spiritual practices, you will find many different systems. The important thing to remember is that despite their differences, all of these systems serve the same purpose: To bring you to a greater awareness of your energy and to guide you closer to joy, peace, health, and enlightenment. Regardless of the system you choose to use, it is important to remember that your practice is only as strong as your personal energetic centers. It is these centers that will lead you on the path to discovering your true nature and becoming a vessel for the Reiki energy that surrounds you—and it should also be the focus of most of your awareness.

The Tanden Energetic System

According to many Eastern traditions, life is only possible because we are all animated by a system of channels of energy that flow throughout our bodies. These channels intersect in certain places, making the energy more concentrated in some areas than others. These intersections are thought of as the body's energetic centers, or *tanden*. *Tanden* is a Japanese word used to refer to the place in the body where its energy—or *ki*—resides (International House of Reiki, 2010f). Specifically, it refers to the point right below your navel, which is thought of as the place through which you can access your full potential. It is also sometimes known as the *hara* or *seika tanden*.

In traditional Japanese Reiki, the human body is said to have three important energetic centers in addition to the point below the navel. These three centers—which include specific points in the head and the heart—are known as the *Three Diamonds* (Shah, 2021). In Buddhism, the image of diamonds is often used to represent the self; and like a diamond, an individual has to "polish" themselves regularly by clearing their energy systems and strengthening their energetic centers.

The lower *tanden*—or *ka tanden*—is situated below the navel, while the *chu tanden* is in the middle of the chest. The upper *tanden*—also called the *sho tanden*—is in the center of the forehead. While other Japanese teachings talk of more than three *tanden* located in other places, the system outlined above was used by Usui and his students in their own Reiki practices (Shah, 2021). It has become the main system around which most Reiki practices from this lineage are centered.

Ka Tanden: Earth Energy

The *ka tanden* is located right below the navel, and this is where the body's earth energy is collected. Earth energy is thought of as the "Original Energy." In the practice of martial arts, it is thought of as the body's "center of gravity," which plays an important role in keeping a body stable and balanced. In energy work, it is the source of life and purpose, and it is what connects you to the universal *ki*. Additionally, your earth energy is the energy you were born into the world with. It is a powerful energy that is the source of both mental and physical strength. It is also what "grounds" Reiki practitioners by keeping them realistic, practical, and situated in the world we live in. The *ka tanden*, in other words, is what connects us to our physical environment; in this way, it not only becomes a source of strength but also of safety.

The *ka tanden* can be thought of as the base that supports the human body and the foundation from which all healing practices should proceed. Although it is the energy you were born with, it is not passive. Instead, it can—and should—be built upon to strengthen your energetic foundation and improve your connection to yourself and the universe. Developing your *ka tanden* can improve your grit and focus. For Reiki practitioners, strengthening this energetic center is particularly important because it can support and ground you in your practice in times when you feel weak or stressed. It is the antidote to insecurity, fear, and uncertainty—and like any structure, having a solid foundation will prevent your "house" from crumbling when life starts to challenge you.

Sho Tanden: Heavenly Energy

The *sho tanden* is also known as the *upper tanden*, and is situated in the center of the forehead. This energetic center is what connects us to our intuition by allowing us to access the expansive energy emanating from the heavens. Unlike earth energy, it is a more ethereal type of energy associated with mental acuity and our spiritual connection to the universal *ki*. Strengthening this energy will help you achieve a state of stillness and improve your ability to act as a vessel for the healing power of Reiki. Individuals who have cultivated this energy may see visions or colors, or they may even have psychic abilities. It is a beautiful energy that can open up the world to you—if you allow it.

Cultivating heavenly energy is essential for successful Reiki practitioners, but it should never be developed on its own. Practitioners who focus solely on the *sho tanden* and neglect the *ka tanden*—as is often the case in contemporary Western training methods—may find themselves unbalanced and ungrounded. A healer with a strong connection to their heavenly energy but a poor connection to their earth energy will often have a good intuition in healing practices, but be unable to resolve their own problems. Your *sho tanden* is the spiritual connection that allows you to see beyond what is in front of you, while your *ka tanden* is the foundation that keeps you grounded and gives you a clear perspective. Thus, in the art of Reiki, balance is key.

Chu Tanden: Heart Energy

The *chu tanden* is the *middle tanden*: It is the source of emotions and human experience and is located in the heart center. It is the balance between the physical *ka tanden* and the spiritual *sho tanden*, and is situated in the place where these two opposing energies meet. Cultivating this energy will teach you to forgive, and it can help you resolve pain, trauma, stress, fear, and anger. It is the source of love, compassion, and peace, it is the balance between body and mind, and the reason why people are able to share their light and sparkle with everyone they meet. To quote Morihei Ueshiba: "'Returning to the heart of things' is the point of balance reached by harmonizing the body, mind, and heart, forming the one perfect diamond—you" (Stiene & Stiene, 2005, par. 4).

Clearing and Building the Tanden

Each of the energetic centers are important in its own right, but the balance between them is even more essential. Cultivating the Three Diamonds—the earth, the heaven, and the heart—will connect you to yourself as a physical, mental, and spiritual being. More importantly, it will increase your connection to the Reiki energy around you while simultaneously keeping you grounded and in tune with yourself. To be a great healer, you need to protect and build upon all of who you are as a human being.

To help his students balance the Three Diamonds, Usui introduced a method of meditation as part of his Reiki system (Shah, 2021). This meditative practice follows the steps below:

1. Sit in an upright position on the floor, a bolster, or a chair. Make sure your spine is straight and aligned with your tailbone and the top of your head.

2. Pay attention to your muscles: Are you clenching your jaw, or is there tension in your shoulders or belly? Take a deep breath in and relax any tightness in your body.

3. Set an intention for your practice. Remember, the aim is to explore each of the Three Diamonds and bring them in harmony with each other. Ask your spiritual helpers to reveal each of these energies to you while you meditate.

4. Start with the *ka tanden*: Breathe in deeply and send your focus to your navel. Inhale all the way into your belly and feel it expand as you draw breath in and empty as you let it out.

5. Place your hands on your belly and allow the life force in your hands to flow into this energetic center. Remain in this position for two to five minutes. After a while, you should start to experience a sense of awareness, safety, and groundedness.

6. Shift your focus from your belly to your chest, where the *chu tanden* can be found. Inhale deeply and feel the chest rise and fall with every deep breath. Pay attention to the physical sensations of your body and your heart. If any emotions arise, allow them to come to the surface.

7. Place both your hands in the center of your chest and channel love into your heart. Remain in this position for two to five minutes.

8. Finally, shift your focus to the *sho tanden* in your forehead. As you send breath to this place in your body, give yourself over to the Reiki energy around you. Allow yourself to connect with your intuition and be inspired by your sense of spirituality.

9. Place both your hands on your forehead and imagine the heavenly energy in the *sho tanden* flowing into your palms. You might feel tingling, warmth, or coolness in your hands or even the rest of your body.

10. Reflect on your meditation: Did one of your energy centers feel more dominant than the others? If there are any imbalances, pay attention to the *tanden* that needs to be cultivated by sending your breath and awareness to that space.

11. When you are ready, slowly come out of your meditation.

Like the chakras, congestion or blockages in these energetic centers cause physical, mental, and emotional imbalances that can only be cured once the flow of energy has been cleared. Balancing the Three Diamonds as well as paying attention to anything you might lack—groundedness, connection, or feelings of love and emotional bonds—is essential for anyone wishing to flourish in life. You are a diamond; simultaneously, you are also human. You can attract dirt that will dim your shine and cloud your sparkle. Even when dimmed, however, diamonds are valuable because they bring beauty into the world. In the same way, you are valuable: You deserve to take care of yourself by taking care of your energy.

Pillar 3:
Process

Chapter 9: Attunement

Most contemporary Reiki courses are centered around taught information—such as hand positions and techniques—but in reality, there is much more to the learning process than just intellect and skill. Rather, becoming a Reiki practitioner requires a student to undergo a sacred ceremony during which knowledge is passed on to them by their teacher in an unconventional and spiritual way. This ceremony is known as attunement, or *reiju* (International House of Reiki, 2010b). It is one of five elements of Usui's Reiki system, and a fundamental part of every healer's training.

Reiju and Attunement

A general definition of *attunement* states that it is the process whereby someone becomes more aware of, or responsive to, their environment (Merriam-Webster, n.d.-a). This could include anything from an increased connection to other people, nature, or business trends, and it has become a popular psychological phenomenon for people who wish to study the relationships between human beings. Like a musical instrument, attunement is how a person is "tuned" to live in harmony with the world around them. In Reiki terms, attunement refers to the connection between a student and their teacher. Additionally, it also refers to a student's increased awareness of the Reiki energy around them: It is the process whereby a master clears their student's energetic pathways and guides their awareness toward the universal *ki* so that they can learn to access that energy at any time. In Japan, this type of attunement is known as *reiju*; directly translated, it means "spiritual blessing or offering" (Steine, 2015a).

Reiju is believed to originate from Tendai Buddhism, which is a spiritual tradition dating back to 8th century Japan (Japan Reference, 2016). In this tradition, the ritual was used to purify the body. As a prolific scholar, devoted spiritualist, and student of Tendai Buddhism, it is believed Usui first came into contact with the practice of sacred attunements while undergoing his training in this tradition. It is also claimed he decided to include such a practice in his own Reiki system because he aimed to heal both the body *and* the spirit, with the majority of his focus placed on the latter (International House of Reiki, 2010b). While later traditions of

Reiki evolved to pay more attention to the physical body, the practice of sacred attunements remains part of every Reiki practitioner's training in contemporary courses.

Reiju is performed by a Reiki master on their student throughout the student's training. Depending on the specific Reiki tradition, a student can receive *reiju* as often as once a week. In contemporary Western training systems, a student of Reiki has to receive four attunements in the first level of their training, three attunements in their second level, and one attunement in their third level. The ceremony is a way for the master to support their student on their spiritual journey by attuning them to—or bringing them into harmony with—the universal *ki*. It is simultaneously a blessing, a clearing, an offering, an initiation, and a way for masters to communicate with their students on a spiritual and energetic plane. During this ceremony, a Reiki master can pass their knowledge to their student, while also giving the student whatever else they may need at that moment. It also opens students up to the Reiki energy so that it can come to flow through them unhindered. Although the attunements originally performed by Usui were based on his intuition, contemporary Reiki masters have developed specific rituals and mantras that they can use to perform *reiju* on their students.

The sacred ceremony of attunement is important, and not just for historical and traditional reasons. Many students claim to experience tangible benefits after a *reiju* ritual. The first is a sense of having access to a universal intelligence; the second is being awakened to the possibilities of true health and flourishing. Students also report that the ceremony has pointed them in the direction of things that needed healing in themselves—such as harmful thought patterns, addictions, unhealthy habits, painful feelings, unconstructive thoughts, and traumatic memories—and that receiving repeated attunements has even facilitated this healing. An attunement can help a student clear their energy, strengthen their energetic centers, and bring the Three Diamonds into harmony. It can also awaken their inner healer, and help them to access—and trust—their intuition.

While it is generally accepted that a student has the most to gain from *reiju*, it is also true that teachers can benefit from practicing these ceremonies. Although the teacher is blessing their student, in a certain sense, they are receiving a blessing as well. Author and teacher Frans Stiene claims that when performing *reiju* on a student, he experiences a sense of openness and emptiness of mind because his ego is in a sense "cut away" (Stiene, 2015). He describes it as a simultaneous process of giving and receiving that reminds him of his True Self. In this way, *reiju* is not just an act performed by one individual on another, but "a union of the teacher, student, and the universe" (Stiene, 2015, par. 2). It is for this reason that teachers are encouraged to perform as many attunements as they can. While it is an opportunity for them to bless and support their students, it also clears their own energetic centers and strengthens their connection to the universal *ki*.

The Attunement Process

Reiju is a deeply spiritual ceremony, and any student who is about to receive one has to spend at least two days preparing their body, mind, and spirit for this ritual. This can be done in several ways: For instance, a student can make sure they are well-hydrated, and that they only consume foods that are easily digested and that exclude meat, dairy, and sugar. Students are also recommended to stay away from alcohol, caffeine, tobacco, or any other mind-altering substances so that they can be in their most conscious state when receiving the attunement. Keep in mind that *reiju* causes certain shifts in an individual—sleep is therefore very important because this can help someone integrate the changes they will experience into their mind, emotions, and energetic centers. Try to stay away from television, cell phones, and social media, and let go of any negative emotions you might be holding on to. A student can ground themselves by meditating, experiencing, and reflecting on stillness, exercising, or spending time in nature. All of these preparations are important, but the most important thing you can do before an attunement ceremony is to trust your teacher, turn your intention toward receiving this sacred blessing, and open up your heart and mind to the Reiki energy.

Although *reiju* is a spiritual and intuitive process, there are certain steps a master can follow when practicing attunement on their student. In contemporary Reiki training, attunements are generally practiced during a Reiki class. The ceremony does not take more than a few minutes, and the student will remain seated throughout the ceremony. Their master will stand over them and perform the ceremony by using hand positions, symbols, breathwork, and most importantly, intention. During the ritual, students may feel energy moving through them in the form of sensations such as warmth or coldness. They may also have visions, or experience other physical sensations. Additionally, the ceremony can trigger certain emotions to be released, and it is not uncommon for students to laugh or cry while receiving *reiju*. Finally, many students report entering a deep meditative state during the ceremony during which they could feel their consciousness shifting.

Reiju does not end when a ceremony does: Once you have been attuned, you can access the Reiki energy around you through intention alone. If you feel it is necessary, you can facilitate this process through meditation, breathwork, or visualizations. An attunement is in part an energetic "detox," which means it will also have other effects on a student after they have received one. Some of these include feeling tired and sore—or in contrast, feeling joyful and light! You might also find that your sleeping patterns have changed and that your dreams have become more vivid. Some students report experiencing heightened intuition and becoming more aware of synchronicities, while others claim the ceremony awakened them to their true purpose in life. It is possible that suppressed emotions can be awakened by the ceremony, and these have to be acknowledged and reflected upon in the days following *reiju*. You may also feel a need to spend time alone or to alter the boundaries you have set for the people in your life. It is important to accept these changes—and yourself—and to embrace your journey of self-transformation.

Meditations After Attunement

Color Meditations

Like any other detox, an attunement will bring out both the good and the bad in you. Although it is a deeply spiritual practice, it also requires you to take care of your body and mind—especially in the days after you have received *reiju*. You can do this by eating healthy and nourishing foods, staying well-hydrated, and getting enough exercise and rest. You can also take salt baths, meditate, or perform Reiki treatments on yourself. Reiki master Justine Melton (2014) suggests using colors as part of your spiritual rituals in the days following an attunement. This is because colors, too, contain energy, and depending on the color, their specific energetic frequencies have healing properties. Melton is particularly drawn to blue because of its ability to ground, relax, and bring about a sense of peace. In order to meditate with this color, she outlines the following steps (Melton, 2014):

1. Prepare the space you want to meditate in by enhancing and clearing the energy or using any of the Reiki symbols that speak to you.
2. Light a candle, preferably in the color you are meditating with, such as blue. Trust your intuition, and let it guide you toward the color you need most for your journey of healing.
3. Lie down on the floor on a mat or blanket. Close your eyes and focus on your breath. Your breathing should be natural and gentle—let your chest rise and fall as you inhale and exhale. Take your time with this step; if you are unsure how long you should remain in this position, try to hold it for at least two minutes.
4. Visualize a ball of blue light hovering over you; watch as the light expands its healing energy into the entire room.
5. Begin to breathe in the blue light and feel its healing energy fill up your body with every inhale.
6. When you exhale, picture yourself releasing anything that is no longer serving you. Watch it as it is carried away by the blue light.
7. Next, visualize an overflowing pitcher full of blue light hovering over you. If you want, you can imagine the pitcher being held by a spiritual helper. Allow them to pour the blue light over you, starting at your head and ending at your feet.
8. As the blue light washes over your body, you will feel it refreshing you while everything negative in your life is swept away by it.
9. Open up your intuition: Now is the time you are most likely to receive messages or visions from your spiritual helpers.
10. Again, imagine the ball of blue light hovering over you and let it surround you entirely. Remain in its loving and protective bubble for the rest of the day.
11. When you are ready, you can release yourself from the meditation by showing gratitude to your spiritual helpers and the color blue for the healing energy they have bestowed upon you.
12. Provided it will not distract you, you can play gentle music while meditating.

Hatsurei Ho

The aim of *reiju* is to connect you to your intuition and to the universal Reiki energy for the remainder of your life on earth. However, this connection has to be cultivated throughout your life and time as a Reiki practitioner. A good way to continuously strengthen your link to yourself and the universe is through *Hatsurei Ho*. This is a Japanese meditative practice used—often daily—by many healers to cultivate their connectedness and strengthen their intuitive and healing abilities.

Chapter 10: Reiki Anatomy

Reiki is a form of energy healing, and therefore it is important for every practitioner to know and understand the energetic pathways and centers that animate living bodies. At the same time, the practice also has a focus on the physical body. This means that a basic understanding of anatomy is required for anyone wishing to heal themselves and others successfully.

The 11 Systems of the Human Body

The human body is a wonderfully complex organization of different cells, tissues, organs, and functions that all come together to form a cohesive whole. Coming to a full understanding of the body can take years of study, and it is a field of specialization in its own right. Thankfully, the complexity of the body can be divided up into eleven different systems to make its overall functioning a little easier to understand. These systems are made up of different tissue types and organs, and have their own unique function. These systems are:

- the circulatory system
- the digestive system
- the urinary system
- the lymphatic system
- the nervous system
- the immune system
- the respiratory system
- the endocrine system
- the integumentary system

- the reproductive system
- the musculoskeletal system

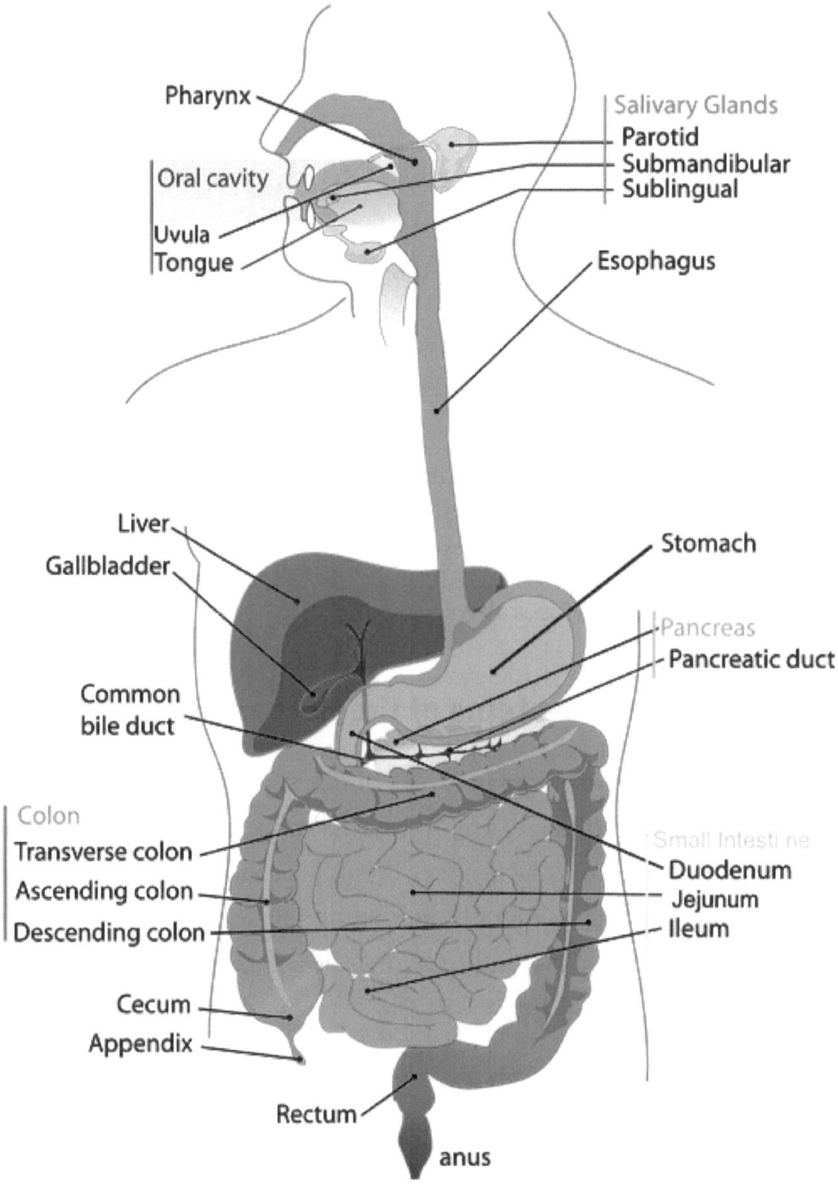

While these different systems do work independently to some extent, it is only when they all come together as a coherent whole that a human body can be said to be working efficiently. Inevitably, an imbalance in one system will impact the health of the others. Simultaneously, by healing one system, you can reduce stress on the other systems. Attaining good health is a journey—oftentimes a long one. Healing yourself will take time and effort, but the benefits of well-being are nearly endless.

The Circulatory System

Your *circulatory system* does exactly what the name says: It circulates oxygen and nutrients to the different parts of your body, and removes toxins and waste products when needed. This system includes the heart—

which is located on the left side of your chest—the blood vessels that can be found all over your body, and the blood carried by the blood vessels. Oxygen from the lungs and nutrients from the stomach and intestines are dissolved in the blood. The blood—along with the oxygen and nutrients—is then circulated by the blood vessels to the parts of the body that need it. The removal of toxins and waste products works similarly, albeit in reverse. For example, carbon dioxide is transported from the rest of the body to the lungs, from where it is expelled and replaced with fresh oxygen.

The Endocrine System

The body's *endocrine system* is a complex set of glands that secrete hormones to control various functions in the human body. Starting from the top of the body, the hypothalamus, thalamus, pituitary gland, and pineal gland can all be found in the brain. The first, the *thalamus*, controls and conveys all the sensory information—except for smell—your body receives. This means it plays an important role in many of the brain's functions, including the sleep cycle, learning processes, and memory production. Below the thalamus is the *hypothalamus*, which is responsible for controlling your heart rate, body temperature, and sensations of hunger and satiety. The *pituitary gland* is beneath the hypothalamus, and its function is to secrete the hormones responsible for metabolism, blood pressure, growth, and reproduction. Further to the back of your brain you will find the *pineal gland* that conveys the information necessary for you to maintain a healthy sleep cycle.

The *parathyroid* and *thyroid* glands are located in your neck. The function of the first is to regulate the calcium levels in your blood, which in turn is necessary for strong and healthy bones. The second, the thyroid, is mostly related to the hormones needed for physical growth and metabolic activity. The *thymus* is in the upper chest behind your breastbone. It plays an important role in your immune system because it is responsible for making the cells your body uses to fight off bacteria and disease. In your upper abdomen, you will find your *pancreas*. This gland produces the enzymes your body needs to break down the food in your stomach, and it is therefore an essential part of the digestive system. It is also important for regulating blood sugar levels. The *adrenal glands* are located on the kidneys on the right and left sides of your lower back. They have several functions: They regulate your blood pressure, metabolism, immunity, and salt levels. Additionally, they are most well-known for the role they play in the body's "fight-or-flight" response.

The Digestive System

To digest food and convert the nutrients into the substances that your cells need to multiply, grow, heal, and maintain themselves, your body requires certain organs. These include the mouth and esophagus, by which food is swallowed and transported to the stomach. From here, it moves to the small intestine into the large intestine, and then into the rectum. Finally, any waste products are excreted through the rectum. In addition to these organs, the pancreas, gallbladder, and liver also play an important role in the digestive process. For example, the liver—which is situated on the upper right-hand side of your abdomen, breaks down toxins in the body. The gallbladder can be found right below the liver, and its function is to produce and release acidic bile into your small intestine so that food can be broken down. All of these organs and glands make up the *digestive system*, which is also known as the *gastrointestinal system*.

The Urinary System

The body's *urinary system* removes toxins from blood and waste products from body tissue. Additionally, this system also removes and excretes any excess fluid in the body. To do all this, the urinary system requires several organs and ducts: The first of these are the kidneys, located on either side of your spine, right below your ribcage. Their function is to filter blood for toxins, waste products, and excess fluid, which is then turned into urine. The urine is passed into the ureters, which are two tubes connecting either kidney to the bladder. Once in the bladder, the urine flows into the urethra, from where it is excreted.

The Lymphatic System

The *lymphatic system* is what is used to drain the body of any excess proteins, fats, fluids, and bacteria. It clears not only substances in the cells but also substances that collect between the cells. For example, fluids are moved into collecting ducts in the system, from where they are transported back into the bloodstream and finally excreted. The different parts of this system are the lymph nodes, lymph vessels, lymph ducts, and various glands. These are spread out all over the body, and the lymphatic system is therefore connected intrinsically to most of the other anatomical systems. For instance, it plays an important role in the circulatory system by regulating blood pressure, and the digestive system. It also creates the cells that fight off bacteria and viruses in the body and is therefore vital to the effective functioning of the immune system.

The Nervous System

Your *nervous system* is what your body uses to communicate with all its different parts. Starting in either your brain or spinal cord, there are nerves connected to every part of your body, including your organs, muscles, glands, and skin. Without nerves, you would not be able to perform any human function, including thinking, moving, digesting, sleeping, or using your senses. Your nervous system includes your brain, spinal cord, and the vast network of nearly seven trillion nerves that connect all the different parts of your body.

The Respiratory System

Respiratory is derived from the word *respiration*, which means "breathing." Thus, the respiratory system is responsible for the movement of air into and out of your body. Additionally, it also transports oxygen and carbon dioxide from and to the bloodstream. A further function of the respiratory system—one that is often not well understood—is its ability to regulate and balance the acids and bases that are found in the body. The different parts of this system are the left and right lungs which can be found in the upper body, the *trachea*—or *windpipe*— through which you breathe, and the respiratory tree, which is a collection of airways scattered through the lungs and throat.

The Integumentary System

In simple terms, your *integumentary system* is your skin. Medically speaking, the entirety of your skin is thought of as a single organ consisting of sweat glands, nails, hair follicles, and nerves. Simultaneously, it is also the biggest organ in the body. The integumentary system has many different functions, but one of the most important is its role as your body's first line of defense against injury or illness. It forms a barrier between the inside of your body and your external environment, and it is also what keeps the rest of your body intact and together. This system is dependent on other systems to keep it in balance. For instance, your skin's temperature is controlled by the nervous system, as well as the hypothalamus in the endocrine system.

The Reproductive System

The *reproductive system* is necessary for human procreation, and its specifics differ depending on your gender. Women's reproductive systems comprise a vagina—which is located in the pelvic area between the bladder and the rectum—as well as a uterus and two ovaries, all of which can be found directly above the vagina. In contrast, men have a penis and testicles as part of their reproductive system. These are situated between the upper thighs outside the body, stemming from the pelvic area.

The Musculoskeletal System

The *musculoskeletal system* refers to all the muscles, ligaments, tendons, and bones that make up the framework of the human body. This system is what keeps us upright and intact. The different parts of this system are spread throughout your body. Muscles make movement possible through their ability to stretch and contract, while ligaments are what attach different bones to each other. Additionally, they also stabilize joints. For their part, tendons join muscles to bone, and they are therefore also important for movement. If any of these components become injured, they can cause various problems in different parts of the body; sometimes, the pain felt as a result of an injury can be in a completely different place than the injury itself. For instance, injuries in the hips can result in pain in the legs, back, or even the neck. Injuries most typically occur when the tissue making up muscles, ligaments, or joints becomes stretched, torn, or inflamed. Bones, on the other hand, have no tensile strength, which means they can be broken if put under too much pressure. Because the components of the musculoskeletal system are scattered throughout the body, they can be the root cause of many different ailments in almost any part of the body.

The Immune System

Your body uses your *immune system* to fight off viruses, bacteria, and any other harmful or foreign cells in the body. This makes it essential for the survival of any human being. Interestingly, despite its importance, all of the components of the immune system are primarily allocated to other organs. These components include organs and glands, such as the lymph nodes, bone marrow, thymus, spleen, and skin, and they are found all over the body. Because of the interconnectedness of the various parts of the immune system with the rest of the body, it is considered one of the most complex systems in the human body.

The human body is complex, and understanding the source of different ailments and injuries can be difficult. However, with some practice, experience, and faith in your intuition, you will soon master the art of healing these ailments with Reiki energy.

Chapter 11:
Symbols and Mantras—Shirushi and Jumon

An important part of the art of Reiki are the five symbols—*shirushi*—and their associated mantras, or *jumon*. Like all the elements of Reiki healing, the five symbols introduced by Usui have their own energy. Knowing, understanding, and working with them will allow the practitioner to focus the healing energy and harness it for a specific purpose. There are five symbols in Reiki healing: The power symbol, the harmony symbol, the distance symbol, the master symbol, and the completion symbol. They are an integral part of every healing session, and they can help you make your practice much more powerful.

Usui's Symbols of Reiki Healing

Symbols form part of our everyday lives, and they serve as characters or marks that represent a specific object, practice, service, or culture. Every logo you pass by on the street or brand name you see on the internet is a symbol of something specific. Each of these symbols has the power to subconsciously evoke far more than their apparent characteristics: The color blue might make you think of the ocean and family vacations at the seaside, while the logo of a car represents the company that makes the car, the type of customer they are targeting, and the lifestyle you imagine to be associated with that car. In the same way, the symbols of Reiki are characteristic of something that stretches far beyond what meets the eye. However, unlike a simple car logo, they represent the power that energy can have when it is focused in a specific direction.

There are various theories as to how these five symbols came to be a part of the Reiki system. Some believe Usui discovered the *shirushi* in ancient Buddhist texts, while others claim they appeared to him in visions. It is also unclear why he decided to incorporate these symbols into his system, but it is generally believed he did so to help his students focus and differentiate between the different energetic frequencies they were exposed to while performing Reiki (Deacon, 2005b). It is a well-known fact that Takata—the woman who first introduced Reiki to the West—believed these symbols to be so sacred that they had to be kept secret. While they are still thought of as divine by contemporary Reiki teachings, knowledge about them is no longer restricted to a select few.

As part of their power, every symbol has a mantra—or *jumon*—that accompanies it. Just as the five precepts discussed in Chapter 4 have magical *kototama*, so too do the *jumon* of the symbols invoke specific cosmic vibrations when particular sounds are made. The symbols are therefore incredibly powerful—so powerful that Takata forbade her students from keeping physical copies of them. Instead, students had to memorize and internalize these symbols. Similarly, those practicing Reiki today are expected to respect the symbols. Furthermore, the strength of the *shirushi* and the *jumon* is not in an intellectual understanding of them, but in the energetic and intuitive experience of their power. Each of the five symbols has a specific quality, and they should all be used together to focus and strengthen the quality of the Reiki healer's capabilities.

Cho ku rei: The Power Symbol

As its name suggests, the *jumon cho ku rei*—also spelled *choku rei* or *chokurei*—is a way to evoke a sense of power during Reiki practice. There is some dispute about the direct translation of the mantra *cho ku rei*, but according to Takata's teachings, it means "put the power here;" another translation is "direct spirits from God," or simply "direct spirit" (Deacon, 2003e). In other words, this symbol is about activating or increasing the spiritual power of a Reiki healer by increasing their ability to channel the universal *ki* to their patient while healing them.

In order to increase their power, many Reiki practitioners use *cho ku rei* before starting a session. This can be done by drawing the symbol—a clockwise or counterclockwise coil—on the walls of the room in which the practice is being performed. Its energy can also be drawn upon through visualization if you feel your power diminishing during a session, if you become aware of negative energy in the room, or if you are healing a particularly serious injury. Additionally, you can use this *shirushi* to protect yourself from imbalanced or impure energy, to avert misfortune, to increase your enlightenment, or to sharpen your intuition. In everyday life, *cho ku rei* can be called upon whenever you require inner strength—such as before a job interview or during a difficult conversation—or if you want to promote a relationship with someone.

Sei he ki: The Harmony Symbol

One of the translations of *sei he ki* is "God and man become one" (Price, 2019a). If you are therefore in need of balance—whether it be in your energy, your mind, your emotions, or some aspect of your life—this is the symbol to turn to. It is also a powerful symbol for protection against negative energy. *Sei he ki* is often used to treat mental and emotional problems, including anxiety, depression, fear, addiction, and chronic stress. Furthermore, it can stimulate memory and help Reiki practitioners retain information better. It is also used to release trauma from the body and the mind by restoring the energetic balance of an individual. It is a particularly useful cure for headaches, in particular those caused by mental or emotional stability, such as tension headaches.

One of this *shirushi*'s most popular uses in the contemporary West is to overcome bad habits and increase self-confidence. It is believed that unproductive behavior and insecurities stem from mental and emotional imbalances and that by rectifying them, you can come to a more positive perspective of yourself and your lifestyle (Price, 2019a). It is also popularly used to increase the power of affirmations and manifestations. In order to do this, people might draw the *sei he ki* symbol after writing down their affirmations or visualize it when manifesting something specific.

Hon sha ze sho nen: The Distance Symbol

Having no present, past, or future: That is the meaning of *hon sha sho nen*. An alternative translation believes the phrase to mean: "Correct thought is the essence of being" (Rhys, 2020b). This symbol is represented by a combination of five *kanji*—or Japanese characters—that are simultaneously the *jumon* of the symbol. There are various interpretations of the distance symbol. Some use it as a way to transcend distance in time and space when using Reiki energy: They use it to send healing to other locations, or even other ages, both in the past and in the future. Others see the symbol as signifying the oneness between the healer, their patient, and the universal *ki*, and they might use it to form a stronger connection with other people or their energetic selves. In this sense, *hon sha ze sho nen* can also be used to connect more strongly to the divine, or a healer's spiritual helpers. In yet other systems of Reiki, this *shirushi* refers to the mental faculties of a specific healer, as well as the power of a state of mindfulness.

In the contemporary West, *hon sha ze sho nen* is most often used to send healing to other places and times. For instance, old wounds can be healed by reframing them as a learning experience rather than simply a traumatic event, or difficult times up ahead can be made smoother by using this symbol to send Reiki energy into the future. Given the virtual and global nature of our culture, it is also often used to heal people from a distance.

The distance symbol is one of the most powerful symbols in the Reiki arsenal. Unlike the other symbols, it works best when used on the metaphysical body, instead of the material body. Additionally, it is most effective when called upon daily by visualizing the symbol or chanting its *jumon*.

Dai ko myo: The Master Symbol

Dai ko myo is thought of as the most sacred symbol in Reiki practices. It translates as "bright shining light" or "great enlightenment," and it is often used to bring healers closer to god (Reiki Info, n.d.). In this sense, *dai* means "great;" *ky myo* has several translations and allusions, including "enlightenment," "nature," "radiance," or "bright light." It is closely related to the universal *ki* and the intuition of the healer, and its purpose is to bring the Reiki practitioner closer to the energy around them by guiding them in the right direction. It is also symbolic of understanding, essence, authenticity, and the ability to know your innermost and truest self. This *shirushi* is sometimes described as the "beating heart of Reiki," (Reiki Info, n.d.) or the "encapsulation of the Reiki phenomenon itself" (Deacon, 2003), and its use should be accompanied by meditative silence and a reverence for the spiritual realm and all it encompasses.

Dai ko myo has the highest vibration of all the symbols, and invoking it can help heal the soul, the aura, and the upper chakras. It also plays a central role when Reiki masters perform attunements on their students. It is a symbol of empowerment and nourishment, and you can use it to increase your healing power so that you can heal yourself and others with greater success. Additionally, it is often used as a tool to increase self-awareness and strengthen your relationship with yourself. Because *dai ko myo* balances the body's energy, it has powerful effects on the immune system; it can also be used to enhance the power of other remedies and medicines or to clear or charge crystals. This symbol can be employed through visualization, meditation, or by drawing it using your third eye.

Raku: The Completion Symbol

The completion symbol—or *raku*—is signified by a zigzag shape thought to be a fire serpent. It is drawn from the top to the bottom, and this symbolizes the *shirushi*'s ability to ground a Reiki practitioner after a session. It is also representative of a path, specifically the path traveled by the *ki* from the universe through the practitioner and into the patient. Using this symbol can therefore help a healer return to themselves and their own energy to cleanse themselves of any negativity they might have absorbed from their patient. Additionally, it helps a practitioner to assimilate the benefits that they experience by healing someone else. Similarly, students often invoke it after receiving an attunement so that they can get the most out of the energy transfer between them and their teachers. It can also be used in your everyday life if ever you need to ground yourself, especially after stressful events. *Raku* can perform these functions because it distributes the life energy of Reiki evenly to all the chakras of an individual.

Raku can be visualized as a pink or violet light, and it is generally only taught to students at the master level of their training. There is some dispute as to its origin, and many practitioners believed it was only introduced to Usui's Reiki system by his later students, in particular, Ishikuro (Rhys, 2020a). Despite this controversy, it is a popular and powerful *shirushi* that has come to play a central role in contemporary Reiki practices.

While the symbols hold great power when used in isolation, they can be even more effective when used in combination. These combinations can include any—or even all—of the symbols, depending on the circumstances.

They can also be used in conjunction with other images—such as photographs of long-distance patients—or items such as crystals or precious stones. Regardless of how they are invoked, the symbols and their mantras hold great power, and they are guaranteed to strengthen your practice, increase your connection with yourself and the Reiki energy, and improve your physical, mental, and emotional health.

Chapter 12:
Techniques For Cleansing, Grounding, Expanding, and Unifying

One of the main goals of a Reiki practitioner is to become a channel for the energy around them. In order to do this, you have to remove yourself from all that exists on this plane of reality—including other people, and your own emotions, thoughts, ideas, and memories. Additionally, to avoid the entrainment of negative energy, you have to purify yourself of any imbalances you may have had before starting a Reiki session. In the same way that it is necessary to purify your own energy after working with a patient. Two other aspects of Reiki healing are focus and unification: The first is important to bring yourself in alignment with the universal *ki*, and the second is to unify your body, mind, and soul so that you can effectively channel the Reiki energy to your patient.

In contemporary Reiki styles, students learn three popular methods to achieve these aims. These are *kenyoku ho*, *joshin kokyu ho*, and *seishin toitsu*. These three techniques are an essential part of Usui's five elements of Reiki, and their respective aims are to purify, focus, and unify the energy of a Reiki practitioner. Depending on the prescriptions, they should be performed during various parts of a Reiki session. Some of them can also be used in day-to-day life to purify yourself of negative energy.

Kenyoku Ho: A Cleansing Technique

Kenyoku ho, or "dry bathing," is a traditional purification technique most commonly used by people before entering a temple or other sacred place. In Reiki practices, *kenyoku ho* is performed to cleanse the energy of the healer before and after a session. Instead of using water, however, the healer uses energy to purify themselves. Its main purpose is to distance the healer from other people and things, including their own emotions, thoughts, circumstances, and energy. This type of distancing is necessary because, although they have to remain in tune with their intuition during a session, they also have to act as an empty vessel for the Reiki energy they intend to channel to their patient.

Dry bathing can be performed through either physical contact or by simply hovering your hands over your body in the space of your aura. You can follow the steps below to cleanse yourself:

1. Perform a *gassho* meditation.
2. After finishing the meditation, continue to pay attention to your breath. Breathe in through your nose and out through your mouth; try to keep your breath natural and effortless.
3. Put your right palm flat onto your left shoulder around the space of your collarbone.
4. Using smooth and controlled downward strokes, move your right hand from your shoulder over your belly to your right hip. Exhale with a "ha" sound every time you sweep your hand across your body.
5. Repeat this on your right shoulder using your left hand.
6. Perform this sequence three times.
7. Next, place your right hand on the outside of your left shoulder.
8. Straighten your left arm out in front of you.
9. Stroke the outside of the length of your arm, starting at your shoulder and ending at your fingertips. Once you reach your fingers, imagine you are throwing negative energy away from you by flicking your right hand into the air. In some versions of *kenyoku ho*, you have to brush your hand along the inside of your arm instead of the outside, while others claim you have to brush your right hand over the inside of the left palm from the wrist to the fingertips. Your choice of method will depend on the style of Reiki you choose to practice, although some masters suggest you follow your intuition when it comes to this part of the practice.
10. Repeat this motion on your right arm using your left hand.
11. End the purification with another short *gassho* meditation.

Dry bathing can be performed when doing other energy work in addition to Reiki healing. It can also be used in everyday life, whenever you feel the need to cleanse yourself of negativity or impure energy.

Joshin Kokyo Ho: Meditation and Breathwork To Expand the Mind

Joshin kokyo ho, also spelled *joshin kokyu ho*, is a combination of meditation and breathwork that is used to cleanse the spirit, focus the mind, and energize the healer. It was introduced by Usui into the Reiki system, and it is taught to students at all levels of their training. When the phrase is broken down, it translates as follows: *jo* means "pure" or "clean," and *shin* refers to the enlightened mind or the essence of a being. *Kokyo* describes the act of breathing, and *ho* means "method" or "principle" (Stiene, 2016). Combined, the phrase, therefore, means "the method of realizing our enlightened mind through breathing in and out" (Stiene, 2016, par. 3). This method requires regular practice, and its ultimate aim is to bring about the realization that the enlightened mind and the universe—when in harmony with each other—are both equally pure and infinite.

In addition to being a breathing and meditation technique, *joshin kokyo ho* also requires you to visualize the universal *ki* as it moves through your body. There are two important components to this practice: The first is to bring your mind to your lower *tanden* located below your navel so that you can become grounded; the second is to let your mind leave your body and open up to the rest of the infinite universe. By allowing your mind to expand endlessly, you are getting rid of any narrow-mindedness you might have, and unifying yourself with the Reiki energy you wish to channel. When your mind opens up into the universe, you are no longer able to hold on to your thoughts or become distracted by them. Instead, you will find yourself surrounded by vastness and endlessness. Any thoughts that come to you will simply dissolve into the space around you if you are willing to let them go without grasping at them. To quote Taisen Deshimaru: "A calm mind not tied to anything lets authentic wisdom appear" (Stiene, 2016, par. 34).

If you are new to Reiki, this type of visualization might be difficult to understand initially. Learning to expand your mind in this way takes time, practice, and patience: Remember, there is just as much value in failing and trying again as there is in "getting it right!" A simple *joshin kyokyo ho* practice will normally follow the steps below (Stiene, 2016):

1. Find a comfortable seat, so that your spine is straight and in alignment with your tailbone and the crown of your head.
2. Place your hands in the *gassho* position and close your eyes.
3. Begin by inhaling through the nose and exhaling through the mouth.
4. Every time you inhale, imagine you are breathing in the Reiki energy through the crown of your head; follow it with your mind as it flows through your energetic centers into your lower *tanden*. Allow the light of the divine to spread through your entire body with every inhale, and let it illuminate everything inside you that is negative, imbalanced, or impure.

5. When your breath reaches the space below your navel, focus on the groundedness it brings you. Keep your mind focused on your body, and try not to get distracted. If you do, acknowledge the distraction and let it gently pass you by.
6. On the exhale, picture the light of Reiki leaving your body. Let it radiate from you into the rest of the universe.
7. Allow your mind to leave your body and let it expand into, and combine with, the energy that is all around you.
8. Repeat this three to five times, or until you intuitively feel you are ready to move on.

Seishin Toitsu: Meditation For Unification

In order to perform Reiki—or to successfully navigate life—concentration is key. Lapses in attention could impede your practice or progress, lead to failure, or even be fatal in some circumstances. A pilot landing a plane cannot afford to lose focus while performing this task, and in the same way, a Reiki healer who has lost their concentration will also lose their energetic connection to their patient and to the energy being channeled through them. To unify the mind, body, and spirit toward performing a single task, many Eastern practices—from martial arts to energy work, calligraphy, and tea ceremonies—have turned to *seishin toitsu* to cultivate focus, avoid hesitation and indecisiveness, and improve the human attention span. In all of these practices, every single movement, as well as the pauses between them, is crucial to the successful execution of the whole—and this is why the unification of everything that makes up a human being is so important.

Seishin can be translated as "pure mind," while *toitsu* means "focusing on the present" or "gathering together" (Ohlenkamp, n.d.). It is an ancient meditation practice aimed to teach concentration and diligence so that the art being performed—whether it be of a physical, mental, spiritual, or creative nature—can be completed effortlessly. In this sense, *seishin toitsu* is a journey: It teaches the practitioner unification of the body, mind, and spirit, but they can only learn this by performing the meditation regularly. On the other hand, *seishin toitsu* can benefit all spheres of life, and its practice should not be limited to Reiki sessions:

1. Begin in a seated position, with your spine straight and your hands in the *gassho* position.
2. Inhale through your nose, and focus your attention on your hands: Picture yourself breathing in through your hands.
3. When breathing into your hands, imagine the Reiki energy around you flowing into your hands with your breath. Follow its flow through your body, all the way to your lower *tanden*. This energy is often visualized as a bright light or a fire that becomes more vivid as it settles into the space below your navel.
4. Exhale, and picture the Reiki energy leaving your hands while its fire remains in your lower *tanden*.
5. You might feel warmth in your hands and belly as the energy moves through you.

6. Feel your mind, body, and spirit come together as a unified whole.
7. When you are ready, gently come out of the meditation.

Just as cultivating concentration—*seishin toitsu*—is about the journey and not the destination, so too is the art of Reiki about the process rather than the end result. Every act and every ritual forms part of the healing process, from unlocking the room in which you aim to perform the session to hovering your hands over your patient. Reiki is an art, not only because it heals, but because it is a complex yet poetic system that comprehensively addresses all facets of who we are as human beings, as well as how we relate to each other, other forms of life, and the universe as a whole. Just like a calligrapher has to pay attention to every single brushstroke and a martial artist has to account for every single movement, so, too, does the healer have to perform every action with precision and decisiveness. Every part of the system has a purpose—and *this* is where the magic of Reiki lies.

Pillar 4:
Training (Shoden/First Degree Reiki)

Chapter 13:
Self-Treatment (Tenohira)

Most people imagine Reiki to be practiced by one person on another. However, it is possible to perform Reiki healing on yourself through daily sessions—and in fact, doing so is considered one of the five main elements of Reiki. *Tenohira* is the art of healing oneself by using your hands to channel energy from the universal *ki* into your own body (International House of Reiki, 2010a). The main purpose of *tenohira* is to unblock and clear energetic pathways in the body. Simultaneously, practicing self-healing strengthens the healer's connection with the divine.

The Reiki system derived from Usui's lineage is complex and comprehensive, and it consists of many different components and rituals. While these are important for effective practices, they can be adapted to fit into a contemporary Western lifestyle. Some practice *tenohira* based on instinct alone, but there are specific hand positions available to anyone who is unsure how to begin the process of self-healing. Remember that Reiki energy is accessible to all, and once you have discovered its healing power, it can never be taken away from you again.

Preparations

The aim of a Reiki practice is to unblock and balance your energy so that you can restore your physical, mental, and emotional health. To do this, you have to be relaxed and focused. To achieve the right state of mind, there are a few practical things you can do before a Reiki session. The first is to pay attention to your clothing: You want to be as comfortable as possible, so make sure you are wearing something loose-fitting and breathable that is appropriate for the external temperature. If you are unsure, it might be wise to layer your clothing or keep something warm handy in case you misjudged the weather! Additionally, if you plan to be barefoot, it is a good idea to make sure you have socks with you to prevent your feet from getting cold.

Next, you have to pay attention to nourishment and hydration. Thirst and hunger will only distract you during a session, so make sure you have a light meal a few hours before a Reiki practice. Simultaneously, it is best to avoid eating too much, as this will direct your body's energy toward digesting your food and away from the treatment. It is also important to use the restroom before starting a session; if you become uncomfortable at any point during the session, stop what you are doing and adjust whatever needs adjusting. Much of the value of Reiki lies in focus and relaxation, so continuing a practice while you are distracted by your body can be frustrating and counterproductive.

Finally, the most important preparation you can make before a Reiki session is to spend some time reflecting. Take a few minutes to pay attention to your thoughts, mood, and sensations. How does your body feel? What state of mind are you in? Are your thoughts racing through your head, or are you focused, centered, and relaxed? In addition to reflection, take the time to set an intention. Why have you turned to Reiki, and what are you hoping to gain from this practice?

If you are performing a treatment on yourself, it is also important to perform the cleansing techniques and meditations required by the Reiki system before beginning the practice. These include *gassho* meditation to focus and calm your mind, and practicing *reiji-ho* to sharpen your intuition. Keeping in mind the principles of entrainment, it is also important to prepare yourself, as well as the space in which you want to perform the session. This could include smudging, meditation, or using the necessary and appropriate symbols. Finally, it is important to perform *kenyoku-ho* to cleanse your energy, *joshin kokyo-ho* to ground and expand your mind, and *sesihin toitsu* to focus your attention by unifying your body, mind, and spirit. These practices are described in chapters 5, 6, 11, and 12 respectively.

How to Perform Self-Treatment

Traditionally, Reiki is practiced by healers on their patients. However, self-healing—*tenohira*—is also possible, and has become more popular in recent years. Reiki master Parita Shah is among those who believe treating yourself is possible, and she practices Reiki daily. Shah (2020) suggests following the process below for anyone who wants to engage in the art of self-healing:

1. Begin by finding a comfortable, quiet place to perform your practice. It is important to be relaxed in body and mind, so find a posture that accommodates this. You can do this by lying down while supporting your head and knees on bolsters, or by sitting in a cross-legged position with your knees below your hips on the floor or on a cushion. If you find either of these options uncomfortable, you can also sit on a chair that supports your back well and allows you to place your feet flat on the ground.

2. Regular practice takes time, energy, commitment, and courage—especially if it is new to you—so celebrate your discipline! Treat yourself with kindness and compassion, and acknowledge your willingness to do what is necessary to improve your physical, mental, and emotional health.

3. Go into a meditative state by turning your attention to your breath. Now begin to notice your body and its sensations: Where do you feel tension, discomfort, or pain? Send your breath to those places, while simultaneously paying attention to your posture. Relax your shoulders, unclench your jaw, and relax the muscles of your face, hands, and feet. If you are uncomfortable in the position you chose, make the necessary adjustments so that you do not become distracted later in the practice.

4. When you feel more relaxed, start paying attention to the way your breath feels in your body. Are you breathing all the way into your belly, or do your inhales get stuck in your chest? Make sure your breath goes all the way into your lower body: Feel your back and ribcage expand as you inhale fully, and collapse when you exhale. Deep breathing is an essential part of a Reiki practicum because it activates all of your energetic centers. Simultaneously, it also stimulates your vagus nerve, which helps you relax.

5. Recall the five precepts of Reiki—as discussed in Chapter 4—and recite them to yourself quietly or out loud. You can say them in either Japanese or English, depending on what you intuitively feel is right for you.

6. Turn to your spiritual helpers, and allow them to guide you through your practice. Shah (2020, par. 7) suggests saying the following words: "I welcome the presence of my Reiki masters, teachers, healers, and guides. I welcome your energetic blessings and messages for the highest good of all. Thank you for gracing us with love and light." Open up your intuition, and feel the presence of those beings who wish you well.

7. Attunements are important when learning to channel Reiki energy, and these can only be performed by a Reiki master. However, even if you have no formal training, it is still possible to channel love and light to yourself. When doing this, your intention and awareness play an important role. Allow yourself to open up to the universal *ki*, and absorb its healing power into your body.

8. Place your hands on your body to channel Reiki into your energetic centers. Begin with the crown of your head,

9. followed by your eyes.

10. Next, put your right hand on your throat and your left hand over your heart.

11. Following this, move them first to the back of your head,

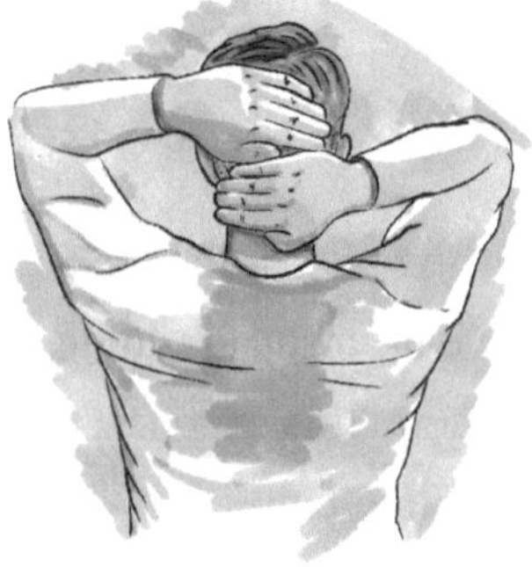

12. and then to your upper chest.

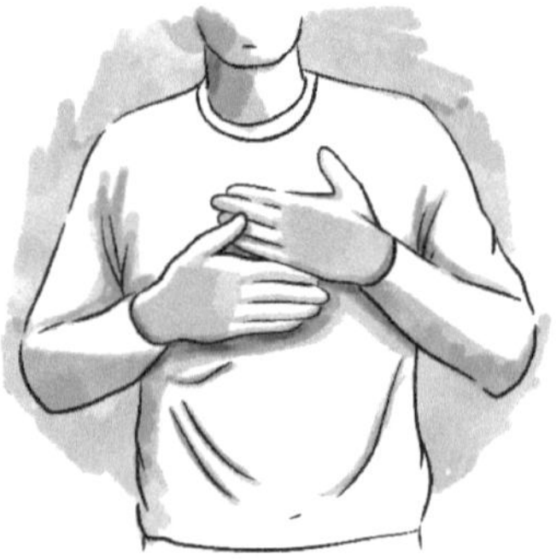

13. Continue moving your hands down to your breast line, and place them so that the middle fingers come together at the point where your breastbone ends.

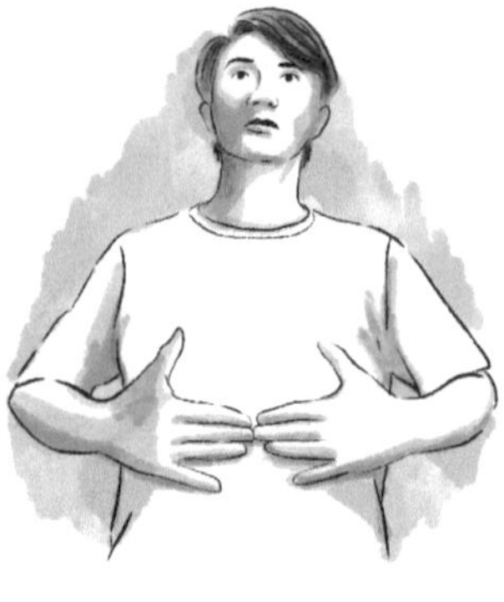

14. Keeping the middle fingers together, move your hands first to your solar plexus in the upper stomach,

15. then to your navel,

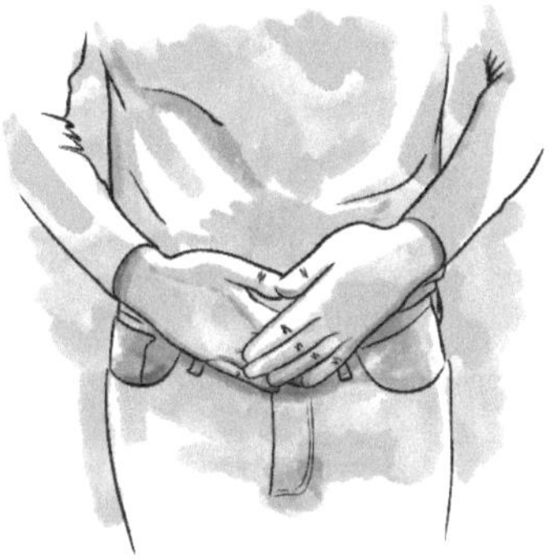

16. and finally to your lower abdomen where your earth energy—or *ka tanden*—is located.

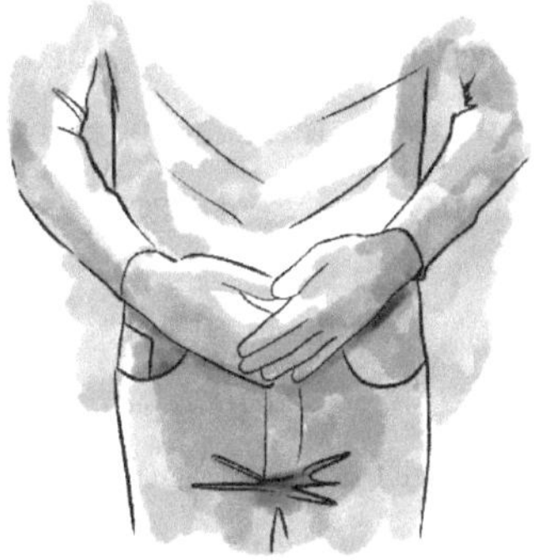

17. Move your hands back to the top of your body, and place them on your shoulders so that the backs of your hands face backward.

18. Next, put your hands on the back of your waistline in the region of your kidneys.

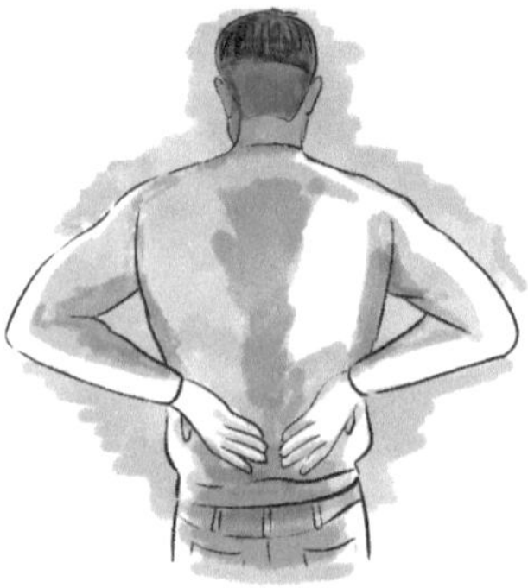

19. Finally, cross your legs if you have not done so already and place your hands on either the tops or the soles of your feet.

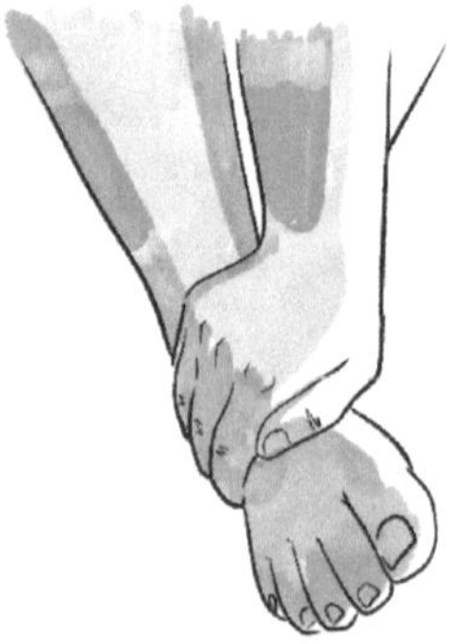

20. Let your hands linger in every position, and allow your intuition to guide you with the length of every placement. If this is difficult, you can also time each placement by using your breath or a gentle Reiki timer designed specifically for this purpose. Most people suggest holding each hand position for two minutes or more.

21. If you ever find yourself unsure during your session, you can turn to *reiji-ho* to sharpen your intuition and increase your connection to the Reiki energy. You can also call on the power of the symbols if you feel it is necessary. The first is described in Chapter 5 and the second in Chapter 11.

22. You can play relaxing instrumental music during your practice, provided this does not distract you.

23. Remember to thank your spiritual helpers and the Reiki energy once you have completed a session! Also, remember to show gratitude for the journey that brought you to Reiki; once you are ready, gently come out of the practice.

Everyone's experience of a Reiki session is different, and you might experience things others don't. Most commonly, people report feeling extremely relaxed, sometimes to the point of being sleepy. You might also feel parts of your body tingle or heat up as the energy moves through it, or you could have a spiritual experience, such as having a vision or seeing a Reiki guide.

Post-Treatment Practices

The power of a Reiki session is as much in the after-effects of the session as it is in the session itself. It is therefore important to integrate the session once you are finished. There are various ways in which you can do this: You can meditate, lie down in corpse pose—or *savasana*—go for a walk in nature, or even take a nap. The last thing you want to do after a Reiki practice is to rush back into the world and resume your busy life, so try to organize your day to give you some time off, and avoid scheduling anything stressful or physically, mentally, or emotionally taxing. Ideally, you should try to spend some time alone so that you can absorb your session and get as many benefits from it as possible.

A Reiki session will most likely bring you new insights, and it is important to reflect on those after the session is finished. You can do this by journaling, drawing, listening to relaxing music, or meditating. It is also good to return to the intention you set before your practice: What did you learn from the session, and how can you incorporate it into your life in the future?

Energy work—whether you are the healer, the patient, or both—takes a lot of energy. While you may feel relaxed mentally and emotionally, your physical body may feel some strain after a Reiki session. For this reason, it is important to nourish yourself with food and water. Drink one or two glasses of water, and if possible, add some electrolytes to it to help revive your body. It is also good to have a light meal or snack to restore your energy and balance your blood sugar levels. Since having food and drink returns your attention to your physical body, it can help to ground you after a session of energy work. Listen to your body and give it what it needs—but try to stick to healthy food that will nourish you without adding toxins to your system.

According to the system designed by Usui, a Reiki healer should perform another *gassho* meditation after a session, as well as cleanse themselves of any negative energy using *kenyoku-ho* dry bathing. If you feel you need to ground yourself, you can also spend some time meditating on your lower *tanden* to return to your physical body. These practices are discussed in chapters 5, 8, and 12. It is unlikely to happen, but if you find yourself in any physical or emotional pain, do not hesitate to contact someone who is experienced in the art of Reiki for advice and help. The purpose of Reiki is to heal—not harm—and there is no shame in turning to others for guidance.

Some people believe that Reiki should only be practiced by someone who has received formal training, while others hold the opinion that Reiki energy is available to everyone, and can be accessed by anyone who decides to do so. There are definite benefits to attending a Reiki class, most notably the attunements you will receive from your teacher. However, what is even more important than your training is your commitment to the practice. For Reiki to truly bring about transformation in your life, it should be practiced regularly. It does not matter when you practice—some people prefer doing it at the same time every day, while others suggest doing it whenever the moment feels right—as long as you do it diligently. Ideally, a session should last 30 to 40 minutes. However, if you have limited time, as little as 10 to 15 minutes a day can still make a big difference. To quote Reiki master Takata: "A little Reiki practice is better than none" (Miles, 2011, par. 12). When it comes to habits and rituals, it is not always the big gestures that count—it is the little things we do consistently that bring about the most meaningful change.

Pillar 5:
Healing

Chapter 14:
Remedies For Different Physical, Mental, and Spiritual Ailments

Your hands have the power to heal. This is no small feat: In a world where countless people are suffering from physical, mental, and spiritual imbalances, having the ability to treat yourself at your very fingertips is almost like having a superpower. Some conditions are worse than others, and many people need Western medical treatment for their ailments. However, even if you are receiving treatment from a doctor or specialist, Reiki can still provide you with a useful form of complementary therapy. For the rest, Reiki is a wonderful way to reconnect with yourself and the universe and address the many medical difficulties our society has to face every day.

Physical Ailments

Energetic imbalances not only manifest as mental ailments or spiritual deficiencies, but they also show up as physical symptoms. Your mind, body, and energy are intrinsically linked, and a disconnect in any one of these areas can have painful consequences for an individual. The list of symptoms that can arise when our chakras are blocked is endless, but some of the most common problems include, but are not limited to:

- headaches and migraines
- pain and stiffness in the neck
- frozen shoulder and shoulder pain
- spinal pain
- skin problems, such as psoriasis, eczema, and acne
- colds and flu
- problems with fertility
- fibromyalgia

- anemia
- heart conditions
- problems with hair growth, such as baldness
- irritable bowel syndrome, irritable bowel disorder, and Chron's disease
- pain in the muscles and joints of the jaw
- muscle spasms
- knee pain
- scoliosis
- issues with eyesight
- pain and stiffness in the legs
- hiccups
- pain in the feet
- kidney disease
- lung problems and difficulty breathing
- problems with weight loss and weight gain
- tuberculosis
- issues with the adrenal glands
- strokes
- sciatica
- gum disease and dental issues
- ankylosing spondylitis
- pain in the solar plexus
- allergies
- throat pain and inflammation
- discomfort and stiffness in the thighs
- tinnitus
- problems with the thyroid glands
- diabetes

- stomach pain and digestive issues
- neurological disorders
- varicose veins
- ulcers

Reiki can also be used as a form of palliative care for people living with serious or chronic illnesses. In order to use Reiki to relieve physical symptoms, try the following method:

1. Sit down in a quiet environment that is free of distractions. To enhance the energy of the room, you can burn incense or candles, or play music, provided this does not draw attention away from your practice.
2. Begin by taking five to ten deep breaths; this will help you to calm your nervous system and center you in your practice.
3. Perform a body scan: Start at the top of your head, and shift your focus down the length of your body to your face, neck, chest, arms, abdomen, legs, and toes. Let your attention linger on every area and notice where the tension is in your body. Are you clenching your jaw? Are you scrunching your shoulders? Are your palms open and your fingers relaxed?
4. Let your focus rest wherever you come across tension or pain. Breathing deeply, send energy to those places to release the tension and alleviate discomfort. You can also hover your hands over these areas, or use the hand positions discussed in Chapter 13.
5. This practice is an ideal opportunity to invoke the Reiki harmony symbol and power symbol. You can bring them into your practice by visualizing them on or above your body wherever you feel tense.
6. Once you have completed your body scan, return your focus to the top of your head and begin the process anew. Again, release any tension you feel in your body.
7. Before you come out of the practice, spend five minutes focusing on your breath and absorbing the peace the session has brought you.
8. When you are ready, give gratitude to your spiritual helpers—and continue the rest of your day surrounded by peace and love.

Mental Ailments

There are few of us who can say we are completely at peace with ourselves and our lives. There is a long list of imbalances that people suffer from, including insomnia and sleep disorders, difficulty managing anger, chronic stress and anxiety, and depression. Other disorders, such as obsessive-compulsive disorder, addiction, and responses to trauma have also become nearly commonplace in the world we live in. Thankfully, we have Reiki—a practice we can all turn to when we are in need of healing. There are many different ways in which Reiki can be used to treat these disorders, but below are some methods you can turn to if you feel unsafe, have difficulty controlling your emotions, or suffer from a painful imbalance or disorder that is disrupting your life.

Reiki to Help You Feel Safe

Disrupted sleep, anxiety, stress, and trauma can be the result of any number of things, including a sense that we are unsafe or unsure in our environment. One of the main benefits of Reiki is the feelings of relaxation and peace it brings about, which makes this form of energy healing ideal for anyone who needs to take some time to recenter themselves. To bring the Reiki energy into your life, try the following (Melton, 2022):

1. Find a comfortable position on your bed and close your eyes.
2. Breathe naturally and deeply, and allow your breath to calm your mind. Focusing on your inhales and exhales, feel the air move your chest up and down.
3. Open your eyes while continuing to focus on your breath, and shift your gaze to the corners of the room.
4. Visualize the golden light of *cho ku rei*—the power symbol—in every corner. Move your gaze to the walls and picture this symbol starting to appear there, too. The symbols of Reiki healing are discussed in more detail in Chapter 11.
5. Focus your eyes toward the middle of the room, where you can imagine a large harmony symbol—or *sei he ki*—hovering in the space above the floor. Depending on the level of training and the number of attunements you have received, you can picture a *dai ko myo* master symbol floating alongside the harmony symbol.
6. Once you have completed your visualization, close your eyes and let the knowledge that you are surrounded by Reiki energy bring you to a place of relaxation. Imagine their golden light washing over you as you lie in bed.
7. Thank your spiritual helpers and the divine energy of the universe for protecting and loving you.
8. You can now go to sleep, safe in the knowledge that you are surrounded by peace, goodness, love, and security.

Reiki for Emotional Regulation

If you find yourself in a constant state of emotional turmoil, you might have difficulty regulating your feelings. This is not a criticism: In a world where things never stop moving, it is impossible to remain in control of your emotions at all times. However, it can result in serious illness that greatly impedes the everyday lives of those who suffer from it. You can follow the steps below in order to perform a Reiki self-treatment:

1. Lie down in a quiet, comfortable place.
2. Cradle the back of your head in your palms and let your elbows fall to the sides of your face.

3. Spend two minutes breathing deeply.
4. Visualize the healing energy from your palms entering your head and travel all the way into your mind.
5. Picture this energy releasing any negativity stored in your thoughts and feelings, and exhale them out into the air around you.
6. Allow the light of Reiki to fill your mind with peace and calmness in the place where your suffering used to be.
7. Next, move your hands to your heart chakra. Again, channel healing energy into this space as you let go of any stress, trauma, pain, or heaviness you are feeling.
8. When you are ready, bring your hands to the sides of your body; spend a few minutes absorbing your practice and giving gratitude to your spiritual helpers and the universal *ki*.
9. Flutter your eyes open and let the light and peace of Reiki surround you for the remainder of your day.

Reiki for Disorders and Addiction Recovery

Contemporary society has become a breeding ground for many serious disorders, such as anxiety, depression, obsessive-compulsive disorder, and addiction. These all manifest in different ways, but what they have in common is the ability to disrupt the normal functioning of those suffering from them. In severe cases, medication may be necessary to treat such imbalances; however, Reiki can serve as a useful complementary therapy to alleviate some of the painful effects of these disorders:

1. Find a comfortable seat in a quiet space.
2. Begin your practice by placing your trust in your intuition and your spiritual helpers: The universe wants nothing but the best for you, and if you want to begin a journey of healing, you have to allow the Reiki energy to guide you.
3. Place your left hand on your third eye chakra and your right hand on your heart chakra. Take deep, natural breaths and allow your body to relax.
4. Think back to all the suffering your disorder has brought you; this might be painful, but it is important that you face what you have been through. Follow your intuition, and allow yourself to express your emotions freely.
5. Imagine each of these painful memories as a black ball; take each one and draw the Reiki symbol of your choice on them.
6. Watch as the pure, white light of Reiki fills each of these balls; imagine them disappearing into the air around you—and out of your life.

7. Think of yourself as a new person with a new start who is free to live their life without suffering or impediment. Your mind has been filled with love and peace, and you are as limitless as the universe.

8. Recite to yourself: "I can maintain the peace I have felt every day. I can call upon it whenever I want, and I am in control of my conscious thoughts."

9. Visualize a protection symbol being drawn on your head.

10. Give gratitude to the divine guidance and the universal *ki*; when you are ready, release yourself from the practice.

11. It is best to perform this meditation every day for at least 21 days.

Spiritual Disconnectedness

It is no secret that we have become disconnected from the universal energy that unites us all with each other and the cosmos. This belief may not hold true for everyone, but there are nevertheless people who feel the need to reconnect their physical bodies with their inner energy, and to reunite with the Reiki energy that makes up the universe. This can be done in various ways, but the simplest method is to simply channel Reiki energy into your body using your breath. To do this, you can follow these steps:

1. Find a comfortable seat.

2. Place your hands on top of your shoulders so that the backs of your palms are facing backward.

3. Begin by breathing deeply but naturally until you begin to feel calmer.

4. Open up your intuition, and picture yourself sending energy from your hands into your shoulders.

5. Let this energy travel from your shoulders through the rest of your body; continue to focus on your breath.

6. You can also place your hands on the back of your head with your palms facing backward and channel energy into your crown chakra.

7. Allow yourself to let go of the blockages you feel in your body, and open yourself up to the universal *ki*.

8. Remain like this for 15 to 20 minutes, or until you intuitively feel you are ready to move on.

Conclusion

Life is not easy, and many of us fall victim to countless daily physical, mental, and emotional ailments. The stress of modern-day existence has taken its toll on the global population, and more people than ever have reason to seek out medical treatment. Despite the historical success of the medical industry in the contemporary West, many are turning to holistic, natural, and alternative practices to heal themselves and their loved ones. Most of these practices have been around for thousands of years, and deserve the new-found attention they've been receiving. They teach us that the ills of the world are deeper than what we see on the surface: Many of our problems occur at an energetic level, and it is only through a return to the interconnected universe that we can find long-lasting solutions to the imbalances that cause so much suffering. The good news is that this very energy—the universal *ki* that animates and links all living things—can be harnessed to bring each and every one of us to a place of peace, harmony, balance, and health.

The art of Reiki has been around since the days of ancient Tibet. Many of these teachings became lost to the world through the tumults of history, but the healer and scholar Mikao Usui and his lineage of students brought them back, first to contemporary Japan, and later to the West. The teachings of Reiki tell us that we can heal ourselves and others by tapping into the energy that surrounds us and by restoring energetic balance within ourselves. By acting as vessels for this energy and channeling it to where it is needed most, we can restore energetic imbalances and restore our well-being.

In order to support his students, Usui established a system according to which Reiki can be practiced. This system is grounded in the five precepts or *gokai*; to help you incorporate these five precepts in your everyday lives, he developed the three pillars of Reiki. These are *gassho* meditations, the art of opening your intuition through *reiji-ho*, and *chiryo*, or action. Other Eastern concepts incorporated into Usui's traditional Reiki system and more contemporary training methods include the chakras or *tanden* energetic centers, *reiju* attunements, and *tenohira* as the art of self-healing. Other important elements are the five Reiki symbols and mantras—*cho ku rei, sei he ki, hon sha ze sho nen, dai ko myo*, and *raku*—and the practices of *kemyoko ho, joshin kokyo ho*, and *seishin toitsu* to cleanse, focus, expand, and unify the body, mind, and spirit. In later Western scientific traditions, the principle of entrainment was discovered and used to describe the energetic interactions that occur between all beings in the living world.

You were right: Everything in the universe is connected, and knowing and understanding this is the way forward if you want to reclaim your power, make better life choices, and get in touch with your higher self. Furthermore, this interconnectedness is possible because of the Reiki energy that unites the entire universe and the infinite realm that lies beyond it. Accessing this energy is the key to health and well-being, and a joyful, peaceful, and fulfilling life; once you have accessed this energy, you will forevermore be able to channel it by your intention alone. Reiki cannot be taken away from you, nor can you forget how to connect yourself to the universe. You have nothing to lose and everything to gain—and all of the universe is ready to help you achieve your full potential.

About the Author

Hailing from a Scandinavian family, author Monique Wagner is no stranger to alternative medicine. For most of her life, she has devoted her time and energy to studying ancient healing methods and the medical wisdom from neo-pagan and occult traditions, as well as other cultures. As an empath, it is her mission in life to share her lifelong experiences with her readers. As a result of many years of research, she has attained comprehensive knowledge, and she is passionate about bringing this knowledge to those who are in need of physical, mental, and emotional healing.

Glossary

Chakras: A Sanskrit term that refers to the "wheels of life." These are energetic centers in the bodies of living things that circulate the energy needed to animate them.

Chiryo: The Japanese term for "treatment;" it implies action, and it is the third pillar of Usui's Reiki system.

Circumambulation: The deliberate, focused, clockwise movement around a space when performing a smudging ceremony.

Cho ku rei: The mantra for the power symbol in Reiki.

Gassho meditation: A meditation performed by placing the hands in a *gassho*—or "prayer"—position. It is the first pillar of Usui's Reiki system, and it forms an integral part of the lifestyle of any Reiki practitioner.

Gokai: A Japanese term meaning "precepts" or "principles," as in the case of Usui's five precepts of Reiki.

Joshin kokyo or **joshin kokyu:** A combined meditative and breathwork practice that aims to cleanse, energize, and focus a Reiki healer before a session.

Jumon: The Japanese word for *mantra*; more specifically, it is the cosmic vibration that is invoked when a specific sound is made.

Kanji: The characters used in Japanese writing to refer to specific words.

Kenyoku ho: A "dry bathing" technique used by Reiki healers to cleanse their energy of negativity before and after performing healing sessions.

Kototoma: A Japanese word that is used to refer to the belief there are mystical powers that reside within words. Can be translated as "the spirit of language."

Mantra: Also known as *seed mantras* or *bija mantras*, mantras are sounds that resonate with the qualities of their assigned chakras. When they are vocalized, they create a unique vibration that facilitates healing.

Mudra: A symbolic or sacred gesture or pose used to channel life-force energy; they can involve the entire body—such as the poses of a yoga practice—or they can be performed with only the hands and fingers, as is the case with hand mudras during a meditation.

Prana: A Sanskrit term referring to the breath, insofar as it is thought of as a source of life-giving energy.

Qi, **ki**, and **chi:** The life-force energy that animates life, and that is vital to all living beings.

Rei: The Japanese word for "universal."

Reiju: A sacred ceremony during which a student is attuned to the universal *ki* through a connection created between them, their teacher, and the Reiki energy. Directly translated from its original Japanese, it means "spiritual blessing."

Reiji-ho: Translated as "indication of the spirit," this Japanese term refers to the intuition of a Reiki healer and the practice whereby they can open themselves up to divine guidance.

Seishin toitsu: An important Japanese concept found in many practices that is centered around concentration by unifying the body, mind, and spirit.

Shirushi: A Japanese word meaning "mark," "symbol," or "token." Regarding Reiki, it refers to the five symbols that form part of Usui's system of healing.

Tanden: A Japanese word used to refer to the energetic center located right below the navel of the human body; also known as the *hara* or *seika tanden*.

Tenohira: The art of self-healing—also known as self-treatment and hands-on healing—by using the hands to channel energy from the universal *ki* to parts of the body where it is needed.

References

Anderson, E. Z., & Wolk-Weiss, C. (2008). Reiki. In J. E. Deutsch & E. Z. Anderson (Eds.), *Complementary therapies for physical therapy*. Elsevier Inc.

Aulinas, A., & Arendt, J. (2000). Physiology of the pineal gland and melatonin. In K. R. Feingold, B. Anawalt, A. Boyce, G. Chrousos, W. W. de Herder, K. Dungan, A. Grossman, J. M. Hershman, H. J. Hofland, G. Kaltsas, C. Koch, P. Kopp, M. Korbonits, R. McLachlan, J. E. Morley, M. New, J. Purnell, F. Singer, C. A. Stratakis, & D. L. Trence, Eds.), Endotext [Internet].. https://www.ncbi.nlm.nih.gov/books/NBK550972/

Barrow Neurological Institute. (n.d.). *About the Pituitary gland.* Barrow Neurological Institute. https://www.barrowneuro.org/resource/about-the-pituitary-gland/

Bedosky, L. (2022, April 12). *All about Reiki: How this type of energy healing works, and its health benefits.* EverydayHealth. https://www.everydayhealth.com/reiki/

Bhogal, R. S. (2020, January 31). A scientific look at balancing your mind, body, and soul. *DaVinci Laboratories.* https://blog.davincilabs.com/blog/a-scientific-look-at-balancing-your-mind-body-and-soul

Billot, M., Daycard, M., Wood, C., & Tchalla, A. (2019). Reiki therapy for pain, anxiety and quality of life. *BMJ Supportive & Palliative Care*, 2019(9), 434–438.. https://doi.org/10.1136/bmjspcare-2019-001775

Biology Dictionary. (2017, December 8). *Muscle.* Biology Dictionary. https://biologydictionary.net/muscle/

Birchler, K. (n.d.). *Gokai: The five Reiki principles.* Sawah Jikiden Reiki Institute. https://sawah.ch/gokai-reiki-principles.php

Brouhard, R. (2022, November 20). *Understanding the 11 body organ systems.* Verywell Health. https://www.verywellhealth.com/organ-system-1298691

Burden, B., Herron-Marx, S., & Clifford, C. (2005). The increasing use of Reiki as a complementary therapy in specialist palliative care. *International Journal of Palliative Nursing, 11*(5), 248–253. https://doi.org/10.12968/ijpn.2005.11.5.248

Cambridge Dictionary. (n.d.). entrainment. In *Cambridge Dictionary.* Cambridge Dictionary. Retrieved November 15, 2022, from https://dictionary.cambridge.org/dictionary/english/entrainment

Cameron, Y. (2021, October 29). *A beginner's guide to the 7 chakras + how to unblock them.* Mindbodygreen. https://www.mindbodygreen.com/articles/7-chakras-for-beginners

Centre of Excellence. (2018, January 8). *Reiki attunement - the process and the purpose.* https://www.centreofexcellence.com/reiki-attunement-process-purpose/

Cho, A. (2022, February 8). *How to smudge your house to invite positive energy: A Feng Shui practice for clearing your home.* The Spruce. https://www.thespruce.com/how-to-smudge-your-house-1274692

Chowang, O. (2016). *Our pristine mind: A practical guide to unconditional happiness.* Shambhala.

Christiano, D. (2018, September 18). *What's the difference between ligaments and tendons?* Healthline. https://www.healthline.com/health/ligament-vs-tendon

Clarke, G. (2022, May 29). *What are chakra mantras and why should you chant them?* The Yoga Nomads. https://www.theyoganomads.com/chakra-mantras/

Clayton, M. (2012). What is entrainment? Definition and applications in musical research. *Empirical Musicology Review, 7*(1-2), 49–56. https://doi.org/10.18061/1811/52979

Cleveland Clinic. (n.d.-a). *Reiki self-treatment.* https://my.clevelandclinic.org/health/treatments/21080-reiki-self-treatment

Cleveland Clinic. (n.d.-b). *Vagina.* https://my.clevelandclinic.org/health/body/22469-vagina

Cleveland Clinic. (2022a, March 30). *Thalamus.* https://my.clevelandclinic.org/health/body/22652-thalamus

Cleveland Clinic. (2022b, April 25). *Integumentary system.* https://my.clevelandclinic.org/health/body/22827-integumentary-system

Cristian-Vital ii, V. (2015, November 14). Anatomy for Reiki. *Reiki News Magazine.* slideshare. https://www.slideshare.net/CristianVasilescu/anatomy-for-reiki

Deacon, J. (2003a). *Kenyoku ho.* James Deacon's Reiki Pages. https://www.aetw.org/d_kenyoku.htm

Deacon, J. (2003b). *Reiki - Tibetan origins?* James Deacon's Reiki Pages. https://www.aetw.org/reiki_tibetan_origins.htm

Deacon, J. (2003c, April). *The Reiki symbols: The "distant" symbol.* James Deacon's Reiki Pages. https://www.aetw.org/reiki_symbolsD.html

Deacon, J. (2003d, April). *The Reiki symbols: The "mental-emotional healing" symbol.* James Deacon's Reiki Pages. https://www.aetw.org/reiki_symbolsME.html

Deacon, J. (2003e, April). *The Reiki symbols: The "power" symbol.* James Deacon's Reiki Pages. https://www.aetw.org/reiki_symbolsP.html

Deacon, J. (2003f, April). *The Reiki symbols: The Reiki "master" symbol.* James Deacon's Reiki Pages. https://www.aetw.org/reiki_symbolsM.html

Deacon, J. (2003g, May). *Shirushi: The four Usui Reiki symbols.* James Deacon's Reiki Pages. https://www.aetw.org/reiki_symbols.html

Deacon, J. (2005a). *The choku rei trail - Interlinking threads.* James Deacon's Reiki Pages. https://www.aetw.org/reiki_symbolsP_links.htm

Deacon, J. (2005b). *The introduction of the symbols into Reiki.* James Deacon's Reiki Pages. https://www.aetw.org/reiki_symbols2.html

Deacon, J. (2005c). *The Reiki symbols: Choku rei & nao hi.* James Deacon's Reiki Pages. https://www.aetw.org/reiki_symbolsP_naohi.htm

Deacon, J. (2006). *More concerning reiju.* James Deacon's Reiki Pages. https://www.aetw.org/reiki_reiju2.htm

Delgado, J. (2016, September 19). *How we kill children's intuition.* Psychology Spot. https://psychology-spot.com/children-intuition/

Energy Healing Info. (n.d.). *Entrainment and the science of energy healing.* Energy Healing Info.https://www.iahe.com/docs/articles/entrainment-and-the-science-of-energy-healing.pdf

Estrada, J. (2019, September 7). *Reiki? I don't know her... So I had experts break down the energy healing practice.* Well+Good. https://www.wellandgood.com/how-to-do-reiki/

EurekAlert! (2022, November 30). Five precepts of Buddhism may be linked to lower depression risk. *EurekAlert!* https://www.eurekalert.org/news-releases/972288

Fox, F. (2021, December 27). *Hatsurei-ho: What it is & how to do it.* International School of Reiki. https://www.freereikicourse.com/hatsurei-ho/

Fox, F. (2022, January 10). *Reiki techniques in practicing reiju meditation.* International School of Reiki. https://www.freereikicourse.com/reiki-techniques-in-practicing-reiju-meditation/

Fraley, A. (2017, December 1). *Gassho meditation: First pillar of Reiki.* Drops of Yoga. http://dropsofyoga.com/blog/gassho-meditation-first-pillar-reiki/

Franklin, S. (2018, May 7). *Blog: A Reiki guided meditation & the 3 pillars of Reiki.* Inis LaMothe, PsyD. https://groundwaterwellness.com/2018/05/07/blog-3-pillars-of-reiki/

Frazier, K. (2018, July 9). *Engaging in the flow of Reiki through its three pillars.* Karen Frazier. https://www.authorkarenfrazier.com/blog/engaging-in-the-flow-of-reiki-through-its-three-pillars#/

Freitag, V. L., Dalmolin, I. S., Badke, M. R., & Andrade, A. de. (2014). Benefits of Reiki in older individuals with chronic pain. *Texto & Contexto - Enfermagem, 23*(4), 1032–1040. https://doi.org/10.1590/0104-07072014001850013

Gatto, R. (2018, May 31). *What these 5 systems of the body can tell us about organizations.* LinkedIn. https://www.linkedin.com/pulse/what-5-systems-body-can-tell-us-organizations-rex-gatto-ph-d-bcc/

Gilberti, T. C. (2004). Reiki: The re-emergence of an ancient healing art in modern times. *Home Health Care Management & Practice, 16*(6), 480–486. https://doi.org/10.1177/1084822304265847

Harris, N. (2014, October 15). *A new look at the five Reiki principles.* International Association of Reiki Professionals. https://iarp.org/new-look-five-reiki-principles/

Hazama, J. (1987). The characteristics of Japanese Tendai. *Japanese Journal of Religious Studies, 14*(2-3), 101–112. https://doi.org/10.18874/jjrs.14.2-3.1987.101-112

heal+h plus. (2018, May 4). *10 conditions linked to stress.* Mount Elizabeth Hospital. https://beta.mountelizabeth.com.sg/healthplus/article/health-conditions-linked-to-stress

Health Essentials. (2021, August 30). *What is Reiki, and does it really work?* Cleveland Clinic. https://health.clevelandclinic.org/reiki/

Hirsch, L. (2019, June). *Female reproductive system.* KidsHealth. https://kidshealth.org/en/parents/female-reproductive-system.html

Institute for Quality and Efficiency in Health Care. (2016, November 17). *How is body temperature regulated and what is fever?* InformedHealth.org.. https://www.ncbi.nlm.nih.gov/books/NBK279457/

Institute for Quality and Efficiency in Health Care. (2018). How does the thyroid gland work? InformedHealth.org. https://www.ncbi.nlm.nih.gov/books/NBK279388/#:~:text=The%20thyroid%20gland%20is%20a

International Association of Reiki Professionals. (2015, October 15). *Exploring Mikao Usui Reiki teachings: Part 1.* https://iarp.org/exploring-mikao-usui-reiki-teachings-part-1/

International Association of Reiki Professionals. (2017, September 24). *The Reiki attunement: A primer on this spiritual ceremony.* https://iarp.org/the-reiki-attunement-a-primer-on-this-spiritual-ceremony/

International House of Reiki. (2010a, February 19). *Hands-on healing.* https://ihreiki.com/reiki_info/five_elements_of_reiki/hands-on_healing/?v=68caa8201064

International House of Reiki. (2010b, February 19). *Reiju and attunements.* https://ihreiki.com/reiki_info/five_elements_of_reiki/reiju_and_attunements/?v=68caa8201064

International House of Reiki. (2010c, February 19). *Reiki meditations and techniques.* https://ihreiki.com/reiki_info/five_elements_of_reiki/reiki_meditations_and_techniques/?v=68caa8201064

International House of Reiki. (2010d, February 19). *Reiki Precepts.* https://ihreiki.com/reiki_info/five_elements_of_reiki/reiki_precepts/?v=68caa8201064

International House of Reiki. (2010e, February 19). *Reiki symbols and mantras.* https://ihreiki.com/reiki_info/five_elements_of_reiki/reiki_symbols_and_mantras/?v=68caa8201064

International House of Reiki. (2010f, February 20). *Reiki energetic system.* International House of Reiki. https://ihreiki.com/reiki_info/reiki_energetic_system/?v=68caa8201064

International House of Reiki. (2010g, March 4). *Earth energy.* https://ihreiki.com/reiki_info/reiki_energetic_system/earth_energy/?v=68caa8201064

International House of Reiki. (2010h, March 4). *Heavenly energy.* https://ihreiki.com/reiki_info/reiki_energetic_system/heavenly_energy/?v=68caa8201064

International House of Reiki. (2010i, March 27). *Historical Reiki inconsistencies.* https://ihreiki.com/reiki_info/reiki_history/historical_reiki_inconsistencies/?v=68caa8201064

Jacobson, J. D. (2022, October 1). *Uterus.* MedlinePlus. https://medlineplus.gov/ency/imagepages/19263.htm#:~:text=Overview

Japan Reference. (2016, May 13). *Tendai Buddhism.* https://jref.com/articles/tendai-buddhism.290/

Jayne, A. (n.d.). *Gokai: Five principles of Reiki.* Jikiden Reiki with Amanda Jayne. https://www.learnjikidenreiki.com/gokai

Johns Hopkins Medicine. (n.d.). *Adrenal glands.* Johns Hopkins Medicine. Retrieved November 19, 2022, from https://www.hopkinsmedicine.org/health/conditions-and-diseases/adrenal-glands

John Hopkins Medicine. (2020). *The parathyroid glands.* https://www.hopkinsmedicine.org/health/conditions-and-diseases/the-parathyroid-glands

John Hopkins Medicine. (2021). *The digestive process: What is the role of your pancreas in digestion?* https://www.hopkinsmedicine.org/health/conditions-and-diseases/the-digestive-process-what-is-the-role-of-your-pancreas-in-digestion

Judith, A. (2016). *Wheels of life: A user's guide to the chakra system.* Llewellyn Publications.

Jules. (2010, February 10). *Japanese Reiki 2 jyoshin koki-ho. Gassho. Seishin toitsu. Reiki principles. Mokunen.* Jules Blogger. https://jules1961.wordpress.com/2010/02/10/japanese-reiki-techniques-2-jyoshin-koki-ho-gassho-seishin-toitsu-reiki-principles-mokunen/

Kawano, Y. (2011). Spirituality and indigenous knowledges: Study of kototoma and decolonization in the school system. In N. N. Wane, E. L. Manyimo, & E. J. Ritskes (Eds.), *Spirituality, Education & Society* (pp. 97–110). Brill. https://brill.com/display/book/edcoll/9789460916038/BP000008.xml

Kryak, E., & Vitale, A. (2011). Reiki and Iits journey into a hospital setting. *Holistic Nursing Practice, 25*(5), 238–245. https://doi.org/10.1097/hnp.0b013e31822a02ad

Lambrou, D. (2020, May 8). *Important nerves in the body and what they do.* Northeast Spine and Sports Medicine. https://www.northeastspineandsports.com/blog/important-nerves-in-the-body-and-what-they-do/

Langlais, S. (2020, November 20). *A Reiki master on how to prepare for & unwind after a session.* mindbodygreen. https://www.mindbodygreen.com/articles/what-to-do-before-after-your-reiki-session

Liachovitzky. (2020). *Human anatomy and physiology preparatory course.* Libre Texts. https://med.libretexts.org/Bookshelves/Anatomy_and_Physiology/Book%3A_Human_Anatomy_and_Physiology_Preparatory_Course_(Liachovitzky)/05%3A_Higher_Levels_of_Complexity-_Organs_and_Systems/5.01%3A_Organs_and_Systems_of_the_Human_Organism

Locke, L. (2012, January 11). The dangers of Reiki. *Catholic Answers.* https://www.catholic.com/magazine/print-edition/the-dangers-of-reiki

Lotus, G. (n.d.). *Reiki really works: A groundbreaking scientific study.* In *Hub Pages.* https://cdn.elebase.io/dbcc75a2-4b9f-4a0e-8e4b-cfa273624e10/6c766633-0ca4-4d05-bc4d-1f485bed2e9a-reiki_really_works-a_groundbreaking_scientific_study.pdf

Mailoo, V. J. (2002). A brief introduction to Reiki. *British Journal of Therapy and Rehabilitation,* 9(5), 190–193. https://doi.org/134.115.005.047

Mason, S. (2010). *Spiritual healing: What is it? Does it work and does it have a place in modern healthcare?* https://www.rcpsych.ac.uk/docs/default-source/members/sigs/spirituality-spsig/su-mason-spiritual-healing-in-modern-healthcare-x.pdf?sfvrsn=4fc21449_2%20(-%20this%20one%20has%20a%20great%20explanation)

Mayo Clinic. (n.d.). *Gallstones.* Mayo Clinic. Retrieved November 19, 2022, from https://www.mayoclinic.org/diseases-conditions/gallstones/symptoms-causes/syc-20354214

McCartney, F. (n.d.). *Intuitive children.* Academy of Intuition Medicine. Retrieved February 6, 2023, from https://intuitionmedicine.org/intuitive-children/

McManus, D. E. (2017). Reiki is better than placebo and has broad potential as a complementary health therapy. *Journal of Evidence-Based Complementary & Alternative Medicine, 22*(4), 1051–1057. https://doi.org/10.1177/2156587217728644

Medline Plus Medical Encyclopedia. (n.d.). *Hypothalamus.* A.D.A.M., Inc. Retrieved November 19, 2022, from https://medlineplus.gov/ency/article/002380.htm#:~:text=The%20hypothalamus%20is%20an%20area

Melton, J. (2014, November 16). *Guided meditation after a Reiki attunement.* Reiki Rays. https://reikirays.com/16395/guided-meditation-for-after-a-reiki-attunement/

Merriam-Webster. (n.d.-a). Attune. In *Merriam-Webster.com dictionary.* Retrieved February 6, 2023, from https://www.merriam-webster.com/dictionary/attune

Merriam-Webster. (n.d.-b). Symbol. In *Merriam-Webster.com dictionary.* Retrieved November 23, 2022, from https://www.merriam-webster.com/dictionary/symbol

Miles, P. (2011, January 1). *How to practice Reiki self-treatment.* Reiki Medicine & Self Care. https://reikiinmedicine.org/daily-practice/how-to-practice-reiki-self-treatment/

Mind Tools. (2019). *Using affirmations: Harnessing positive thinking.* https://www.mindtools.com/pages/article/affirmations.htm

Morero, J. A. P., Pereira, S. de S., Esteves, R. B., & Cardoso, L. (2021). Effects of Reiki on mental health care: A systematic review. *Holistic Nursing Practice, 35*(4), 191–198. https://doi.org/10.1097/hnp.0000000000000456

National Institute of Diabetes and Digestive and Kidney Diseases. (2018, June). *Your kidneys & how they work.* https://www.niddk.nih.gov/health-information/kidney-disease/kidneys-how-they-work

Nicole, A. (2020). *Gassho meditation.* Insight Timer. https://insighttimer.com/spiritofnorton/guided-meditations/gassho-meditation-12mins

Nield-Anderson, L., & Ameling, A. (2000). The empowering nature of Reiki as a complementary therapy. *Holistic Nursing Practice, 14*(3), 21–29. https://journals.lww.com/hnpjournal/Abstract/2000/04000/The_Empowering_Nature_of_Reiki_as_a_Complementary.6.aspx

Ohlenkamp, N. (n.d.). *Seishin toitsu: Concentration in Judo training.* Judo Info. https://judoinfo.com/concentration/

Parikh, D. (2018, February 6). *Reiki to heal OCD.* Reiki Rays. https://reikirays.com/40490/reiki-heal-ocd/

Patel, K. (2022, July 26). *Reiki healing for beginners.* Goop. https://goop.com/wellness/spirituality/reiki-for-beginners/

Patel, K. J. (2017, August 9). *How to use Reiki to calm anxiety.* mindbodygreen. https://www.mindbodygreen.com/articles/reiki-healing-for-anxiety

Phillips, C. (2021, December 28). *What is reiji-ho, and how to do it?* International School of Reiki. https://www.freereikicourse.com/reiji-ho/

Pikörn, I. (2020, June 1). *What prana is and how to feel it.* Insight Timer Blog. https://insighttimer.com/blog/what-is-prana/

Powell, C. (2012, August 11). *Mikao Usui, Reiki founder.* Reiki, Medicine & Self Care. https://reikiinmedicine.org/popular/mikao-usui-reiki-healing/

Powers, L. (2017, August 24). *Did Dr. Usui use hand positions with Reiki?* Online Reiki with Lisa Powers. https://onlinereiki-course.com/dr-usui-use-hand-positions-reiki/

Price, N. J. (2019a, September 29). Universal symbols: The calming sei he ki. *Kindred Spirit Magazine.* https://kindredspirit.co.uk/2019/09/29/universal-symbols-the-calming-sei-he-ki/

Price, N. J. (2019b, October 27). Universal symbols: The grounding fire symbol raku. *Kindred Spirit Magazine.* https://kindred-spirit.co.uk/2019/10/27/universal-symbols-the-grounding-fire-symbol-raku/

Rand, W. (2012, September 1). *Giving an advanced Reiki session.* The International Center for Reiki Training. https://www.reiki.org/articles/giving-advanced-reiki-session

Rand, W. (2014, March 10). *Reiki before Usui.* The International Center for Reiki Training. https://www.reiki.org/articles/reiki-usui

Rand, W. L. (2001, December 19). *Strengthen your Reiki energy.* The International Center for Reiki Training. https://www.reiki.org/articles/strengthen-your-reiki-energy

Rand, W. L. (2004, January 1). *Kenyoku, dry bathing.* The International Center for Reiki Training. https://www.reiki.org/articles/kenyoku-dry-bathing

Rand, W. L. (2014a). *An evidence based history of Reiki: A selection of articles from Reiki News Magazine.* International Center For Reiki Training.

Rand, W. L. (2014b, October 15). *What is the history of Reiki?* The International Center for Reiki Training. https://www.reiki.org/faqs/what-history-reiki

Rapport, L. (2022, September 12). *Cancer cases rising "dramatically" in adults under 50.* Everyday Health. https://www.everyday-health.com/cancer/cancer-cases-rising-dramatically-in-adults-under-fifty/

Rataic, T. (2017, June 13). *How to do gassho meditation.* The Reiki Guide. https://thereikiguide.com/gassho-meditation/

Reiki Info. (n.d.). *Dai ko myo - The great shining light.* https://www.reiki.info/World/English/Reiki-Symbols/Dai-Ko-Myo-Reiki-Master-Symbol.htm

Reiki Therapy Resources. (2018, March 10). *Using Reiki to deal with anger.* https://www.reikitherapyresources.com/reiki-anger/

ReikiJane. (2020, July 27). *Using your intuition with Reiki - Reiji-ho: Treating humans and horses*. Reiki Jane. https://www.reikijane.co.uk/using-your-intuition-with-reiki-reiji-ho-treating-humans-and-horses-2/

Reshel, A. (2016, June 15). *The Tibetan science of healing*. Uplift. https://uplift.love/the-tibetan-science-of-healing/

Reville, W. (2011, February 17). The pseudoscience of creating beautiful (or ugly) water. *The Irish Times*. https://www.irishtimes.com/news/science/the-pseudoscience-of-creating-beautiful-or-ugly-water-1.574583

Rhys, D. (2020a, August 25). *Raku symbol - meaning and importance*. Symbol Sage. https://symbolsage.com/raku-symbol-meaning-significance/

Rhys, D. (2020b, August 26). *Hon sha ze shon nen - Meaning and uses of this Reiki symbol*. Symbol Sage. https://symbolsage.com/hon-sha-ze-sho-nen-reiki-explained/

Robertson, A. (n.d.). *Raku Kei Reiki: The way of the Fire Dragon*. Reiki Online. https://reikionline.info/products/raku-kei-reiki-the-way-of-the-fire-dragon

Rosenbaum, L. (2020, July 31). *Reiki 101: Everything you need to know about this energy healing practice*. Yoga Journal. https://www.yogajournal.com/lifestyle/reiki-101/

Sadhguru. (2015). *Body: The greatest gadget*. Jaico Publishing House.

Saling, J. (2021, August 23). *Pain types and classifications*. WebMD. https://www.webmd.com/pain-management/guide/pain-types-and-classifications

Shah, P. (2018, August 30). *How reiju transformed my practice*. Reiki Rays. https://reikirays.com/43684/how-reiju-transformed-my-practice/

Shah, P. (2020, October 6). *I'm a Reiki master, and here's how I practice self-healing on a regular basis*. Well+Good. https://www.wellandgood.com/reiki-self-healing/

Shah, P. (2021, December 15). *Try this: A Reiki meditation to balance earthly and heavenly energies*. Chopra. https://chopra.com/articles/try-this-a-reiki-meditation-to-balance-earthly-heavenly-energies

Shah, P. (2022, August 24). *The essential guide to Reiki attunements: Levels 1, 2 and 3*. Parita Shah Healing. https://paritashahhealing.com/reiki-attunements/

Shevchuk, D. (2011, November 11). Reiji-ho: The Reiki prayer. *Find Your Way Home Holistic Healing*. https://findyourwayhome.ca/140/reiji-ho-the-reiki-prayer/

Shirleytwofeathers. (2019, February 20). *Reiji-ho and chiryo*. Twofeathers Reiki. https://shirleytwofeathers.com/The_Blog/twofeathersreiki/reiji-ho-and-chiryo/

Shrivastava, A. (2022, January 18). *Reiki sleep technique*. Reiki Rays. https://reikirays.com/91740/reiki-sleep-technique/

SōhōT. (1988). *The unfettered mind: Writings of the Zen master to the sword master* (W. S. Wilson, Trans.). Kodansha. (Original work published 1986)

Stelter, G. (2016, October 4). *A beginner's guide to the 7 chakras and their meanings*. Healthline. https://www.healthline.com/health/fitness-exercise/7-chakras#The-takeaway

Steine, B., & Stiene, F. (2005). *The Japanese art of Reiki*. O Books.

Steine, B., & Stiene, F. (2008, July 14). *Are the Reiki precepts affirmations?* International House of Reiki. https://ihreiki.com/blog/are_the_reiki_precepts_affirmations/?v=68caa8201064

Steine, B., & Steine, F. (2011, September 9). *The energetic system*. International House of Reiki. https://ihreiki.com/blog/the_energetic_system/?v=68caa8201064

Steine, F. (2015a, February 18). *Reiju - giving and receiving, together as one*. International House of Reiki. https://ihreiki.com/blog/reiju_-_giving_and_receiving_together_as_one/?v=68caa8201064

Steine, F. (2015b, August 11). *The roots of the system of Reiki*. International House of Reiki. https://ihreiki.com/blog/the_roots_of_the_system_of_reiki/?v=68caa8201064

Steine, F. (2016, November 10). *Insights into jōshin kokyū hō*. International House of Reiki. https://ihreiki.com/blog/insights_into_jshin_kokyuu_h/?v=68caa8201064

Streich, M. (2009). The story of Dr. Chujiro Hayashi. *Reiki News Magazine*, 40–53. https://www.reiki.org/sites/default/files/StoryOfChujiroHayashi.pdf

Sunrise Reiki Centre. (2015, June 15). *Reiki lineages & systems*. https://sunrisereikicentre.com/about-reiki/reiki-lineages-systems/

Suttkus, L., & Suttkus, J. (2011). *Reiju Reiki*. Ascension Reiki. https://www.ascensionreiki.com/ReijuReiki.html

Takase, E. (1999, January). *Seishintoitsu*. Takase Studios. https://www.takase.com/library/seishintouitsu-concentration-of-mind/

TanDen Concepts. (n.d.). *What is TanDen?* http://www.tandenconcepts.com/blog/?page_id=576

TaosHerbCo. (n.d.). *About sacred herbs and smudging ceremonies*. TaosHerbCo. https://www.taosherb.com/store/sacred-herbs.html

Thapa, P., & Farber, D. L. (2019). The role of the thymus in the immune response. *Thorac Surg Clin.*, *29*(2), 123–131. https://doi.org/10.1016/j.thorsurg.2018.12.001

Thaut, M. H. (2015). The discovery of human auditory–motor entrainment and its role in the development of neurologic music therapy. *Progress in Brain Research*, *217*(2015), 253–266. https://doi.org/10.1016/bs.pbr.2014.11.030

The International Center for Reiki Training. (2015a, March 17). *Anatomy for Reiki - English*. https://www.reiki.org/resources/anatomy-reiki-english

The International Center for Reiki Training. (2015b, September 14). *Learn the Usui principles in Japanese*. https://www.reiki.org/learn-usui-principles-japanese

The Reiki Guild. (n.d.). *A history of reiki*. https://www.thereikiguild.co.uk/topics/13-history-of-reiki

University of Michigan Health. (2022). *Parathyroid disorders*. Michigan Medicine. https://www.uofmhealth.org/conditions-treatments/endocrinology-diabetes-and-metabolism/parathyroid-disorders

University of Minnesota. (n.d.). *Where does Reiki come from?* University of Minnesota.https://www.takingcharge.csh.umn.edu/where-reiki-from

Urdinlaiz, D. (2021, November 12). *Reiki symbols and their powerful meanings*. Thought Catalog. https://thoughtcatalog.com/daniella-urdinlaiz/2021/11/reiki-symbols/

vanderVaart, S., Gijsen, V. M. G. J., de Wildt, S. N., & Koren, G. (2009). A systematic review of the therapeutic effects of Reiki. *The Journal of Alternative and Complementary Medicine*, *15*(11), 1157–1169. https://doi.org/10.1089/acm.2009.0036

Vitale, A. (2007). An integrative review or Reiki touch therapy research. *Holistic Nursing Practice*, *21*(4), 167–179. https://doi.org/10.1097/01.hnp.0000280927.83506.f6

Vorvick, L. J. (2020, August 13). *Tendon vs. ligament*. MedlinePlus. https://medlineplus.gov/ency/imagepages/19089.htm

Weingus, L. (2018, May 8). *Reiki symbols & their meanings: Everything you need to know*. Mindbodygreen. https://www.mindbodygreen.com/articles/reiki-symbols-meanings

Wilson, M., & Cook, P. F. (2016). Rhythmic entrainment: Why humans want to, fireflies can't help it, pet birds try, and sea lions have to be bribed. *Psychonomic Bulletin & Review*, *23*(6), 1647–1659. https://doi.org/10.3758/s13423-016-1013-x

WordHippo. (2022). *What does 印 (Shirushi) mean in Japanese?* https://www.wordhippo.com/what-is/the-meaning-of/japanese-word-50c9aa8612bc8594dc095ff7aabff3410fecc718.html

World Health Organization. (2022, June 8). *Mental disorders*. https://www.who.int/news-room/fact-sheets/detail/mental-disorders

Yasuka. (2021, June 23). *Understanding kanji and kana*. KCP International. https://www.kcpinternational.com/2021/06/15398/

Yogapedia. (n.d.). *Definition - what does chakra mantra mean?*https://www.yogapedia.com/definition/11152/chakra-mantra

Yogapedia. (2020, September 10). *Definition - what does mudra mean?* https://www.yogapedia.com/definition/5027/mudra

Zins, S., Hooke, M. C., & Gross, C. R. (2018). Reiki for pain during hemodialysis: A feasibility and instrument evaluation study. *Journal of Holistic Nursing*, *37*(2), 148–162. https://doi.org/10.1177/0898010118797195

Images

Clker-Free-Vector-Images. (2012, April 24). *Digestive system human digestion labelled* [Image]. Pixabay. https://pixabay.com/vectors/digestive-system-human-digestion-41529/

THE 7 PILLARS OF CRYSTAL HEALING

63 Techniques & Strategies to **Transform** Your Health With the **Power of Stone Magic.** Have a More Balanced Life by Protecting Your Energy. Gem Remedies for 50+ Symptoms

MONIQUE WAGNER

Table of Contents

Introduction

If you're like most spiritual people, you've probably felt a strong connection between your mind, body, and the world around you. You're not the only one. Many other people throughout history have noticed this. What you are feeling is the inherent interconnectedness of the universe and everything in it. Forces we cannot even fathom are at work in our world, shaping our every move and thought. These are not scary or chaotic forces, though. Some might be, but most work to bring the universe into balance; restoring the inherent harmony at the core of our world is their mission. If we can harness these forces, or at least understand them, then we can start building a more connected and balanced life that is as in sync with the universe as possible.

You might find that this feeling waxes or wanes during particularly difficult phases of your life. This is your natural forces attempting to realign themselves during a transition. On one hand, trials in your life might cause you to want to turn away from the universe and its forces. On the other hand, they might want you to turn toward them more than ever. This is the right path. When dealing with the powerful forces of the universe, we want to be as much on their side as possible, working in tandem with them rather than against them. There is a lot to be gained from harnessing the universe's power, especially during difficult periods of your life. Connecting with these powers can help us understand what the universe might be trying to tell us through our hard times and will help us manifest the kind of life we want instead. If you are struggling, feeling like you just can't get ahead in the world no matter how hard you try, you should know that there are ways to make the universe work for you instead of the other way around.

So, what are these mysterious methods for learning about and manipulating the universe? Well, there are learning methods, like Tarot and astrology, which help you chart the course of your life and understand where your destiny and temperament come from. But if you want to have control over your life through mystical means, then crystals are the best way to go about that. Crystals and crystal healing have been around for literally thousands of years. They began in Ancient India and have continued to grow and evolve in their practice over time, eventually culminating in the modern practice we know today. Crystals all have unique mineral properties that can help link us with spiritual forces and attempt to guide those forces to help us. Crystals can aid in a number of life's problems, helping you with almost any facet of life from money to relationships to career goals. Making a serious change to your life by using crystals is possible and has been done throughout all of human history, making it a tried and true practice.

In this book, I will share with you the seven basic pillars of crystals and crystal healing. We will look at each of the fundamental qualities of crystals to help you get started on your crystal journey. Over the course of this book, you will learn how forces like vibrations can shape you, the people around you, and the universe as a whole. You will find 63 techniques, tips, and strategies to help you transform your health and find inner peace. These techniques, tips, and strategies are peppered throughout the entire book. And it's intentionally designed this way to serve as your guide along each step of the process.

You will learn to harness these vibrations with crystals. I will also teach you about the many different kinds of crystals, what they do, and the effects they can have on different areas of your life. There are hundreds of different kinds of crystals and a myriad of different ways you can use each of them, so the world of crystal practice is vast and anything but simple. After reading this book, you should have a good idea of how to choose the right crystals to achieve the results you are looking for in your life.

There was a time in my life when I felt lost and out of control. I felt that there were forces flying around me that were wreaking havoc in my life, yet I didn't know how to tame them. I was inspired by my Scandinavian neo-pagan roots to look into different spiritual practices to try and solve these deep problems I was grappling with in my life. I did my research and came to crystal healing. The more I learned about crystals, the more I realized that they could help me. I read up on many different kinds and began incorporating them into my everyday life, using them to correct a negative wavelength in my life or to manifest the things I had secretly dreamed of but was always too afraid to pursue. To my delight, I began to see amazing results. I am proud to say that I am no longer a sufferer of burnout and now feel that I have truly realigned myself through crystal healing to be the best person that I can possibly be. By writing this book, I want to help you discover the power of crystals and learn how to implement them to improve your life as I have improved mine.

This book takes a powerful but practical approach to crystal healing. I will be going through the seven pillars in a linear fashion so that you can ease into the process of crystal healing little by little. The first pillar will deal with the fundamentals of crystals. This is the section where I will give you an overview of the history of crystals as well as some of their most important applications and cross sections. Pillar 2 is where I will start to get into the practical aspects of crystals. Here, I will give you crucial information on which crystals you should buy and where you can buy them as well as some important classifications within the crystal family. In the third pillar, I will start to talk about some of the applications crystals can have in your life. In this section, we look at how you can use crystals and what they can help you with. After that, in the fourth pillar, we will step back and I'll guide you on how to prepare for a crystal session. This involves priming your crystals for practice and taking good care of them. Along the same lines, the fifth pillar will deal with storing and caring for your crystals, especially when you are not actively using them. The magic doesn't go away when you do, so you have to be very careful with dormant crystals and where and how you store them. In Pillar 6, I will give you a list of some of the most common types of crystals and how they can be used. Here, you will get an at-a-glance look at many different types to decide which ones you want to use for your own practice. And finally, in Pillar 7 we will deal specifically with the healing aspect of crystals, and I will show you how to use them to promote healing in your life and those of others. Through these seven pillars, you will learn the ins and outs of crystal healing, gaining new knowledge of a practice that can have a profound effect on your life and your relationship with the universe.

Pillar 1: Fundamentals

Crystal healing is for everybody. It is one of the most common and ancient spiritual practices in the world, but what is it exactly, and how can we use it? You are probably curious about all the different things crystals can do as well as how they connect to other spiritual practices. In this pillar, I will be giving you a basic breakdown of crystals and all the things they can do. First, in Chapter 1, we will look at the definition and origins of crystal healing. This is the chapter where I will really lay down the foundation of what we call crystals. Then, in Chapter 2, we will examine the relationship between crystals and energy, investigating how crystals carry energy and what that energy might entail. Following that, Chapter 3 will deal with the relationship between crystals and chakras, another important spiritual practice that also originated in Ancient India. Chakras are very important to the energy and alignment of the body, so they have a very close connection to crystals. Finally, in Chapter 4 the last fundamental we will be examining is the connection between crystals and auras, which are also very important to current and ancient spiritual practices. Through these four chapters, I will give you a clear explanation of the basics of crystals so you can then move forward with acquiring them for yourself.

Chapter 1:
What Is Crystal Healing?

Essentially, the process of crystal healing is to utilize the energy of certain crystals in order to have an effect on the body. Crystal healers and users believe that each crystal has a unique set of powers that are stored deep in its geological core. These crystals naturally hold this power but can be used by people to channel that power toward all sorts of things. You can thus select certain crystals based on their properties and attempt to channel them into the kind of healing you want to practice. This is the basic format for crystal healing, but the actual practice is much wider and deeper. Since crystal healing has been practiced for much of human history all over the globe and still continues strongly to this day, there are many different schools of thought and cultural practices that use different methods of crystal healing simultaneously. There are also many different aspects of crystal healing, even within certain practices. You can wear crystals on your body, use them in tandem with meditation or massage, or incorporate them into certain rituals. Crystals can also be used in medicinal practices, psychological healing, and to help repair relationships. In this chapter, we will look at some of the fundamental aspects of crystal healing, helping you to understand where crystals came from, what they can do, and how you can use them in your spiritual practice.

History of Crystal Healing

Crystals have a rich history stretching back at least 6,000 years. It's hard to pin down exactly where the use of crystals started because there were simultaneous origins all over the world; however, we will focus on the three main traditions that got crystals going: Native American, South Asian, and European. These three cultures form the backbone of modern crystal practice, having each developed core concepts and distinct practices around the concept of crystal healing. In this section, I will give you a brief overview of how each of these cultures formed their understanding of crystal power.

Native American Crystal Practice

In America, crystal healing was practiced in particular by the Cherokee and Apache nations. The traditions were very standardized within these cultures and were taught explicitly through generations using a consistent methodology, yet they also evolved over time. Cherokee and Apache practices emphasize the core concepts of meditation and respect. These two aspects of crystal healing show great weight given to the power of crystals, emphasizing their evident importance. When handling crystals, according to the Cherokee and Apache nations, you must think about channeling your desires very carefully and clearly and treat them as though they are extremely powerful objects by showing them great respect. Looking at this practice, we can see where our current concepts around clarity of mind and respect for crystals come from.

South Asian Crystal Practice

On the Indian subcontinent, a crystal tradition was also brewing. In this part of the world, crystals were invariably tied to their main religion, Hinduism. Hinduism is one of the oldest currently practiced religions and is still the dominant official religion of India. In Hindu texts, called the Vedas, crystals came from the body of the demon Vala, thus harnessing his power within their materiality. This perspective on crystals emphasizes their intense power, being literally divine in their makeup, as well as their potential for evil. If you do not channel your crystals properly, they have the potential to bring chaos and destruction. All the more reason to treat your crystals with care and respect.

European Crystal Practice

In Europe, many pre-Christian cultures developed a crystal practice as well. Britain in particular has a rich history with crystals. In Western crystal practice, crystals are very closely related to the stars, particularly in astrology. Crystals were assigned meaning based on their associations with astrological signs, thus linking them with the mystery and power of the heavens. One unique aspect of European crystal practice is that, because of their link with natal astrology, people had certain crystals that they were particularly connected with. Your sun sign in astrology might relate to a certain crystal, which means that you would use that type of crystal if you were sick or needed help in some way. This system of having "patron crystals" is a particularly European invention, which later came to relate to the concept of patron saints. In this practice, we can see how individual identity and astrology were closely related to crystal practice.

Benefits of Crystals

So, now that you understand what crystals are and where they come from, you probably want to know what they can actually do for you. There are many ways crystals can benefit you. The benefits of crystals are generally divided into three main groups: physical health, mental health, and manifestation. Here, we will give you a short description of these three categories of crystal benefits and how you can harness them.

Physical Health

There are many people who feel left behind by the modern medical world. Either because they have a chronic illness that they just can't get a diagnosis for, or maybe because they're a woman and feel that medical science doesn't care about the female body, or even simply because it is prohibitively expensive. For these reasons, many people are turning to alternative forms of medicine to feel more heard and to seek additional treatments not traditionally practiced by Western doctors. Though you should never take your health care completely into your own hands, especially if you have a life-threatening disease like cancer, you can supplement your existing medical treatment with crystals. For those with less life-threatening ailments, crystals are suitable. Crystals can also be a great form of alternative medicine for illnesses that don't have discovered causes or treatments within the medical community, such as migraines or chronic fatigue. Many people who experience these conditions feel left behind by the medical world and have found a lot of healing using crystal practices. They can help to align your energies and soothe the body to harness its natural immune responses, among other things. If you are suffering in a way that doctors just don't seem to be able to cure, then it's worth giving crystals a try.

Mental Health

An even more complicated component of the medical world is mental health care. Many people feel at the end of their rope when it comes to getting care for their mental health. They feel that they are dismissed, pigeonholed by rigid diagnoses, or overly medicated without much concern for individual needs. Crystals will help you ground yourself and forge a stronger connection with the earth and the universe around you, which can do wonders for your mental health. If you feel like your mental health issues are not being adequately addressed with modern psychology and nothing seems to work, then crystals can be a great thing to try.

Manifestation

Finally, you can use crystals even if you are not particularly suffering or if your problems are more external. Because crystals have such a strong power and connection to the universe, you can use them to make things happen outside your own body. Many people use crystals to help them with things like their careers, relationships, family, and even creativity. If you are looking for some answers that lie outside of yourself—in your destiny or your relationships with other people or the world at large—then you can definitely use crystals to try and bring a little more order to your life.

Difference Between Crystals and Gems

You might be wondering whether crystals are always the same as gems. After all, we use crystals in non-spiritualist jewelry on occasion alongside gems, so it can be hard sometimes for people to tell the difference between them. While there is some overlap between gems and crystals, they are not necessarily the same. Gems are mainly categorized by their purity. When you see something like a sapphire or diamond, they are usually ones that have been found to have a high purity of chemical makeup and thus will be cut and sold for value. Crystals, on the other hand, are not valued or even categorized by purity, but instead by their chemical shape. There is no inherently more "pure" crystal because they are just categorized by their material properties. A crystal also doesn't need to be shiny or reflective like a gem. Many crystals resemble rocks, completely opaque and hard. The final distinction, of course, is that crystals have spiritual properties and are used for healing purposes. Gems are not necessarily used for this purpose, so I won't be talking about them in this book. Now that you are familiar with the basic essentials of crystal healing, we can start to look at some of the things crystals interact with. In the next three chapters, we will be exploring the relationships crystals have with things like life energy, chakras, and auras.

Chapter 2:
Crystals and Energy

In the world of crystals, there are several cornerstone concepts at the core of the practice, one of which is the concept of energy. In crystal theology, each crystal has a particular energy that will help you harness that particular aspect of crystal power. When crystal healers are selecting a crystal, they will be using these energy concepts in order to choose which crystal is right for the occasion. If you choose the wrong crystal for your practice, then you will likely have a much harder time attaining the results you want. For this reason, you should educate yourself well on the concepts of crystal energy before you attempt your crystal practice. In this chapter, we will look at a few different aspects and applications of crystal energy to further your understanding of how crystals interact with our inherent spiritual sides.

Body Energy

The concept of crystal energy would not be complete if we did not address the energies that humans give off as well. In fact, everything in the universe is vibrating at a particular frequency. All these frequencies have to do with forces like heat, electricity, and chemical makeup. All humans vibrate at a particular frequency which denotes their specific energy. Have you ever noticed that certain people have "higher" energies than others or that certain people are more exhausting to be around than others? This is directly related to that person's energy. Just as crystals do, every person has their own particular energy that they give off. Moreover, humans also have different sections of our bodies that give off different frequencies than others. Many things might affect our energies in different parts of our bodies, such as relationships, stress, or even health problems.

When we are experiencing these misalignments in our body's energy, we can use crystals to rearrange our energies and try to bring them to a more balanced state. This is why people use crystals to heal their bodies and minds through energy and vibrations. So, for example, if you are vibrating at a lower frequency because of something in your life, you can use high-vibration crystals in order to bring balance back into your body through osmosis. Similarly, you can use crystals with lower vibrations to absorb some of the higher energy in your body and help you to get your energies lowered again. This is a fairly basic explanation with simply positive and negative values, but it gets the general concept across. In reality, there is a whole rainbow of energies that your body can be experiencing, with specialized crystals acting as a balancing agent for all your body's misalignments. In short, crystals help to regulate your energy with their own.

Stone Vibrations and Power

The idea that crystals vibrate is not a purely spiritual concept. In fact, crystal vibrations are a well-documented scientific phenomenon. In fact, crystal vibrations actually have the power to run small mechanical devices. For example, quartz has been used to power watches since the late 1960s. Because quartz has such a reliable and regular vibration pattern, watchmakers can channel the battery through it. This creates an extremely steady beat that helps the watch to keep time. As we can see from this example, quartz and other crystals create a very real physical energy field, and if this energy can be used to regulate mechanical devices, it can certainly be used to regulate people's energies. This is the real science behind the spiritual vibration changes that many people report when they use crystals in their healing practices. So, next time someone tells you crystals are all mumbo jumbo, you can ask them what's powering their watch!

Chi

Many assert that the idea of crystal energy has roots in the Chinese concept of life energy, or Chi. Chi is essentially the core energy of your body, your true self, or your deepest alignment. All the aspects of your mind and body flow back into your Chi energy. The things you eat, how you move your body, the people you interact with, and the practices you choose to engage in all feed into your overall Chi. So, if you are not living a happy or healthy life, your Chi will reflect this. To take proper care of your Chi, you must first take proper care of yourself. In return, your Chi creates your overall identity and helps to center your sense of self. Your Chi also connects you with the universe at large, which represents a mass or higher Chi. In a sense, the universe's Chi flows through all of us, taking individual forms but always flowing back into the same pool.

The core concept of Chi is the distinction between the formed and the formless. The formed world is the physical world, which consists of your physical body, the earth, and the people around you. These are the things we can touch, see, and feel. All of these things have a formless quality to them, even seemingly dead things like rocks, but the world of the formed only deals with the physical properties of everything. The world of the formless is the spiritual reality. It cannot be seen, heard, or perceived by the senses in any way, but it is deeply felt by everyone and everything on earth. You will not meet a person, even the staunchest atheist, who has not felt some sort of higher connection at some point in their life, whether they call it God, energy, or even just love between people. This formless world is clearly mapped onto the formed world, but the degree of their connection is paramount. These two worlds are distinct from one another, but we must find connections between them.

So, how does this relate to crystals? Well, in the world of Chi, crystals intend to form a strong connection between the formed and formless worlds. When you use crystals, you are helping to reconnect with your inner Chi energy and draw a clear connection between the formed world of your body and the formless world of your spiritual mind. When these things are in alignment, you will be in a much happier and healthier state. With crystal healing, you can create this connection, centralizing all your energies and drawing your mind and body closer than ever.

Chapter 3:
Crystals and Chakras

Another aspect of the energy of crystals is chakras. We discussed chakras briefly when we mentioned the different energies in different parts of your body. Chakras are essentially a framework by which we can categorize our bodies according to energies. It is similar to the ideas in Chi but breaks down the energies into distinctive parts. Chakras are just as responsible for modern thought around crystal healing and form a major aspect of current crystal practice. In this chapter, I will lead you through the main concepts surrounding chakras and how you can use them to enhance your crystal practice.

What Are the Seven Chakras?

As we have mentioned, unlike Chi, there are actually multiple chakras in your body; in fact, there are seven, all responsible for a different type of energy within your body. This system identifies different key points throughout your body that can be targeted for a healing practice. When you use the chakras to heal yourself, you will be targeting one of these key areas. Each area corresponds to a different aspect of your life or potential ailment. By identifying these different areas and the part of the body with which they connect, you can construct a much more targeted spiritual healing process. In this section, I will outline the seven chakras and explain what they are, how they relate to your life and body, and how they can be used for healing.

Root Chakra

The first chakra we will be looking at is your root chakra, which is located at the lowest point in your body's core: the base of the spine. This is considered the root of your body because the entire nervous system derives from the spine. It is also the part we sit on, making it our connection to the ground below us, or our roots. This chakra connects us to the earth, forming our bonds with the ground beneath our feet and keeping us centered in reality. The root chakra is associated with the color red, indicating the blood and life force that are so central to this chakra's theme.

As with most spiritual ideas, such as astrological signs and tarot cards, all chakras have good and bad manifestations. Rather, there is a condition where this chakra is not aligned and a condition where it is. When your root chakra is misaligned, this translates to your sense of security and groundedness. Physical symptoms of a misaligned root chakra can be constipation, arthritis, or colon issues. Emotional symptoms can be anxiety about your financial or living situation and a general feeling of being lost and not knowing your place in the world. When your root chakra is aligned, you should be feeling a strong sense of control over your life and a connectedness to the world around you. Opening up this chakra and keeping it aligned is essential to maintaining your sense of self and identity from which all the other aspects of your personality will spring.

Sacral Chakra

The sacral chakra is located in the groins. This chakra governs the realms of sexuality, creativity, and self-esteem. These might seem like dissonant ideas, but they are actually closely related. For many people, the energy associated with their libido is strongly connected to their creative energy. The desire to create things, impact others, and connect are all things that apply to both creative pursuits and sexuality. Likewise, self-esteem is also related to both of these realms. Creative expression and sexuality are both very intimate topics where people show a side of themselves that they don't typically display for the whole world. You are showing a lot of vulnerability in these pursuits, and thus rejection can hurt all the more. For this reason, many people's self-esteem is firmly connected to their creative talents and sexual performance. You really can't understate the power these things have. The sacral chakra's color is orange, representing the intensity of its subject matter.

When your sacral chakra is misaligned, this can lead to issues with the associated organs. Physical symptoms might include chronic urinary tract infections, lower back pain, and sexual impotence. Emotional symptoms might include sexual repression, anxiety, or creative blocks. When your sacral chakra is blocked, you will find that these areas of your life feel like something is stuck, unable to get out. This can be a very frustrating chakra to have blocked since it governs over areas that you might feel shame around. For this reason, it can be hard to get help when this chakra is out of alignment. When your sacral chakra is aligned, though, you will experience a free flow of creative and sexual ideas. You will be able to perform well in both of these areas and feel a strong sense of self-esteem as a result. Keeping this chakra aligned is central to your sense of confidence in yourself and your abilities.

Solar Plexus Chakra

Moving upward on the body, you come to the solar plexus chakra. This chakra is located in the stomach or upper abdomen. As such, it rules things like hunger and basic needs as well as confidence and self-esteem. While the sacral chakra deals with self-esteem as related to more intimate settings, the solar plexus chakra deals with self-esteem as related to more public settings. So, while your sacral chakra might deal with your insecurities in close relationships or in the bedroom, the solar plexus chakra deals with insecurities around your body image, larger friendship groups, and things like public speaking. You'll notice a trend that the higher we move up the body, the more outward we begin to look. The first few chakras are in relation to the self, but as we approach the halfway point—the heart chakra—we begin to look more outward. The solar plexus chakra's color is yellow, and it deals with more social insecurities than the sacral chakra.

When the solar plexus chakra is misaligned or blocked, then the areas of life described above will become challenging. Physical symptoms will usually take the form of digestive issues, such as ulcers or heartburn. You might also have a lot of sensitivity to certain foods, with your stomach not being able to handle very much. In terms of psychological symptoms, you will likely suffer from a lot of confidence issues around how you are perceived. Body image issues leading to eating disorders are a common manifestation of a misaligned solar plexus chakra. For those who find their solar plexus chakra to be blocked, there might also be issues around power or feeling powerless. Therefore, if this chakra is aligned, you will likely be a very confident and sociable person. Moving forward from the confidence and groundedness of the root and sacral chakras, which are inner confidence, those with a free-flowing solar plexus chakra will also feel comfortable sharing these things with the world. They will feel like they can freely express who they are and not fear judgment of their words or appearance.

Heart Chakra

As the center chakra on the list, the heart chakra occupies a very important place. This chakra is the transition from the inner world to the outer world, bridging the connection between the self and others. It's no coincidence, then, that the facets of life this chakra deals with are love and relationships. The heart chakra is located exactly where you would think: in the middle of the chest. In yoga, this chakra is very important as the body's center, with yoga instructors often returning to this position frequently throughout the practice to re-center the body. As a transitional chakra, the heart chakra takes up a very important position on this list. It represents the crossroads between many things: self and other, inside and out, upper and lower chakras, and individualism and collectivism. The heart chakra corresponds with the color green. When you focus on your heart chakra, you are essentially focusing on core connections.

As you can imagine, having your heart chakra misaligned or blocked can leave you in a state of individualized loneliness. Failing to forge a connection between self and other will result in one of two things. On one hand, you may focus entirely too much on your own needs, never considering the needs of others. This will turn you into a highly selfish and individualistic person who no one will receive much love and care from. On the other hand, having your heart chakra misaligned could also cause you to lean in the other direction and become too focused on others' needs, completely forgoing your own. Either way, it will cause you to have very one-sided relationships that don't result in mutually beneficial and satisfactory circumstances. The misalignment of the heart chakra can also have physical symptoms, including actual heart problems and breathing problems such as asthma. Regardless of your symptoms, a blocked heart chakra will leave you in a state of deep loneliness. When your heart chakra is open, however, you will enjoy strong and fruitful connections with others in which everyone's needs are being met and everyone is able to express themselves freely.

Throat Chakra

Even higher on the body is the throat chakra, which is obviously located in the throat area. It governs parts of the body such as the mouth, tonsils, and anything in that general area. The throat chakra deals primarily with your verbal communication with others and the world. As we move up the body, we are moving further outward. While the heart chakra deals with love and connection, the throat chakra deals with all forms of communication, not necessarily of an intimate nature. The throat chakra is blue in color, and its alignment will cover a lot of your public identity, presiding over your ability to express yourself clearly to others as well as how to use your power of speech for good.

When your throat chakra is blocked, you will have problems with communication. Some physical symptoms can be throat infections or even dental problems, anything to do with the hygiene of the mouth and throat area. Emotional symptoms include a failure to express yourself properly, perhaps becoming extremely shy or simply being inarticulate. In the worst cases, those with a blocked throat chakra might start using their speech maliciously, engaging in harmful gossip or insulting behavior. You might also find that you don't have control over your speech and tend to speak without thinking. When you align this chakra properly, however, you will recapture this aspect of your speech and be able to communicate more effectively and honestly. A big part of an unblocked throat chakra is the ability to speak with compassion and remain truthful to yourself as well as to educate others.

Third Eye Chakra

Your third eye chakra is located just at your brow, a little higher than the space between your eyes. If you want, you can imagine another eye there, but that's not quite what the third eye chakra is trying to express. The third eye chakra is not about being able to see the world around you but instead being able to see past it into the intuitive world beyond. This might sound like we are going back to the base, interior world of the root chakra, but it is actually beyond even that. The third eye chakra is moving past the social world into the world of the unknown or the unformed. Your ability to trust the implicit forces around you and to see reality for what it really is are all connected to your third eye chakra. This chakra is all about reaching beyond the everyday and becoming more in touch with the vibrations of the universe. Your third eye chakra is purple. If you learn to really see through your third eye chakra, then you will have a much clearer, more intuitive picture of what is going on around you.

Those with blocked third eye chakras will often be somewhat obtuse. They are the kind of people who really can't see past the end of their noses and constantly fail to consider the bigger picture in any situation. They will not trust their intuition or even really be aware of it. Instead, they will make decisions purely based on immediate results or from information that is readily available. There are also physical symptoms associated with a third eye chakra block. Seeing and hearing problems can occur as well as chronic headaches or migraines. People who are able to open up their third eye chakra will really see the world for what it is and be able to make more long-term, spiritually aligned decisions.

Crown Chakra

The crown chakra is the top of the body's equivalent of the root chakra. This is the top of the head, or the highest extent of the nervous system. While the root chakra represents the base of all your other chakras, leading up into each of them, the crown chakra represents the apex of all your other chakras and trickles down to the others. In itself, it represents your connection to your destiny and spiritual identity. Your crown chakra should lead you through your life's path and help to align all your other chakras. They work symbiotically, each affecting the other in turn. Thus, if you don't have all your other chakras aligned, your crown chakra is likely to suffer, just as your life plans and spiritual faith tend to suffer when you are experiencing difficulty in one or another aspect of your life. Similarly, if you don't have your crown chakra fully aligned, you will likely struggle with some of your other chakras. Basically, the crown chakra cannot be properly aligned without the other chakras, and vice versa. The crown chakra corresponds either with the color indigo, to represent the apex of the color wheel, or white to represent all colors combined.

Blocked crown chakras might manifest in a number of different ways. Usually, someone with a misaligned crown chakra will seem to be a very backward or stubborn person. They will not have a strong sense of where they are going in life and will likely experience frequent ruts due to their inability to connect with their life's purpose. Often, these people will end up very lost, wasting a lot of their potential because of their inability to truly evaluate who they are or where they are going in life. They might have a strong foundation, but if they don't put it to good use, they will squander a lot of their potential. Physical symptoms might include chronic full-body pain or confusion as the entire nervous system will be affected. When you open up your crown chakra, you will find that you have set yourself on a clear course and feel strongly connected to the spiritual world above.

How to Use Crystals for Chakras

So, what does this all have to do with crystals? Well, many crystal healing practices will map themselves onto the chakra system in order to better isolate the areas of your body that need healing. Throughout the last section, I pointed out the dichotomies between a blocked and an unblocked chakra. Well, you might be wondering now how to align these misaligned or blocked chakras. This is where crystals come in. Crystals have been used throughout the centuries to create stronger connections among chakras and to help unblock the places where there have been blocks. Traditionally, crystal healers will assign different crystals to certain chakras, helping the patient to target specific crystal energies toward corresponding energies in their bodies. Certain crystals have particular powers that are more useful for some chakras than others. Sometimes, this process simply means incorporating certain crystals into your practice to target your chakras that are misaligned. Other times, this means actively touching those crystals to the part of your body corresponding to that chakra. For example, you might wear a crystal necklace if you are trying to target your throat chakra or participate in a crystal chakra healing session where crystals will be placed at different intervals along your back to match up with the chakra hierarchy. Using these methods, chakra crystal healers combine the spiritual knowledge of both crystals and chakras to help unblock and set free all aspects of your mind and body.

Chapter 4:
Crystals and Auras

The third facet of crystal healing is auras. Besides Chi, your inner core energy, and chakras, your seven central energies, you also have an external aura of energy vibrating around your body at all times. These fields are in constant motion around the perimeter of your body, modifying and influencing your every move. The concept of auras is not new. In fact, it dates back to the Ancient Greeks, using the same Greek root as the word "breeze." Thus, we can see how, from the beginning, auras were something of the air, constantly flowing and changing shape. In this chapter, we will look at the essential qualities of auras and how they can interact with the concept of crystal healing.

Aura Colors

Much like chakras all have a corresponding color, auras are usually understood through the lens of color as well. People who read auras will usually assign a specific color to someone's aura, reading the energy. This is not by accident. Colors are actually frequencies that change based on the speed at which they vibrate. On the color scale, violet has the highest frequency, while red has the lowest frequency, with the gradient of the rainbow bridging the two. If you think back to the chakras, you can see how this maps neatly onto them, with the root chakra corresponding to red, both the lowest on their respective scales, and the crown chakra corresponding to indigo, both the highest. When you read someone's color aura, you are picking up on their levels of vibration, assigning them an energy level. Colors are not just vibrations, though. Besides the chakra assignments, most people have strong associations with certain colors. Colors hold a lot of meaning, even for people who don't know about chakras at all. Once you start to learn the colors and their meanings, you will have a much easier time identifying certain color associations in your life.

How to Read Auras

Auras take a special kind of person to read. You need to have both a keen eye and a strong sense of the person and who they are. If you are going to read an aura, make sure you spend some time with the person first. When someone knows you better, they will be able to let their guard down and allow their full personality to shine through. Once they are in this state, you must concentrate very closely on the line between them and the wall. This is where the aura lies. If you look very closely, you should be able to see the faint outline of a certain color radiating just around the edge of their body. You can also read your own aura. To do this, you will need to hold up your hand in front of a wall or stand in front of a mirror. From there, you should be able to discern your aura. Once you have determined your or another person's aura, you will be able to interpret it.

What Do Auras Mean?

So, you've figured out your aura color, now what does it mean? Well, there are several ways to interpret the colors of your aura. One is to map your aura color onto its corresponding chakra. If your aura is associated with a chakra, it generally means that that chakra is unblocked for you. Furthermore, it might even mean that you are particularly ruled by that chakra, with your basic personality aligning closely with that chakra's qualities. You can think of this as being similar to your astrological sign, with a particular facet of life that you are focused on. So, if your aura is red, you are likely a very grounded person who is probably a rock for others in your life with a strong sense of self and purpose. If your aura is orange, you might be a particularly sexual person who has a strong penchant for passion and connection. People with yellow auras are usually the life of the party with a wide social circle. People with a green aura will likely have very close intimate relationships in their life and be exceptionally caring. If your aura is blue, it might mean that you are a very verbal person who communicates remarkably well and takes a lot of pride in your language skills. If you possess a purple aura, you are most likely a very spiritual person with strong foresight. And finally, if your aura is indigo, then you are most definitely a powerfully aligned person who finds balance in most facets of your life. Through all these colors, we can see how colored auras can have a powerful impact on how you conduct yourself throughout your life and what forms your base personality.

How Crystals Affect Auras

So, how can crystals interact with your aura? Similar to how certain crystals have corresponding chakras, they also have corresponding auras. You can choose a specific crystal to heal the specific aura that it has a relationship with. But, you might ask, if auras are just something that describes your personality and values, much like an astrological sign, then what needs healing? We know that chakras can become misaligned, so what can happen to auras? Well, auras have their own version of misalignment, which is called an auric tear. Auric tears are vulnerable points within your aura that risk letting negative energy into your body. If you are experiencing an auric tear, then you might have anxiety, depression, or general misalignment. Things just might seem to never go your way. Enter crystals. When you are experiencing difficulties with the areas of your life that correspond to your aura, you need to do something about it. You can use the vibrations of various crystals to help restore your aura back to the state it is meant to be in. When you do so, you are creating a protective layer around your aura, which works to heal existing auric tears and prevent future ones. As always, crystals are there to help align and center your energies.

Pillar 2:
Sources

Moving on to the second pillar of crystals, we arrive at sources. When you are planning to use crystals in your healing practice, you will need to know how to get them. Not all crystal sources are made equal, so you will have to do a little bit of research to ensure that you are buying the right product and not engaging with fake or inferior crystals. In this pillar, we will dive into everything you need to know about sourcing, helping you to figure out the best place to purchase your crystals.

Chapter 5:
What to Buy

The first step in obtaining your crystals is figuring out which ones you want to buy. The world of crystals is so vast and complex that it can really be hard to know where to start. You might have a wide range of interests in their healing power as well as ailments you want to fix, so choosing just one or a few crystals can be extremely difficult. For this reason, you need to seek out all the information you can possibly find on crystals and crystal healing in order to determine the precise crystals you need. In terms of crystals, there are a few primary factors to consider when determining what kind of crystals you should buy. In this chapter, I will give you some concrete guidance on how to identify and choose crystals.

Crystal Shapes

Back in Chapter 1, I stated that crystals are defined by their molecular structure. Well, there are actually several different molecular structures that crystals can take on, each denoting a different quality. Understanding the meanings of these different molecular structures can help you to better identify what kinds of crystals you want to buy. There are seven main shapes in the world of crystals, all of which convey their own unique meaning.

1. **Cube Crystals**
   Crystals that come in cube shapes are grounding crystals. Much like the root chakra, these crystals help keep you grounded and remind you of the simpler, basic things in life that are important to keep in mind.

2. **Pyramid Crystals**
   When you buy crystals in the shape of a pyramid, you are intending to connect with your desires. This shape resonates with the sacral chakra, which deals with passion and pleasure. Manifesting with pyramid crystals will help you connect with the things you really want.

3. **Sphere Crystals**

   Sphere crystals resemble a planet or a globe, resonating with their purpose of connecting you with the greater world as a whole. These crystals can help put your life into perspective, reminding you of the greater forces at work in the universe.

4. **Tumbled Crystals**

   These are the smallest form of crystal and come in tiny shapes much like a pebble. These are travel-sized crystals that can help you continue to feel a crystal's energy everywhere you go. You can also make these into jewelry so you always have a crystal touching your skin for protection.

5. **Pointed Crystals**

   These crystals focus on… well, focus! If you have a very specific goal or problem to target, then manifesting with pointed crystals is an excellent idea. You will be able to sharply focus on your task at hand, channeling energy in a very specific way.

6. **Heart Crystals**

   While crystals don't naturally occur in heart shapes, they can be cut as such to enhance their overall meaning. Using a heart-shaped crystal is intended to channel your heart chakra, helping you to connect with others and show your compassion.

7. **Cluster Crystals**

   Using a cluster crystal is all about unity and connection. Much like the crown chakra, the cluster crystal presides over all the other crystals, helping them to bind together and form a cohesive healing pattern.

Choosing a Crystal

The next step comes when you have to decide what actual crystal type you want to choose. In Chapter 17, I will list a more definitive selection of crystals, but here I'll outline some important factors for you to consider when choosing a crystal to purchase. First of all, you should be very clear about your intentions with your crystals. If you don't state up front what you want out of your crystal journey, then you will be more lost than you need to be. Being aware right away of what you want your crystals to do for you will help you in the initial narrowing process. The second step in choosing a crystal is discovering things about yourself. We've already talked about crystals and auras to help you to choose a crystal that particularly corresponds to your aura, but you might also want to consider your astrological sign in the mix. As I stated in the crystal history section, European crystal practice traditionally associated people's astrological signs with crystals. Take a look at your birth chart and make a list of crystals that correspond to some of your major signs, specifically your sun, moon, and rising signs. From there, you will have a definitive list of your intentions with your crystals and the ones that will particularly help you in your own personal journey. And finally, once you have made these lists, you can simply choose the crystals you gravitate toward. Colors or shapes that draw you in might be your subconscious looking for those crystal properties in your life. As with most spiritual practices, intuition lies at the core of your crystal healing practice.

Chapter 6:
Where to Buy

Once you have decided on which crystals or what kinds of crystals you want to buy, then you will have to start looking for sources. This can be just as confusing a task as choosing crystals in the first place. With the recent boom in crystal popularity, it seems like crystal stores are popping up all over the place, both online and in physical locations. For a person who wants to start getting into crystals, the options can seem overwhelming. You might find that there is just too much out there for you to feel like you can make an informed decision. Luckily, in this chapter, I will provide you with some guidance on the main sources people use to get their crystals as well as a helpful guide for identifying which crystals are authentic and which aren't. By the end of the chapter, you should have a firm sense of where you want to buy your crystals.

Buying in Person

The first thing that sprang to mind for you when thinking about buying crystals was likely going into a store. You probably imagined a long row full of boxes containing sparkly stones, each brimming with hidden power. However, there are actually a lot of different contexts in which you can buy crystals in person. In this section, we will look at the different aspects of buying crystals in person as well as the pros and cons of doing so.

Types of In-Person Crystal Sources

As you can imagine, there are many ways to buy your crystals in person. You may have even encountered some of these sources in your life. Here, we will look at some of the most common types of crystal retailers and their qualities.

Occult Stores

Often, crystals are sold alongside other occult or spirituality wares in a general-purpose occult store. These places are good because they offer a wide variety of other spiritual items and are generally more common than crystal-only stores. However, you might find that, depending on the size of the store, there will be a more limited crystal selection and the staff might be less knowledgeable about crystal healing.

Crystal Stores

Sometimes, you will come across a store that sells only crystals. These are far less common and will generally only be found in major towns and cities. They are, however, one of the better options since they tend to have an excellent selection of different types and cuts of crystals as well as a very knowledgeable staff.

Independent or Market Salespeople

Occasionally, independent sellers will set up temporary stalls in marketplaces or run a crystal business alongside their psychic or tarot reading practice. These people can be more hit-or-miss than more permanent crystal and occult stores. On one hand, you might get someone who is extremely knowledgeable and passionate and who can use some other psychic skills they have to personally tailor crystals to your life situation. However, there is also more room for dishonesty here, meaning you run more risk of being sold fake crystals, being overcharged, or possibly even being scammed. If you are going with an independent seller, make sure they are trustworthy.

Pros and Cons of Buying in Person

Obviously, there are some benefits as well as drawbacks to buying crystals in person. As you go through your crystal journey, you will gradually figure out what you prefer. Here, we will explore some of the pros and cons of in-person crystal shopping.

Pros of Buying in Person

The most obvious upside of buying in person is that you get to have a physical experience with your crystals before purchasing them. Provided the owner lets you, browsing a crystal store will involve physically holding the crystals you are intending to buy. From this, you can get a clearer sense of that crystal's vibrations. The intuitive aspect of crystal shopping that I mentioned at the end of Chapter 5 will be much easier to lean into at an in-person store. You might find that you are drawn to a crystal you didn't expect to be all because you were able to see and touch it in person first. You will also be able to interact more with the owner or staff and, provided they are knowledgeable, discuss your crystal intentions with them. All in all, in-person shopping gives you a more personalized, intimate experience with your crystals before you buy them.

Cons of Buying in Person

The main downside of buying your crystals in person is availability and selection. Not everyone lives in a big city that has a lot of crystal store options to choose from. You might be stuck with a very small store that has incredibly limited options. When it comes to market stalls and independent sellers, you might run into the problem of lack of accountability. You might buy a crystal from a retailer that turns out to be fake, but if they have up and gone, you have no one to give you a refund. Always make sure to keep the business card or contact information of anyone you buy from. All in all, though, if you are willing to travel to a bigger crystal store, you should do at least some of your crystal shopping in person, just for the physical connection.

Buying Online

If you live in a more remote location or find traveling difficult, you might want to look toward buying crystals online. A large portion of the recent surge in crystal popularity has happened online, so you will find that there is a huge variety of options for buying your crystals through an online space. Likely, you have already encountered some crystal people on social media who may have associated stores, so you are no stranger to the online crystal business. In this section, I will give you some important guidance on how to buy crystals online.

Types of Online Crystal Sources

As with in-person stores, there are a lot of different ways you can buy crystals online. Many different kinds of people and companies sell crystals online, from the most independent crystal healers to large corporations like Amazon. You will certainly find no shortage of crystals online, which is why it can be somewhat overwhelming to choose where you should be looking for them. Here, we will give you an overview of the three most common types of online crystal stores to help you decide where you want to seek out your crystal collection.

Mega-Retailers

Since crystals have taken off so much recently, many larger retailers have begun selling them. You will certainly find a large variety of crystals on certain mass retailer websites, such as Amazon, Aliexpress, and Shien. These larger corporations might lack personal connection, but they make up for it in price. You will usually find the lowest prices for crystals on these websites, so if you are a crystal user on a budget, then this might be where you want to turn. However, for those who are very new to crystals, these websites don't offer very much guidance, so you might find yourself overwhelmed. Mega-retailers are ideal for those who already know exactly what they want and are searching for the lowest possible price.

Online Crystal Stores

A step down in size from the mega-retailers are online stores dedicated to selling crystals. These are usually run by crystal healers or enthusiasts and thus will be able to offer much more guidance about what kinds of crystals you should buy. Some might even be accompanied by blogs that explain the complex meanings behind each crystal. Many online crystal stores are still large enough to have a wide selection and, in fact, might even have a wider selection than the crowd-pleasing mega-retailers who only stock the most popular crystals. Thus, if you are looking for more obscure crystals or a little more guidance around the crystals you want to buy, then you should look toward specialized online crystal stores.

Spirituality Influencers

The most independent sellers you will find online—the virtual equivalent of the marketplace stall—are social media crystal influencers. Many of these people run blogs, Instagram pages, or TikTok accounts dedicated to crystals. If you learned something about crystals from these people, you might be incentivized to buy from them. Many of these influencers offer a highly personalized crystal experience. Depending on how popular and busy they are, they might even be available to personally chat with you to discuss your crystal needs. Some will sell through their own personal website and some through larger platforms like Etsy. However, be aware of the same dangers as with independent in-person retailers and be sure to get their correct contact information before buying from an independent online retailer to avoid any scams. If something seems fishy, it's best to avoid it.

Pros and Cons of Buying Online

As you can see, there are a lot of reasons to buy your crystals online, but there are still things you have to be aware of and watch out for. Here, we will look at the positive and negative aspects of online crystal shopping.

Pros of Buying Online

What online shopping really has going for it is availability. You are no longer limited by the options at your local crystal shop or required to drive to faraway cities to find the crystals you want. If you're looking for something more obscure, you can bet that you will be able to find it online sooner than in person. Online shopping also might cut out the middleman. You don't always know where in-person crystal retailers source their crystals, especially the more independent ones. For all you know, it might be an online store! Buying online is also often cheaper for this very reason since the retailers don't have to pay rent on a storefront or staff to work there. So, for those who want to save a bit of money and time, as well as access a much wider array of crystal options, online is likely the best option.

Cons of Buying Online

Online shopping's biggest flaw has always been a lack of certainty about the product before you buy. This is usually a big problem for things like clothes, which aren't guaranteed to fit, and it can be just as big a problem for crystals. Holding a crystal in your hand is the only sure way to know if you connect with it. Even if you do all the research you can, shopping online will always lack this physical aspect. You might also miss out on some personalized help. Barring certain crystal influencers, there really isn't much personalized help online. If you are more of a beginner who is looking to talk to someone about your crystal needs, then you will certainly be lacking for this online. All in all, the online option is recommended more for intermediate to advanced crystal practitioners, with beginners requiring more guidance than many online platforms are able to provide.

Identifying Crystal Authenticity

As I stated a few times above, there are a lot of opportunities for people to sell you fake or subpar crystals. Especially if you are a beginner in your crystal journey, you might have a difficult time discerning what's real from what's fake. And since you are intent on harnessing the very real power of authentic crystals, you don't want to get stuck with something fake. Fake crystals that don't have the same chemical qualities as real crystals simply won't work. If you attempt to heal using fake crystals, you will not get results and may become discouraged with the crystal healing practice altogether. Here, we will discuss some of the aspects of crystal fakery and what you can do to protect yourself from it.

What Is a Fake Crystal?

So, what is the difference between a real crystal and a fake one? Well, it's all in the chemical composition. You see, real crystals always come from the earth. They are naturally formed substances that absorb earthly vibrations and energy. However, some sellers will provide crystals that are not naturally formed in the earth but are instead man-made. This could be a manipulated rock that is dyed or shaped to look like a crystal or a completely artificial substance like fiberglass that is artificially shaped to resemble a crystal. These things are simply not crystals and will not work in the same way. Trying to pass them off as authentic crystals is wrong and does a lot of harm to the crystal community. Unfortunately, these things still circulate, so you have to be wary of them.

Red Flags for Fake Crystals

Fortunately, there are some clear "tells" when a crystal is not authentic. Most crystal healers will have a keen eye for what a crystal should look like, but for a beginner, it can be really difficult. In this section, I will describe some clear red flags around crystal shopping to help you identify crystals that might not be real.

Red Flag #1: Shady Selling Practices

Right off the bat, you should be evaluating the perceived honesty of the seller. Dishonesty can happen at any level, from a street vendor to a major chain retailer. For this reason, you can't always judge by appearances, but you should judge by the way the product is being sold. Are there clear indications of what the crystal is made of? Does it seem to be factory-made or mass-produced? Is it being pushed on you with very vague information or a lot of haste? All of these things can indicate a shady crystal business that is not selling the real thing. Whether you are buying online or in person, you need to keep a sharp eye out for these "snake oil" salespeople.

Red Flag #2: Strange Names

One of the most common ways to spot a fake crystal is if it has a weird or fake-sounding name. All crystals have official geological names like amethyst, quartz, jade, and so on. Normally, when you are buying crystals, they will simply be called these names. However, for some reason, many fake crystal sellers will add descriptors to these existing geological names, calling them "sunset quartz" or "starry night amethyst." These are often actually dyed quartz (which is not a real gem) or even just glass. Reputable crystal salespeople will not need to use these quirky or mystical-sounding names because they trust their product and their customers enough to be up front and authentic. Even though they might sound cool, these funky-named crystals are often fake.

Red Flag #3: Too Perfect-Looking

Real crystals come from the ground and thus have irregular coloring and shapes. When you look at real marble flooring, you can see how the lines in the marble are naturally formed. The same goes for real wood, which will have organic-looking lines throughout. Well, crystals will also have these same kinds of patterns. Fake crystals, on the other hand, often will have more regular patterns, since they are man-made and not formed in the earth. Even though the manufacturer might try to make the formation look natural, most people will be able to see through this pretty quickly. Look closely at the formation of the crystal and judge for yourself whether it looks like it could be a rock that came from the ground. If it doesn't look like it, then you might be dealing with a fake crystal.

Chapter 7:
Vogel Crystals

In the world of crystals, there is one innovator in particular who stands above the rest. His name was Marcel Vogel, and he was one of the pioneering crystal scientists of the 20th century. Vogel worked for IBM developing scientific principles behind things like crystal-powered computers and watches. He also authored some of the most important writings on crystals and how to utilize their power properly. One of the most influential things he came up with was a particular way to cut crystals that harnesses their power in the most efficient way possible. These crystals, cut according to Vogel's research, are called Vogel crystals and are considered one of the highest-quality crystal cuts in the world. In this chapter, we will explore different aspects of the Vogel crystal, exploring what makes it one of the best ways to cut crystals and how you can find and identify a Vogel crystal for yourself!

How Do Vogel Crystals Work?

First of all, all Vogel crystals are quartz. You won't really find a Vogel crystal in any other material. This is because quartz is one of the purest crystals and thus has the ability to channel more effectively than others. In terms of shape, the Vogel crystal is cut in a very specific way with one point at both ends. The idea is that one end acts as a receiving port and the other as a transmission antenna. You can think of these like the speaker and microphone on a headset, with one end for input and one for output. The idea is that this cut harnesses the natural vibrations of the crystal in the best way possible and thus has the ability to transmit energy at a much more efficient rate. This cut is also used for technological purposes as it is able to channel the quartz's vibrations very efficiently into the battery of a computer or watch. You can still get effective results with non-Vogel quartz, of course, but this is considered the height of crystal innovation. For these reasons, many crystal practitioners opt for Vogel crystals to ensure they are practicing crystal healing to its fullest potential.

How to Identify a Vogel Crystal

Considering these qualities of the Vogel crystal, you are probably curious about how to identify whether a crystal is a Vogel crystal. Here, I will provide you with the basic criteria for something to be considered a Vogel crystal.

1. **Natural Quartz**
   For a crystal to be considered Vogel, it has to be a naturally occurring crystal. You cannot make a Vogel crystal without completely natural quartz because the vibrations simply will not work.

2. **Doubly Terminated**
   Double termination is the technical name for the Vogel crystal shape, which comes to a point at either end. Furthermore, the crystal must be shaped to this arrangement with the exact right measurements as specified by the Vogel design. You should make sure it comes from a certified cutter so you know you are getting the exact right shape.

3. **Cut With the C-Axis**
   All quartz has a "c-axis" which is the natural molecular structure of the crystal. You can think of this as being like the grain of wood. You want your crystals to be cut with the grain rather than against it so that they are as smooth as possible and able to conduct energy with maximum efficiency. Vogel crystals are stipulated to be cut along this axis.

4. **51-Degree Reception End**
   The reception end of the crystal, sometimes known as the female end, must be cut at an angle of 51 degrees. This is a reference to the dimensions of the Great Pyramid of Giza, which inundates the crystal with more power. Connecting with one of the most important monuments of the ancient world helps to center the spiritual energy of the crystal.

5. **Less Than 51 Degree Transmitter End**
   Your transmitter end, sometimes known as the male end, must have a more acute angle than the reception end. The idea behind this is to refine the energy as it passes through the crystal. If you have a wider receiver than transmitter, the crystal is working to focus the energy flowing through itself, thus creating a more accurate channel.

6. **Four or More Side Faces**
   Another essential attribute of a Vogel crystal is the number of sides it has. Your crystal must have at least four sides in order to be considered a bona fide Vogel crystal.

How Can I Use Vogel Crystals

Vogel crystals are very useful for focusing energy. Many people approach crystal practice with a very unfocused mind. They are searching for meaning and purpose in their lives and thus want to find some kind of focus for their thoughts and goals. Incorporating a Vogel crystal into your practice is an excellent way to add some of that extra razor-sharp focus to your life. One great way to use Vogel crystals is to approach them with a question that you are agonizing over or a problem that feels like it is running in circles through your mind. The Vogel crystal will help you gain clarity on these messy situations and give you guidance as to the direction you should be going in life.

Pillar 3:
Purposes

As you can probably see from all the previous chapters, there are a lot of ways you can use crystals. Crystal healing is obviously the most common, which we will get into in Pillar 4, but there are also many other ways that you can implement crystals in your life. They are all important to consider and give you an opportunity to integrate crystals deeper into your life and practices. These other uses will help you practice crystal healing more casually and frequently. They allow you to make crystals a part of your everyday life, not just your dedicated practice. In this pillar, we will look at three distinctive ways in which you can use crystals. The first way is around your house by decorating with crystals. The second way is to wear crystals on your body so that their powers can always be with you. And the third way is to incorporate crystals into your existing meditation practices. With these three methods, you can see that there are more integrated and diverse ways to use your crystals.

Chapter 8:
Decoration

Who doesn't love the idea of beautiful crystals all over your house? Incorporating crystals into your home's decor is one of the most interesting ways to bring energy flow into your everyday life. Having crystals around the house can help you to recalibrate your energies throughout the day without even having to engage in active crystal practice. They can bring a sense of peace and balance to your spaces, inundating your home with their healing powers. As a nice bonus, they also lend a great aesthetic as decorations! Many crystal practitioners incorporate crystals into their home decor for these reasons.

One of the most important things to consider when decorating with crystals is the compatibility of the crystal's qualities and the uses for the specific space. Each room in your house has a particular purpose and thus a particular energy profile you want to follow. Failing to consider the specific uses for the rooms you are intending to decorate with crystals is one of the biggest mistakes you can make. Let's just say you don't want to put high-energy crystals in the bedroom or relaxation crystals in your home office. When you are decorating your house with crystals, the ways in which each room is used are of the utmost importance. In this chapter, I will lead you through a room-by-room guide for what kinds of crystals work best in certain spaces.

Exteriors

The first part of this chapter will not be devoted to your house but to the space around your house. It might not seem like it, but your outdoor spaces provide lots of opportunities to incorporate crystals. Since outdoor spaces look different for every house, you should really consider what yours looks like and how you use it. Whether you have a small balcony or a sprawling yard, there are many different ways to spend time outside. Maybe you have a dedicated eating area where you love to entertain and have dinner parties, or perhaps you have a cozy hammock area surrounded by tranquil ferns where you love to go and read. You might even have a large enough space to play sports or do your morning exercises. Deciding what kind of energy you want to be encouraging all depends on your specific uses for your outdoor space. In this section, I will walk you through some of the considerations around outdoor crystal design.

Types of Crystals to Use

As I said above, the types of crystals you will choose for your outdoor space will hinge significantly on what kind of outdoor space you have. For eating and entertaining outdoor areas, you want to use crystals that enhance connection and pleasure. Eating with others is one of the most powerful ways to connect, so what better way to streamline that connection energy than with a crystal? If you use your outdoor area for relaxation purposes, then you want to choose crystals that focus on meditation and rejuvenation. Relaxation is all about recharging your batteries, so cleansing and tranquilizing crystals are perfect for a relaxation area. Finally, if you are using your outdoor area for sports or exercise, especially practices like yoga, then you want to choose crystals that forge a mind-body connection and ground you in the earth. We go outside to exercise because it better connects us to the earth around us, so crystals that focus on spiritual connection are great for this purpose. Putting some serious thought into the purpose of your outdoor space will help you choose the crystals you want to incorporate there.

How to Incorporate Them

Backyard decorations can be as creative as you want them to be, so why not integrate some crystals? One creative way to add crystals to your outdoor space is by making them into a beautiful set of chimes. You can make one from scratch or add your favorite crystals to an existing chime. You can also use crystals in tiling, creating a tile display at the center of your outdoor table or to attach to a tree. The most important thing about crystal incorporation is to place them strategically. If you want to enhance connections while eating, then you should place your crystals at the center of the table to help channel the energy toward one cohesive center. Likewise, you should include your crystals in the specific area of your outdoor space that you use the most. However you choose to incorporate your crystals into your space, make sure it's creative and cohesive!

Bedroom

Moving indoors, many people decorate with crystals in their bedrooms. The bedroom is actually a more multipurpose room than you might think. People obviously use their bedrooms for sleeping, but they are also used for dressing, grooming, and intimate relations. Some people even work at a desk set up in their bedroom or read books in bed, among many other things. That's a lot of purposes for one room! Thus, when considering the vibrations you want your bedroom to have, you have to find a way to center them all. Try to think about all the ways in which you use your bedroom and all the different energies you want to enhance there. You might find that you want to use different crystals in different parts of your bedroom to try to section off the sometimes conflicting energies there. Here, we will look at the best ways to use crystals in your bedroom.

Types of Crystals to Use

Similar to using crystals outside, you will want to use a few different types of crystals in order to focus different kinds of energies in your bedroom. The first major use for your bedroom is sleeping. You might think to just use relaxation crystals here, but there is actually so much more to sleeping than just relaxing. Sleeping and dreaming are very important processes for brain development, imagination, memory, and spiritual identity. Dreams can be very powerful experiences, either for good or bad. You likely want to use a few different kinds of crystals to enhance your sleep: one to relax and wind down from the day, one to encourage positive dreams, and one to encourage meditation or philosophical thought. Combining these will ensure that you have relaxing and fruitful sleep. The second major use for the bedroom is intimacy and sex. Whether you have multiple partners a week or have been happily married for decades, you likely want to bring some element of excitement to your bedroom. Crystals that encourage arousal, pleasure, and comfort in the body are essential here. Self-esteem is crucial for a healthy sex life, so you want to forge a strong connection with your own body in order to explore someone else's. Speaking of comfort in your body, you will also want to encourage self-esteem in relation to the third most common use for the bedroom, which is dressing and grooming. Feeling like you can put together a strong look that complements your body and makes you feel good about yourself is essential. Crystals that encourage mind-body connection and confidence are great for your dressing and grooming area. No matter the use, there is a crystal to help you in the bedroom.

How to Incorporate Them

Bedrooms are a great place to bring crystals since there are so many hidden places for you to put them. The trick with such a versatile room is to strategically place certain crystals to enhance the different uses of the bedroom. So, for crystals that are intended to help you sleep, you should place them lower down and closer to where your head is when you sleep. The bedside table or your headboard can be great places for these crystals to radiate into your mind while you sleep. During intimacy, you might be more upright on the bed, so you might want to place these aphrodisiac crystals on a higher plane, perhaps hanging on the wall above the headboard to create a second layer of psychic space. Finally, for dressing purposes, you should incorporate these crystals around your vanity. You could create a crystal frame for your mirror or have a crystal dish for your precious jewelry. By sectioning off different places to put your crystals, you are helping to compartmentalize the room and keep all the different energies separate so they don't conflict with one another.

Kitchen

One of the most dynamic rooms in the house is the kitchen. The kitchen is a place for many things. It is a place for creativity, enjoyment, pleasure, and connection. Some people describe the kitchen as the heart of the home, so you want to make sure that this room has the right energy. Crystals are a great way to enhance the flow of your kitchen, bring people together, and stimulate creativity in your culinary activities. When you use crystals in the kitchen, you are giving yourself an opportunity to push yourself toward a happier family and a better life for all. Here, we will look at some of the best ways to incorporate crystals into your kitchen.

Types of Crystals to Use

Since we mentioned that the kitchen is like the heart of the house, you would do very well to use crystals connected with the heart chakra. This will help center the room in the house and redirect flow from other rooms back to the kitchen. The heart chakra is also all about love and intimate family connections, bringing the closest people in your life together. Eating together, cooking together, and doing so in the presence of crystals can really help strengthen your connection with your family. You might also want to use some creativity-stimulating crystals, ones that help you connect with your imagination and that will motivate you to try new things in the kitchen. These two types of crystals will help you balance connection and creativity in your food-preparing spaces.

How to Incorporate Them

Where you place the crystals will depend on the type you are using. For connection-based crystals, place them where your family normally gathers to eat. This could be your eat-in kitchen space, your breakfast bar, or even your dining room table. Creating a beautiful centerpiece out of crystals can be a great way to seamlessly introduce crystals into your food spaces. For creativity-sparking crystals, you want to put these where you will be actively preparing the food. Try placing some crystals on your windowsill or hanging them above the oven or main prep space. Using these two methods, you can bring a distinct sense of strength and purpose to your kitchen space.

Living Room

The living room is also a space that is focused on connection, but a slightly different kind. While the bedroom focuses on connection with the self and intimate partner, the most intimate form of connection, and the kitchen focuses on connection with the immediate family, the living room is the space that has the strongest relationship to the outside world. This will be the space where you spend time both with your immediate family and with visitors. Thus, you want to focus on energies that are both homey and connected but also inviting and outward-reaching. You can think of this space as your home's gateway to the world beyond, creating an inviting atmosphere for everyone to enjoy. Here, we will look at the best ways to create this environment in your living room using crystals.

Types of Crystals to Use

Crystals that enhance interpersonal connections are the obvious choice for the living room. The purpose of the room is for conversation and bonding, either with family or friends, so you want to bring in crystals that bring people together. Another important aspect of the living room to harness is a sense of open-mindedness. This is the room through which new perspectives and ideas will be introduced to your home, so you should create a space that invites those new ideas in. For this reason, openness and welcoming crystals are ideal picks for your living room. Choose these wisely, and you will create energy that invites anyone in and makes them feel like a close family member.

How to Incorporate Them

The living room is typically a well-decorated room full of trinkets, so you will likely find many opportunities to incorporate them. One great place to put crystals in your living room is near the fireplace if you have one. The expression "home and hearth" emphasizes the fireplace, or hearth, as the heart of the living room. This is the component that releases heat and is the focal point of the room. Even if you are not actively lighting it, many living rooms with fireplaces arrange their furniture around it so it acts as a kind of psychic focus. Placing crystals on your mantel will thus help spread their energy around the room evenly. You can also place crystals on the coffee table, especially if this is a place where you are serving snacks. Using these centering methods, you can create a strong circulation of positive and inviting energy in your living room.

Chapter 9: Wearing Crystals

Another effective way to passively incorporate crystals into your life is by wearing them. Wearable crystals have a very long tradition. Many jewelry practices and styles in cultures around the world have incorporated crystals. To this day, it's extremely easy to buy crystal jewelry, even without realizing you are doing so or knowing anything about crystals. Chances are, you actually already own a piece of crystal jewelry and don't even know it! But if you are aware of the benefits and select your crystals right, there are so many ways wearing crystals can help improve your life! In this chapter, I will talk about how wearing crystals can help you as well as the things you should consider when selecting a crystal to wear around with you.

Benefits of Wearing Crystals

There are numerous benefits to crystal healing, and many of those can be especially enjoyed when you are wearing your crystals around. For this reason, many people swear by their crystal bracelets or necklaces. People also wear their crystals as earrings or even have tiny ones stuffed inside their bras! There are countless ways to benefit from your wearable crystals. Here, we will look at some of the most compelling ways wearable crystals can help you.

Integrating Your Crystal Practice

Depending on your crystal practice, you might have isolated times of day when you engage with your crystals. These might be during meditation or crystal healing sessions. Doing these things is great since it gives you some solid, dedicated crystal time. However, it is also helpful to integrate your crystal practice into your life more continuously. If you wear your crystals throughout the day, you will be able to reap their benefits all the time rather than just during isolated occasions. You might also be able to benefit even when you are not paying attention to your crystals, meaning that you are achieving a subconscious symbiosis. Essentially, wearable crystals make your crystal practice a 24/7 occasion.

Creating a More Intuitive Mind

Because of this stronger and more consistent connection to your crystals, you will likely forge a deeper connection with your subconscious. You will be letting your subconscious mind become more vocal in your relationship, allowing it to speak louder to you. After a while, you will likely find that you have an easier time listening to and learning from your intuition. From this, you can really see how constantly wearing crystals can lead to a much more intuitive mind overall, even after you have taken your crystal jewelry off.

Health Benefits

Many healers will also preach the physical health benefits of wearable crystals. Ailments such as skin conditions and arthritis can benefit a lot from prolonged contact with vibrating crystals. You might find that wearing crystals can have a positive effect on some of these ailments. Talk to your doctor or homeopathic care provider to discuss whether you might be able to incorporate crystals into your existing healing practice for these things.

Aesthetics

Let's be honest, another major attraction of crystals is how they look! With all the beautiful colors, shapes, and textures that come out of the crystal family, they make wonderful jewelry even without considering their healing powers. You can buy or make some truly beautiful jewelry from your crystal collection to wear in style while also benefiting from their powerful energies.

Things to Consider

Before you start strapping on your quartz necklaces and jade bracelets, you should give some careful consideration to what they are going to be used for. Wearing crystals and constantly absorbing their energy can actually be very draining, and if you don't consider their uses, you might end up confusing your energies around certain activities. Wearing a crystal around your body is much more drastic than incorporating it into your practice. The wearing of a crystal involves constant contact with that crystal's vibrations and thus means that you will be more closely and consistently exposed to its energy. In this section, we will explore some aspects of crystal wearing that should be considered before you start.

Context Matters

As with decorating your home, you need to cater your crystals to the situation at hand. Wearing the wrong crystal at the wrong event or to the wrong location can have serious consequences on the energy you are bringing into that situation. Think back to our discussion of the home and the energies involved in the different rooms. Now think of your life as being like a house, with different rooms that serve different purposes. Your life is full of diverse experiences that all require different energy levels and types of energy to flow properly. You're probably going to want to bring different energy levels to your workplace than you would bring when hanging out with friends or on a relaxing day at the beach. All these contexts will require you to have different energies. Bringing a relaxation-focused crystal to a work brainstorming session would likely not be a good idea, just as bringing a focus crystal to your Saturday night out on the town may not be optimal either. These can confuse your energies and make your experience worse and unfulfilling. When choosing crystals to wear for your various experiences, make sure to tailor them to the energy you want to bring into that experience.

Be Careful About Who You Interact With

Another facet of life that has a lot of variabilities is the social world. Besides where you are going, it also matters who you are with. Crystals will also affect those around you, their energies subtly radiating to the other person. Thus, you should carefully consider who you are with and how the crystals you are wearing might affect them as well as the general dynamic between you. You certainly don't want to encourage any romantic feelings between you and your boss or contentious feelings between you and your new partner's family. Making sure that you are wearing crystals that encourage the type of relationship you want to have with the person or people with whom you are interacting and that nourish their natural energy is essential to a healthy crystal-wearing practice.

Give Yourself a Break

Finally, wearing crystals constantly, especially very intense crystals, can be exhausting. Some crystals have very strong energy and encourage a lot of change and rebirth, which you don't always want to be bringing to your life every day. If you have a favorite crystal necklace that you find yourself wearing frequently and you are noticing that its vibrations are affecting you a lot, then you should consider giving yourself a break from that crystal, maybe leaving it off for a day to see how you feel or avoiding wearing it in situations that don't suit its energy. Remember: Your crystals should be serving you, not the other way around, so if you ever feel like the energy is too strong, you can always take a break.

Chapter 10:
Meditation

Meditation is one of the fastest-growing practices in the West. Over the past few decades, more and more people on this side of the world, even those who don't practice Buddhism or Hinduism, are discovering the amazing benefits of meditation. Mindfulness and meditation have even taken over in the corporate world, with many workplaces offering mindfulness workshops for their employees. In the age of hustle culture and mass burnout, with a pandemic on top of it all, it's no wonder many people are finding meditation beneficial. It can help refocus your mind and rid yourself of some of the more harmful mindsets you may get into. It can even help improve your physical health by reducing stress. Suffice it to say, there are a number of reasons meditation is becoming so popular these days. Crystals are also very popular, leading many people to incorporate them into their meditation practice. In this chapter, I will talk all about the purposes, benefits, and methods of using crystals to meditate.

Why Meditate With Crystals?

Alongside meditation in popularity are crystals, so it's no wonder that many people have been combining them. In fact, the practice of meditating with crystals dates back to the very origins of crystal practice itself, so putting the two together makes a lot of sense. Meditation is all about letting the energies of the universe pass through you as you absorb and attempt to be at one with them. So, why not incorporate some of the specific energies from crystals into that practice? Crystals can work to give your meditation more focus and help with some of the main purposes of crystals, such as manifestation and energy absorption. If there is a crystal whose energy you are particularly interested in or a particular conundrum in your life that you want to bring focus to, then incorporating crystals into your meditation practice can be a great idea. In short, meditating with crystals can enhance both your meditation practice and crystal practice, creating something that is greater than the sum of its parts. Here, we will look at some of the most compelling reasons to use crystals in your meditation practice, illustrating some of the ways they can help push you further along in your spiritual journey.

Focus

The first main reason you might use crystals in your meditation practice is to try to focus on a specific issue or question. This relates to the more Western meaning of the word "meditate," which means to ponder or think over. In Western culture, meditation is often associated with Christian monks or philosophers who would spend their days pondering theological questions, poetry, and art. With this type of meditative practice, you are trying to use the power of crystals to really think a question through. It could be a personal question, such as whether or not you should pursue a relationship with someone, a professional question, such as trying to find your path in life, or even a spiritual question, such as the order to the universe. Whatever question you choose, a focus crystal can help direct your ideas to a more streamlined train of thought, leading you toward something truly enlightening.

Specific Energies

Even if you are not looking for an answer to a specific question, you might want to harness a more specific type of energy in your meditation. Meditating can be an intimidating practice for a lot of people since it requires total concentration. It can be easy for your mind to wander, especially if you are not an experienced meditator. Thus, bringing certain crystals in can help you really focus your meditation energy, resulting in a more concentrated meditation practice. Using crystals to guide your feelings and thoughts in a certain direction is one of the best ways you can incorporate them into your practice.

Deepen Connections

When you use crystals in your meditation practice, you have the ability to deepen your meditative process and draw stronger connections between your spiritual practices. You can see how your relationship with crystals can echo in your relationship with your meditation practices and see how this symbiosis informs both. Creating this connection allows you to see the higher aspects of spirituality and the core aspects of spiritual practice as well as how many of these practices are attempting to access the same universal energy. You can even take this a step further and start incorporating astrological practices, numerology, or Tarot into your crystal meditation, perhaps choosing certain phases of the moon or days of the week to meditate to enhance the experience. All spiritual practices are inherently connected, and practicing them together is a powerful way to start seeing the higher plane that they are all reaching for.

Understand Your Crystals

More than just using crystals to enhance your meditation, meditation can also help you understand your crystals more deeply. Taking special time with each of your crystals is an amazing way to really dive into the very specific way each crystal works for you. This is especially effective if you really go one crystal at a time with your meditation. When wearing crystals or keeping them around the house, you aren't really spending intentional, focused time with them. However, when you are sitting individually with one particular crystal, then you can really notice the way it affects you. Observe yourself a little during this meditation practice. How does the crystal make you feel? What thoughts come to mind? Is it making you feel relaxed or energized? You can even write a short reflection after this meditation if you want to record your experience. You might find that you end up wanting to do this reflection every time you buy a new crystal so you can really get to know how it affects you!

What Crystals Should You Use?

If you are going to try different kinds of meditation, then you should experiment with different crystals. Focus crystals tend to be popular for meditation since they help you to streamline your ideas. However, you can choose different kinds of crystals for this practice, not just focus ones. It all depends on what your goals for the meditation session are. If you intend to have a purely relaxing session, then bringing along crystals that will help with that relaxation is prudent. However, if you want to dig deep into your soul, then you will need crystals that focus on truth and revelations. Or perhaps you are interested in manifestation meditation, in which case you should choose a crystal that relates to the facet of your life in which you are trying to manifest. Basically, the crystals you choose should correspond to the goals you have for your meditation practice. In Chapter 17, when I list all the pertinent crystals, you should consider how each one can be used during meditation. Reflect on your meditation goals, as well as the crystals you personally connect with, and you will be able to choose the right one that will fit your meditation practice perfectly.

How to Use Crystals in Your Meditation Practice

So, now that you know why you should use crystals for meditation and what crystals are best to use, you can start learning how to use them. The long and short of it is that there is no one way to integrate crystals into your existing meditation practice. It's all up to the way you prefer to meditate and your relationship with crystals. Some people feel the effects of crystals very strongly and thus can't be too close to them without becoming overwhelmed. On the other hand, many people feel that they need to have their crystals very close to them in order to feel any effect at all. In another vein, there is also the issue of parts of the body, or chakras, where you feel your crystals have the strongest effect. In order to harness a crystal's meditative power, you need to find the method that works best for you. There is no one way of doing so, but there are some established methods that might be a good jumping-off point for you. In this section, I will share some of these methods so you can begin to explore the ways crystal healing can be incorporated into your meditation practice.

The Holding Method

The simplest way to meditate with crystals is to simply hold one while you meditate. This is best to use with focus crystals when you are attempting to channel a particular thought or feeling through your crystal. When you hold a crystal, you want to center its power and channel your thoughts through it. Sit down or stand, depending on what you prefer, and hold the crystal out in front of you. Concentrate on the crystal and how it feels in your hand. Whether or not you have your eyes open, make sure you know where it is in space. Then, think about the topic you are meditating on very carefully, concentrating on the crystal at the same time. This should help your energies work together well and channel the questions through your crystals. Even if you aren't using a focus crystal, the holding method requires you to channel your energies through your hands and the crystal inside of them. If you are intending the crystal to have more of an effect on you, try to feel the ebb and flow coming from your palms up your arms and radiating throughout your body. This way, you should be able to really concentrate on the energy of that one crystal, either channeling your thoughts through its prism or allowing its energy into your body.

The Chakra Method

As I talked about in Chapter 3 with chakras, crystal practice is linked with the chakras of the body, so you might want to incorporate those concepts into your practice. This meditation method will involve concentrating on a certain part of your body and the crystal it is associated with. To choose a crystal for your chakra meditation process, you should use three frameworks: crystals associated with the particular thing you are manifesting or unblocking, crystals associated with the chakra you are targeting, and of course, crystals you personally connect with. If you are able to find the crystal that fits all these criteria, you will be well on your way to unblocking your chakras and creating balance throughout your body.

The method by which you should use crystals to target your chakras during meditation involves lying face-down and placing crystals strategically along your back at your central chakra points. So, if you are targeting your root chakra, you would place the crystal over your tailbone, and if you are targeting your heart chakra, you would place the crystal right between your shoulder blades, and so on. You might need a friend or masseuse to aid you with this practice. Lie there for as long as you think you need to and really concentrate on that part of your body and the crystal's impact on it. Try to feel that same ebb and flow entering that part of your body as a loosening agent. At the same time, you can also concentrate on issues pertinent to that chakra. For example, if you are targeting your sacral chakra with your crystals lying on your lower back, reflect on some issues you might be insecure about and feel them being cleansed and leaving your body. You'll likely find that this targeted practice will help you with more specific problems that relate to clear facets of your life. Crystals can be a very effective way to open up blocked chakras.

The Surrounding Method

For those who are more sensitive to crystal power or who want to incorporate a wider array of crystals into their practice, you can try the surrounding method. The surrounding method involves laying your crystals out in a formation around your person as you meditate. The formation, the amount and type of crystals, and the placement of each individual crystal are all up to you. The advantage of this method is that it welcomes many different crystals so that you can mix and match, creating a wonderful variety of energies. However, you should be wary that this benefit can also be a drawback as mixing too many crystals together can be challenging and potentially dangerous for the inexperienced crystal user. Combining two incompatible or hyperintense crystals can create a confusing meditation experience. Since most people want meditation to be relaxing, clarifying, or even rejuvenating, creating conflicting energies is probably the last thing you want to do. Thus, you should make sure to do your research and learn about the crystals you are using and their effect on one another.

To perform your meditation using the surrounding method, you can incorporate some of the above techniques. For example, you can use the concentration of the holding method by selecting a particular crystal to place in front of you and concentrate your energy on. You can also incorporate chakras into the surrounding method by placing certain crystals strategically to match up with your chakras. You can achieve this either by lying down and placing the crystals around you at chakra points or by hanging your crystals at chakra points while sitting up. Combining these methods can help you really enhance the surrounding method and can even be a good modification for those who find touching crystals to be too intense.

The Yoga Method

Another method of meditating with crystals is to incorporate them into a meditative yoga practice. Just as there are different kinds of meditation and crystal practices, there are also many different kinds of yoga practice. However, if you are practicing more meditation-driven yoga, then you might want to consider incorporating some crystals. You can use the surrounding method by placing crystals around the area where you want to do your yoga practice or even wear your crystals while you practice your yoga. This method can also cross over with the chakra method, especially if you are trying to unblock a certain chakra and want to use its corresponding crystal to do so. No matter the spiritual practice, they can often be intertwined to help benefit you on your spiritual journey.

Pillar 4:
Preparation

Moving away from the purposes and possible applications of your crystals, we will now get into the core of crystal practice: the actual preparation and use of your crystals. You might not know it, but preparation is actually a huge part of using crystals. Treating your crystals properly is integral for them to be effective. In this pillar, I will be showing you all the essential ways you need to prepare your crystals.

Chapter 11:
Cleansing Your Crystals

The first step of the preparation process is to cleanse your crystals. You may not realize it, but the outside world can actually have a huge effect on your crystals. Similar to how your crystals impose their vibrations on the rest of the world, so too does the world impose vibrations on your crystals. These other vibrations can have a great influence on how your crystals work and can sometimes completely decimate their intended purpose. Cleansing is especially important to do when you first purchase your crystals. They have either been in a store, being touched by many people every day, or in a shipping warehouse, where they may have been tossed from person to person. All those people had their own energies that they were bringing and which might have had an effect on your crystals. You don't want to be encountering all those people's energies when you engage in your own crystal practice. Thus, cleansing is essential when you first purchase your crystals, no matter what. But it's not just at the beginning that they need to be cleansed. Your crystals are exposed to many different energies throughout the time you are using them. Whether it's the people you encounter while you are wearing your crystals, people who are invited into your home, or simply your own different energies rubbing off on them, your crystals should be cleaned regularly to make sure that they are always fresh and ready to use to their full potential.

Now, what do I mean by cleaning? It's not a physical cleaning, although you can always do that too. No, what I am talking about is a spiritual cleansing of the crystal's vibrations. You can think of this as a kind of reset, like restoring your laptop to factory mode or clearing a hard drive. All the debris and bugs that have accumulated in the crystal's vibrations are wiped clean and you can start fresh. You're probably wondering how this is done since there is no clear physical process to "wipe" a crystal. Well, I am here to help. There are a few different methods for cleansing crystals, all of which bring their own qualities to the table. The method you choose will be up to you and your crystal practice as well as the degree of cleansing you are going for. In this chapter, I will outline for you the fundamentals of crystal cleansing so you can ensure that you always have properly reset crystals.

Method #1: Plain Water

Sometimes, you just have to cleanse your crystals the old-fashioned way: with plain water. Water is the root cleansing material, the substance that humans and animals alike have washed themselves with for millions of years. For cleansing crystals specifically, running water is essential. Bathing your crystal in a tub of standing water will keep its old vibrations surrounding it. Running water, on the other hand, is able to completely wash away any negative energy. You want your water to be cold and free-flowing for this purpose. For the best results, you should try using a natural water source, such as a stream. This will imbue your crystal with energy from the earth. However, if you don't have access to a natural river or stream, then you can use tap water, but make sure it is flowing freely. To achieve a proper cleanse, hold your stones under the running water for at least a full minute. This technique is great for a quick cleanse to breathe some fresh life into your crystals.

Method #2: Salt Water

For a deeper, more chemical cleanse, you can use salt water. While fresh water is associated with the clean mountain springs of the earth, salt water is associated with the deep and powerful oceans. Salt water has natural disinfecting and purifying qualities, which is why doctors will often prescribe it for infected wounds or mouth sores. You can also use this purifying quality to cleanse your crystals. This kind of cleanse is for a more deeply disrupted stone as opposed to running water which really only cleans the surface. The technique to cleanse your crystals with salt water is to submerge them for at least a few hours, if not a few days. This will allow the salt water to fully penetrate your stone to its core and allow all the unwanted vibrations to seep out. You might want to perform a post-cleansing rinse using the above method with fresh water, just to ensure everything is washed off and you don't have any negative vibrations or salt water residue still clinging to your crystal. As with fresh water, you will have the best results with natural salt water. Obviously, this is not really feasible for anyone who doesn't live in a coastal location, so you can make your own using salt and water. If you are landlocked but still very serious about using natural seawater, you can always order some online and have it delivered to you. However, salted water will still be suitable. For a more natural touch, you can use a raw salt source, such as Himalayan pink salt or sea salt. This technique gives your crystals a deep, thorough cleanse that will completely reset the way that they heal.

Method #3: Rice

Have you ever heard the advice about putting a waterlogged phone into a bowl of rice to try to save it? That technique is based on the fact that rice has natural absorption properties. Rice is naturally porous, so it tends to soak up any moisture around it. Crystal healers, however, will use rice to not only absorb water but negative energy as well. Instead of soaking into your crystals as with salt water, rice instead draws the negative effects out of your crystals. The method of soaking is done in almost exactly the same way as with salt water. You place your crystals in a bowl of rice and soak them for at least 24 hours. This should be enough time to pull out any negative energy that you don't want in your crystals. Rice can do wonders for drawing any conflicting vibrations out of your crystals and creating a fresh environment.

Method #4: Sunlight

Besides water and grain, the other life-giving element on this earth is the sun. Anyone who has stepped outside on a beautiful day knows how rejuvenating just a few hours of sunlight can be. It can make you feel like a big solar panel, having your batteries recharged by the warm light. Well, the same actually goes for your crystals. Even though it might not seem like much, exposing your crystals to a healthy amount of sunlight can actually be a powerful cleansing agent. Putting your crystals outside on a sunny day in an exposed area can give them the heat and light cleanse they need to reset.

Method #5: Moonlight

As an alternative to cleansing with sunlight, you can also soak your crystals in moonlight. Moonlight is simply a reflection of the sun's light, so it has already been filtered and subdued. Cleansing with moonlight is less harsh than cleansing with sunlight, but it is equally important. If you want a softer, more mystical approach to cleansing with light, moonlight can be a great option. Of course, you can always time it so that your crystals get a little bit of both. Try to find a sunny day followed by a full moon so that you get the best possible effect for your crystals.

Chapter 12:
Charging Your Crystals

Once your crystals are nice and cleansed, you can now start charging them. Charging your crystals is an integral part of the process of infusing them with energy. As much as crystals bring their own energy to the table, their energy comes from a connection to the earth. Just like batteries, and even people, they need to reconnect with a power source every once in a while to replenish their energy. When you are embarking on your crystal journey, you will need to learn how to charge your crystals in order to maintain their energy throughout your time with them. All the best crystal practitioners regularly charge their crystals and swear by some of their favorite methods. In this chapter, I will teach you all about the process of charging crystals so that you, too, can participate in this important aspect of crystal healing. First, I will give you an overview of the difference between charging and cleansing. Next, I will describe a general timeline and schedule for when you should give your crystals a good charge. And finally, I will enlighten you about some of the ways in which you can effectively charge your crystals. By the end of the chapter, you should have a solid grasp of the process for charging your crystals and be ready to start doing it yourself.

What Is Crystal Charging?

So, what exactly is going on when you charge your crystal? And what is exactly the difference between charging and cleansing? Well, the main difference is output versus input. When you cleanse your crystals, you are removing negative energy from them, allowing them to recalibrate their vibrations and come to a more balanced state. When you charge your crystals, on the other hand, you are imbuing them with positive or energizing vibrations. Though crystals retain their natural vibrations indefinitely, exposing them to positive energies can do a lot for their productivity. Thus, charging is like giving your crystal vibrations a boost. It's like flavoring a cast-iron skillet. The skillet might work on its own, but taking proper care of it—washing it with sea salt and allowing flavors to soak into it—can really enhance its performance. Charging your crystals gives them a recalibration in a different way than cleansing does by infusing them with energy rather than removing energy from them.

When Should You Charge Your Crystals?

So, we know that you should cleanse crystals when you first get them and when you feel they have been exposed to excessive negative or conflicting energies. These experiences can confuse your crystals and cause their energies to become imbalanced. But when do you charge your crystals? Well, we can think of the relationship between cleansing and charging as being like washing and moisturizing your skin. After you take a shower—washing your skin—you want to moisturize your body to restore some of the hydration lost during washing. Because cleaning with soap can strip the body's natural oils, adding moisturizer afterward is essential to help your skin retain moisture. The concept is similar for cleaning and charging crystals. If you have recently cleaned your crystals, they will be much more vulnerable than before as they have been completely stripped down to their natural vibrations. Thus, they could use a boost to help recalibrate their energy. For this reason, it's a good idea to combine your charging schedule with your cleansing schedule, doing one after the other. This way, your crystals will get a dual energy replenishment and be able to come back as strong as possible.

How to Charge Crystals

Now that you know why and when you should charge your crystals, we need to talk about how to do so. As with cleansing, there are many ways in which you can charge your crystals. Many of these substances will have slightly different effects on your crystals, so you should make sure that you know the specific qualities of everything that you are using to charge each crystal. Similar to choosing the crystal yourself, you should make sure you are in tune with the vibrations you are giving to your crystals. In this section, I will outline some of the most common methods and materials people use to charge their crystals.

Burial

Crystals come from the earth. It's no wonder, then, that they draw so much energy from it. It is the ground that first imbues your crystals with all their potent energy, drawing all their vibrations out of the very core of the earth. When we mine them, we sever that connection. Yes, we are still able to harness the powers of the crystal continuously after this, but we must remember that it is the ground that formed the crystal and gave it its natural vibrations. When you restore this connection, even for just a few hours, you give the crystal a boost from its natural home that it needs in order to really shine.

The general method for charging your crystal through burial is very simple. All you have to do is dig a hole anywhere in the ground. This could be in your backyard or even a safe public space that is very secluded where the crystal is not likely to be stolen. If you don't have access to a burial place in the ground, you can try burying your crystal in a large potted plant to simulate the experience of being buried in the ground, but this does mean that your crystal won't have access to the strong earth connection of being buried directly in the ground. For another modification, if you have a crystal that is apt to get dirty and is hard to physically clean, such as a very jagged one, you can put it in a protective container. However, you should know that burying your crystal bare will have the most powerful effects. For the best results, you should leave your crystals buried underground for at least a week each time you recharge them. This will allow their temperature to fully regulate and absorb all the vibrations of the earth. You can leave them there for less time, but you might not get the full effect you want. Burying a crystal in the ground allows it to reconnect to its roots (literally) and restore some of its most primal vibrations.

Singing Bowls

Vibrations are a huge part of crystals, as we have discussed at length throughout this book; vibrations are also a core aspect of sound. Sound might not seem like something powerful, since you cannot see or touch it, but it can actually have an immense impact on your crystals. Now, almost any sound can affect your crystals. Your own voice even has an effect. You can try singing or chanting to your crystals to try and align them with your energy. These strategies are very popular and have proven effective. But one of the most common ways people use sound to charge their crystals is with singing bowls. These are the round metal bowls you can find at most spirituality stores that have a stick that goes along with them, sometimes resembling a mortar and pestle. When you drag the stick along the outer edge of the bowl, you create a beautiful sound. These bowls are not just used for crystals but to generally help people with their vibrations. The sound has a powerful quality that can really ignite energy. For this reason, singing bowls are absolutely perfect for charging crystals.

You can charge crystals using singing bowls by sounding them in the vicinity of your crystals. The closer your crystals are to the sound, the more intense the effect will be on them. If you have small enough crystals or a big enough bowl, you can even put your crystals inside the bowl to get the maximum effect. Some crystal healers refer to this as giving your crystals a "sound bath." Bathing your crystals in the beautiful vibrations of your singing bowl is a powerful way to charge them. This is especially true for those who already incorporate singing bowls into their existing spiritual practice. For those people, sound baths are one of the ideal methods of charging your crystals as they will help align all the vibrations of your different spiritual practices.

Incense

Another one of the senses you can use to charge your crystals is smell. There are so many herbs and spices with different qualities that can be useful for charging. Look at the incense you normally use and evaluate how it might be compatible with your crystals. Try to match different kinds of incense with crystals that are also attuned to that particular quality. If you are able to do this, then you will be able to charge your crystals with the exact kind of energy that will really make them sparkle.

There are a few distinct ways you can charge your crystals with incense. One method involves burning the incense and then allowing your crystals to pass through the smoke. This exposes them to the vibrations in the smoke, coating them with a thin film of residue. This can help the healing effects of the incense truly soak into the crystals. The other method involves smudging or rubbing the soot from the incense smoke on your crystals. Both of these methods involve coating your crystals with the incense residue, which is an important way to really allow the two energies to contact one another. Some popular types of incense to use include herbs or pure incense like lavender, sandalwood, and jasmine. When you do this technique right, you will be infusing your crystal with certain energies, just like with singing bowls.

Salt

If you want to infuse your crystals with another crystal, you can actually use salt! Technically, salt is chemically a crystal. It is not generally used in crystal practice, except perhaps Himalayan pink salt, but it has a strong relationship to your spiritual crystals because of this quality. Thus, you can actually use salt to charge the crystals in your practice. We talked back in the last chapter about using salt water, which is water infused with salt, for cleansing. But for charging, you need something a little bit more powerful. Soaking your crystals in a bowl of salt, especially a more natural salt, can infuse them with all sorts of energies. Just like burying your crystals in the ground, immersing your crystals in salt reconnects them with their roots and allows them to exchange energies with other crystals.

Human Breath

Believe it or not, you also have strong spiritual energy and vibrations that can really rub off on your crystals! Just being around your crystals is inherently charging to them since your presence asserts your vibrations onto them. If you own crystals that you wear or otherwise interact with a lot, then you are already infusing them with your vibrations. But if you are actively charging your crystals, then you will want to make sure that they have as much exposure to your vibrations as possible. When we talk about human vibrations and auras, we mean a lot of things. Heartbeat, nervous system, breathing rhythms—all these things contribute to your overall aura frequency. Since it's hard to expose your crystals to the former two, many crystal healers use the latter in order to create a strong connection between their own vibrations and their crystals'. Breathing directly on your crystals exposes them not only to the rhythm of your breathing but also to the natural vibrations of your voice box. You can also try singing directly into your crystals to get the maximum vibration effect. This technique charges your crystals with powerful vibrations and ensures that they are strongly connected to you and your body's particular aura.

Connect Them With Your Spiritual Guides

If you are very embedded in the spiritual community, then you will likely have your own spiritual guides. These are figures, such as gods or astrological entities, who you feel you have a strong connection to and who you look to for guidance in your spiritual life. Many of the techniques we have talked about in this chapter focus heavily on connection. These techniques help you to form links between different aspects of your spiritual life and create pathways that will help you on your journey toward spiritual unity. If you are able to link your spiritual guides with your crystals, charging them with the right kind of energy for you, then you will be further enriching your spiritual web and creating strong connections all around.

Chapter 13:
Programming Your Crystals

The third major step before using your crystals is to program them. Programming is the natural progression from cleansing and charging. When you charge your crystals, you are infusing them with energy and boosting their abilities to serve their natural purpose. Programming, however, is a more focused kind of charging. If you think of charging as charging up your laptop, programming is like setting your desktop picture and downloading the software you want to use. While some of the charging methods I talked about in the previous chapter are helpful to steer your crystals toward your intention, programming is about directly stating your intention and setting your crystals on the exact path. In this chapter, I will lead you through the process of programming your crystals so that you can make sure they are on the best path of intentionality. First, I will give you the general definition and parameters of crystal programming. Then, I will explain some of the distinctive benefits of programming your crystals. And finally, I will show you a few of the many methods you can use to program your crystals toward the purposes you want them to serve. By the end of this chapter, you should have some very purposefully programmed crystals!

What Is Crystal Programming?

So, we know that crystal programming is all about setting your crystals toward specific intentions, but how exactly does that work? Well, programming your crystals is all about setting intentions. When you go to meditate, you likely already have an intention in your mind. You want to recharge, reflect on some ideas, or let go of your anxieties. Well, it's the same with crystals. Before you start using your crystals, you need to really set your intentions with them. What are you really using your crystals for? What kind of energies are you looking to bring into your life with them? What are the energies you are hoping they will help you banish? Where do you see your crystal journey taking you? Toward enlightenment about the higher things in life? Toward the kind of life you want to have? Toward a deeper connection with the universe and others? Considering all these important questions will greatly help you to program your crystals in the direction that is right for you.

Crystal programming also relates to the material qualities of your crystals, meaning that you have the ability to program your crystals with material conditions as well as with intentions. Some of the charging methods I talked about in the last chapter relate to specific things, but that was mostly just with alignment and forging connections between your spiritual practices. The methods outlined in this chapter will focus on more specific ways to guide your crystals in a certain direction. They will infuse your crystals with a particular quality which will allow you to focus the natural qualities of your crystals toward the exact use you are intending them for. In other words, programming is a more precise version of charging, one being revving up your engine and the other setting your course.

Benefits of Crystal Programming

There are many ways programming can completely revamp your crystal experience. You might have had exceptional experiences with crystals so far and can certainly go on using them without necessarily programming them every single time you use them, but you will assuredly get better and more focused results if you do program them. However, you will not get your desired results if you are attempting to go against the natural properties of the crystal. Stating your intentions should always be a narrowing-down process. You should consider your intentions before you even buy your crystals, and then you should continue to narrow down as you go. Trying to make a relaxation crystal into a manifesting crystal will only mean that you aren't getting what you want and are confusing the crystal's energy. As long as you are able to thoroughly match the crystal's qualities to your intentions, you will easily be able to program them to the intentions you have in mind.

Crystal Programming Methods

As with cleansing and charging, there are many ways you can program your crystals. Some of these ways will be more effective with certain types of crystals than with others. Certain methods will also be more effective with certain types of intentions than others, especially if you have very specific plans for your crystals. In this section, we will explore some of the most common methods people use to program their crystals. Some of these methods will involve pure manifestation on your part, while others will require specific ceremonies to be conducted. It all depends on what you feel is right for you and your crystal.

Manifestation

The clearest way to really program your crystals properly is to incorporate them into your manifestation process. Hold them while you are manifesting or meditating, and try to really link the thoughts going through your mind and the crystal you are holding in your hand. Visualization is a very important part of this process. Think about the thing you are trying to manifest in your life. Is it love? Creative inspiration? Money? Whatever it is, you need to connect with it. But connecting to it doesn't just mean thinking about the thing itself but rather how it specifically fits into your life. Think about the exact way in which you would experience the things you want and clearly visualize an image of your life with this newfound thing. If you do this while deeply connecting with your crystal, then you will be able to actually manifest what you want as well as program your crystal at the same time.

Chakra Method

Back in Chapter 3, we talked about how crystals relate to the chakras. There are often crystals that correspond to different chakras, and crystals can even help you to unblock or open up some of your chakras. But did you know you can also use your chakras to program your crystals? Because crystals are heavily connected to manifestation, the best chakra to use is actually your third eye chakra. This chakra is connected to your far-reaching goals and life plan. If you use this chakra to program your crystals, then you will forge a strong connection between these long-term plans and your chakras. The exact way in which you can accomplish this is to lie down and place your crystal of choice over your third eye chakra. Then, you can practice some of the same manifestation and visualization techniques listed above. You can think of this method as a sort of elevated version of the manifestation technique, using the specificity of the third eye chakra to help you guide your intentions toward your crystal's energy.

Crystal Grids

Another important method you can use to program your crystals is to actually use other crystals. Crystals obviously have strong vibration patterns that both affect and are affected by other vibration patterns. So, it follows that crystals are able to be influenced by one another. Your crystals, especially if they have different vibrations or are for different purposes, can have a massive impact on each other. They can pick up on each others' vibration patterns and exchange energies. Creating this symbiosis between crystals is a very important aspect of programming them, especially if this is a group of crystals that you intend to use in conjunction with one another. Just like syncing your crystals up with your own energies and the rest of your spiritual practices, syncing your crystals up with each other is also crucial. Plus, if you sync your crystal combinations properly, you can actually create a more dynamic effect than you might have had otherwise.

So, how do you sync your crystals? Well, one of the most popular methods of doing so is to use something called a "crystal grid." A crystal grid is essentially an arrangement of crystals designed so that they can feed off of one another's energies. You can use crystal grids to program and just practice in general. Crystal grids do all of what I listed above: construct a relationship between your crystals and help you to gather multiple energies in one place for a more powerful crystal healing session. When you use a crystal grid to program, you are subtly creating a dynamic and hierarchy among your crystals. You are introducing them to one another, setting the precedent for the way they will be used in tandem in the future.

The arrangement of the crystals is, of course, paramount when it comes to a crystal grid. Most crystal grids are constructed as a circle, with one "dominant" crystal in the center and the other crystals surrounding it. However, you can decide what arrangement suits you best. If there is a particular shape or pattern that you feel speaks to you spiritually, such as a triangle or a star, then feel free to use that shape. Most shapes will have a crystal placed so that forms some sort of center or peak. Where you place each crystal within the hierarchy will have a great impact on the way the crystal functions in regard to the others. If placed in a strong position, this crystal's vibrations might have dominance over the other crystals, thus setting a definitive precedent for the vibrations of the collection as a whole. For this reason, you should choose which crystal goes in this position wisely, picking the one you feel the strongest connection with and the one you feel has the most bearing on your intentions. This way, you will charge all of your crystals with your favorite one, aligning them with your chosen energy.

Chapter 14:
Setting Your Intention

In order to use crystals effectively, you have to know what you are using them for. You don't want to go manifesting the wrong things. Even if you are aware of the vague ideas you want to manifest, you might not be specific enough in those intentions. Manifesting vague things with your crystals is almost as bad as manifesting the wrong things since you are basically not giving your crystals the proper directions. You might find that you end up in a "be careful what you wish for" kind of situation, where you are in a negative version of your intended manifested purpose. For this reason, setting your intentions properly is one of the most important aspects of crystal use. In this chapter, we are going to step back from hard crystal knowledge and discuss your reasoning for using crystals. I will take you through the step-by-step process of ironing out your clear intentions for your crystal practice and creating a plan for how you are going to use your crystals.

Step 1: Determine the Facet of Life You Are Manifesting

It's always good to narrow your ideas down before coming up with something major. When you are embarking on a journey of manifestation, you need to start by identifying where in your life you are trying to manifest positive energy. Is it in your love life, your professional life, your creative life, your friendships, or something else? This area doesn't necessarily have to be an area in which you are extremely deficient. For example, many people who are working in their dream field still have goals and aspirations related to their careers, and many people in happy marriages still pray for longevity in their relationships. Thus, the facet of life that you are manifesting in can be any facet in which you have goals, hopes, dreams, or aspirations. Anywhere you feel like you could have more or go further can be an area for manifesting. You might also want to manifest in multiple areas of your life at the same time. If that is the case, you should still follow these steps individually for each one. For the purposes of this step, you should decide what category you are trying to manifest within.

Step 2: Determine Where You Are Now

The next step of the process is to take a good hard look at what that facet of your life looks like now. As much as many happy people still want to manifest, you might also be experiencing a hard time. Knowing how you currently feel in that facet of your life will be integral in figuring out what exactly you are trying to manifest. Ask yourself this question: "What do I feel is lacking in this part of my life?" It might be everything. For example, you might be single and desperate for a relationship, and therefore you are simply lacking the presence of romance in your life. Or, you might already be in a relationship but experiencing a rough patch with your partner, so you are lacking some of the more nuanced aspects of love. Career-wise, you might be happy in your job but feel like you are due for a promotion and are therefore feeling somewhat of a lack of professional appreciation. Or, alternatively, you might be in a completely dead-end job and feel like you are lacking any professional satisfaction. Whatever your degree or type of deprivation, you need to identify the missing piece that is driving you to want to manifest change in that area.

Step 3: Determine Where You Want to Be in the Short and Long Term

Once you have determined your current state of affairs, you need to really investigate what you want them to turn into. Just identifying your lack is not enough; you have to identify what you want to take its place. Failing to do so might result in you manifesting the wrong kind of energy to replace it. So, for example, if you are single and want to be in a relationship, you can't just manifest for the alleviation of your loneliness—you have to manifest for the actual type of relationship you are seeking. Otherwise, your spiritual guides won't have a clear idea and you could end up in an unhealthy or unsatisfactory relationship because you failed to really define the details of what you actually want. This is where you start to form the basis of your manifestation. You are creating clear aspirations out of your dissatisfaction.

One important element of this step is to consider the difference between the near future and the more distant future. Most goals will have both components to them, with the short-term goals merely being stepping stones to your longer-term goals. So, in regards to your romantic life, your long-term goal might be to be happily married with kids, but your short-term goal is simply to get a date. In the professional world, your short-term goal might be a promotion, whereas your long-term goal is to become CEO of your company. All of these goals are important to consider. So, when you are looking at how you want your deficiency to be transformed, you have to think about how you want it to be addressed immediately as well as down the road. This will give you two distinctive visions to concentrate on as you move forward in your manifesting journey.

Step 4: Create a Mood Board

After you've really dug deep into what your goals are, you need to start visualizing them more carefully. One of the most popular ways to visualize goals for your life and yourself is to create a mood board. Conventionally, a mood board is a collection of photographs or other images representing an idealized version of what you want. Think of a mood board as a bulletin board for your future. You can add clothes you would like to wear, places you would like to live or visit, professions you would like to have, and so forth. They don't have to represent the exact things you want, but their purpose is to give you a visual representation of the type of life you want. When people plan their weddings, they will often create mood boards with images of things like dresses, decorations, food, cakes, and other wedding-related items. They won't necessarily have those exact flower garlands or centerpieces, but they will have a clear visual guide to show a wedding planner so that they can create something similar. This is what you are going to do for your future self.

Mood boards help you visualize the life you want more clearly, showing you the life you could have if you achieve your goals. Since manifestation relies so heavily on visualization, mood boards help you to create that mental picture of what your future life is going to look like. That being said, a mood board does not necessarily need to be completely visual. You can simply collect things that inspire you. So, if you are looking to become an entrepreneur, you might not find it helpful to create a picture collage of people in business suits, but you might find it helpful to create a list of entrepreneurs who inspire you or a YouTube playlist of some talks about starting a business. These items aren't necessarily pictures per se, but they still give you something definitive to look at in order to help your manifestation brain visualize what you want.

Step 5: Connect Your Desires to Your Core Self

In psychology, there is a dichotomy known as intrinsic motivation versus extrinsic motivation. Extrinsic motivation is motivation that is unrelated to the actual task at hand but instead is based on the pursuit of a material reward, such as a paycheck or a prize. Intrinsic motivation, on the other hand, is the desire to do something for its own sake, reaping pure satisfaction from accomplishment itself. So, if you bake because you love creating interesting combinations of flavors and get satisfaction out of completing the task well, that would be intrinsic motivation, whereas if you bake because you work in a bakery and need to make your weekly paycheck, that is extrinsic motivation. Even though some extrinsic motivation is effective, many psychologists believe that intrinsic motivation is actually more powerful. When you connect the task you are doing with your deepest desires and values, then you will be more likely to accomplish it well because it's the accomplishment itself that is of value.

When you get to the manifestation stage, you really need to be able to find intrinsic motivation for the goal you have set. This is important to do for two reasons. The first reason is that your goals will be more focused and easier to achieve. If you want a promotion because you want to make a higher salary versus because you want to make a difference in a way that only the higher position can really achieve, then you might not get as far. The other reason you should try to find as much intrinsic motivation as possible is that, for manifestation to be effective, you need to really believe it at the core of your being. The crystals respond to your innermost vibrations. If the desire isn't vibrating at the very core of your body, the crystals will not be able to truly pick up on it, even if you are screaming it in your conscious mind. In order to really achieve results with your crystal manifestation, you have to ensure that your goals are strongly aligned with your innermost values.

Pillar 5:
Care

So, you've prepared your crystals, you've set your intentions, and you've been able to manifest great things. You are truly reaping the benefits of all your amazing crystals have to offer. But now you need to take a bit of a step back and ask yourself what you are offering to your crystals. By now, you really understand that crystals are like living things. They are rife with vibrations, life, and energy. You can't just treat them like inanimate objects. As I talked about in the chapter on cleansing, crystals are very susceptible to outside influences, and vice versa. If you don't take care of them properly, your crystals can easily become misaligned, or worse, misalign other things too. In this pillar, we will be focusing on how to properly care for your crystals. This is an extremely important aspect of working with crystals, helping you to give back to your crystals and treat them right after they have given so much to you.

Chapter 15:
Storing Crystals

The way you store your crystals can have a huge impact on how they work. You can think of crystal storage as kind of like your crystals' off time. This is their time to relax, recharge, and rest for the next time you want to use them. But storing them is not quite as simple as that. Where you choose to store a crystal can have an effect on the crystal as well as the space. The combination of crystals that can be stored together is also an important complexity to acknowledge. You might also be interested in how long you should store your crystals. All these questions and more are important to investigate. In this chapter, I will guide you through proper storing practices for your crystals, helping you to create a healthy environment in which your crystals can rest in between healing sessions.

What Your Crystals Need Protection From

As we stated above, your crystals are very open to outside influences. You saw in the previous few chapters how many different influences and elements have the ability to strongly affect your crystals. Any kind of vibration can completely alter the way your crystals work. This is good if you are trying to influence them in a certain way since it allows you to really customize your crystals to your specific needs, but it is not good in the sense that, if gone uncontrolled, your crystals can pick up a lot of outside influences without you realizing it. When you are storing your crystals, there are a few things that you need to be concerned with. In this section, I will give you a list of the major things you need to keep your crystals away from during their storage period in order to protect them from these influences.

Light

As we talked about in the chapter on cleansing, crystals can actually be greatly affected by light. Sunlight and moonlight in particular are very activating to crystals. If your crystal is exposed to natural sunlight or moonlight without being properly regulated, these can have an excess influence on its vibrations and possibly cause it to go out of whack. On another note, some crystals can be physically damaged from too much sunlight. Have you ever removed a picture from the wall in a brightly lit room only to realize that the sun has faded the wallpaper over time and there is a much more saturated square under where the picture used to be? Well, if sunlight can have this effect on wallpaper, it can certainly have an effect on crystals. So, for both their physical and spiritual well-being, try to keep your crystals in a dark place when storing them.

Water

The other major influence on crystals is water. In the chapter on cleansing your crystals, I talked about how running water and salt water can significantly influence your crystals. While you do want to cleanse your crystals regularly, you also don't want them to be constantly exposed to water. As with light, this can have a destabilizing effect on their vibrations, so it is best to keep your crystals' water exposure very controlled. Likewise, water can also damage certain crystals physically. Water has a corrosive or erosive effect on rocks if they are exposed to it for too long, so make sure your crystals are not stored in any place where they could get wet or rained on, both for the sake of their vibrations as well as their physical integrity.

People

People have energies and vibrations that can actually affect a crystal's energy. This is why I advised you to cleanse your crystals after they come in contact with other people, especially the general public, because all of the energies they bring to the table will have an effect on your crystals. This is why you should make sure to store crystals in a space where they won't be consistently exposed to people. This will make sure that their vibrations are kept pure and uninfluenced by people. It is for this reason that many people don't keep their crystals displayed, at least not unless they are actively trying to influence that room. Keeping your crystals displayed can cause their vibrations to be disrupted, especially if that area is used frequently by a lot of people. So, keep your crystals in a space where they will have lots of privacy, such as a closet or secured drawer.

Each Other

And finally, your crystals can also have an effect on one another. In the last chapter, I talked about crystal grids and how they can be used for programming. They can influence each other's vibrations and thus change the nature of each other's healing abilities. Well, the same goes for storage. If you store two crystals together, they will have an influence on one another. Unless this is something you want, you should probably store your crystals as separately as possible. Even putting them in different compartments of a jewelry box is a good way to get a small amount of the separation that they need.

What Needs Protection From Your Crystals

On the other end of the spectrum, crystals also will influence other things with their vibrations. Again, you do want this in some capacity, but making sure that your crystals don't have any undue influence on yourself and the people and world around you is responsible. For this reason, you should not only be very careful about which crystals you wear around whom but also about where those crystals are when you're not wearing or using them. You might inadvertently be exposing your friends or family to powerful crystal vibrations that should really only be used consciously and in small doses. This is especially true for very powerful crystals or crystals that have transformative energy. These can be very disruptive to someone's life, so they need to be handled with care. Leaving them lying around can potentially cause a lot of problems. So, for example, you might accidentally leave your crystal storage kit in the guest room of your house only to have a guest stay over and unwittingly experience the effects of the crystals in the kit. Or, you might think it's safe to store crystals in your bedside table drawer but are actually being affected by them in your sleep. Crystal vibrations are very powerful, so make sure you store them wisely.

Pillar 6:
Directory

Throughout this book, I have talked at length about the various uses for crystals and how different types of crystals can correspond to all sorts of things, like chakras, astrological signs, ailments, and so on. But what are these specific crystals? What are the names of some of the crystals you can use and what is each one generally used for? I have thus far avoided mentioning any specific crystals, but in this pillar, I will finally be answering this question. Here, we will look at some actual crystals and the purposes they serve in crystal healing practice.

Chapter 16:
Crystal List

You're probably wondering what exact crystals you should be using for your practice. I've already given you some advice about how to choose crystals, such as to trust your intuition or to select based on your intentions, but now I will get into the different crystals and what they are best used for. In this chapter, you will find a list of some of the most commonly used crystals and a brief description of each one's various applications.

Clear Quartz

When you think of crystals, you are probably picturing clear quartz. Clear quartz looks like the archetypal crystal: It is a clear, glassy stone that shines with white light. It is easily the most common crystal you can buy in stores. Moreover, clear quartz is also extremely versatile. This crystal can be used in almost any kind of crystal practice as a key grounding or protection crystal. What people mainly use clear quartz for is banishing negative energy. It can be used for any chakra because of its versatility but is especially useful for the third eye and crown chakras, which deal with clarity.

Rose Quartz

As you might be able to guess from its name, rose quartz is a beautiful pink stone. It is generally connected to the world of romance, earning it the nickname "the love stone." Rose quartz is probably the second most common crystal after clear quartz. It generally deals with the more emotional aspects of life, helping you to connect with others and even humanity at large. It is also known as a de-stressing stone, helping you to ease some of those tight anxieties that can build up over time. Many people also connect the rose quartz to their feminine side, and it has even been known to regulate menstrual cycles. The chakra that corresponds to rose quartz is of course the heart chakra, which is responsible for the more interpersonal side of life.

Smoky Quartz

The final type of quartz I will talk about is smoky quartz. Smoky quartz is a very powerful crystal known for banishing negative energy from your life. This stone is known to work best alone as it is a very foundational crystal and has an extremely powerful independent energy, so it may not be the best choice for your crystal grid. It is generally considered to be a rebalancing stone and can help you let go of old or stale belief systems. Its corresponding chakra is the root chakra since this crystal has the power to both destabilize your core beliefs as well as to ground you in new ones to find a way forward. Between these three types of quartz, we have the bottom, the middle, and the top chakra covered. Many people like to have all three so they can deliberately target different chakra areas comprehensively.

Amethyst

Moving away from the transformative power of the smoky crystal, amethysts are a very low-key stone. They are thus also very common crystals for people to own. In fact, many people have amethysts purely for decoration because of their sparkly texture and gorgeous purple shade. Most people will use amethyst as a balancing crystal, helping them to restore peace to their lives. It is also very commonly used for chronic pain issues. The amethyst is associated with the crown chakra, helping you to balance and regulate all your body's systems.

Angelite

As its name suggests, angelite has strong celestial connections. Its coloring echoes this as well—a soft sky blue. This crystal is all about purifying. If you feel like you have a very cluttered life and are losing connections to the things that you believe in, angelite can help you clear away some of the debris and breathe some fresh air into your life. It is also a deeply calming crystal and is especially good at helping you sleep. Hanging or placing an angelite crystal near your bed at night can help you achieve a more serene sleep. The angelite crystal is associated with the higher three chakras, including the throat, third eye, and crown, connecting to its regulating and purifying powers.

Green Jade

One of the most popular crystals used in jewelry, the green jade crystal is a beautiful opaque green, suggesting serenity and earthiness even in its coloring. Green jade is one of the best crystals to use for meditation. It has a calming effect that can really take your meditation abilities to the next level. Its corresponding chakra is the heart chakra, which connects it also to the spheres of love and romance, even family. Use green jade to connect more deeply to others and your spiritual self.

Tiger's Eye

The tiger's eye crystal is a smoky brown crystal that evokes an earthy but mysterious tone. As you might gather from its name, this crystal really promotes boldness. It is a crystal that can help you find your courage in a given situation. It is also associated with creativity. If you feel like you are experiencing a creative block or are having trouble sharing your creative side with others, tiger's eye can really help with that. Its corresponding chakra is the sacral chakra, which connects to the confidence-building and creative energy of the stone.

Malachite

This stone is not for the faint of heart. Its dark green wavy patterns represent the depths of the sea and all the powerful, unknowable entities that lie down there. Malachite is typically used for transformation purposes. It has the power to really banish negative energy from your life but often from a place or in a way that you weren't expecting. You might find that after using this crystal you lose friendships or experience intense upheavals in your life. While these things might be alarming, they are necessary for your growth. Malachite balances the heart and throat chakras, connecting with the communication and interpersonal honesty this crystal promotes.

Black Onyx

Black onyx is one of the prototypical protection crystals. It is imperative for your life to retain its positive energies and move toward a purely positive existence and mindset. As with malachite, black onyx is mainly used to expel negative energy from your life. Although it is somewhat less potent, it can still be a dangerous crystal to use because of the amount of change it can bring. Again, expect to see toxic people leave your life abruptly and for other major changes to take place. The main difference between malachite and black onyx is their chakra connection as black onyx is linked with the root chakra. Fundamental changes in your life will usually take place with the black onyx.

Fluorite

If you are looking for clarity in your life, you will want to use fluorite. This aqua-colored crystal is perfect for seeing the world realistically. Some people describe using this crystal as like wiping the fog off their windshield, allowing them to see clearly for the first time. Fluorite is also all about living in the moment. It can help you stop dwelling on past experiences or fretting about future possibilities. In short, fluorite can bring a groundedness and realism to your life and is great for trying to work out problems. Fluorite is linked with the throat chakra due to its focus on clarity and honesty.

Lepidolite

If green jade and rose quartz are about connecting with other people, lepidolite is all about connecting with yourself. This dark purple stone is one of the most visually striking crystals on this list. It is a great tool if you want to start practicing some more rigorous self-love in your life. It can help you get in touch with your higher spiritual self, creating a powerful connection. This can also lead to you becoming a more naturally intuitive person, allowing yourself to listen to your subconscious mind a little more closely. This crystal is linked with the higher chakras, including the heart, third eye, and crown, connecting with its high spiritual significance.

Turquoise

Turquoise is often considered to be the stone of luck. It is a powerful tool for manifestation meditation. It helps to guide you toward your ideal life, the path you are best suited for in your highest life. When you use turquoise during meditation, you can more clearly visualize your deepest desires. In this way, it can actually help you learn a lot more about yourself than you might have previously thought possible. This stone is connected with the throat chakra and is often used to help people who have a fear of public speaking find their voice.

Black Tourmaline

This dark, charcoal-looking crystal is one of the subtler crystals of the bunch. This is a purifying crystal that can be used to ward off and clear the air of negative energies in your space. It is very slow to work, but the results it can get are spectacular. Because of this slowness, it is one of the best candidates for wearability or interior decoration, as we talked about back in Chapters 8 and 9. You might not notice a profound difference in your life right away after using black tourmaline, but if you keep it in your space long enough, over time you will realize how clean and pure your space feels, all thanks to this crystal's slowly powerful energy. This stone is connected with the root chakra, helping to connect you with your space and banish negative energy.

Green Calcite

If you have gone through trauma in your life or experienced debilitating mental health issues in relation to your self-image, then green calcite is the crystal for you. Green calcite can help you to process difficult events from your past, letting go of the possible negative feelings about yourself that they might have caused. This stone can also help rid you of limiting beliefs about yourself, such as insecurities telling you that you can't do something or that you're not good at certain things. This crystal is associated with the heart chakra, reverberating through yourself into all your relationships.

Pillar 7:
Healing

So, now that you know the most common crystals that are used in the practice, we can move on to how they are used for healing. Those who have had issues in their lives, whether psychological, physiological, or circumstantial, have likely searched for healing in some way. There are many avenues that you can take for healing, and not all of them are for everybody. Sometimes you find that you just can't find exactly what you're looking for in mainstream medical circles. You have to search for that kind of healing elsewhere. If you are someone who values holistic healing—that is, including both the mind and body in your healing process—then crystals can be a very helpful avenue for you. Crystals can bring all the faculties of the body together and help you to heal in a way that makes you feel good all over. In this pillar, we will look at the process of using crystals to heal yourself.

Chapter 17: Healing

No matter what aspect of your life you are looking to heal, there is likely a crystal that can help you with it. Furthermore, there is also a particular way of using crystals that can especially target that area of your life. If you are able to properly match your crystals with the facet of your life that you are intending to heal, then you will be well on your way to constructing an effective healing practice. In this chapter, I will go through some of the most common areas in which people heal themselves using crystals and explain some of the fundamental aspects of that practice.

Anxiety

One of the most common reasons many people will turn to practices like crystal healing and meditation is stress. Nowadays, many people live very stressful lives, so practices like these are all the more necessary. Crystals regulate the body's natural rhythms, which is ideal for anxiety sufferers. Because anxiety is all about speeding up our rhythms to create a high-stress body, regulating our vibrations is essential. Amethyst, tiger's eye, and aquamarine are three of the most commonly used crystals for anxiety. In terms of methods, many people will either meditate with these crystals when they are experiencing immediate anxiety, or they will wear them around when they are experiencing lower-level, constant anxiety. If you follow these methods, your crystals should be able to help you regulate your moods and create a less anxious you!

Change

We all go through changes in our lives, but most of us wish that we could have a little more control over the changes we experience. There are two main ways in which people use crystals for change. One is to cope with changes outside of our control. Things like deaths, divorces, marriages, and births all have a huge impact on our lives, and crystals can help you manage these changes. Angelite is one of the most common stones used for change acceptance. Consider keeping some by your bed at night during transitional periods to help guide you into your new life. The other way people use crystals for change is to manifest change in areas that feel stale. This means that you are trying to bring about new experiences, relationships, and thoughts. For this side of change, you want to use either clear quartz for clarity or malachite for purging negative energy. Both of these crystals will guide you toward a new future worth pursuing. To use these crystals properly, incorporate them into your manifestation or meditation practices so you can be very clear about what you want.

Connection

Forging better connections is one of the things crystals are particularly good at. Similar to change, there are three main ways in which people use crystals for connecting purposes. The first kind is connection with the self. This is usually a building of intuition and a mingling of the conscious and subconscious minds. For this purpose, you should use a crystal such as turquoise to help open yourself up to your innermost desires. Second of all, there are connections with other people, both romantic and platonic. To help boost your ability to communicate, empathize, and care for others, you should choose stones like rose quartz and green jade. Finally, there is a connection with the universe at large or the spiritual world. This means opening yourself up to some of the higher forces that tend to go unnoticed in everyday life. For this purpose, you should choose either amethyst or clear quartz to bring that higher knowledge into your life.

Balance

Creating harmony in your life is one of the most important things to do on your spiritual journey. An unbalanced life can lead to a myriad of problems, including misalignment, confusion, and misdirection of life goals. If you are experiencing a lack of balance in your life, it can be a hard thing to pinpoint. There are a lot of consequences to having a lack of balance, which can reverberate throughout your entire body and every aspect of yourself. For this reason, an imbalance in your body can lead to all kinds of serious complications, such as low confidence, lack of groundedness, and suffering relationships. Thus, bringing balance to your life is essential. If you want a crystal that is good for balance, you should choose either a crown chakra crystal like amethyst or a strong variety of crystals. Creating a wide range of crystals to use in a grid or to wear together can ensure that all your bases are covered and you are able to make certain bodily faculties work in harmony with one another.

Concentration

Concentrating is something a lot of people struggle with, especially those with concentration-based disorders such as obsessive-compulsive disorder (OCD) or attention deficit hyperactivity disorder (ADHD). Issues with concentration can have an effect on your work performance, your interactions with other people, and your creative pursuits. But concentration means more than just your ability to pay attention to something in the moment. Concentration can also mean your level of focus in your life or your ability to choose a lane and commit to things or truly consider what you want to do with your life. People who lack concentration in a major way often switch between jobs frequently, never able to settle on what they like. They might also struggle to maintain long-term relationships because they find themselves overwhelmed by the number of options available to them. In these cases, people might be lacking in direction and purpose, which can leave them feeling really lost in life. For this mental state, you will want crystals that are associated with the third eye chakra and focus in general. Clear quartz, especially in the Vogel cut, is a great place to start. These crystals will help you see past the immediate clutter to the higher purpose you want to have in life.

Grounding

Another thing many people struggle with is feeling grounded. If you are someone who moves around a lot or moved around a lot as a child, you might find that you lack a place that feels like home or where you have roots. Those experiencing cultural diaspora might also feel a lack of groundedness. But it's not just a place that people might feel grounded in. You might have lived in the same place your whole life but don't feel grounded in your relationships or your career. You may feel that these things are not stable and could crumble around you at any moment. Sometimes this lack of feeling grounded results in something called an anxious attachment style, which can cause you to feel constant anxiety over whether you are accepted and loved, unable to truly trust the people in your life to be committed to you. Whether or not a traumatic incident triggered this, you likely feel a lot of pain around this. When using crystals to heal yourself for grounding, you want to get crystals that target your root chakra, such as black tourmaline or black onyx. These crystals will help you start to gain a more grounded perspective on your life and self and settle into where you are.

Conclusion

Crystals reaped their vibrations from the very core of the earth. Coincidentally, we share these vibrations. At our cores, we are made from the same substance and share a profound connection with the earth and thus crystals. Crystals are the way we connect to those core vibrations from whence we came, creating a strong relationship with the earth. It's no wonder, then, that crystals can have such a strong influence over us. We respond to them on a very deep level, recognizing that core connection and allowing it to influence us. There are many spheres of life in which crystals can influence us. They can help us connect with our sense of self, our purpose in life, others' feelings, and the universe at large. They can bring clarity to our life, helping us see through the debris of everyday life. They can create a more balanced mind and body that acknowledges the inherent connection between all the faculties. If we can let in the power of crystals, we are able to heal many aspects of our lives in a deep, long-lasting way.

In this book, I have led you through some of the most fundamental aspects of crystals and their healing practices. First, I showed you the basics of crystal history, helping you to see where the crystal practice comes from and how it has strong roots in many cultures around the world as well as connections to other practices like chakras, meditation, religion, and astrology. Then, I advised you on the ways in which you can purchase your crystals, leading you through all the main options available and listing the pros and cons of each so that you can make an informed decision for yourself. Following that section, we looked at some of the ways in which you can incorporate crystals into your everyday life, such as decorating your home, wearing them, or meditating with them. These purposes can help you to see the many different applications that crystals have, showing you that there are numerous aspects of your life in which crystals can be beneficial. Next, I led you through the processes of taking care of your crystals, from when you first buy them and ongoing maintenance to optimization and storage. This section is incredibly important for crystal users since it reminds you that your crystals are like living things that need to be cared for just like a plant. Finally, I gave you two comprehensive lists: one of some of the most popular crystals out there and the other about some of the facets of life that crystals can help you heal. With these lists, you get a strong sense of the fundamental crystals and their uses, helping you to start to choose which crystals you think are right for you and your intentions with them. After reading, you should now have a basic comprehensive knowledge of crystal healing and should be excited about using crystals going forward!

You now have a window into one of the most powerful healing practices in the world. Many of the ailments and predicaments you have found yourself in over the years can be helped immensely by this crystal practice. Take this knowledge and apply it to your crystal practice, using it to heal your life. After seeing the benefits, you'll wish you had introduced crystals into your life sooner!

Glossary

Amethyst: A purple crystal excellent for balancing.

Angelite: A blue crystal used for purification.

Aura: The vibrations surrounding someone's body.

Black onyx: A black protection crystal corresponding to the root chakra and associated with groundedness.

Black tourmaline: A black purification crystal associated with the root chakra and used for self-help.

Body energy: Natural vibrations that are given off by the body that can be targeted in certain spiritual healing practices.

Chakras: A set of points on the body that correspond to both physical and psychological spheres.

Chi: Core energy of the body that connects the physical and spiritual worlds.

Clear quartz: A clear crystal used for focus.

Cluster crystal: A crystal shape associated with connection.

Crown chakra: The highest chakra on the body, connected to higher knowledge and the spiritual world.

Crystal grid: A method of crystal use that involves placing your crystals in a grid position to bounce their energies off each other.

Cube crystal: A crystal shape that is associated with groundedness.

Fluorite: An aqua-colored crystal associated with clarity.

Green calcite: A green crystal used for trauma healing.

Green jade: A green crystal used for love and connection.

Heart chakra: The chakra at the center of your body, associated with love and connection.

Heart crystal: A crystal shape associated with love and connection, often rose quartz.

Lepidolite: A dark purple crystal used for self-love and confidence.

Malachite: A dark green stone used for radical transformation and growth.

Manifestation: The act of envisioning an event in order to make it happen.

Pointed crystal: A crystal shape used for focus.

Pyramid crystal: A crystal shape associated with desire.

Rose quartz: A type of crystal associated with love and relationships.

Root chakra: The bottom chakra on your body, associated with your sense of self and belonging in the world.

Sacral chakra: The second-lowest chakra on the body, connected to creativity and sexuality.

Smoky quartz: A type of crystal used for banishing negative energy.

Solar plexus chakra: The third chakra on the body, associated with self-esteem and image.

Sphere crystal: A crystal shape associated with greater purpose and connection to the world at large.

Third eye chakra: The sixth chakra on the body and the second from the top, associated with long-term plans and inner truth.

Throat chakra: The fifth chakra on the body, associated with communication and honesty.

Tiger's eye: A type of crystal associated with strong purpose.

Tumbled crystal: A shape of crystal that is very small and portable.

Turquoise: A type of crystal associated with luck.

Vogel crystal: A particular make of crystal created by Marcel Vogel that is cut with specific dimensions to promote focus and clarity.

References

Amethyst meaning: Everything you need to know—Healing properties & everyday uses. (n.d.). Tiny Rituals. https://tinyrituals.co/blogs/tiny-rituals/amethyst-meaning-healing-properties-and-everyday-uses

Ancillette, M. (n.d.). *How to store crystals and gemstones to avoid negative influences.* Angel Grotto. https://angelgrotto.com/crystals-stones/storing/

Avalon, A. (2019, November 3). *Vogel crystals explained.* Avalon InLa'Kesh Blessings & Welcome. https://www.avaloninlakesh.com/vogel-crystals-explained/

A beginner's guide to crystal healing. (n.d.). Therapy Directory. https://www.therapy-directory.org.uk/blog/2014/01/16/a-beginners-guide-to-crystal-healing

Black onyx meaning: Healing properties, uses, & benefits. (n.d.). Tiny Rituals. https://tinyrituals.co/blogs/tiny-rituals/black-onyx-meaning#:~:text=Black%20Onyx%20is%20a%20root

Carlos, K. (2018). *Crystal healing practices in the Western world and beyond.* https://stars.library.ucf.edu/cgi/viewcontent.cgi?article=1283&context=honorstheses

Chee, C. (2021, September 10). *Angelite: Meaning & healing properties of this blue crystal.* Truly Experiences Blog. https://trulyexperiences.com/blog/angelite-crystal/#:~:text=What%20Chakra%20Is%20Angelite%20Good

Clear quartz crystal: Meaning & healing properties. (2021, September 20). Truly Experiences Blog. https://trulyexperiences.com/blog/clear-quartz/

Crystal shapes. (n.d.). The Australian Museum. https://australian.museum/learn/minerals/what-are-minerals/crystal-shapes/

Crystals 101. (n.d.). Adelphi. https://home.adelphi.edu/~sa21715/Crystals101.html

Crystals for accepting change. (n.d.). Crystal Vaults. https://www.crystalvaults.com/crystal-reference-guide/crystals-for-change/

Ekhart, E. (2021, April 14). *What is Chi?* Ekhart Yoga. https://www.ekhartyoga.com/articles/practice/what-is-chi#:~:text=Chi%20is%20your%20life%20force

Energy reading 101: What your aura colors say about you. (2020, July 19). Mind Body Green. https://www.mindbodygreen.com/articles/aura-colors-and-their-meanings

Enhance your meditation practice with crystals. (2018, July 17). Chopra. https://chopra.com/articles/enhance-your-meditation-practice-with-crystals

Estrada, J. (2019, October 25). *Crystal shapes matter—Here's what they mean and how to amplify their power.* Well+Good. https://www.wellandgood.com/crystal-shapes/

Fluorite meaning: Healing properties & everyday uses. (n.d.). Tiny Rituals. https://tinyrituals.co/blogs/tiny-rituals/fluorite-meaning-healing-properties-everyday-uses

Guhr, A., & Nagler, J. (n.d.). *Crystal healing: The ancient tradition—The therapeutic power, magic and mystery of gems, stones and crystals.* https://www.earthdancer.co.uk/wp-content/uploads/2011/03/aaCrystalpower.pdf

Healing crystals for your home or office. (2021, April 20). Desert USA. https://www.desertusa.com/dusablog/healing-crystals-for-your-home-or-office/

Healing properties and benefits of malachite. (n.d.). Gempundit. https://www.gempundit.com/blog/malachite-stone-uses-meaning-and-healing-properties#:~:text=The%20empowering%20Malachite%20balances%20the

Houston, D. (2018, December 23). *Green-calcite: Meanings, properties and powers.* Crystals and Jewelry. https://meanings.crystalsandjewelry.com/green-calcite/

Houston, D. (2019, May 17). *How to program crystals.* Crystals and Jewelry. https://meanings.crystalsandjewelry.com/how-to-program-crystals/

How to arrange crystals in your home, according to the experts. (n.d.). Eva Gems & Jewels. https://evagemsandjewels.com/blogs/insights/how-to-arrange-crystals-in-your-home

How to charge your crystals. (2020, April 22). C Magazine. https://magazinec.com/beauty/how-to-charge-your-crystals/

How to cleanse, charge, and activate healing crystals. (2022, April 27). Healthline. https://www.healthline.com/health/how-to-cleanse-crystals#using-smaller-stones

How to meditate with chakra stones. (n.d.). Conscious Items. https://consciousitems.com/blogs/practice/how-to-meditate-with-chakra-stones

How to meditate with crystals. (n.d.). Verywell Mind. https://www.verywellmind.com/how-to-meditate-with-crystals-5214020

How to tell if a crystal is real in 7 easy ways. (n.d.). Tiny Rituals. https://tinyrituals.co/blogs/tiny-rituals/hw-to-tell-if-a-crystal-is-real

An introduction to gem identification. (n.d.). International Gem Society. https://www.gemsociety.org/article/how-gems-are-identified/

Lepidolite meaning: Healing properties & everyday use. (n.d.). Tiny Rituals. https://tinyrituals.co/blogs/tiny-rituals/lepidolite-meaning-healing-properties-everyday-use

Mael, M. (2021, October 25). *How often should you cleanse and charge crystals?* Michal & Company. https://michalandcompany.com/how-often-cleanse-and-charge-crystals/

Marcel Vogel and healing crystals. (n.d.). Crystal Light and Sound. https://www.crystallightandsound.com/who-was-marcel-vogel/

Meditating with crystals. (n.d.). Better Sleep. https://www.bettersleep.com/blog/meditating-with-crystals/

Need more courage & motivation in your life? Reach for this powerhouse crystal. (2022, May 30). Mind Body Green. https://www.mindbodygreen.com/articles/tigers-eye#:~:text=Tiger%27s%2Deye%20is%20closely%20related

The one crystal your collection is missing for grounding & protection. (2022, March 12). Mind Body Green. https://www.mindbodygreen.com/articles/black-tourmaline-healing-properties-how-to-use-more#:~:text=Which%20chakra%20is%20associated%20with

Palermo, E. (2017, June 23). *Crystal healing: Stone-cold facts about gemstone treatments.* Live Science. https://www.livescience.com/40347-crystal-healing.html

Regan, S. (2021, June 15). *How to know if your crystals need charging + 9 potent methods.* Mind Body Green. https://www.mindbodygreen.com/articles/how-to-charge-crystals

Roberts, T. (2022a, March 22). *25 of the best crystals for balance and healing.* Sarah Scoop. https://sarahscoop.com/25-of-the-best-crystals-for-balance-and-healing/

Roberts, T. (2022b, March 30). *25 of the best powerful crystals for health & wellness.* Sarah Scoop. https://sarahscoop.com/25-of-the-best-powerful-crystals-for-health-wellness/

Rocha, U. (2017, August 30). *What is an aura and how do crystals help or heal it?* Stonebrick. https://stonebridgeimports.ca/a/500-what-is-an-aura-how-do-crystals-help-or-heal-it

Scoop, S. (2022, June 1). *25 best crystals to use for grounding and healing energy.* Sarah Scoop. https://sarahscoop.com/25-best-crystals-to-use-for-grounding-and-healing-energy/

Seeing aura colors may reveal inner truths. (n.d.). Goodnet. https://www.goodnet.org/articles/seeing-aura-colors-may-reveal-inner-truths

6 tips for buying and using crystals (A beginner's guide). (2014, March 11). Thought Catalog. https://thoughtcatalog.com/claudia-st-clair/2014/03/your-essential-guide-to-buying-and-choosing-crystals/

16 crystals for prosperity & abundance. (n.d.). Tiny Rituals. https://tinyrituals.co/blogs/tiny-rituals/crystals-for-prosperity

Smoky quartz: Meaning & healing properties of this mysterious crystal. (2021, September 10). Truly Experiences Blog. https://trulyexperiences.com/blog/smoky-quartz/

The spiritual science of crystal healing: Chapter 7 working with Vogel. (n.d.). Satya Center. https://www.satyacenter.com/pages/crystal-wisdom-of-marcel-vogel-chapter7

Stelter, G. (2016, October 4). *Chakras: A beginner's guide to the 7 chakras.* Healthline. https://www.healthline.com/health/fitness-exercise/7-chakras#The-takeaway

Stone energy: How to choose a crystal that will rock your world. (n.d.). Cosmic Cuts. https://cosmiccuts.com/blogs/healing-stones-blog/stone-energy-how-to-choose-a-crystal-that-will-rock-your-world

10 healing crystals for concentration and focus. (n.d.). Cosmic Cuts. https://cosmiccuts.com/blogs/healing-stones-blog/healing-crystals-for-concentration-and-focus

3 simple ways to charge crystals with intentions. (n.d.). WikiHow Health. https://www.wikihow.health/Charge-Crystals-with-Intentions

Top 10 reasons why you should wear crystals & gemstone jewellery. (n.d.). Nature's Magick. https://naturesmagick.com.au/blogs/natures-magick-blog/top-10-reasons-why-you-should-wear-crystals-gemstone-jewellery

Turquoise chakras. (n.d.). Durango Silver. https://www.durangosilver.com/turquoise-chakras.html#:~:text=Turquoise%20is%20a%20stone%20of

The 20 best crystals for communication. (n.d.). Tiny Rituals. https://tinyrituals.co/blogs/tiny-rituals/crystals-for-communication

20 healing crystals for anxiety & stress. (n.d.). Tiny Rituals. https://tinyrituals.co/blogs/tiny-rituals/crystals-for-anxiety

Use these 6 crystals to connect with the universe. (2018, April 18). Yoga Journal. https://www.yogajournal.com/yoga-101/use-these-6-crystals-to-connect-with-the-universe/

Using crystals for chakra healing. (2021, May 17). Ohana. https://ohanayoga.com/crystals-for-chakra-healing/

Vogel crystals explained. (2019, November 3). Avalon. https://www.avaloninlakesh.com/vogel-crystals-explained/

What is an authentic Vogel crystal? (n.d.). Crystal Light and Sound. https://www.crystallightandsound.com/what-is-a-vogel-crystal/

Why you need to program your crystals and how. (n.d.). Unique Fengshui. https://uniquefengshui.com/programming-your-crystals/

Your guide to charging crystals with intention. (n.d.). Bustle. https://www.bustle.com/life/how-to-charge-crystals-intention-experts

THE 6 PILLARS OF CHAKRA HEALING

89 Beginner Techniques & Hacks to Heal Your **Body, Mind,** and **Spirit**. Transform Your Life Through Energy Balancing. Guide to Practical Remedies for Health and Wellness

MONIQUE WAGNER

Table of Contents

Introduction

The human body is a complex machine full of numerous systems and organs; it performs millions of actions a day, some conscious, some unconscious. In fact, the vast majority of tasks the human body performs are actually unconscious. Heartbeats, digestion, immune responses—all of these things happen without your conscious mind needing to be involved. Most people really have no idea what's going on inside their bodies at any given time. This is why people can live with a serious illness and not be aware of it or fight viruses while they are asleep. But there are more unconscious things going on inside the body than just basic health functions. Underneath all the physical processes of your body, there are also spiritual systems that underpin the very core of who you are, systems that work parallel to your body's physical functions but that are just as unconscious. Some people call it the soul, some the spirit self, but there is one system that categorizes this inner network according to parts of the body called chakras.

Chakras are an ancient South Asian philosophy that endeavors to explain these unseen systems that work throughout the human body. A lot of research has been done lately around the connection between the body and mental health. Many researchers are finding that there are great mental health benefits to things like exercise, healthy eating, and even gut bacteria. Western medicine is realizing more and more that there is a strong connection between the mind and the body and that all of our body systems are connected. Well, practitioners of chakra medicine have always known this. Chakras aim to explain and explore the complex ways in which our minds are linked to our bodies and how these links can be manipulated in order to ensure that all our faculties are working at their highest capacity.

So, what are chakras exactly? Well, chakras are essentially points identified in our bodies that have a certain significance. Each body part has a corresponding mental facet—an aspect of life or the self that is ruled by that particular body part. This is similar to how back pain is related to stress or how chronic fatigue is linked to digestive problems. Chakras attempt to define aspects of our bodies that are connected to aspects of our minds. The elements of life that chakras deal with, however, are often much deeper than Western medical science will really examine. For example, Western doctors will often talk about stress, grief, or trauma, but they won't talk about relationships, long-term goals, self-esteem, or spiritual identity. These things can be seen as a little too abstract or vague and sometimes are not even taken seriously at all by Western doctors.

But chakra healers know that the bodily impacts of self-esteem can be just as powerful as those of trauma. In chakra healing, everything you feel has a reflection in the body and vice versa. By forging and recognizing this connection and explaining its intricacies, chakra healing aims to heal the mind through the body and the body through the mind.

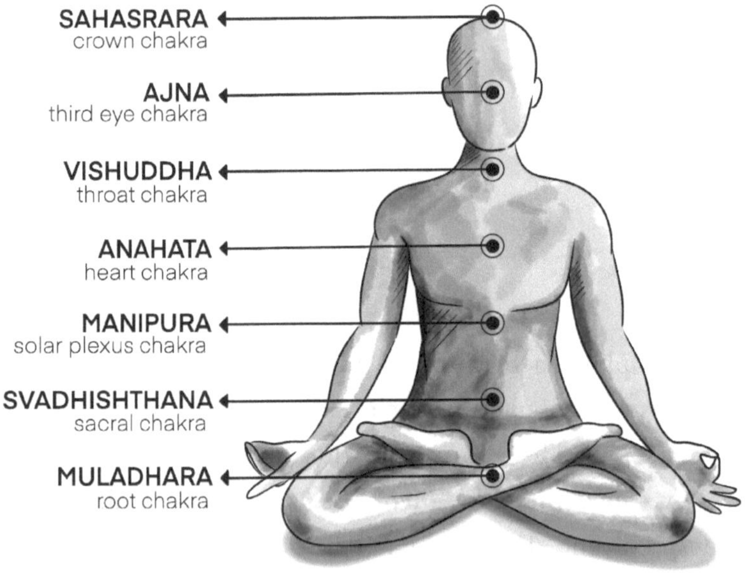

There are seven main chakras on the body which each correspond to a specific aspect of your life. The seven main chakras are the root chakra, the sacral chakra, the solar plexus chakra, the heart chakra, the throat chakra, the third eye chakra, and the crown chakra. Each of these seven has a corresponding body part, bodily system, set of possible ailments, and aspect of the self. In terms of physical assignment, this list goes from the bottom of your core, the tailbone, to the top of your head. The bottom, or root chakra, deals with the baser things in life, kind of like the bottom of the pyramid of needs. As you move up the body, you get to higher and higher purposes on the emotional chain, eventually culminating in the crown chakra, which deals with your spiritual self. Because of this scale, the chakras are often divided into two groups: the higher chakras and the lower chakras. Using this system of seven, you can categorize your body in terms of the ways it influences your mind.

So, how do chakras work exactly? Generally, chakra healers talk about chakras being "blocked" or "unblocked." When a chakra is blocked, you will usually see both psychological and physiological responses—a reflection in both your mental and physical health. For example, your throat chakra deals with not only your communication with others but also your general sinus, throat, and mouth area. So, if your throat chakra is blocked, you might find that you have sinus issues and feel like you aren't communicating very honestly or effectively with others. What chakra healing aims to do is help you identify which chakras on your body might be blocked and how you can go about unblocking them. Only by closely connecting the mind and the body can you really heal both.

In this book, we will give you a complete overview of chakra healing through six distinctive pillars. These pillars aim to divide chakra healing into six easy parts to help even the most inexperienced beginner become knowledgeable in the subject. In the first pillar, we will look at the foundations of chakra healing, explaining how they work and a little about their history. In the second pillar, we will dive deeper into the actual systems of the chakras, looking at each individual one and its role in your life. Then, in Pillar 3, we will branch out a little bit and look at the relationships that chakras have with other systems in your body as well as the world at large. After that, Pillar 4 will look at the ways in which you can activate your chakras, showing you more concrete and practical tips about fine-tuning your chakras. In Pillar 5, we will then talk about how to balance your chakras and ensure that they have strong relationships with one another. Finally, in Pillar 6, we will discuss the specific healing practices you can use with your chakras. Through these pillars, you will be able to see how understanding chakras and their applications can drastically improve your life and your connection with your body. You will also find 89 techniques, tips, and strategies to help you heal your body, mind, and spirit. These techniques, tips, and strategies are peppered throughout the entire book. And it's intentionally designed this way to serve as your guide along each step of the process. With this information, you will be able to live a more balanced and spiritual life.

Pillar 1:
Foundations

Chakras have been around for a great portion of human history. For millennia, they have helped people gain a more holistic understanding of their minds and bodies. This system helps us section off different facets of our lives to explain why we think and feel the way we do. For those who are seeking a stronger relationship with their bodies, chakras have served a very important purpose. In this pillar, we will start you on your chakra journey by outlining some of the key aspects of chakras. First, we will provide a general definition of chakras so that you are more aware of what they are and what they do. Then, we will talk about some of the common misconceptions associated with chakras. Following this, we will explain some of the origins of the practice, tracing its history from ancient times up to today. Finally, we will discuss chakras and their relationship with energy. By the end of this pillar, you will have a basic understanding of chakras to take forward into the rest of the book.

Chapter 1:
Chakras Explained

In the Introduction, we gave a vague description of the concept of chakras, describing them merely as "energy centers," but here we will get into the specifics of what chakras really are. In this chapter, we will be thoroughly defining the chakras and their meanings by listing the main ones and giving you a solid understanding of how they connect the mind and the body. We will also give you a list of common misconceptions surrounding chakras to help you recognize what chakras *aren't* as well as what they are.

What Are Chakras?

So, what are chakras exactly? What parts of the body do they encompass and how do they work? What is their purpose and how do they help us? Well, the word "chakra" in Sanskrit actually means "wheel." The individual chakra wheels are envisioned like discs on the spine. The seven chakras are then positioned as seven individual discs representing different spinal altitudes. Given the prevalence of the nervous system throughout the body and the importance of the spinal cord as the center of that system, it makes sense that this would be the center of the chakras as well. The idea of the chakras as wheels also speaks to their dynamic nature. Our chakras are all spinning, creating lively energy centers at these distinct points in our bodies. Essentially, chakras are seven energy-holding wheels marking specific points on our spinal cord.

Chakras are mainly described as being "balanced," "blocked," or "unblocked." When a certain chakra is blocked, it means that you will have problems in that particular part of your body, and this can also translate to having similar problems in the area of your life to which that chakra corresponds. Identifying the specific chakra in your body that is blocked can greatly help you to connect physical and psychological ailments. The process of chakra healing thus generally centers around unblocking or opening up your chakras. You can do this through energy healing, yoga, or many other practices, which we will discuss in more detail later in this book. When your chakras are opened up, you will have a stronger connection between your mind and body as well as relief in many of your systems. By harnessing the power of chakras, you can bring a strong sense of holistic health to your body and mind, clearing up many ailments that cannot be reached by any other kind of medicine.

Crossover Practices

There are many other spiritual healing practices that have a strong relationship to chakras. Many of these traditions evolved alongside one another, sharing philosophies and incorporating each other into their practices. They might also have characteristics that correspond to one another, encouraging you to combine certain ideas from one practice with its corresponding elements in the other one. Often, combining these practices with one another can help enhance each one individually. In this section, we will talk about some of the main spiritual practices that have crossover with chakras.

Crystals

Crystal healing is another important part of spiritual practice. Crystals that come from the ground have strong vibrational powers which can preside over certain aspects of life and the body, similar to chakras. Most crystals have a corresponding chakra with which they connect strongly. Many people will incorporate crystals into their chakra healing, and vice versa, using corresponding crystals to help heal specific chakras.

Astrology

Another spiritual practice that corresponds with chakras is astrology, particularly the planets. In ancient astronomy, there were seven planetary bodies: the sun, the moon, Mercury, Venus, Mars, Jupiter, and Saturn. The outer planets had not been discovered yet, so ancient astrology operated on a system of seven. If you notice, there are also seven chakras, which is no coincidence. Each chakra is associated with a different planet. The root chakra is associated with Mars, the sacral chakra with Mercury, the solar plexus chakra with Jupiter, the heart chakra with Venus, the throat chakra with Saturn, the third eye chakra with the sun, and the crown chakra with the moon. Each of these chakras also corresponds with those planets' associated qualities in astrology. On your birth chart, you will be able to see the position of all your planets within the zodiac. For example, your Mercury might be in Gemini or your Mars in Sagittarius. When looking at your birth chart, consider how some of these planetary positions might relate to your chakra system.

Yoga

Yoga is probably the spiritual practice that is most closely related to chakras. Yoga evolved alongside chakras and is inextricably linked to chakra philosophy. Like chakras, yoga is a practice that aims to connect the mind and the body, incorporating both physical movement and mindfulness in order to create this connection. Many yoga poses and sequences are based on certain chakras or chakra systems. In the practice of chakra healing, yoga is often used extensively to help unblock certain chakras. Yoga promotes balance in the body, building strength, and always returns to the core, or the spinal cord. It helps you to balance your chakras and unblock certain ones that might be closed. In other words, you will need to know at least a little bit about yoga in order to practice chakras, and vice versa!

Common Misconceptions

As with any spiritual practice, there are a lot of misconceptions people have about chakras. How many people have told you that astrology is "nonsense" because everyone born in June can't possibly have the same personality? Or that crystals are just rocks that may offer a placebo effect? Skeptics and misinterpreters are a source of aggravation for many spiritual healers. People who don't understand the nuances of a particular spiritual system can be extremely frustrating. The same goes for chakras. Here, we will look at some of the most common misconceptions people tend to have about chakra healing.

Misconception #1: There Is Only One Chakra System

Because of how old and widespread the concept of chakras is, there are a lot of different systems people have practiced over the years. The system that we are discussing in this book is just one of many that have evolved over time. Because chakras are so fluid as a system, there are many ways to practice them, and no one way is necessarily right or wrong. If you get very into chakras, you can try different practices for yourself. However, it is never advisable to mix practices with one another. This will result in unsatisfying results and create a mixed relationship with your chakras. So, no matter the practice you choose to follow, make sure that you are consistent about it.

Misconception #2: The Chakras Exist in Physical Space

Although we did talk about how the chakras are located in specific areas of the body, they are not actually physically located in your body. Likewise, they do not necessarily physically resemble or associate with the qualities we ascribe to them, such as colors. Instead, they are focal points for visualization. They help us to see past the simple biological functions of the body and into the more minute functions of the visualizing mind. Thus, it is not very helpful to think of your chakras as a physical reality like your actual spinal cord. Instead, think of your chakras as focal points, parts of your body that need attention, not literal discs spinning around your spinal cord.

Misconception #3: There Are Only Seven Chakras

As we said above, there are many different chakra systems in the world. Some involve the seven-chakra system, which is the one we are focusing on in this book. However, there are many systems that include different numbers of chakras—anywhere from five to hundreds. You can think of the differences in the number of chakras as some systems involving more focus and attention rather than other systems leaving things out. Systems with fewer chakras tend to condense ideas into larger sections, whereas systems with more chakras tend to split the body into smaller parts that preside over more specific areas. Thus, when you are choosing a chakra system, reflect on the level of specificity you want.

Chapter 2:
Origins and History

Chakras did not come out of nowhere! Moreover, the ways we practice chakra healing today, especially in the Western world, did not come out of nowhere either. Current chakra practice is the result of a long history that spans the whole world. Those who know a lot about chakras will tell you that there is a lot more to them than meets the eye and that it took us a long time to get to where we are today. In this chapter, we will be looking at some of the most essential aspects of chakra origins. We will first be looking at the geographic origins, tracing the places that made chakras what they are today. Then, we will be looking at the timeline of the history of chakras, telling the story from their earliest origins through their maintenance over the course of history up until the current chakra practices of today. By the end of this chapter, you will be well-versed in where chakras came from and how they've changed over time, giving you a clearer picture of how their current practice came to be.

Where Are Chakras From?

Chakras have spread far and wide throughout the world today. In almost every country on Earth, you will find someone who practices chakra healing. Most people around the world have heard of chakras, and there are countless people across borders and cultures who have brought a version of chakra practice into their spiritual healing journeys. But it wasn't always this way. In fact, chakras actually have very specific origins in the Indian subcontinent, known today as South Asia, or the collection of countries of India, Sri Lanka, Bangladesh, and Pakistan. In this part of the world, we can trace the origins of chakras. To this day, chakras are still practiced widely throughout South Asia and are very commonly associated with other aspects of South Asian culture and spiritual practices. Often, dedicated chakra healers will make pilgrimages to parts of India to try and trace the geographical roots of the practice that has brought so much joy and healing to their lives.

Religious Origins

A discussion of chakra healing would not be complete without a discussion of the religions with which chakras are associated. There are two main religions with origins in South Asia: Hinduism and Buddhism. Both of these religions have strong relationships with chakras and warrant a thorough discussion of the ways they have incorporated chakras into their practices throughout history. In this section, we will discuss how chakras fit into Hinduism and Buddhism in both historical and contemporary practice.

Hinduism

Chakras are inherently a Hindu concept. Hinduism is one of the oldest widely practiced religions in the world. It has its origins in Ancient India, dating back thousands of years. The beginnings of Hinduism are all contained within certain Sanskrit texts called the "Vedas." These are a dense collection of texts that detail the main philosophies of the Hindu religion. They are a compilation of many different documents throughout history, so it is difficult to date their origins. Chakras have their roots in these documents and thus can be said to be at least a few thousand years old. Evolving alongside the Hindu tradition, chakras also have Hindi names along with their English names. So, the root chakra is the *muladhara*, the sacral chakra is the *swadhisthana*, the solar plexus chakra is the *manipura*, the heart chakra is the *anahata*, the throat chakra is the *vishuddha*, the third eye chakra is the *ajna*, and the crown chakra is the *sahasrara*. For the purposes of this book, we will be using their English names, but it's important to remember that they were originally used in Hindu practice.

Chakras are linked to many different Hindu practices and are still used in the contemporary Hindu religion. The way chakras work in this practice is through the passing of knowledge from the bottom to the top. The chakra energy is believed to be sacred and to come from above from the highest form of life known as Brahman. Naturally, these energies tend to pool around our root chakra, concentrating in the lowest part of our bodies. With meditation and yoga, the goal is to raise these energies through the chakras. As this energy moves up the chain of the body, we become more attentive to higher knowledge and gain a more enlightened view of life and the universe. The crown chakra is the ultimate goal of this practice, concentrating our energies in the highest place on our spiritual body to become aware of things beyond the visible universe and to gain deeper insight.

Besides yoga and meditation, another aspect of Hinduism that relates to the chakras is the gods themselves. As you might already know, Hinduism is a polytheistic religion, which means that they worship more than one god. Unlike Christianity or Islam, which have one central spiritual being, Hinduism has many different gods that all relate to different ideas or facets of life. This is similar to the Greek gods, such as Aphrodite and Dionysus, who preside over love and wine respectively, or even the patron saint system of Catholicism, which assigns different areas to different saints. Consequently, all the gods in Hindu theology have their own unique role to play in the cosmic system. And, as you might have guessed, they each have a chakra that they are associated with. The root chakra is associated with Ganesh, the god of beginnings who takes the form of an elephant; the sacral chakra is associated with Vishnu, the god of preservation and benevolence; the solar plexus chakra is associated with Siva, the god of destruction and renewal; the heart chakra is associated with Ishvara, a more conceptual god who is a center of spiritual enlightenment; the throat chakra is associated with Sadasiva, the highest form of Siva representing fulfillment and longevity; the third eye chakra is associated with Ardhanarishvara, the composite of Siva and his consort Parvati representing the harmony between male and female; and finally the crown chakra is associated with Lord Siva, or the highest form of Siva. When you focus on a particular chakra in Hindu theology, you are also channeling or asking for help from a particular god in the pantheon.

Buddhism

Compared to Hinduism, Buddhism is actually a relatively new religion, though it still has origins in ancient times. Buddhism started around 500 B.C.E. in what is now the northern region of the nation of India. It began with a prince named Siddhartha who chose to leave his aristocratic existence to achieve a more collective understanding of reality through charity and living among the poor. Buddhist teachings thus purport that there is no true boundary between people, nor between humans and animals, and therefore selflessness is the only true expression of reality. From there, Buddhism spread throughout the subcontinent and into parts of Asia such as China, Korea, and Japan, where it continues to be very widely practiced today.

Buddhism is very different from Hinduism, but because Buddhism began in South Asia as well, there are many Hindu concepts that were carried over to it. Though there are technically no mentions of chakras in the original Buddhist texts, there are prevalent ideas that can be seen to have origins in Hindu chakra practice. Buddhist use of the chakras is found most prominently in Tibetan Buddhism, which is a particular sect of Buddhism that has carried over many Hindu aspects to Buddhist theology. In Tibetan Buddhism, there is a strong tradition of chakra meditation similar to that in Hinduism. However, there are also other Buddhist systems that use chakra or energy exercises. For example, Chinese or Zen Buddhism acknowledges three main chakras: the lower *dantian* (similar to the solar plexus or sacral), the middle *dantian* (similar to the heart or throat), and the upper *dantian* (similar to the third eye or crown). In this chakra practice, we can see the roots of Hindu chakras. So, while chakras aren't as embedded in Buddhist theology as they are in Hindu theology, there are still aspects of chakra healing found within Buddhism.

Chakra Timeline

Now that you are familiar with the religious origins of chakras, we can talk a bit about how chakras have evolved throughout history. As we said earlier in this chapter, they do have their roots in the present-day country of India, but they have been found to spread far outside its borders, influencing many other cultures and spiritual movements over the course of history. In this section, we will give you a brief overview of the evolution of chakra practice.

Ancient Period

As we discussed in the religion section of this chapter, chakras are ancient in origin. They find their roots in texts thousands of years old and are thus one of the oldest continuously practiced traditions. In the ancient period, chakras were fairly confined to Hindu communities and kingdoms. They formed a significant component of Hindu practice and were also used in healing. Many different regions throughout South Asia practiced a version of chakras, some being different from others. At that time, things like the number of chakras, their exact meanings, and their relationships with things like colors were not yet fixed. Communities in different areas believed in different numbers of chakras and ascribed different meanings to them. At that time, there was not the same seven-chakra system we have today, especially not in relation to specific psychological states. This system was still in flux, made unique by every region that put its own spin on the practice.

Middle Ages

During the Middle Ages, the most important thing to happen throughout Afro-Eurasia was the rise of Islam. As the religion took off in the Middle East, it began to spread outward, both west into Europe and North Africa as well as east toward South Asia. The northern region of modern-day India, which you will remember was the place of origin for Buddhism, was colonized by a Muslim empire known as the Mughals. The Mughal Empire was extremely powerful in this region and lasted from the early 1500s to the late 1800s. Much of contemporary Indian culture and architecture has its origins in this period, including the iconic Taj Mahal itself. The wealth and influence of this empire were staggering, meaning that much of the subcontinent was Muslim for a time. Because Islam is a monotheistic religion that is more focused on scholarship and prayer than meditation and yoga, chakra practices were not as common during this time. However, there were still many autonomous Hindu regions that continued to practice chakras as before. But once the Mughals were no more, an even greater force was coming for India that would have another massive effect on their religious identity: the British.

Modern Revival

Starting in the 1500s, or the "Age of Exploration," Europeans began to grow dependent upon an economic system based on conquest and trade, resulting in a colonial hold over a large portion of the world. Alongside this age of colonialism, a new movement sprang up in French and English philosophy called "Orientalism," starting around the 1700s–1800s. During this period, many French and British scholars became fascinated by "Eastern" religions and philosophies as well as art and decor. Many would travel to places like China and South Asia to learn about religious practices and to purchase decorative items. While these French philosophers were furnishing their houses with Chinese pottery and Indian textiles, they were also furnishing their minds with these new ideas. Orientalism as a concept eventually gave way to many New Age movements that sought to incorporate elements of Eastern religions like Hinduism and Buddhism into their lives. One of the concepts that they incorporated was chakras. Throughout the 19th and 20th centuries, chakras gradually became more and more popular in the West. This coincided with movements like spiritualism, occultism, and New Age philosophy. It is here that we truly see the rise of the seven-chakra system and the contemporary Western chakra system in general.

Chapter 3:
Energy

Moving on to a more in-depth understanding of the chakras, we are now ready to talk about the specificities of the chakra system. One of the most important concepts in chakra practice is energy. We have already mentioned energy as a concept thus far, but only vaguely. You might think of energy as simply the opposite of fatigue. This is how we typically use the word in the Western world. We say, "I have no energy," when we really mean we are tired or feel that our bodies don't have enough fuel to function. However, from a spiritual standpoint, this would always be a false statement. You always have energy flowing through you, no matter how tired you feel. More than that, in certain spiritual systems, you have many different kinds of energy that all relate to one another in different ways. Systems like the chakra framework can help you to understand the different kinds of energies within you and to harness these energies and nurture them so that they can work properly. Chakra practice in particular has a very specific relationship with the concept of energy. In this chapter, we will talk about the precise ways in which chakra practice describes and categorizes energy.

Prana

Many different religions and practices have a specific word to mean "energy," and chakra practice is no different. In this particular philosophy, energy is known as "prana." Prana is a way of describing the life force within all of us, much like the concept of "Chi" in Chinese philosophy. Prana is present in all things on earth, including things that might seem to be inanimate, which means that humans, animals, plants, and rocks alike have prana at their core. This is a guiding concept in the world of crystal healing which operates on the idea that rocks and minerals have an essential energy to them that can be used for healing purposes. Some people also believe that prana is a vital principle in life. There is an element of oneness to prana that connects all the living things that have it at their center. It helps us to see and connect with the vital life force at the core of our beings as well as the core beings of others. We can see how this Hindu concept influenced the core life force aspect of Buddhist theology, connecting all things on Earth with a common thread. However, there is still more to prana than just a central life force; it is also channeled through pathways known as "nadi."

Nadi

The division of prana is done by nadi, which shape prana into the form it needs to take in order to successfully create life force. The nadi are actually very similar to the chakra system itself, sectioning off the body into different parts that are defined by certain characteristics and functions. However, unlike chakras, which run from the bottom of the body to the top, nadi run from side to side. These intersect with the chakras in very interesting ways and can change or add nuance to the existing meanings of the chakras. If you don't consider your nadi, then you might be getting an incomplete version of your chakra readings. This is very similar to astrology, which has multiple different signs that interact with each other. Knowing your main sign, or sun sign, can be useful and tell you a lot about yourself, but if you aren't aware of your moon sign, rising sign, planets, or houses, then you will always have an incomplete picture of your astrological identity. The same goes for chakras. Think of the nadi as your moon sign, another facet of the chakra system that can help you further expand your knowledge of the chakras in your body. Now, just like with chakras, there are actually many different nadi systems that identify different numbers of nadi in the body. Some identify three, some fourteen, and some many more. Each of these systems will have a varying degree of complexity based on the number of nadi it identifies. However, for the purposes of this book, we will be looking at three of the most important nadi. In this section, we will list these three for you and explain their significance within the body.

Ida Nadi

First off, we have the ida nadi, which is located on the left side of the body. Some people call this the "negative" side of the body, or your negative nadi. However, negative doesn't necessarily have a, well, negative connotation in this context. Oftentimes in spirituality, negativity doesn't mean bad or malicious but merely one side of a duality. Thus, you can think of "negative" things in spirituality with a more neutral connotation, meaning simply the inverse of a positive thing. Imagine them as the negative numbers on a number line, running parallel to the positive numbers but in the opposite direction. You can also think of them as the negative side of a battery or the south pole of a magnet. You can even think of them like negative space in a painting or a photograph, not full of dynamism, but a necessary aspect of the composition which gives the piece clarity and freshness. So, there is no need to avoid or look away from your ida nadi, even though it is categorized as technically negative.

The nadi are essentially categorized according to dualities, so the ida nadi will be everything the pingala, its corresponding nadi, is not. Ida is often associated with feminine energy. We can see in many other spiritual dualities that feminine energy is commonly associated with the moon, coolness, and emotions. The elements of earth and water are also associated with the ida nadi. Many female goddesses throughout the world are also associated with these things, such as the Greek goddess Artemis, who presides over the moon. Other aspects of ida nadi are creativity and inspiration as well as introversion. Think of the stereotypical "reserved genius," and you will have some idea about the central philosophy of the nadi. One interesting aspect of the nadi is that they recognize one fundamental concept in brain science, which is that the left side of the brain actually controls the right side of the body and vice versa. Therefore, you might have been confused about this nadi, since we typically think of the right brain as the creative side and the left side as the logical side. Well, don't worry because this is actually true of the nadi. Ida might preside over the left side of the body, but it presides over the right side of the brain as well. Ida also connects with the nervous system of the body and thus controls much of your body's physical functions, being the inherent link between the brain and the body. For this reason, it is a central aspect of your body and mind.

One of the most common misconceptions about the ida nadi, and the nadi in general, is that only women can really connect with it. Because it is associated with feminine energy, male chakra practitioners might be reluctant to lean into it. However, this is a much too literal interpretation of the concept of the ida nadi. Just as negative energy does not mean bad energy, feminine energy does not necessarily mean biologically or literally female. Basically, you can be any gender and associate strongly with your ida nadi. If you want to get in touch with your feminine side or bring some free-flowing energy into your chakra practice, you should try to channel your energy through this side of your body, allowing your prana to flow properly and release its powers.

Pingala Nadi

In contrast to the ida nadi is the pingala nadi. This nadi is associated with masculine energy and is the mirror image of ida nadi in every way. It is located on the right side of the body but controls the left side of the brain. As you might expect, it is associated with the sun, meaning that it is the warm, enlightening force to the ida's shadowy, cool force. The pingala nadi also leans more heavily into logic and reason. Elements like fire and air are also associated with the pingala nadi. We can see these associations in other religions as well. For example, the Greek god Apollo is Artemis's twin brother and is associated with the sun, while the hypermasculine god Ares is associated with fire and vigor. These associations are baked deeply into many religious systems from around the world, and thus it is highly important to recognize them in tandem with one another. Again, you don't have to be male to connect with your pingala nadi. Anyone can focus on this force in their life. It can help you realize some of the deeper ideas formed in the ida and put them into motion. Channeling your pingala nadi will help you bring things into action and create dynamism throughout your life.

Sushumna Nadi

So, you might be wondering, if the former two nadi are mirror images of each other, how can there be a third nadi? Well, the third nadi is actually located directly in the middle of the spine and represents the merging of the two. This nadi is the most important as it represents an existence free of dualities and contradictions. Only by truly balancing and awakening your ida and pingala nadi can you come to activate your sushumna nadi. This highlights the importance of your ida and pingala nadi as collaborators rather than enemies. You should not think of them as two sides of a chessboard but rather as two sides of a married couple. Separated and working independently, these nadi will only have themselves to rely on, working only with the tools they have within their own realms, but together, they can combine their energies to become greater than the sum of their parts. All the deep ideas forged in your ida nadi can finally be freed and come to fruition in your pingala nadi, and all the energy found in your pingala nadi can be used to nurture and care for others using your ida nadi. This is very similar to the concept of yin and yang, which also constructs opposing forces that strongly influence one another and need to be merged in order to truly reach enlightenment. Unfortunately, most people do not find the strength to connect these two nadi in order to fundamentally awaken their sushumna nadi and thus spend their lives with two divided halves. In order to truly create harmony in your body, you must learn through chakra healing to merge these energies to create a balanced whole.

Pillar 2:
Systems

In Pillar 1, we discussed all of the basic information associated with chakras. We let you know how the chakras work and where they came from. By now, you should be starting to get a firmer grip on the working world of chakras. In this section, we will be moving into a more detailed understanding of the chakras. First, in Chapter 4, we will discuss the chakras as a system, illustrating how they work in tandem with one another to form a harmonious whole. Next, in Chapter 5, we will give you a thorough explanation of the individual major chakras themselves. These are the seven chakras we have already talked about that form the basis for the Western chakras. Then, in Chapter 6, we will talk about the higher chakras, which is a separate system made up of five different chakras that exist on a different plane from the major chakras. Finally, in Chapter 7, we will discuss the minor or lower chakras, which center around smaller, more specific sections of the body. In these chapters, you will get a stronger sense of the main chakras themselves as well as more context around how they function in relation to other chakra systems.

Chapter 4:
Chakra Systems

The chakras are not forces that act in and of themselves. We have touched a little on the individual meanings of the chakras thus far in the book, but it is important to take a step back and assert that the main aspect of chakras is their connection to one another and their flow throughout the body. As we have seen with the nadi, the ability to truly merge and connect your chakras with one another is a central aspect of how they operate within the body. Only by treating your chakras as a single unified system can you come to understand them and their flow. You cannot fix one without the others being finely tuned. You can think of your chakra systems just like ingredients in a recipe. Has it ever happened that you had all the right ingredients for a recipe, all of excellent quality, but you mixed them together in the wrong order and the recipe completely fell flat? Well, that's how you have to think about chakras. Even if you balance or unblock them all individually, you will only be able to truly heal them if you think of them as a single system that needs to be balanced. In this chapter, we will discuss how the chakra system treats itself as a system of balance and harmony.

What Are Chakra Systems?

So, first of all, what are chakra systems and how do they work? How do these distinctive areas of the body connect to one another? Well, the chakra system all goes back to the discussion we had in Chapter 2 about the Hindu origins of chakras. In this philosophy, chakras are not distinctive aspects of your body at all but a network of areas that channel energy through them. You can think of this system as being multiple floors in an office building with the spine as an elevator connecting them all. The bottom floors are basic functions like electricity, bathrooms, power sources, and of course, the foundation of the building itself. Then, as you move to the middle floors, you get administration and communication departments, which manage the functions of the company and connect it to the outside world. On the top floors of the building are the executives, the creative teams, and the CEO, all of whom deal with the highest functions of the company, planning its future and coming up with groundbreaking ideas that will take it far. As you can see, all of these areas work independently, but they have clear relationships with one another and a movement from top to bottom. If you center yourself too much on your bottom floors, or lower chakras, then you will never gain higher knowledge or foresight. But conversely, if you neglect these foundational chakras, or basic company functions, the rest of the building will suffer. From this analogy, we can see how the energy flow throughout the chakras is crucial for their spiritual function. Using meditation and yoga to facilitate the spread of this energy, especially from the bottom to the top, is a central part of chakra practice and philosophy.

What Is in a Chakra?

There has been a lot of discussion in modern Western culture about the body's role in psychological states. Books like Bessel van der Kolk's *The Body Keeps the Score* detail how many of our experiences, both good and bad, can be stored in the body's organs and nervous system (2014). You can even see this playing out in real time with physical anxiety symptoms or physical triggers associated with trauma. According to chakra theory and practice, the body really does keep the score. For millennia, chakra healers have asserted that chakras not only store energy centers but also core aspects of our lives, both mental and physical. Chakras can keep track of your memories, your experiences, and your habits. They have a keen memory and serve as a way to create who we are. But as you probably know, the things that make you who you are can also be the things that limit you. Understanding your chakras and what they are storing inside them is integral to forming a more complete understanding of yourself and where you have come from.

Chakras can store even more than the past; they can also store the future. The state your chakras are in determines what your future self or life will look like. Furthermore, your chakras also hold your dreams, goals, and beliefs about the future. We see this more literally played out in the higher chakras, which deal with foresight and planning, but also in the lower chakras which deal with identity and self-esteem. The beliefs you have about yourself and your future are stored deep within your chakras, meaning that your chakras have an important influence on your future. Thus, with this future influence, we can see how chakra energy flows freely between the body and the outside world. Just as chakras are influenced by your ideas and experiences, so too are your future experiences influenced by your chakras. From this, you can really see how the body creates reality and how reality creates the body. Use this knowledge to feel a stronger connection to the world around you.

The Importance of Chakras in the Body

So, now that you know how connected the chakras really are, you can begin to see how a blockage in any of your chakras can really affect your ability to function. One chakra being blocked does not just mean that the certain aspect of your life controlled by that chakra is blocked but also that energy cannot freely flow throughout your whole system. You can think of this like a drain being blocked. Water can flow above and below the block but not through it, so your drain is unusable simply because one small part of it is not functioning properly. For a more complex analogy, we can turn back to our seven-floor office building. Let's say floor five is the communications department, representing the throat chakra. If this department stops working properly, the other departments might not be affected right away as they are still going about their business. But slowly, the company's relationships with other firms will deteriorate, beginning to erode their capacity for outreach. They will lose advertisements, which will lead to fewer new clients, and eventually reduced profits. They will also not be able to respond to customer complaints, which might lead to losing even repeat customers who were previously loyal. All of these repercussions will eventually lead to cuts in other departments, and if not fixed, a complete shutdown of the company. As you can see, just removing one essential aspect of the function of the company can lead to a massive restructuring and possibly even bankruptcy.

Let's map this back onto a human being and their chakra identity. If you have a blockage in your throat chakra, you might struggle with communication, be dishonest, or have social anxiety. These kinds of things won't necessarily directly affect your other chakras and their functions, since they will be operating on different wavelengths. However, over time, the struggles you are facing because of your throat chakra block will eventually come to affect the other facets of your life. Struggling with communication can ruin relationships, which touches your heart chakra. Being dishonest hurts your social reputation, which can affect your self-esteem and relationships. Having social anxiety can mean you withdraw from the world, even your friends and family, which disrupts your sense of home and self, affecting your root chakra. All of these reverberations will eventually block your ability to flow energy up to your crown chakra and truly have foresight in the world. What you will be left with is a mind preoccupied with the petty issues of the everyday and the inability to truly seek enlightened thought.

Chapter 5:
Individual Chakras (Major)

Understanding the role the chakras play in each others' function is extremely important, but just as important is understanding how they work individually. Only by deeply exploring each chakra can you begin to recognize which ones you might have blocked and learn how to go about unblocking them. This will help you identify areas in your life that you feel might be affected by the chakra blockages and create a stronger sense of who you are. In this chapter, we will talk in-depth about each of the individual major chakras by giving you core information about the facets of life each one presides over as well as additional information about them and associations they might have.

Root Chakra

Associated Color:

Red

Associated Element:

Earth

Associated Body Parts:

The base of the spine, also known as the pelvic floor, where the earth and the body make contact

Description

The root chakra is the base of the whole chakra system. This means that it exists in a duality. On one hand, it deals with the baser aspects of human life, meaning that it is the least important chakra. But on the other hand, it is also the root of many aspects of your sense of self, including your core identity, your origins, and your connection to your bodily functions. It forms a large part of both your everyday living and your unconscious mind. Some people even think of the root chakra as representing a more animalistic side of human nature, showing us the basest of our instincts. However, this is one of the worst chakras to have unbalanced. Since energy tends to be concentrated here, with the goal of moving up toward the crown chakra, having a blocked root chakra means that your energy can't even move up to the next chakra, the sacral chakra. If your root chakra is unbalanced, then there is a very strong likelihood that your whole chakra system in general is badly unbalanced and lacks any flow whatsoever. Your higher chakras will be cut off from their energy source, and you will be left feeling like you have neither roots nor wisdom. Making sure this chakra is open and flowing freely is essential to the function of the entire chakra system.

Sacral Chakra

Associated Color:

Orange

Associated Element:

Water

Associated Body Parts:

The lower abdomen or genitals

Description

The sacral chakra is the center of your desire function. Thus, it presides over both sexuality and creative drive. It is the area in which many of your core ideas form. You need this chakra to give you a kind of life force. If your root chakra is your connection to the earth, then your sacral chakra is the drive that allows you to soar from it. Another big part of your sacral chakra is self-esteem. This relates not to the general self-esteem we might associate with the social world but to a deeper inner self-esteem that relates to our most intimate selves. This is a side of our personality that we might only share with ourselves or our intimate partners. When this self-esteem is threatened, it is much more serious than just being embarrassed—it is crushing to our sense of self. Thus, the sacral chakra represents another facet of our foundation of self, this time relating to our abilities more than our origins.

When your sacral chakra is unbalanced, you might very well react with frustration or anger. This can either be directed at yourself or others, but it stems from deep feelings of inadequacy. A blocked sacral chakra might find you failing to live up to your own expectations, which can result in you feeling frustrated with your situation and lashing out. You might also experience blocks both creatively and sexually. Creatively, this can look like writer's block or even just a lack of energy to complete the creative tasks you want to complete. Sexually, it can either come in the form of aversion or repression, or it can go in the other direction toward sexual obsession. Sometimes, this symptom can be physical, leading to sexual dysfunction or bladder issues. However, when this chakra is well-balanced, then you will feel a strong sense of accomplishment and pride in your achievements. You will also have the inner confidence to trust your own intuition and feelings.

Solar Plexus Chakra

Associated Color:

Yellow

Associated Element:

Fire

Associated Body Parts:

The stomach area or upper abdomen

Description

Your solar plexus chakra is where the ego tends to come in. As we move upward through the body's chakras, we start to get into the more social aspects of the world. Because it is still in the lower half of the chakras, the solar plexus chakra deals with the view of the self as it pertains to others. This is similar to the self-esteem-based sacral chakra but takes a particular focus on relationships with others. Your solar plexus chakra is thus connected more to your general acceptance by society or your friends rather than your evaluation of your own abilities. Things like popularity, social standing, and even just generally feeling loved by people can influence the self-esteem related to your solar plexus chakra.

When your solar plexus chakra becomes blocked, you will likely struggle to feel relevant in the world. You might feel isolated, unloved, unattractive, or useless. These feelings are directly related to a damaged ego, which feels like it is not performing for others in the way it wants to. Because the physical stomach is such a delicate organ, this is also an area with a lot of room for physical symptoms. A blocked solar plexus chakra can lead to a host of digestive problems, including food sensitivities and a tendency to throw up easily. However, if you gain the ability to balance it properly, then you will be able to face the world with more confidence and focus.

Heart Chakra

Associated Color:

Green

Associated Element:

Air

Associated Body Parts:

The chest

Description

It's easy to guess the heart chakra's purpose: love, compassion, and connection with others. As the center chakra on the body, it deals with neither personal nor outward-looking self-esteem but instead equally balances the two. This chakra is the connecting force between you and others, thus constructing an important link between the upper and lower chakras. Your heart chakra presides over everything regarding your relationships, helping you to empathize with others, understand their needs, and communicate your own needs to them. In other words, it weighs yourself and others equally, striving to create strong two-way relationships in your life.

An unbalanced heart chakra can lead to many difficulties in your relationships. This will often take the form of hostility toward others. Negative feelings about other people, such as jealousy and anger, will usually be the manifestation. You might find yourself lashing out at loved ones or expecting the worst of people even though they haven't done anything wrong. Another common way your unbalanced heart chakra might manifest is through trust issues. You might find your attachment style turns anxious, leading you to struggle to keep your relationships close. You might also experience physical symptoms like chest pain or heartburn from an unbalanced heart chakra. Someone whose heart chakra is well-balanced will be open to others, ready to give and receive love, and feel genuinely part of a strong community. This is the ideal state to be in and helps you build intimate relationships and feel truly fulfilled.

Throat Chakra

Associated Color:

Blue

Associated Element:

Space

Associated Body Parts:

The throat as well as the neck area and sinuses

Description

The throat chakra is particularly concerned with the workings of the voice box, especially metaphorically speaking. The throat chakra presides over all things relating to your communication and vocal qualities. The way you speak and what you choose to use your words for are strongly influenced by the throat chakra. Consequently, it is also focused on a more public version of the interpersonal heart chakra. While the heart chakra focuses on your strong bonds with the important people in your life, the throat chakra focuses more on the public relationships in your broader life, looking further outward to things such as how you conduct yourself in the public sphere and how you convey your ideas to others. Being the communication chakra, the throat chakra deals with the wider social world and your ability to share yourself with it.

If your throat chakra is unbalanced, your communication and self-expression skills will suffer greatly. There are two ways this can go. The first way is that you become an incredibly timid person who struggles to express yourself. You might become socially reclusive or shy away from things like public speaking or performing in any way. This creates a very insular person who might have an excellent inner life but who struggles to bring that out into the greater world. The second way it can go is that you become a manipulative person who is confident in your social abilities but uses them for bad instead of good. You might be dishonest, prone to gossip, and possibly even outright cruel to people's faces. Both of these outcomes are not desirable and result in a person who struggles to have a healthy relationship with the outside world. Physical symptoms might also ensue; illnesses such as frequent head colds, sore throats, enlarged tonsils, and sinus infections are all related to a blocked throat chakra. When you finally manage to balance your throat chakra, you will be able to enjoy healthy and honest communication with others and be able to project yourself as a trustworthy and articulate person.

Third Eye Chakra

Associated Color:

Indigo

Associated Element:

No associated element

Associated Body Parts:

Between the eyes

Description

The third eye chakra is the second-highest chakra in the system and is where we first reach an area that is beyond everyday human life. The "third eye" is a commonly used term in the West, usually used to describe someone "opening their third eye" in order to see a higher reality. In chakra healing, the third eye is somewhat related to this concept, but it is more related to knowledge of the self and intuition. Essentially, when you use your third eye, you are stepping outside of your life and seeing it from a more objective standpoint. This allows you to get some distance from situations you might have grown too accustomed to and are thus struggling to see past. It will help you make long-term plans for your life and sort out what values are really and truly important to you. At the same time, the third eye chakra is also about connecting more strongly with your intuition and feeling more present in yourself or your body. So, it is simultaneously about intuition and greater objectivity.

When your third eye chakra is blocked, you will be very shortsighted in the way you think about and plan your life. Some might say this state is like not being able to see the forest for the trees—you cannot see your life's grand plan because you are too distracted by the day-to-day minutiae. You might feel as though you lack focus in your life, or you might not be able to see the higher purpose or goal of what you're doing. This can lead you to end up in meandering careers or relationships that seem to just go on without any clear trajectory or end goal. You might also experience physical symptoms. One of the most common symptoms is migraines, which affect a lot of people. You might also experience bouts of blurred vision or feelings of eye strain. When you work hard to unblock your third eye chakra, you will be able to see more clearly in order to plan your life and to connect more powerfully with your deepest intuition.

Crown Chakra

Associated Color:

White

Associated Element:

No associated element

Associated Body Parts:

The very top of the head

Description

The crown chakra is the pinnacle of all the chakras. It is the height of the chakra system and is responsible for your connection with the higher spiritual worlds. The goal of the whole chakra system is to eventually flow upward into the crown chakra, concentrating your energy there in order to achieve ultimate enlightenment. There is a lot of power to this chakra, so when or if it becomes unbalanced, it can create a lot of problems for the sufferer. You might feel constantly frustrated or cut off from your spiritual self. You might struggle with your faith or have a hard time committing to your view of the cosmic order of the universe. When this chakra is balanced, however, you will enjoy a strong connection to your higher self and gain a stronger understanding of the universe at large.

Chapter 6:
Higher Chakras

Thus far, we have only talked about the chakras that are represented on the physical body. Each chakra has a clear relationship with a particular body part and will therefore manifest in particular physical as well as psychological issues. However, there is actually another set of chakras that have an impact on how you live your life. These chakras are not located on the physical body but in spaces around the body. These are called the "higher chakras." The idea of the higher chakras is directly linked to body energy. When we talk about the body's energies, we are not just talking about actual locations on the body but the energy that your body radiates. According to the higher chakras, there are particular nodes of energy around the body that concentrate into individual chakras. This is called the "etheric body." These chakras work similarly to the rest of the body's chakras. They can become blocked or unbalanced and thus influence aspects of your thoughts and life. Again, as with the major chakras, there are a varying number of them depending on the chakra system you are using; here, we will be looking at five in particular. These five are the earth star chakra, the soul star chakra, the universal chakra, the galactic chakra, and the divine chakra. In this chapter, we will look at each of these chakras in detail and discuss their relationships with your chakra healing process.

Earth Star Chakra

Location:

Twelve inches below the feet

Description

The earth star chakra is inherently related to the root chakra. It is located below our feet and thus is almost always located within the earth. What this chakra implies is that much of our chakra energy spends time in the ground. This is a good thing! It means we have a strong connection to the earth below us and can find groundedness in its soil. So, since it's so closely related to the root chakra, what's the difference? Well, the main difference is in connection and a sense of something outside yourself, as the location of the chakra implies. This chakra focuses on your relationship with the earth below your feet, unlike the root chakra, which is more focused on your sense of identity. The earth star chakra is incredibly important not just for your sense of groundedness, but for your feelings of being a part of the organic material of the earth. It reminds us that we come from the earth and are made from its materials. We are inherently connected and will return to it one day. Your earth star chakra might also relate to your sense of mindfulness or feeling present in your day-to-day activities. Basically, the earth star chakra is your gateway to the earth below you and helps you mingle these energies together.

When your earth star chakra becomes unbalanced, you run the risk of losing this groundedness. You might feel like you are floating in space or not really human. Oftentimes, people who live lives that are very disconnected from nature experience earth star chakra blocks. For example, if you don't go for walks outside very often or if you live in an area that is very concrete-heavy, you might feel a disconnect from your earth star chakra; this can also happen if you live or work in a high-rise building and spend most of your time hundreds of feet above the earth. All of these situations are ways in which we disconnect from the earth, meaning that our earth star chakra is constantly floating around in space. To heal your earth star chakra, you should spend more time in nature to ensure that this energy node is actually making contact with the earth. Hiking, doing outdoor yoga, or even swimming in a lake can do wonders for the health of your earth star chakra.

Soul Star Chakra

Location:

Six inches above the head

Description

The soul star chakra is physically in the opposite position of your earth star chakra. It is an extension of your crown chakra just like your earth star chakra is an extension of your root chakra. The soul star chakra relates to your higher self, the core of your being that remains through reincarnations. In fact, the soul star chakra is often the path by which many people try to explore their past lives. Past lives are also known as "Akashic records" and can be used to gain powerful insight into the nature of your soul. We can carry so much from a past life that can greatly influence fears and talents in this current life. Discovering past life experiences is just as informative as discovering your childhood trauma—it can give you a lot of insight into who you are today. Some people also find that this chakra helps them to connect with their psychic side. Many people will use crystals to activate this chakra more powerfully by holding them in the spot above their heads where the soul star chakra is located. Those who have effectively opened their soul star chakra might feel as though they can see a higher plane of reality and have a stronger relationship with supernatural forces.

Universal Chakra

Location:

Twelve inches above the head

Description

Located just above the soul star chakra is the universal chakra. The universal chakra is directly related to that oneness of being we talked about in our section on Buddhism. The core energy to the universe will become available to you through the magic of the universal chakra. This chakra connects you to the unconditional love and inherent connection between all beings that pulses through the core of our world. The universal chakra also does not recognize time, so by unlocking it you can shed the oppressive shackles of linear time for something more everlasting. Crystals and crown-focused meditation can do wonders to help you unlock this chakra and start living among those cosmic realities in the great beyond.

Galactic Chakra

Location:

Two to fifteen feet above the head

Description

The galactic chakra's location surely lives up to its name being that it's the highest of the chakras we've seen so far. This chakra is further away from your body, and thus your body's energy does not have as strong an influence on it, but that does not make this chakra any less important. This chakra really allows you to connect with those intergalactic possibilities that are floating out in the universe. Some people call the galaxy chakra the "prophecy chakra." It gained such a reputation because it aids with things like divination and fortune-telling. Many professional psychics will tap into their own galactic chakras to help them connect with those future-connected forces out there in the universe. However, it is not just the future that this chakra helps with but also uncovering secret meanings and deeper truths. Psychics will also evoke their galactic chakra to help see past the debris of everyday life to the things that have not yet been revealed. If you want to have stronger insight into the future, or even achieve full-on psychic level, then you need to get actively in touch with your galactic chakra.

Divine Chakra

Location:

Above the galactic chakra to infinity

Description

The divine chakra is the highest chakra on this entire list and, in fact, the highest chakra in the entire chakra system. This chakra begins where your galactic chakra ends, assisting in your connection to important eternal forces. The divine chakra is how you connect with the highest form of knowledge and truly ascend to the uppermost point in the universe. You finally understand the oneness of everything and have completed your spiritual journey. Those who have successfully connected with their divine chakra are some of the most tranquil and zen people you will ever meet. They seem to take everything in stride as nothing seems to bother them at the roots of their being. Balance your divine chakra and you will have a life full of supreme knowledge and spiritual guidance.

Chapter 7:
Individual Chakras (Minor)

Besides the seven major chakras of the body and the five outer chakras beyond the body, there are also some less significant chakras that influence your body and behavior. These are called the "minor chakras." Some of these minor chakras are elevated to major status in certain chakra practices, but for our purposes, we will talk about them as part of the minor set. Even though they are called "minor," they can still have a significant impact on your body and mind, influencing the feelings you have or decisions you make. While the major chakras focus simply on key points in your body's core, the minor chakras are associated with more specific parts of your body. These concentrated chakra points can help you gain more specific knowledge of the body and its effect on the mind. In this chapter, we will discuss three individual minor chakras, helping you to distinguish their unique qualities and meanings. The chakras we will discuss are the foot chakra, the knee chakra, and the pubic chakra. By learning about these specific chakras, you will be able to more clearly define the areas on the body and their meanings.

The Foot Chakra

Location:

The feet

Description

The first chakra on the list of minor chakras is the foot chakra. This chakra is strongly related to the root chakra as well as the earth star chakra. In other words, it is associated with your sense of groundedness and connection to the earth. Your foot chakra is responsible for connecting your crown chakra back to the ground, thus utilizing your body as a sort of lightning rod that connects the sky energy with the ground energy. When you have a particularly blocked foot chakra, you will likely experience a lot of symptoms related to fatigue, restlessness, and disorientation. You might feel like you don't have a strong sense of home or know where your true support system lies. You might also find yourself getting frequently confused and lacking direction surrounding life plans. If you are experiencing these symptoms, then you badly need to balance your foot chakras, and the way to do this is similar to balancing the earth star chakra: Connect your feet with nature by running through grass in your bare feet or soaking them in a natural water source like a pond or spring. You can also use crystals, especially those associated with groundedness, to help unblock your foot chakras. If you are able to unblock your foot chakras and open them up to the light, then you will enjoy a life full of groundedness and certainty.

The Knee Chakra

Location:

Knees

Description

We might not think about them a lot, but our knees are actually very important parts of our body. They are the main connecting force in our legs and help us to walk properly. They are a focal point of a lot of our energy and facilitate free movement. However, like many major joints in the body, the knees also tend to be rife with problems. Many people, especially as they get older, have problems with their knees. They might have trouble walking, going up stairs, or kneeling. For this reason, it's essential to take good care of your knees and treat them well in your spiritual practice. One important way to spiritually care for your knees is through your knee chakra. This is an important minor chakra and can be used to promote energy and dynamism in your life. One of the best treatments for unblocking the knee chakra is yoga. Yoga promotes strength and connects us with the beautiful ways our bodies can move. Practicing some knee-centric yoga poses can help you to give that part of your body some love and unlock all the exciting potential at their core.

The Pubic Chakra

Location:

The genitals

Description

This chakra is a more refined version of the sacral chakra, occurring further down on the sexual organs and creating a concentrated perspective on sexuality. This chakra is solely concentrated on sexual functioning and thus touches other aspects of life such as relationships, self-esteem, and anxiety levels. Experiencing a blocked pubic chakra will inevitably lead to sexual issues, repression, or hypersexuality. This chakra can be balanced by practicing healthy attitudes toward sexuality and the body. Whether you are alone or with a partner, try to cultivate an environment in which you feel comfortable and safe. Experiment with different positions (many of which can be found in the Hindu text *Kama Sutra*) to help you with your feelings about yourself and help to unblock any frustrated sexual energy that you might be experiencing.

Pillar 3:
Relationships

As we have seen throughout the previous chapters of this book, the chakras are inextricably linked to the many systems of the body as well as many other spiritual systems. Chakras do not exist in a vacuum. This is why it is so imperative that you develop a strong understanding of your chakras and the way they affect your body—because they affect many different areas of the body and mind very strongly. Now, we have already talked about chakras and their relationships to many things like religion, astrology, crystals, and other spiritual practices, but here we are going to examine two specific systems with which chakras have a very strong relationship in greater detail. In this section, we will explore this very close relationship between the chakras with one system of the body—the endocrine system—and one spiritual system—the elements. Through these comparisons, you will gain a more holistic understanding of chakras and be able to better implement them into many of the practices that you already partake in throughout your life.

Chapter 8:
Chakras and the Endocrine System

The endocrine system is interesting because it is a very important system within the body, but it doesn't get a lot of attention in the mainstream. We talk a lot about the nervous and digestive systems, which have clear functions in relation to the way we eat and manage anxiety. We are also building increasing awareness as a culture around things like the gut bacteria system and the chemical workings of mental health, but these are just a few pieces of the puzzle when we talk about all the complex systems of the body. There are so many functions the body performs without us even realizing it, and the endocrine system is one of them. Now, the endocrine system is not one hidden organ that you didn't know you had, but it is in fact a series of well-known organs that you were probably not aware had a connection to one another. This system has a very important role to play in many hormonal functions of the body. It also happens to be strongly linked with the system of the chakras and thus is relevant to bring up in a book about the subject. In this chapter, we will discuss the relationship that this system—the endocrine system—has with the chakras. First, we will give you some background on the endocrine system itself, helping you to understand its specific functions. Then, we will give you a breakdown of how this system interacts with each individual chakra as well as the chakra system as a whole.

What Is the Endocrine System?

In a way, the endocrine system is actually a kind of medicalized version of the chakras. This system divides the body up into parts, each represented on a different part of the core going from the base to the top. It also asserts that these systems are connected and, even though each performs its own specific functions, they can also greatly affect one another as well. This is what makes them a system. So, essentially, every aspect of the endocrine system has a core function, while its relationships with the other organs are expressed through the flow of hormones instead of energy. The various parts of the endocrine system thus have the same flow as chakras and are able to have as profound an impact on the mind and body. The main areas that the endocrine system deals with are metabolism, overall mental state, stress levels, pain response, energy, reproduction, and development of the body. That's a lot of aspects to preside over—important ones at that! No wonder this system is considered so important and can be seen as similar to the chakras in that way. The system consists of many organs and glands, which all have varying degrees of effects on the above list and are all required for the proper functioning of each. In short, the endocrine system is a highly important system responsible for many of the body's psychological and physiological problems.

Parts of the System

As we mentioned, there are many different organs and glands associated with the endocrine system. In many ways, this system functions similarly to that of the chakras, encompassing parts of the body from the top of the head to the bottom of the core. In this section, we will talk about the various organs of the endocrine system, detailing the way in which each one affects the body and mind as well as its relationship to the chakra system. For the sake of symmetry, we will be sorting the list from bottom to top, just like we did with the chakras, helping you to see the connections between the two systems.

Testicles/Ovaries

The first major body parts in the endocrine system are the organs that perform reproductive functions. This can be either ovaries or testicles depending on the biological sex of the person. These organs are the lowermost organs but also serve a very important function. Interestingly, these organs are not essential for survival. After all, many people have them removed or blocked off and are still perfectly healthy. However, they are necessary for some people to have in order to continue the human species. Thus, they serve an interesting function in the body—to perpetuate the human species but not the human body itself. Though they are technically the lowest organ on this list, their corresponding chakra is not actually the root chakra but the sacral chakra. This chakra presides over reproduction and, by proxy, sexual function as well. They also serve the important purpose of producing sex hormones like estrogen and testosterone in both men and women, which are hormones that help with sexual function and the development of the body. When we talk about the sacral chakra, we are thus also talking about reproduction and the ability to bring life into the world.

So, how does the dysfunction of these organs relate to the blocking of the sacral chakra? Well, the sacral chakra is also connected to creativity and self-esteem. Some people feel shame or disappointment in themselves at the inability to have children. This is something they will have to work through in order to accept themselves as they are, but nevertheless, there might be a certain bump in the road to try and recover their self-esteem. Many people also connect creativity with reproduction, viewing their children as creative projects to be sculpted properly. They might also feel the opposite way—that their creative projects are like their children. People might call their novel or film their "baby," referring to the laborious process of creation that can sometimes feel like parenting a child. Thus, reproductive dysfunction can also be metaphorically linked to creative stagnation or writer's block. In this sense, there are a lot of important physical and thematic links that connect the sacral chakra with the testicles or ovaries.

Pancreas

The pancreas is one of the more overlooked organs in the body, but it still serves a very important purpose. It is located in the abdomen just behind the stomach, and its corresponding chakra is the solar plexus. The pancreas performs one of the most important functions for the body's hormones by producing insulin, which helps to keep the body's blood sugar levels in check. It also produces hormones and helps you to digest things properly. You need your pancreas very badly. Having a dysfunctional pancreas is actually the main component of diabetes, sufferers of which are forced to regulate their blood sugar manually with synthetic insulin, which is very difficult to do and takes up a lot of time. Basically, you want your pancreas to be functioning properly.

The main way the pancreas relates to the solar plexus chakra is through its regulation of certain digestive issues. The pancreas helps to make sure your digestive system is functioning properly, which is also the main job of the solar plexus chakra. The pancreas therefore works in tandem with this chakra, meaning that blocks or malfunctions of either can have a disastrous effect on both. What you see psychologically when there are difficulties with the solar plexus chakra can also manifest in the pancreas—feelings of no control and dysregulation of the body. This regulating organ connects strongly to the highly balance-focused solar plexus chakra.

Adrenal Gland

Another part of the endocrine system that is closely related to the solar plexus chakra is the adrenal glands. These are glands that sit on top of both of your kidneys and help them to perform their main functions. These glands are also strongly connected to other glands within the body's system, such as the pituitary gland and the hypothalamus. These three glands form their own mini-endocrine system, helping the body to regulate many different essential hormones. In particular, the adrenal gland is responsible for distributing hormones such as epinephrine, which is also known as adrenaline. Adrenaline is responsible for your body's energy levels and can give you that important energy boost and sense of vigor in times of extreme stress. What these hormonal functions essentially accomplish is the regulation of things like blood pressure and metabolism. These are two highly essential aspects of the body, the mismanagement of which can result in some serious chronic issues that can eventually lead to fatal problems like heart disease. We can see how both of the organs that we have talked about so far in relation to the solar plexus chakra are highly connected to regulation. These organs help the body maintain balance, which is again strongly related to the solar plexus's functions.

Thymus

Moving up on the body, the thymus is located in the chest. I'm sure you can already surmise which chakra is connected with this organ: the heart chakra. The thymus performs some very important functions in the body's immune system. When you are fighting a virus, your thymus is the one fighting against the body's invaders. It helps keep you healthy and strong. This is related to the heart chakra's focus on health and happiness, especially around family. You can think of your body as a family and your thymus as the protective parent trying to keep danger away. It's an organ of nurturing and is essential in helping you stay strong against many different illnesses that can potentially attack the body and cause great harm.

Thyroid

The thyroid is located just by the voice box at the front of the neck. Because of its location, it is of course directly related to the throat chakra. The thyroid is responsible for your metabolism. Many people with thyroid dysfunctions have a lot of trouble maintaining a healthy weight, often remaining underweight despite a healthy diet or overweight despite calorie restrictions. Many people with thyroid issues, particularly those that are undiagnosed, feel that they are out of control of their bodies and might experience self-esteem issues as a result. A dysregulated thyroid can also lead to chronic anxiety issues, so many people with thyroid issues might experience social withdrawal or extreme anxiety around things like speaking in public. Interestingly, this has many parallels to some of the issues outlined in our section on an unbalanced throat chakra. If you find that you are experiencing extreme anxiety, then you might have a problem with either your throat chakra or your thyroid.

Hypothalamus

Finally, we reach the brain and thus the third eye chakra. The hypothalamus is a gland within the brain that is responsible for a wide variety of brain functions. It is located directly below the optic nerve, which physically links it very closely with the third eye chakra's relationship to sight. There are many things it does though—much more than anything related to sight. The hypothalamus controls things like your blood pressure, appetite, general body temperature regulation, and even sleep. All of these things are very important. Most significantly, all of these regulations feed back into your cognitive function. Things like having high blood pressure, an unregulated eating schedule, or not getting enough sleep all have a significant negative impact on the brain and its function, but of course, if the brain is not functioning properly, then these things aren't either. We can see the vicious cycle the hypothalamus can get into if it is not regulated. This also connects to the long-term goals and planning of the third eye chakra. Regulating these foundational functions of the body helps to keep your body healthy and your mind sharp and has a strong effect on the way you think.

Breakdown of the Chakra Connection

The connection between the chakra points and the key organs of the endocrine system is certainly striking. It seems that even before we had the technology to dissect the human body, we were acutely aware of the fact that these points were very important to an interconnected web. By comparing the endocrine system to the chakra system, we can see that the system of the chakras actually has a sound medical basis. These points on the body are not chosen at random, and we can see how they actually have similar functions to the body's overall purpose. We can also see how the chakras have a strong connection to the actual functions of the body, and we can observe the specific ways in which a blocked chakra can affect the body. This is not to say that chakra healing needs medical science to legitimize it but merely to point out that they do not come from nowhere and their relationship to the body can be observed as well as felt.

Chapter 9:
Chakras and the Elements

Back in our section on individual chakras, we listed an element that coincides with each chakra. This might not have seemed that important at the time, but the connection with the elements is one of the things that links the chakras to many other spiritual systems. The elements each carry meanings associated with them that can help further inform your chakra healing practice. Additionally, linking the elements in your chakras to the elemental associations of other spiritual practices such as astrology, crystal healing, and tarot can help you incorporate these other practices into your chakra healing. In this chapter, we will talk about the association between the elements and the chakras. First, we will give a detailed definition of the specific elemental system we will be using so you understand the specifics of this system and where it came from. Next, we will list each individual element and give you a description of all the things it is associated with as well as the specific sides of each spiritual practice it presides over.

What Are the Elements?

First of all, let's identify what elements we are talking about here. You might be familiar with the periodic table of elements, which you may have learned about in chemistry class. This system is an ever-expanding chart of every single chemical that human beings have discovered on Earth so far. However, we will not be discussing this system of elements. Instead, we will be focusing on ancient elemental systems that were developed before things like microscopes could reveal more division among the elements. One such elemental system, which is probably the most famous of the ancient ones, is the Greek system of the four elements. These elements are earth, fire, water, and air. They feature very prominently throughout ancient Greek science, philosophy, and astrology. Systems like the zodiac, tarot cards, and crystal healing are all designed to correspond to one of these four elements. For this reason, you can often divide many of these spiritual systems into groups of four to help you distinguish or specialize your healing practice. However, again, this is not quite the system we will be talking about. In chakra healing, there are actually five elements. The first four are earth, fire, water, and air, similar to the Greek system, but the Hindu or chakra element system includes a fifth element called "ether," or space. This element has a higher connection and does not necessarily map onto other spiritual systems in the same way, though it does map onto the chakras. Each chakra relates to one of these elements, except the top two which don't have elemental connections. In the rest of this chapter, we will look at the five elements of the chakras, explaining both their meanings and their connections.

Earth

Ah, the Earth. Our home, our protector. Feeding us, sheltering us, clothing us. It's no wonder people nickname the Earth "mother." In a way, the Earth gave birth to us all. Though most of the elements on the periodic table are found in the earth, in this system it is a whole element in itself. In most spiritual systems, the earth is associated with a grounding force. You can think of the earth as either things that are associated with the ground, such as plants, dirt, or rocks, or you can think of this element as the core of the Earth itself. Whichever is easier for you to visualize is best. Most people feel a strong connection to the earth, especially if you are someone who has powerful feelings of connectedness or belonging. Thus, in most spiritual systems, the earth is in some way associated with rootedness or down-to-earth qualities. In the chakra system, the earth is associated with the root chakra, as we talked about back in Chapter 5. Here, we will look at all the spiritual systems that include the earth and explore how it interacts with your chakra healing journey.

Associated Zodiac Signs

Virgo, Taurus, and Capricorn are the signs on the zodiac that are associated with the earth. These are all signs that are known for being very practical and straightforward. There is no messing with earth signs since they tend to see through to the truth of everything. If you have earth in your sun sign or birth month, then you will probably be a highly pragmatic person, very protective of your loved ones, and might even feel a particular connection to earthly things in general. If you are experiencing a root chakra block, look at some of the earth signs that might be in your birth chart. Your sun, moon, or some of your planets might be in earth signs, which can help you gain insight into your connection to your root chakra and this element in general. You also might want to coordinate your chakra healing practices around earth signs in the sky. Consider waiting until an earth sign birth month to start your chakra healing journey. Making this connection with your chakras and your birth chart, as well as the current celestial sky, can help you specify and clarify your chakra healing practice.

Associated Crystals

Many crystals involved in healing have significant associations with the earth. This makes sense as most crystals are mined out of the ground and therefore come from the earth. Three of the main earth-associated crystals are tiger's eye, smoky quartz and amazonite. Tiger's eye is particularly useful for giving you energy and confidence. If you feel insecure in your grounding energy, a tiger's eye can help you reconnect with your self-esteem. Smoky quartz, on the other hand, is a protective stone, both against actual illness and negative energy in general. This crystal is perfect if you want to build a deeper connection with the earth. Finally, amazonite is strongly associated with material abundance. This might not seem like it is associated with the earth, but as we will see below in the tarot section, abundance is actually related to crop success, which is connected to the earth. Using crystals associated with the earth can really help you with unblocking or opening up your root chakra. If you have a root chakra block, consider using one of these three crystals in your meditation practice to give it some attention.

Associated Tarot Suit

Tarot is another popular spiritual practice. Tarot cards are similar to conventional playing cards in the sense that there are four suits, each of which has a set of number and face cards. The suits, however, are different in a tarot deck. Instead of diamonds, hearts, clubs, and spades, you have pentacles, cups, wands, and swords. People use these cards to gain insight into their lives and futures. The four suits are also associated with specific elements. The other major difference between tarot cards and other card decks is that there are two parts to the deck: the major arcana and the minor arcana. The minor arcana is the four suits with their number and face cards—the part of the deck that most resembles a conventional deck—totaling 56 cards. The major arcana is a series of individual cards which don't belong to a particular suit but relate to archetypes or ideas. You might have even seen some cards in popular culture, such as death, the hermit, or the hanged man. Some of these cards have elemental associations, so we will include those in our chakra discussion as well as the suit cards.

In this case, the suit in a tarot deck that is most associated with the earth is pentacles. Pentacles are gold coins that symbolize money and prosperity in the world. As we said above, money and material prosperity have long been associated with the earth, dating back to the days of widespread agriculture. People's money quite literally came out of the ground and so the association was born. For this reason, many tarot decks feature nature-based themes and colors in the artwork for their pentacle suit. There are several ways to incorporate tarot practice into your chakra healing. You can inquire as to whether there might be a root chakra block in the first place by doing a reading for yourself or going to a professional psychic and taking notice if a lot of pentacles are coming up in your reading, especially if they are reversed, as this may indicate a blockage. If you already feel like you are experiencing a blockage, you can try an isolated reading. Some tarot readers will isolate parts of the deck, such as a single suit, to try and determine a particular problem. You could try an isolated reading with just the pentacles to get a more specific idea of your relationship to the earth element. You can also see if any earth-associated major arcana cards come up. Some major arcana cards that are connected with the earth element include the devil, the hierophant, the empress, the hermit, and the world. Using these methods, you can employ the tarot to help you both ascertain and improve your relationship with the earth.

Water

The next element we will be talking about is water. Water is the element most closely associated with flow as is represented by the fluid currents of the ocean or the meandering trajectory of a brook. We are just as connected to the element of water as we are to that of earth. First of all, our bodies are about 70% water, meaning that water makes up the vast majority of what is inside us. Furthermore, we need to drink water in order to survive, cook food, bathe ourselves, wash things for protection from disease, and even navigate the world. Water has a huge impact on not only individual human lives but on entire civilizations. Most major cities in the world were built on a coast or a river, ensuring that every inhabitant had an adequate water source. This element is thus extremely important to us. The chakra most linked to water is the next one up from the root chakra—the sacral chakra. This chakra is tied to water through its focus on inner emotions and sexuality. In this section, we will look at how water figures into other spiritual systems as well as its impact on the sacral chakra.

Associated Zodiac Signs

Similar to how there are three earth signs in the 12-sign zodiac system, there are also three water signs. These water signs are Pisces, Cancer, and Scorpio. All three of these signs are known for being very emotional. Pisces are emotional in a sensitive way, being extremely self-conscious and vulnerable to criticism. Cancers, on the other hand, are more emotional in the way that they are very focused on love and family and protective of those they love. Finally, Scorpios are emotional but in a very secretive way. They hold their cards close to their chests and take a long time to let people in. We can see this play out in the sacral chakra, especially with some of the extremely intimate relationships the sacral chakra covers. This chakra is associated with some of the most sensitive and vulnerable emotions, especially when they are related to sexuality and the most inner self. As we said in the above section on earth, you can use the water-associated zodiac signs to help time your sacral chakra healing practice by either locating them on your birth chart or performing your healing practice at times when that sign is in sun or moon.

Associated Crystals

Most of the crystals associated with the element of water are focused on bringing you inner peace and fostering healthy relationships with the people in your life. Three of the main water-associated crystals are aquamarine, turquoise, and amethyst. Aquamarine is a calming crystal. This crystal is designed to create a sense of tranquility within your life and, by proxy, help reduce stress and anxiety. It is also helpful for focusing your energies. Turquoise, on the other hand, is a powerful cleansing stone. This crystal is especially useful for banishing negative energy from your life which, in the context of relationships, might mean cutting out some particularly toxic people. Finally, amethyst is a healing stone particularly useful for emotional trauma. It can help soothe those wounds that you might have endured throughout your life and help you to rebuild a new life. If you are suffering from a block in your sacral chakra, then you can use one of these three crystals in your healing practice to help open it up.

Associated Tarot Suit

The tarot suit associated with water is cups. The cups of the suit are designed to hold water, and whether or not they are full, or the degree to which they are full, is often laden with meaning within the deck. Often, illustrations for the cups suit will feature water in other places as well, not just inside the cups. Some of the most common motifs are a waterfall or river. These symbolize new beginnings but also an abundance of love or emotional energy. The major arcana cards that are associated with water include the moon, the priestess, the chariot, the hanged man, and death. With your sacral chakra, you want to be able to open yourself up to the most intimate parts of this energy. Do a tarot reading, either with the whole deck or just the cups, and see what comes up. If you are getting a lot of reversed water cards or negative water cards, such as the five of cups, then you might have an imbalanced sacral chakra. Use the readings to construct a path toward opening that chakra.

Fire

The third element on this list is fire. As you can probably guess, fire is often strongly associated with passion, confidence, and boldness. It can also be associated with creativity, being the spark or the light bulb that enlightens the creative mind. And of course, it is also associated with sexuality, especially when people speak of the fires of passion or a burning desire. This element is, perhaps unexpectedly, associated with the solar plexus chakra. This chakra connects with the driven aspect of fire which forms a large part of your self-esteem. Fire also connects to some of the physical properties of the solar plexus chakra, which some refer to as your "digestive fire." In this section, we will look at how the element of fire relates to your solar plexus chakra and its themes in other spiritual practices.

Associated Zodiac Signs

Fire is very important to some of the zodiac signs. The signs that are under the influence of fire are Leo, Aries, and Sagittarius. Leo is the sign of confidence and social influence. Basically, Leos just can't help but be charming. This relates to the social connection aspect of the solar plexus chakra. Aries is the sign of competition. Aries love to spar with people in a friendly (or not-so-friendly!) manner, which connects to the desire to perform well that sits at the core of the solar plexus chakra. And Sagittarians are known for their ability to mediate, which can provide a different perspective on the social personalities of Leo and Aries. Therefore, we can see that these fire-associated signs in the zodiac have a lot in common with the solar plexus chakra and can thus be used in tandem with your chakra healing process. Timing your solar plexus chakra healing with one of these three signs will help you align with the fire element more closely and create a more focused healing practice.

Associated Crystals

Crystal healing can help you greatly with balancing your solar plexus chakra, especially ones that have a strong association with fire. Three of the best crystals to use in your solar plexus chakra healing journey are garnet, red jasper, and carnelian. Garnet is one of the most potent and powerful crystals. It is strongly associated with love and relationships as well as balancing your sexual self. It is also associated with perseverance and forward momentum, which resonates with the social achievement aspect of the solar plexus chakra. Red jasper is more of a calming, protective crystal. This gemstone has the ability to balance your intense emotions and bring a sense of tranquility to your life. It is also a great manifestation crystal, helping you to bring positive energy into your life. Finally, carnelian is one of the best success-bringing crystals, resonating with the confidence and drive you are trying to manifest through your solar plexus chakra. Using any of these three crystals in your meditation or chakra practice will help you link better with the fire element and your solar plexus chakra more specifically.

Associated Tarot Suit

The suit in the tarot most associated with fire is wands. This might be a strange association, but the wand is meant to represent spark and creativity, with magical fire pouring out of its tip. Usually, the wand suit is used to talk about your feelings toward creativity or even professional pursuits. We can see this reflected in the way the solar plexus chakra is often linked to our social pursuits and self-esteem in relation to how we are perceived by others. Some of the major arcana cards associated with the element of fire are the sun, the tower, the emperor, and the wheel of fortune. If you want to learn more about your relationship with your solar plexus chakra, then you can do some tarot readings and focus on the placement of the wand suit and the above-mentioned major arcana cards in your reading.

Air

Coming to the final of the Greek elements, we have air. Air is, of course, the lightest element, consisting mainly of gas. As with the other elements, air is also necessary to sustain life. Air not only nourishes us by giving us oxygen to breathe in and power our bodies with, but it sustains many other things as well, like plants and animals. It's no coincidence, then, that the chakra most associated with air is the one right next to our lungs: the heart chakra. Physically, the oxygen we breathe from air is one of the most important aspects of powering our physical hearts, so air as an element is quite literally involved with this part of our bodies. Moreover, air is also metaphorically linked to our heart chakras, representing the expansiveness and higher knowledge of unconditional love. In this section, we will look at the ways in which the element of air intersects with aspects of other spiritual systems and how to harness it in order to help you on your chakra journey.

Associated Zodiac Signs

The three zodiac signs associated with the element of air are Gemini, Libra, and Aquarius. These three signs all have strong associations with malleability as a person. This might seem like a bad thing since we tend to think of people who hold steadfast to their beliefs as stronger; however, this malleability can also be a strength, allowing these air signs to make compromises and be more open-minded in order to help those they love and adopt new worldviews. When healing your heart chakra, look at the qualities of the air signs and connect with some of the ones in your birth chart or that are in the current sky's chart.

Associated Crystals

Despite being rocks from the ground, there are actually many crystals that have a strong association with the air. Three of the best crystals to use for air-connected heart chakra healing are fluorite, clear quartz, and blue lace agate. Fluorite is a great crystal for promoting more focused, rational thinking. In the context of the heart chakra, this can help you bring clarity to your relationships and perhaps help you evaluate which ones are important. Clear quartz is also useful for clarity, but it is also considered to be the leader of the crystals, so to speak. You can use this crystal in tandem with other crystals to create a lightness and clarity in your manifestation of chakra healing practice. Blue lace agate is a tranquilizing stone that helps you to bring a sense of peace to your life. All these crystals are excellent for strengthening your connection to the air element and your heart chakra.

Associated Tarot Suit

The tarot suit associated with the element of air is swords. Swords are the suit of enlightenment and sharp rational thinking. Often, illustrations on cards in the sword suit will feature clouds, birds, or the sky very prominently. Many tarot readers will interpret this suit as being related to both your academic pursuits, if that is relevant, as well as your higher thoughts or spiritual pursuits. This is the suit in which you will find clarity of mind and where logic will prevail. The major arcana cards associated with the element of air are the fool, the lovers, the magician, and the star. When you are using this suit in relation to your heart chakra, you can evaluate the place of these logical ideas and higher realities within your relationships as well as at the core of your being.

Ether

Now that we have completed the four Greek elements, we can move on to the three additional Vedic, or Hindu, elements. These higher elements are different from the previous four in the sense that they do not have a physical reality. They also do not feature prominently outside of Vedic philosophy, which is why they don't have corresponding tarot cards, crystals, or zodiac signs. From here on out, we will simply describe the element as it pertains to the relevant chakra and what it means for connecting with that chakra or opening it up.

The first of the higher three elements we will be looking at is ether, or empty space. This is essentially the absence of physical matter. It's what you would get if you sucked out all the air from the space around us. This element is actually very important to Vedic philosophy since it is thought to be the first element ever created. It is the empty space into which the universe expanded and thus is the base for all life. However, this element does not just exist in empty spaces but in fact all around us; thus, it is the linking force between all things in the universe. The connecting chakra to the element of ether is the throat chakra. The way that this chakra connects to ether is through the theme of authenticity. Because of the extreme clarity of emptiness, there is no room for bamboozlement. Channeling this element can help you if you have blocks with your throat chakra, clearing the air for you to live a more honest and authentic life.

Light

Recently, quantum physics has been doing a lot of research into the behavior of light in physical space. Light travels through things called photons, but physicists still can't agree on whether photons are particles or waves. This ambiguity is what makes photons so interesting. Photons are also extremely fast. In fact, the speed of light is the highest recorded speed in the universe. This element is thus perfect for association with the third eye chakra. The third eye chakra is all about enlightenment, stretching the boundaries of everyday perception. Light is the element that makes sight possible. Everything you see is actually just different colors and shades of light, and thus your eyes work merely as light receptors. Metaphorical light, or enlightenment, also forms a connection between the third eye chakra and the element of light. Consider connecting with different light sources in your life to help unblock your third eye chakra. Evaluate how much natural versus artificial light you use in your daily life and perhaps try to use more natural light. You could even try to change up your light sources by introducing a new light source. Try meditating by moonlight to recalibrate your body and your third eye chakra's relationship with light.

Thought

The final and most immaterial element on this list is thought. Although scientists mainly talk about thought as a series of neurological connections, almost every spiritual philosophy categorizes the human mind or soul as being separate from the physical body. Thus, thought in this context is immaterial thought—not the workings of neurons. This element cannot be measured, seen, or even perceived by anyone other than the thinker, and this is why it is ultimately strongly connected to the crown chakra, which is all about the highest realities of our minds and our connection to the universe beyond. This is why mindfulness is such an important aspect of enlightenment and spiritual healing. It allows us to truly focus and be at one with our thoughts, allowing them to pass by us and be noticed without being sources of stress. If you want to learn to balance your crown chakra, you need to put a strong emphasis on your thoughts and the ways in which they connect with the outside world and the universe at large.

Pillar 4: Activation

Now that you understand all about chakras, their history, their individual meanings, and the connections they have to your physical body and other spiritual systems, you are ready to start learning about the actual process of using them to heal. This is the point in the book where we move away from theory toward a more practical approach to the chakras. In this pillar, we will talk about all the different ways you can start to activate your chakras. In the first chapter of the pillar, we will talk about the benefits of opening and activating your chakras. This section will list the reasons why you should care for your chakras, all the hidden problems that can arise when they are blocked, and what opening them up can do for your life. In the second chapter of this pillar, we will talk about the specific ways you can activate your chakras, helping you begin your journey of chakra healing. Throughout this section, we will make a strong case for why and how you can start activating your chakras for a more fulfilled life.

Chapter 10:
Why Should You Open Your Chakras?

Throughout this book, you have probably been wondering about the specific reasons you should be balancing your chakras. After all, you've gone your whole life without even knowing about them, so what's the big deal? Well, as you might have ascertained throughout the last few chapters, there are actually a lot of compelling reasons as to why you should be trying to activate, or open, your chakras. Your chakras are gateways to your body and mind, useful tools for understanding and remedying many of the difficulties you might be facing throughout your life. In this chapter, we will be outlining some of the most compelling ways in which chakras can help enhance your life. First, we will discuss how chakras can help you pinpoint issues in your life that you might previously have struggled to recognize and articulate. Next, we will look at how chakras can greatly enhance your relationship with yourself and your sense of personhood. After that, we will talk about how you can enhance your general spiritual life by incorporating chakra practice. And finally, we will discuss how chakras forge a strong mind-body connection that will help you bring these forces together. By the end of this chapter, you'll be ready to start activating your chakras!

Target Issues in Your Life

Many people experience problems in their lives that they may not be able to really explain or put their finger on. It could be a mysterious physical problem that doesn't have a clear cause, such as migraines or chronic fatigue, or it could be a psychological problem like depression or anxiety. For these vaguer conditions, many people go through the medical system without getting a definitive answer about their condition from doctors; thus, many people end up very frustrated by their conditions and begin looking elsewhere for answers. What chakra healing does is break down the body into parts and help you identify where on the body your ailment might be originating. For example, if you have persistent headaches, it might relate to your third eye chakra being imbalanced, or if you have a lot of anxiety around speaking in public or meeting new people, it could be caused by a block in your throat chakra. The ability to pinpoint the exact causes or location of your issue can be a dream come true for sufferers of vague or unidentified illnesses. Chakra healing can help people with this very thing because it creates a clear system of division in their body, helping to identify and connect more specific problems.

Learn About Yourself

Connecting with your chakras can also teach you a lot about yourself. If you have certain personality traits that are linked to a particular chakra, then you might be able to investigate why that particular chakra is important. Notice if any of the other qualities of that chakra resonate with you so that you can see the impact it might have had on you and your life. By investigating aspects of the chakras, you might also have noticed that there were certain chakras you connected with more than others and possibly some things that may have triggered particular anxieties. In this case, you will be able to see what areas of your life might need more work and attention. The chakras help you with this because they compartmentalize different aspects of life, perhaps pointing out areas that we might not have thought of. To aid in this aspect of chakra healing, consider going through each chakra one at a time and really evaluating your relationship to that area of your life as well as any physical symptoms you tend to experience related to the particular chakra.

Enhance Other Spiritual Practices

As we talked about back in Chapter 9, there are many other spiritual practices that have elemental links to the chakras. However, the connections go far beyond merely associating with similar elements. Almost every other spiritual practice in existence can be enhanced through the amalgamation of chakras. Things like mindfulness, meditation, tarot readings, and astrological practice can all benefit from a thorough knowledge of your chakras. Mindfulness can help chakras by focusing on specific areas of the body in your meditative practice. Likewise, meditation also benefits from a more focused approach and especially an awareness of the higher chakras that are meant to connect you with the universe at large. Having a keen awareness and openness toward your upper chakras will vastly improve your meditative experience and help you reach higher spiritual enlightenment through it. Tarot and astrology might also become more clear once your chakras are activated, helping you to see how different aspects of your birth chart relate to your chakras or how tarot readings might interact with them, helping you to make better decisions for the future. Crystals, too, can benefit from activated chakras. The more awake your chakras are, the more receptive your body is to crystal energy, and thus the more effective your crystal healing practice will become. Whatever combination of practices you are engaging in, you will certainly benefit from activated chakras.

Strengthen Mind-Body Connection

Finally, chakras are all about the inherent connections between the body and the mind. Your understanding and concept of your body will fundamentally change after the inclusion of chakra healing into your practice. Most of us walk around with a sort of harsh mind-body division. We think of our body as simply a machine performing the baser functions and our brain as the thing that has the most profound impact on our lives, where all the important stuff happens. But through chakra healing, you can really see how both physiological and psychological processes are stored in the brain and the body. You can then develop a stronger connection between these two. Activating your chakras will help you create a reciprocal healing process in which you can heal your mind through your body and your body through your mind. Perhaps targeting your physical stomach with a healthier diet can actually help your social anxiety. Conversely, working on your social anxiety with a therapist might help cure your chronic stomachaches. Chakra healing gives you the tools to make these connections and allows you to work toward a more holistic healing practice for yourself. By activating your specific chakras, you are awakening this connection, meaning that your old dichotomy between the intellectual workings of your mind and the basic functions of the body will be no more. You can enjoy a strong connection as well as more opportunities for growth!

Chapter 11:
How to Awaken Your Chakras

Okay, you're convinced—activating your chakras is important! But how do you actually do it? What are the processes whereby you can start to actually awaken your chakras? Likely, this is the moment you've been waiting for as you've been reading this book. Though we have discussed some chakra-opening methods already, such as using crystals or astrology, we have not yet discussed the actual process behind the opening of the chakras themselves in isolation. Well, in this chapter, we will be discussing exactly how you can activate your chakras. First, we will explore what actually happens when your chakras become activated to help you be able to judge the difference between an activated and unactivated chakra. Then, we will look at a step-by-step approach to opening up your chakras. We will guide you through the actual stages, starting with the root chakra and ending with the crown chakra. Though we will not be touching on the other sets of chakras we mentioned earlier in this book, many of the ideas we will be talking about will help you in case you do want to move on to activating those other chakras. By the end of this chapter, you should be all ready to start using some techniques for opening your chakras!

What Happens When Chakras Are Activated?

First of all, what does an opened chakra feel like? Because the chakras allow you to look at a specific aspect of your body and life, you will have a better idea of how they feel because you can laser focus on just that one area. There are two aspects to the feeling of a chakra being either opened or closed: the body and the mind. In the body, you will likely feel less tension in that area if the chakra is open. You might be relieved of bad neck muscle tension, for instance, after balancing your throat chakra, or you might have relief from constipation after balancing your root chakra. You might also feel a stronger connection to that body part and be relieved of shame about it. The second aspect is the mind, which connects to the facet of life over which the individual chakra presides. If you are able to unblock your chakra in that area, that part of your life should see some improvement. You might notice a more active appetite for healthier foods by balancing your solar plexus chakra or a greater capacity for care by balancing your heart chakra. Ensuring that you know very well how to balance these areas of your life will help you to see growth and change. When you successfully open all your chakras, you will be able to facilitate the energy flow between your root and crown chakras. This creates a sense of fluidity and helps your chakras work together toward a more holistic approach to health and happiness.

Where Do You Start?

All this advice might seem overwhelming, especially if you are not sure which chakras you need to be balancing. You have likely already done some reflection about this, but even so, it's hard to know for sure as there is some crossover of symptoms, especially psychological symptoms. For example, struggles with self-esteem can manifest through the root, sacral, or even solar plexus chakras. Therefore, even if you have strong insight into your individual issues, you still might not be completely clear as to the chakras that need activation. From there, you have two options. You can either isolate one or a few chakras that you think need work and follow the process of activating just those. This is advisable for those who already have a good idea of what their chakra needs look like, having narrowed it down to just one or two individual chakras as the source of their issues. Alternatively, you can do a full-body chakra heal. This is where you start from your root chakra and focus on each chakra in sequence until you reach your crown chakra. This is advisable to do if you're not sure what the sources of your chakra difficulties are or if you want a more holistic healing process. It's also advisable that you do this every so often. After all, just because you aren't having an issue with a particular chakra doesn't mean it couldn't use some attention. Therefore, you should do a full-body chakra heal if you haven't identified the source of your chakra issues as well as periodically to promote the health of all your chakras and to support the connections between them. In the next section, we will go chakra by chakra, giving you the best ways to balance those individual areas for a better quality of life.

Chakra by Chakra

Because each of your chakras is responsible for a different area of your body and life, they all need to be approached in a slightly different way. In this section, we will look at the different methods you can use to help heal your chakras and make sure they are taken care of properly. These methods will all involve simply your body and your mind, so no materials are necessary! However, if you want to use some aids, they certainly can help enhance your chakra healing process. There are two main types of aids people use for their chakra sessions. The first kind is environmental aids. These are simply things you can do to your room to put yourself in a relaxed, contemplative, or meditative mood. This can be anything that helps you relax, such as candles, soft lighting, or instrumental atmospheric music. These things are not essential but can certainly make the process better than trying to do chakra awakenings in a crowded room or brightly lit space! Basically, this kind of aid is about finding your comfort zone so you can do the difficult work of activating your chakras without distractions or added stress. The other kind of aid is spiritual aids, such as the ones we talked about in Chapter 9. If you are into another spiritual practice, such as crystals, incorporating that practice into your chakra healing can actually do a lot for your connection to your chakras. Since you already have a strong connection to your crystals, for instance, you can have an even stronger connection to your chakras by combining the practices. This aspect isn't necessary either, but it can enhance the experience if that sort of thing is important to you. In this section, however, we will just give you aid-less techniques to which you can add these aids if you wish. We will go from the root to the crown to help you envision the process as a cohesive sequence.

Root

To activate the root chakra, you can engage in some simple meditation. This isn't just any meditation, however, it is the kind of prototypical meditation you will often see in advertisements for yoga classes. This posture involves sitting cross-legged on the ground and putting your hands on your knees in the "okay" position facing up, your thumb and index finger pointing toward the sky. This hand position is called a "mudra" and is very important in Hindu philosophy. Sitting cross-legged on the ground is essential for accessing your root chakra as it creates a connection between your body, specifically the root chakra, and the earth. Some modifications can be to sit cross-legged with your nondominant leg on top, just to build better awareness in your body, or to sit in the lotus position or upside-down crossed legs to build some stretching into the process. For the best results, you should do this outside, actually touching the earth, but if that is not an option, pick the lowest floor in your home that you have access to so you are as close to the earth as possible. Another aspect of this posture is the chant. You should build a chant into your root chakra healing process. One of the ideal ones is "lam," which you can chant over and over. Try to really lose yourself in the chant and feel the vibrations of your voice in your root chakra. Doing this exercise regularly can help you to build a stronger connection to your root chakra and hopefully work on activating the best of its powers.

Sacral

This chakra, which is located slightly above your root chakra, should be activated with a slightly different pose. This pose involves sitting on your knees with your heels underneath you. Place your hands on your knees, palms up. This is another mudra that is connected to the sacral chakra. Try to focus your mind on your sacral chakra area as well as any concerns you have that you know are directly related to the health of your sacral chakra. The chant that goes along with the sacral chakra position is "vam," which you should chant while you are in this pose. Just as with your root chakra exercise, this should help to stimulate your sacral chakra and hopefully build a stronger connection between your mind, your body, and the spiritual energy of that chakra.

Solar Plexus

To activate your solar plexus chakra, you should assume the same pose that you did with your sacral chakra—sitting on your knees. However, this time your hand position will be different. Instead of on your knees, you should rest your hands on your stomach, directly touching your solar plexus chakra. You should also incorporate the specific chant that goes along with the solar plexus chakra, which is "ram." Again, try to lose yourself in this chant and feel its vibrations in your solar plexus chakra. Connecting these areas of your body should help stimulate energy flow into the solar plexus chakra and remove some of the blockages that might have arisen within them.

Heart

The next position on this list involves sitting on a chair. Because this chakra is higher on the body, you want to physically raise yourself off the floor to symbolize its higher energy. However, because it is also in the middle of the body and not the top, you are not standing all the way up but instead creating a halfway point. This aspect of the heart chakra posture ensures that you will be channeling the intermediary energy of the heart chakra. Besides sitting on a chair, there is also a mudra associated with this chakra. It involves both hands: Simply place your thumbs together and your index fingers together to form a sort of diamond in front of your chest. Assume this mudra while you are sitting to help channel the energy of the heart chakra. You should also incorporate your chant. In this case, the chant is the word "yam." Hold this posture and try to feel the energy flowing through your heart chakra.

Throat

To activate your throat chakra, you are going to go back to the same position you were in for the sacral and solar plexus chakras. This time, though, there is no corresponding mudra. Instead, you are to focus on elongating your body, especially your neck. Straighten your back and look slightly up and ahead. This helps open up the physical space of your neck, leaving room for spiritual energy to flow throughout. You should also close your eyes to help facilitate your concentration in this pose. The chant associated with the throat chakra is "ham," which you should try to feel especially clearly in your voice box. After all, this chakra is especially about speech, so your chant will be particularly important. Try to feel all that negative verbal energy spilling out, making way for more positive communication.

Third Eye

The pose you want to assume for your third eye chakra is a cross between those for the root and throat chakras. You want to sit down cross-legged, with your back elongated and your eyes closed. This time, closing your eyes is especially spiritually connected to making way for other forms of knowledge to enter your head and to practice seeing with your mind rather than just your blunt senses. The chant for the third eye chakra is simply "om," a chant you have likely already heard of in connection to conventional meditation. Activating your third eye chakra can be achieved using this pose.

Crown

Finally, for your crown chakra, you want to assume a posture similar to the previous one but this time sitting cross-legged on a chair. This gives you the same raised quality as with the position for the heart chakra, but it still incorporates postures from the other chakras, signifying the unity within the chakra system. The final chant for the crown chakra is the same as for the third eye, "om," again borrowing from the previous chakras to symbolize the crown chakra as being above all the others. Using all or some of these poses can be an amazing way to truly activate your chakras and lead you toward a more dynamic relationship with their power.

Pillar 5:
Balance

Besides activating your chakras, there are other aspects of them that need to be accounted for. As we have reiterated throughout this book, your chakras are meant to work together as a system. They have unique qualities individually, but they don't exist in isolation from one another. First of all, the energy flow that we've been talking about makes it so that all of your chakras need to be activated and opened in order to work at their fullest potential individually. However, it is also necessary for your chakras to be in balance with one another, to share common vibrations. You can think of this as similar to a home entertainment system. Even if you have the best devices—speakers, screen, Blu-ray player, and so on—they still need to all be connected to the same Wi-Fi and hooked up to one another in order to create that cohesive system. It's the same with chakras. Not only do they all need to be activated, but they also all need to be in line with one another in order for the entire unit to work as it should. In this pillar, we will shift into a discussion of the chakras as a balancing act. First, we will look into how to evaluate the relative balancing of your chakras, examining how you can tell whether your chakras are blocked or unbalanced. In the next chapter, we will instruct you on how to actually go through the process of balancing your chakras. By the end of this pillar, you should clearly understand the distinct qualities of chakra balancing and know how to do it properly.

Chapter 12:
What Is Chakra Balancing?

Alright, so now you know that chakra balancing is different from chakra activating, but what exactly is it? Well, the main idea of chakra balancing is that it is possible for chakras to be overactive as well as underactive. While it might seem positive for your chakras to be overactive, meaning they are working harder, it isn't necessarily a good thing. In fact, a chakra being overactive is often a sign that your chakras are overall unbalanced. Sometimes when a chakra is underactive, it means that other chakras are leaned on harder. You can think of the chakras as classmates working together on a group project. When everyone is putting in equal effort, then no one should be doing more than their share since the slack is being picked up equally. However, if there are those who are underperforming, skipping group meetings, or not completing their portions of the task, then often the other people will have to overperform, doing more than their due because they need to overcompensate for their classmate's failings. You can see this kind of dynamic played out more subtly within people themselves. Sometimes, when a person feels like they are underperforming at something, they will try to overcompensate in other areas. So, kids who struggle in school might try extra hard at sports, or kids who don't fit in might cultivate an artistic persona outside of school to gain self-esteem. In this sense, we can see how chakras being blocked or underperforming might cause other chakras to become overactive in compensation. You can boost those underperforming or blocked chakras by activating them, but often you will also need to learn not to rely on your other chakras so much to stop them from having to overperform and ensure that your chakras are all functioning equally and in tandem with one another.

What Is the Difference Between Balancing and Activating?

In the previous pillar, we only discussed chakras as being either blocked or unblocked. If one of your chakras was blocked, that meant that it wasn't working at all and there was something stopping it. Well, this is only half true. In fact, most of your chakras will work on some level since each one has a relationship—good or bad—to the facet of life it presides over and the body part it resides in. It's simply a matter of degree. Therefore, some chakras might be more active than others. As we discussed previously, this is the reason activation alone does not necessarily work perfectly, and why you need to balance them as well to make sure all the chakras are operating at the same frequency. If you don't balance, then your activation might result in you relying unevenly on one chakra or another. Balancing ensures that all the chakras are working just enough—not too hard and not too little—allowing each other to have an equal part in your overall health. After all, each chakra is important in its own way, functioning as part of a necessary whole.

How to Tell if Your Chakras Are Imbalanced

Back in Chapter 5 when we discussed individual chakras, we talked a little bit about how to tell when your chakras are blocked. Here, we will go a bit deeper and dive into how your chakras might look if they are overactive or underactive. Understanding why both of these things are negative is essential to the practice of balancing your chakras. In this section, we will first look at overall signs of imbalance then go into the individual chakras and outline some of the signs that the chakra is either overactive or underactive.

Overall Chakras

When your chakras are generally unbalanced, you will likely feel it in your body and your mind. Your health might be all over the place, being healthy one month but sick the next. You might also have uneven pains throughout your body. Psychologically, you might feel like you have a very skewed sense of self-esteem, perhaps being extremely confident in some areas but very shy in others. You might also struggle with relationships, being able to open up to people in some circumstances but not others, or struggling to connect on every level with a partner. This can cause frustration for yourself and others. Finally, you will likely feel spiritually disconnected, unable to truly transcend the everyday and think about those big spiritual questions with any clarity. These symptoms often mean that you have overactive and underactive chakras, leading your body to be severely unbalanced.

Root

When your root chakra is unbalanced, you will feel unrooted in some way; however, the way you feel this and how it manifests will look different depending on whether your root chakra is over- or underactive.

Overactive

An overactive root chakra looks like survival mode. You will feel like you need to greatly overcompensate for your feelings of uprootedness and insecurity. This might lead to an insecure attachment style or very conscious feelings of lostness.

Underactive

If your root chakra is underactive, on the other hand, this will likely manifest slightly differently, creating a more dreamy existence that isn't exactly aware of its lack of roots. You might tend to live in a fantasy world, not truly connected to those around you. It might not be as uncomfortable an existence as an overactive root chakra, but it will likely feel empty and as though it doesn't have much substance.

Sacral

Your sacral chakra's unbalanced symptoms will always affect your relationship to work versus pleasure. However, the side of the spectrum on which it falls will be greatly affected by whether your sacral chakra is over- or underactive.

Overactive

If your sacral chakra is overactive, then your appetite for pleasure will be insatiable. While this might sound like fun, it can end up manifesting as addictive behavior. Addiction to unhealthy food, alcohol, sex, or even dangerous drugs can follow from an overactive sacral chakra, which is completely focused on pleasure.

Underactive

When your sacral chakra is underactive, however, then you will most likely swing to the other side of the spectrum, depriving yourself of even the most harmless pleasures in life. This can lead to you becoming antisocial, prudish, depressed, and even impotent. Through excessive restriction, those with underactive sacral chakras end up with a stunted ability to experience pleasure in life.

Solar Plexus

Because the solar plexus chakra is related to self-esteem, the relative balance of that chakra will almost always manifest in the form of one's level of self-consciousness and feelings of power over others. As with the sacral chakra, the difference between an overactive and an underactive solar plexus chakra will put you on either end of the spectrum.

Overactive

If you have an overactive solar plexus chakra, then you will likely have a highly overinflated sense of self. You might feel superiority over other people and tend toward manipulative or controlling behavior. Those with overactive solar plexus chakras might be perceived as narcissistic by others, and they might even lack empathy and struggle to feel compassion for others.

Underactive

However, when this chakra is underactive, then there is a serious danger of becoming extremely low in confidence, ultimately struggling to have any sense of your own worth. These people will be the complete opposite of the narcissistic overactive chakra, becoming doormats or failing to speak up for themselves.

Heart

Your heart chakra's relative activity manifests itself through relationships. More specifically, it deals with your prioritization of needs and the way you manage boundaries. Where you fall on this spectrum will correspond to the relative over- or underactivity of your heart chakra.

Overactive

Those with overactive heart chakras will be very overeager in relationships and devote themselves entirely to their partner. Though this may sound like a good thing, it can have two distinct negative consequences, one for the individual and one for their loved one. For the individual, this often leads to a loss of self to the relationship, creating a sense that they are completely in that relationship and have no sense of autonomy anymore. For their loved one, this can result in added pressure and crossing of boundaries. A person with an overactive heart chakra might be hurt when loved ones set boundaries or take time for themselves, not understanding the concept of personal space.

Underactive

When someone's heart chakra is underactive, they will be very closed off to love. While they might not be outwardly cold or cruel to others, they might really struggle to let others in, meaning that their relationships struggle to progress past the initial stages. They might be afraid of the vulnerability that comes from loving someone or even of just pursuing someone and thus avoid relationships at all costs.

Throat

The throat chakra is all about voice. Not just your physical voice, but your metaphorical voice as well—how comfortable you feel expressing yourself and arguing your case in front of others. Your degree of confidence in your voice will ultimately be determined by the relative activity of your throat chakra.

Overactive

People with overactive throat chakras will appear similar to those with overactive solar plexus chakras. That is, they will seem overconfident and uninterested in others. However, for the person with an overactive throat chakra, it will manifest in the way they speak. They might tend to talk over others or interrupt often, while at the same time struggling to listen effectively. They might want to seem more intelligent than they really are, causing them to speak with authority on matters they don't really know much about or even outright lie to make themselves look better.

Underactive

On the other hand, those with underactive throat chakras will struggle to express themselves and lack faith in what they say. They might have a strong sense of self-esteem, perhaps coming from a well-balanced solar plexus chakra, but it will be very internal and not easily expressed to others.

Third Eye

The way relative activity manifests in your third eye chakra is through your sense of the world around you. This makes it somewhat similar to the root chakra in terms of its effect on your perception of reality.

Overactive

Having an overactive third eye chakra might not on the surface seem like a bad thing. After all, seeing ahead is good, right? But it can often lead to a kind of perception of reality similar to the underactive root chakra. Those with an overactive third eye chakra might tend to be disconnected from reality or life, seeing only the grander picture and forgetting to appreciate the little things or the earthly pleasures that make life worth living.

Underactive

If you have an underactive third eye chakra, you will be the opposite. Interestingly, most people actually have an underactive third eye chakra. It means that you have not yet come to realize the grander narrative of your life. It is very hard to have a well-balanced third eye chakra early in life as the narrative of your life starts to take shape later as you begin to gain more spiritual wisdom.

Crown

As we know, the crown chakra is associated with the highest realities and your relationship with your spiritual life. It is not something that can actually be over- or underactive. It is merely the summation of your other chakras. Thus, an unbalanced crown chakra is caused by imbalances in your other chakras. Balance all of your chakras equally, and you will unlock the key to a properly balanced crown chakra.

Chapter 13:
How to Rebalance Your Chakras

So, what do you do if your chakras become unbalanced? Well, there are certain techniques you can use to balance them. You already know how to unblock your chakras by using the techniques we discussed back in Chapter 11, but balancing can be trickier. Overactive chakras can especially be difficult to balance since most of them involve major blind spots that can be difficult to acknowledge. In this chapter, we will lead you through some essential techniques for creating balance and harmony among your chakras.

Are Your Chakras Overactive or Underactive?

The first step to balancing your chakras is to determine whether they are underactive or overactive. It might be hard to tell at first, especially if you are experiencing physical symptoms. Even for psychological issues, it might be difficult to determine what exactly your issues are in relation to a particular chakra. Use the diagnostic traits in the last chapter to really ascertain where you stand on the scale of underactive to overactive. This might take a fair amount of self-reflection, especially for those with overactive throat or solar plexus chakras, which tend to manifest as overconfidence. When you are determining this scale, you have to be willing to see the negative side of yourself and possibly confront some very ugly truths. If you are willing to do this, then you will be able to successfully place yourself on the scale of underactive to overactive.

Chakra by Chakra

Now, the process of actually balancing your chakras is slightly different from the process of activation. When it comes to activation, it's all about connecting with each chakra. However, unbalanced chakras tend to be the result of an unmet need somewhere in your life. The unbalanced chakra is either responding to a deficiency by shutting down or overcompensating. In this sense, underactive and overactive chakras are two sides of the same coin; it just might take longer for those with overactive chakras to accept that they have a problem. Thus, the answer to balancing your chakras properly is to feed that unmet need it is responding to. Here, we will go chakra by chakra, explaining the core need that must be met in order for that chakra to be balanced properly.

Root

An imbalance in your root chakra is almost always a response to a sense of rootlessness in your real life. Maybe you've been moving around a lot lately or don't really have a permanent home. Maybe you just exited a long-term relationship and are struggling to redefine your identity independent of that person. Or maybe you are recently retired and don't know what your new life is going to look like. Consistent uncertainty and major changes in life will often manifest through an imbalance in the root chakra. To balance, try to anchor yourself to something concrete. Find something important to you that isn't changing and try to concentrate on it during your meditation practice. This will help you to create a context in which you feel safe without having to change your circumstances permanently.

Sacral

Over- or underactive sacral chakras are usually a response to a lack of constructive or fulfilling pleasure. Both people who abstain from and overdose on pleasure do not have a healthy relationship with it. Those who tend toward addiction struggle to find pleasure that fulfills them in a lasting way. They are always searching for their next "fix" because they lack truly fulfilling pleasure. Similarly, those who abstain from pleasure probably have a hard time connecting to pleasurable activities and are bogged down by shame. In both cases, you need to find an activity that is pleasurable in a more lasting way. Higher quality "junk food" such as cookies from an artisanal French bakery might help you get your sugar fix while also learning something about another culture and expanding your palate. If you're a TV junkie, try putting on a show you've never seen before or an interesting film. It's the same action, but you are expanding your mind at the same time. For both over- and underactive sacral chakras, you need to learn to appreciate "higher" pleasures or pleasures that expand your mind and yourself, leading to a more lasting feeling of fulfillment.

Solar Plexus

Because over- and underactive solar plexus chakras often manifest in terms of your levels of insecurity, you need to find ways to boost your confidence. Even though they might not seem like it, those with overactive solar plexus chakras can often be just as insecure as those with underactive ones. Their excessive boasting is often a kind of overcompensation wherein they feel the need to constantly project their greatness into the world. If you fall into either of these categories, you need to face your insecurities. Try to have a vulnerable moment with a friend where you are neither bragging nor holding back—simply show yourself in an honest light. Or, you can try to face some of your fears: speak in public, meet a new person, fly on an airplane. Any of these things will help you build a strong sense of inner confidence that does not rely on bragging for its foundation.

Heart

People with both over- and underactive heart chakras often have what's called an "insecure attachment style." An insecure attachment style is a method of connecting to other people wherein you never feel truly secure in your relationship with them. You might constantly fear that your loved ones are going to leave you, even if they have given no indication that they are going to do so. Interestingly, the main symptoms of an insecure attachment style include both the signs of an overactive heart chakra (excessive clinginess, lack of boundaries) and an underactive heart chakra (social withdrawal, fear of intimacy). Clearly, we can see that there is a connection and that your heart chakra being over- versus underactive are two sides of the same coin. To help combat both of these reactions, you need to build a stronger faith in the people around you. Remind yourself that they are there for you and that they will love you even if you make mistakes. Maybe even reach out to one of these people and let them know about the insecurity that you have. Even if you are someone who seeks reassurance often and your loved one is sick of giving it, approaching this in a more honest way and framing it around your own self-reflection will help them to give you more meaningful reassurance of their commitment to you. You should also remind yourself of your commitment to others. Often an unbalanced heart chakra, especially an underactive one, can result in fear of commitment since you are afraid of getting hurt. Therefore, reinforcing your own commitment to others is just as important as being reassured of their commitment to you.

Throat

Both overactive and underactive throat chakras are a direct response to a misuse of the voice. A lack of true confidence in your voice or a lack of interest in others' voices will usually be the cause of your overactive or underactive throat chakra. The solution, then, is to work on your communication skills, both input and output. For output, try to isolate the cause of your difficulty speaking. Do you tend to speak over people because you are afraid of not being heard? Are you reluctant to speak up because you are afraid you have nothing interesting to say? One good exercise is to engage in some reflective writing. This allows you to use your "voice" outside the presence of other people. Write about something you're interested in and notice how you feel differently when you are writing versus speaking. For input, you need to do some exercises to improve your listening skills, both as a model for how you should be speaking and to help you listen better to other people. Put on some podcasts and try to be a really active listener. Note what the people are saying and truly take in their information. Then, write another reflective piece about what you liked about their words and how they said them. Reinforcing the two-way nature of communication will help you achieve more balance within your throat chakra.

Third Eye

The main cause of an unbalanced third eye chakra, whether it is manifesting as overactive or underactive, is a lack of connection between your spiritual life and your everyday life. Those with overactive third eye chakras tend to overlook the little everyday things in life, and those with underactive third eye chakras tend to miss the spiritual world. Both of these outcomes are negative since you lack the connection that allows you to live a more spiritually connected life. The best way to help balance your third eye chakra is to practice mindfulness. Mindfulness is the perfect remedy to an unbalanced third eye chakra because it endeavors to do just what you need: connect the spiritual and everyday realms. Noticing the unique tranquility or beauty of a leaf or a butterfly can do wonders for making the everyday spiritual and the spiritual everyday. By cultivating a strong mindfulness practice, you will be able to effectively balance your third eye chakra and create a stronger connection between your spiritual and physical self.

Pillar 6:
Healing

The third major way people interact with their chakras is through healing. Healing your chakras is an ancient practice and happens when people feel like their chakras are blocked or severely unbalanced. You can even experience chakra trauma which can lead to terrible repercussions for the rest of your body. In this pillar, we will be exploring some of the ways in which people specifically use healing practices to help their chakras. First, we will be discussing five different specific healing traditions: Ayurveda, yoga, meditation, psychotherapy, and Reiki. Through these five techniques, you will learn some alternative ways you can interact with your chakras. Then, we will talk about different areas of your life in which chakra healing can have a powerful effect. By the end of this section, you should know how to heal your chakras and what that healing can be used for.

Chapter 14: Practices

There are many different ways to interact with your chakras. We've already talked about a few of them in the last two pillars when we shared techniques for activation and balancing. But here, we are going to talk about some of the methods that are commonly used in healing specifically. These practices range from ancient to modern and cover a wide range of different chakra needs. Selecting a method will depend on a number of factors, including the chakra you are needing to heal, the depth of your trauma, and how you want to go about healing as well as your involvement with other spiritual practices. In this chapter, we will explore five of these methods so that you can construct your own version of chakra healing that incorporates the best of all worlds. At the end of this chapter, you should have a solid understanding of these techniques and a good idea of which ones might be most beneficial to you.

Ayurveda

A system of medicine that runs adjacent to and is often associated with chakras is Ayurveda. It originated in ancient South Asia, just like the chakras. You will probably notice the word "Veda" as part of Ayurveda, which is no coincidence since it is also derived from the same texts as chakras. However, this medicinal practice focuses on holistic healing that incorporates aspects like diet, exercise, psychology, and spirituality, among other things. This approach to medicine is often adopted in the West as a response to the relatively single-minded approaches in Western medicine. With Ayurvedic medicine, you will be able to treat and check in with the whole body. Similar to chakras, it acknowledges that the body is a system, not just a series of unrelated organs, and thus is aware that the process of healing will always involve more than one healing practice. When you engage with Ayurvedic medicine, you will not be able to heal one area of the body without checking in on all the others, which helps to bring a more holistic awareness to the body.

The Four Pillars of Ayurveda

There are actually four main pillars of Ayurveda healing that can be used to help your body. In this section, we will give you an overview of these four pillars.

1. *Tridosha*

   The Tridosha are the three basic bioenergies that circulate through your body. These energies regulate all of your body's functions, helping you to stay alive and healthy.

2. *Triguna*

   The Triguna are the three basic properties of the universe. These consist of the pure, the dynamic, and the inert. They circulate through both our bodies and space to bring connections throughout the world.

3. *Five Mahabhutas*

   The five Mahabhutas are actually something we've already discussed. These are the five basic elements of the world: earth, water, air, fire, and ether.

4. *Chorashi Ousodhi*

   Finally, the Chorashi Ousodhi are the 84 herbs that are central to Ayurveda healing. These herbs are incredibly important and will be vital to our discussion of Ayurveda and the chakras.

Ayurveda and Chakras

So, how do you use this medicine alongside chakras? Well, we have already discussed some of the other aspects of Ayurvedic healing in tandem with the chakras, so in this section, we will focus on the herbs associated with each chakra. This is a fascinating way that we can see the connection between what we put in our bodies and how we feel. These herbs or foods can target specific chakras and help to heal them through the supplementation of necessary nutrients. In this section, we will list the seven chakras alongside the Ayurvedic recommendations for foods or herbs to add to your diet.

Root

For your root chakra, the Ayurvedic texts recommend, unsurprisingly, root vegetables. These will help you quite literally connect with your roots and with the earth. These vegetables often contain traces of dirt or organic matter which can actually be quite healthy to ingest in small doses. This organic matter contains microbes that can do wonders for your guts. Try incorporating more vegetables like carrots, beets, and even potatoes into your diet to help your root chakra heal and grow.

Sacral

For the sacral chakra, you want to eat things that are beneficial to your digestive tract. These are usually anti-inflammatory or gut health-promoting herbs or foods that can do wonders for your sacral chakra's function. There is also a lot of evidence that the way you treat your gut has strong implications for your mental health. Thus, even the psychological aspects of your sacral chakra can be healed through your gut. In general, fermented foods such as kombucha, kimchi, or sauerkraut can be great ways to heal and repair your gut. Two other important herbs have been mentioned in Vedic texts in relation to the sacral chakra for centuries: nagarmotha and gurmar. These are both easy-to-find plants that will do wonders if you are experiencing blocks with your sacral chakra.

Solar Plexus

For your solar plexus chakra, you want to eat things that target your digestive tract as well, but more in the stomach rather than the gut territory. Thus, you want to focus more intensely on anti-inflammatory spices. Cardamom and fenugreek are two of the best herbs to keep your stomach calm and facilitate healthy digestion.

Heart

For your heart chakra, you want to eat for cardiovascular health. Fiber and iron are two very important nutrients to help with your heart and blood systems. From the Ayurveda perspective, garcinia and sandalwood oil are two of the most important herbs to take if you are experiencing a blocked heart chakra.

Throat

For your throat, you want to focus on things that are going to prevent the most common illness associated with a blocked throat chakra: sinus infections. Foods with a high vitamin C content are great, especially fruits like berries and citrus. According to Ayurveda, you should also be taking things that are clarifying since clarity and honesty are traits associated with a well-balanced throat chakra. Thus, sage and guggulu are some of the best ones to take to help balance out and promote health within your throat chakra.

Third Eye

Your third eye chakra needs brain-nourishing food as well as food that promotes clarity of thought and a sound balance between your mind and body. For this, one of the best things recommended by Ayurveda is ginkgo biloba, which helps you to gain that clarity of sight so central to the third eye chakra.

Crown

For your crown chakra, you want to be awakening your highest forms of thinking and self. For this, you should be promoting beauty in your life. This is why Ayurveda promotes lavender as the herb of choice. You can bring lavender into your life in the form of tea, edible lavender, or even burning lavender incense or candles in your space to form that close connection.

Yoga

One practice that we haven't talked about too much directly throughout this book is yoga. We have addressed it peripherally, but it is really one of the most important chakra-adjacent practices. Yoga is incredibly important to your chakra healing journey because it is all about opening up the body. With yoga, you are moving your body in ways you never thought possible, using muscles and stretching joints you didn't even know you had. By engaging in the practice of yoga, you are helping to build better awareness of your body and creating a connection to your chakras. Here, we will list for you some of the best yoga poses for healing each of your chakras.

Root

To heal your root chakra, you should try poses that help to ground you in the earth. Mountain pose and warrior pose are the best for this since they help you with balance and energy flow between your body and the ground below it.

Sacral

One of the leading causes of digestive issues is lack of exercise and movement in the core. For this reason, expanding and compressing your abdomen is especially helpful for the sacral chakra. Forward bends, either standing or sitting, are some of the best ways to release tension within your sacral chakra and help build a better core.

Solar Plexus

The solar plexus is connected with the element of the sun, hence the name. Thus, yoga sun salutation sequences are strongly associated with the solar plexus chakra. Performing a whole sun salutation every day, or at least often, will help you connect with your solar plexus chakra and start your journey toward healing it.

Heart

For your heart, it's all about opening up your chest. Back in Chapter 13, we talked about how embracing vulnerability and opening yourself up to the world is essential for the heart chakra, so you really need to build this into your yoga practice. Cobra pose is a great one because it lifts the chest to the sky, exposing it, stretching it, and elevating it at the same time. Practicing poses like this will build strength in your heart chakra.

Throat

As with the heart, we want to expose this chakra to the world to help banish insecurity and negative thoughts. Cat pose, where you alternately round and arch your back, can help you to really get that flow moving in your neck, creating a sense of positive vulnerability that can help you start getting over some of your communication-based fears.

Third Eye

The third eye chakra is all about gaining a certain perspective on the world. Since our eyes are always at the top of our bodies, it can be good to reverse this by going into child's pose. In this pose, your forehead is on the ground, helping to build that connection between your third eye and the earth.

Meditation

Along the same lines as yoga, we have meditation. Again, we have already brought up meditation periodically throughout this book. When it comes to meditating with your chakras, it's all about connecting that certain facet of life with that certain part of your body. Sometimes, we feel disconnected from our bodies, so focusing on them can help you to find solutions to problems that you never would have thought of otherwise. It can also help you to feel more validated in some of your concerns. If you have had chronic anxiety your entire life but don't know why, it's very useful to be able to point to something concrete that is causing it and have multiple techniques ready so you can work on that anxiety going forward. Thus, meditating with your chakras brings awareness to your meditation practice and to your body as a whole.

Psychotherapy

Some people, especially those who have already been to therapy or are currently in therapy, find it useful to incorporate chakra healing into the process. Looking at your issues through the lens of chakra imbalances can help put some of your thoughts and feelings into words. You might be able to pinpoint certain times in your life, even traumatic incidents, wherein you felt like your chakras might have been thrown out of balance for whatever reason, preventing you from living your life to the fullest. It can help certain psychiatric practices take shape, especially in the form of creating a narrative. However, because of the medical nature of many psychiatry degrees, not all psychiatrists will take chakra healing seriously. If you are serious about chakra healing, you will either want to find a psychotherapist who specializes in chakra healing or at least is open to it as an aspect of your therapeutic journey. After all, there's nothing worse than being dismissed by the person who is meant to help you!

Reiki

Finally, you can use Reiki, a Japanese form of energy healing that can do wonders for your mind and body, especially when used in tandem with your chakras. This practice involves a Reiki healer using their energies to help you promote your own. It is based on a very similar ideology to that of chakras, and thus the two practices can be used in tandem with one another for maximum effect. Find a Reiki healer to help you promote your healing journey. Many healers can be found in most major towns and cities, so consider trying it out to ensure that you are maximizing all resources in relation to energy healing.

Chapter 15: Remedies

Almost everyone has gone through some kind of hardship in their life. And for a lot of people, these struggles can be ongoing. You might suffer from a particular ailment, be it physical or psychological, for many years. If you don't have the tools to help yourself heal from these things, they can seem very scary. Throughout this book, we have listed a number of solutions to many problems that a lot of people face in their lives. In this chapter, we will go more in-depth about each of these ailments that can be helped through chakra healing. You can think of this section as being a kind of index to help you keep track of all the things you can do with the power of chakras. By the end of this chapter, you should have a firm grasp on all the amazing things chakras can do to help you!

Allergies

Seasonal allergies can be a nuisance, but did you know that chakra healing can actually do a lot to alleviate them? This ailment is most often associated with an unbalanced or traumatized heart chakra. Because allergies are related to an overactive immune system, it can often actually be an overactive heart chakra that can be at the root of the issue. By healing your heart chakra, you might be able to relieve your allergies.

Anger Management

Who among us hasn't gotten angry before in their lives? Sometimes anger can be healthy, fueling your sense of justice or self-worth. However, anger can just as often be unhealthy. Some people might even find that they struggle with chronic anger management issues. Fortunately, chakra healing might actually be able to help you with this. Oftentimes, anger stems from deep feelings of being underappreciated or unloved. Thus, the heart chakra and solar plexus chakras—the ones most responsible for your relationships with others—might be blocked if you are experiencing chronic uncontrollable anger. Consider healing these chakras in order to get a better hold on your anger.

Anxiety

Generalized anxiety is one of the most common issues people experience. Especially in a world as chaotic as ours, it's almost impossible not to feel anxious all the time. Chakra healing can do wonders for anxiety. However, since anxiety is so general, almost all chakras have a part to play. Doing some inner work, either alone or with a therapist, can help you trace the specific type of anxiety you happen to be experiencing and thus pinpoint the specific chakra you should be targeting to help it.

Back Pain

Related to anxiety, and therefore to the chakras, is back pain. Because the back is long, it actually connects to all the chakras as well. The spinal cord, which covers your entire back, is said to be the central point of all the chakras. As with anxiety, it is useful to pinpoint where on your back you are experiencing pain in order to identify the correct chakra to heal.

Codependency

It's healthy to depend on other people and have others depend on you. After all, that's what friend circles and family units are for. However, there is a type of dependency that can become unhealthy. This is when someone relies on someone else to an unhealthy degree, perhaps even preventing that other person from being happy in order to stay connected to them. If you are struggling with codependency, then you likely also have an imbalance in your heart chakra—probably overactive. Setting boundaries and balancing out your heart chakra will help you to create healthy relationships with proper distance.

Confidence

Confidence is a topic we have talked about fairly extensively throughout this book. Generally, confidence is like anxiety and can be connected to many of the chakras. However, the lower ones, especially root and sacral, will contain the deepest confidence issues. If you struggle with chronic low self-esteem, it would be best to start with these lower chakras to target those deeper insecurities and then gradually work your way up the chakra system.

Headaches

Migraines or chronic headaches are also common problems for many people. They can be caused by a variety of things ranging from poor gut health to iron deficiencies to eye strain. Thus, a complete balancing of all of your chakras is needed in order to help ameliorate headache issues you might be experiencing. That being said, you might also want to check specifically on your third eye chakra since this tends to be the chakra most associated with headaches.

Joints

Many people also suffer from joint pain. We in the West live very sedentary lifestyles, often with sedentary jobs and hobbies. Sitting too much and not incorporating proper stretching techniques into your everyday life can have devastating consequences on your physical and mental health. Chakra healing, especially if it is combined with yoga practice, can help you to open up some of those joints and build flexibility and bring flow back into your body.

Sex

Even though it remains a taboo topic in many parts of the world, sexual issues are all too common. Whether it's addiction or repression, many people struggle to maintain a healthy relationship with their sexuality. The first step in this process is to focus on your sacral chakra, which is the sexual center of your body, among other things. If you are having sexual issues with a long-term partner, you might also want to check in with your heart chakra to make sure you are providing enough care to one another as well as with your throat chakra to ensure that you are communicating properly. At the end of the day, self-esteem and communication skills are the backbone of a healthy sex life.

Trauma

Finally, it's an unfortunate fact that many people have experienced trauma in their lives. Incidents such as deaths, assaults, or even dramatic moves can cause a person to become traumatized for life. Oftentimes, we hold this trauma in our bodies as well as our minds, which makes chakra healing perfect as a trauma healer. Identifying the source of your trauma will help you to determine which chakra you need to address in order for you to start to heal.

Conclusion

The chakras are a complex system. They consist of many different systems, coincide with countless other spiritual practices, and account for a multitude of functions throughout your body. However, if understood properly, they can be a great asset for your happiness and your health. Throughout this book, we have endeavored to enlighten you on some of the most essential aspects of the chakra healing process. We have led you through all the essential aspects of chakra healing, helping you to see how chakras work. We have detailed the history of the chakras, showing you where they came from and the cultural context in which they evolved. Then, we discussed each of the chakras in isolation and discussed the aspects of life as well as body parts over which each of the chakras presides. Moving forward, we talked about ways you can manage your chakras, either through activation, balancing, or healing. Through all of this, you have gained priceless knowledge about the chakras and the place they can have in your life. You now have the tools to get out there and start healing your chakras!

If you learned from this book, we would really appreciate seeing a review from you. We take a lot of pride in our books and would love to hear what our readers think. Building community and sharing your experience is what spiritual learning and healing are all about. We ensure that our books inform people about things that can help them in their real lives. After reading this book, you are now equipped with the knowledge of one of the most powerful and ancient systems in the world, leading you toward a path of enlightenment and health. Chakra healing isn't for the faint of heart—it's for the ones who really want to dig deep into their innermost selves and heal themselves in ways they didn't know were possible. It might be a long journey ahead, but you are now prepared to go out and do it for yourself. So, go out into the world and get healing!

Glossary

Astrology: A spiritual system based on the positions of stars and planets. Conventionally, it consists of 12 zodiac signs, 7 planets, and 12 houses.

Ayurveda: A type of Vedic healing that focuses on holistic practice, including diet and spirituality.

Blocked chakra: A chakra through which energy is not flowing properly.

Buddhism: A religion that started in Northern India in the 4th century B.C.E.

Chakra: A point on your body that consists of a specific kind of energy. Originating from the Vedic text of Ancient South Asia.

Chakra activation: Helping your chakras to open and work to their full potential.

Chakra balancing: Making sure your chakras are operating at the right frequency relative to one another.

Chakra healing: Bringing your chakras back to proper health.

Chorashi Ousodhi: The 84 herbs that form the foundation of Ayurvedic healing.

Crown chakra: The highest chakra on the body, located at the top of the head. Associated with the highest forms of spiritual learning.

Crystal healing: A spiritual practice that uses the natural vibrations of crystals to heal the body.

Divine chakra: The fifth and highest of the higher chakras, located in infinite space and associated with divine knowledge.

Earth star chakra: The first of the higher chakras located a foot below the feet, associated with the spiritual knowledge of the earth.

Endocrine system: A medical system that connects some of the major organs and glands of the body and which can easily be mapped onto the chakra system.

Five Mahabhutas: The five elements as represented in the Ayurveda system.

Galactic chakra: The fourth chakra in the higher chakra system, located two feet above the head.

Heart chakra: The fourth chakra located in the chest, associated with love and relationships.

Hinduism: An ancient but currently practiced religion developed thousands of years ago in South Asia.

Ida nadi: The nadi on the left side of the body associated with femininity.

Nadi: A parallel chakra system that runs from the left to the right of the body.

Overactive chakra: A chakra that has overcompensated, resulting in exaggerated, often negative versions of that chakra.

Pingala nadi: The nadi on the right side of the body associated with masculinity.

Prana: The chakra word for energy.

Reiki: A type of healing that involves transferring energy through the hands.

Root chakra: The first chakra located at the bottom of the spine, associated with groundedness and stability.

Sacral chakra: The second chakra located in the lower abdomen, associated with intimacy and creativity.

Solar plexus chakra: The third chakra located in the stomach, associated with self-esteem and socializing.

Soul star chakra: The second chakra in the higher chakra system, located six inches above the top of the head.

Sushumna nadi: The center nadi located in the center of the spine, associated with the balance between the ida and pingala nadi.

Tarot: A spiritual system of cards that can be used for divination or self-discovery.

Third eye chakra: The sixth chakra located between the eyes, associated with foresight and wisdom.

Throat chakra: The fifth chakra located in the throat, associated with communication and honesty.

Underactive chakra: A chakra that is operating at a lower frequency in comparison to the others.

Universal chakra: The third chakra in the higher chakra system.

References

Anatomy of the endocrine system. (2019). Johns Hopkins Medicine. https://www.hopkinsmedicine.org/health/wellness-and-prevention/anatomy-of-the-endocrine-system

Ayurveda. (2019, December 2). Hopkins Medicine. https://www.hopkinsmedicine.org/health/wellness-and-prevention/ayurveda#:~:text=What%20is%20Ayurveda%3F

Balanced chakras reduce anxiety. (n.d.). Anxiety. https://www.anxiety.org/balance-your-chakras-let-your-anxiety-melt-away

Burney, R. (2017, January 21). *Chakra levels of consciousness.* Codependency Recovery. https://codependentrecoveryexpert.wordpress.com/2017/01/21/chakra-levels-of-consciousness/

Chakra | religion. (n.d.). Encyclopedia Britannica. https://www.britannica.com/topic/chakra

Chakra elements and their meanings. (n.d.). 7 Chakra Store. https://7chakrastore.com/blogs/news/chakra-elements

Chakra endocrine system | PDF | thyroid | adrenal gland. (n.d.). Scribd. https://www.scribd.com/document/200345709/Chakra-Endocrine-System

Chakra yoga explained—A full guide to the 7 chakras. (n.d.). TINT Yoga. https://tintyoga.com/magazine/chakra-yoga/

Chakras and Buddhism. (2019, August 15). The Zen Universe. https://thezenuniverse.org/chakras-and-buddhism-the-zen-universe/

Chakras, colors & Hindu gods: A closer look at the Hindu system. (n.d.). Lotus Sculpture. https://www.lotussculpture.com/blog/chakras-colors-hindu-gods/

Chakras: A beginner's guide to the 7 chakras. (2016, October 4). Healthline. https://www.healthline.com/health/fitness-exercise/7-chakras#Chakra-101

Complete guide to the 7 chakras: Symbols, effects & how to balance. (2019, June 13). Arhanta Yoga Blog. https://www.arhantayoga.org/blog/7-chakras-introduction-energy-centers-effect/#:~:text=Symptoms%20and%20Effects-

Doniger, W. (2019). *Ganesha | meaning, symbolism, & facts.* Encyclopædia Britannica. https://www.britannica.com/topic/Ganesha

Earth star chakra: What it is & why it matters. (2022, April 12). Be My Travel Muse. https://www.bemytravelmuse.com/earth-star-chakra/

Element of air in tarot cards. (n.d.). Corax. https://www.corax.com/tarot/element-of-air.html

Element of earth in tarot cards. (n.d.). Corax. https://www.corax.com/tarot/element-of-earth.html

Element of fire in tarot cards. (n.d.). Corax. https://www.corax.com/tarot/element-of-fire.html

Element of water in tarot cards. (n.d.). Corax. https://www.corax.com/tarot/element-of-water.html

Feeling out of sorts? Here's how to balance your chakras. (2020, January 4). Well+Good. https://www.wellandgood.com/chakra-balancing/

Fire element crystals: 9 best healing stones to balance your elements. (2021, November 14). Crystals Alchemy. https://crystalsalchemy.com/fire-element-crystals

5 common misconceptions about chakras. (2018, October 1). Himalayan Institute Online. https://himalayaninstitute.org/online/5-common-misconceptions-chakras/

5 ways to heal your knee chakras. (2012, September 12). Mindbodygreen. https://www.mindbodygreen.com/articles/how-to-heal-your-knee-chakras

The genital or pubic chakra. (n.d.). Malankazlev. http://malankazlev.com/kheper/topics/chakras/Pubic.htm

Get to know the seven chakras. (n.d.). Yoloha Yoga. https://yolohayoga.com/en-ca/blogs/yoloha-life/get-to-know-the-seven-chakras#:~:text=A%20person%20with%20an%20overactive

Hindu deity Vishnu. (n.d.). Khan Academy. https://www.khanacademy.org/humanities/art-asia/beginners-guide-asian-culture/hindu-art-culture/a/hindu-deity-vishnu#:~:text=Vishnu%20is%20the%20god%20of

How attachment styles affect adult relationships. (n.d.). Helpguide. https://www.helpguide.org/articles/relationships-communication/attachment-and-adult-relationships.htm#:~:text=Attachment%20styles%20and%20how%20they%20shape%20adult%20relationships&text=Those%20with%20insecure%20attachment%20styles

How do you know if your chakras are open? (2020, May 12). Beadnova. https://www.beadnova.com/blog/12981/how-do-you-know-if-your-chakra-is-open-or-blocked

How to activate chakras in your body? (2021, February 4). Best Wellness Resort. https://www.dharanaretreat.com/blogs/how-to-activate-chakras-in-your-body/#:~:text=Sit%20on%20your%20knees%2C%20with

How to identify & heal blocked chakras. (2019, January 27). Mindvalley Blog. https://blog.mindvalley.com/symptoms-of-blocked-chakras/

Hueneburg, K. (2021, October 19). *The complete guide to understanding the chakras.* One Yoga. https://oneyogathailand.com/the-complete-guide-to-understanding-the-chakras/

Importance of foot chakra. (2015, May 1). Reiki Rays. https://reikirays.com/21123/importance-of-foot-chakra/

Jackson, D. (2020a, August 18). *Higher chakras series: Exploring the universal chakra.* AskAstrology. https://askastrology.com/universal-chakra/

Jackson, D. (2020b, August 29). *Higher chakras series: Exploring the galactic chakra.* AskAstrology. https://askastrology.com/galactic-chakra/

Jackson, D. (2020c, September 4). *Higher chakras series: Exploring the divine gateway chakra.* AskAstrology. https://askastrology.com/divine-gateway-chakra/

Learn about your seven chakras and how to keep them in balance. (2020, January 8). Chopra. https://chopra.com/articles/learn-about-your-seven-chakras-and-how-to-keep-them-in-balance

Mughal dynasty | history, map, & facts. (2018). Encyclopædia Britannica. https://www.britannica.com/topic/Mughal-dynasty

9 powerful air element crystals for inspiration. (2021, November 15). Crystals Alchemy. https://crystalsalchemy.com/air-element-crystals

9 powerful water element crystals for love and inner peace. (2021, November 17). Crystals Alchemy. https://crystalsalchemy.com/water-element-crystals

Peters, J. (2021, August 3). *Exploring the spiritual meaning of lower back pain.* Spirituality & Health. https://www.spirituality-health.com/exploring-the-spiritual-meaning-of-lower-back-pain

Planets and chakras. (n.d.). Sahaja Yoga Portal. https://www.sahajayogaportal.org/en/astrology/planets-chakras.html#:~:text=Chakras%20display%20the%20nature%20and

A primer of the chakra system. (2020, August 20). Chopra. https://chopra.com/articles/what-is-a-chakra#:~:text=The%20chakra%20system%20holds%20your

Raveesh, B. (2013). Ardhanareeshwara concept: Brain and psychiatry. *Indian Journal of Psychiatry, 55*(6), 263. https://doi.org/10.4103/0019-5545.105548

Ray, D. A. (2021, February 20). *Ayurveda and the 7 chakras: A step by step guide.* Amit Ray. https://amitray.com/ayurveda-and-the-7-chakras-a-beginners-guide/

7 chakras in human body, significance & how to balance them. (n.d.). Art of Living (India). https://www.artofliving.org/in-en/meditation/meditation-benefits/seven-chakras-explained

Seven crystals associated with the earth element. (n.d.). Exemplore. https://exemplore.com/healing/Seven-Crystals-Associated-with-the-Earth-Element

Symptoms of allergies, how to cure and get treatment of allergies. (n.d.). Rudraksha Ratna. https://www.rudraksha-ratna.com/articles/allergies

Tantrik studies. (2016, February 6). Tantrik Studies. https://hareesh.org/blog/2016/2/5/the-real-story-on-the-chakras

Vail, L. F. (2018). *The origins of Buddhism.* Asia Society. https://asiasociety.org/education/origins-buddhism

van der Kolk, B. (2014, September 25). *The body keeps the score: Brain, mind, and body in the healing of trauma.* Viking Press.

What are nadis? Your guide to energy channels in your body. (2021, April 19). Brett Larkin Yoga. https://www.brettlarkin.com/nadis-in-yoga/

What is ida nadi? (n.d.). Yogapedia. https://www.yogapedia.com/definition/5374/ida-nadi

What is ishvara? (n.d.). Yogapedia. https://www.yogapedia.com/definition/5296/ishvara

What is nadi? (n.d.). Yogapedia. https://www.yogapedia.com/definition/5028/nadi

What is sadashiva? (n.d.). Yogapedia. https://www.yogapedia.com/definition/7680/sadashiva

What is the origin of the chakra system? (n.d.). Indigo Massage & Wellness. https://indigomassagetherapy.com/uncategorized/what-is-the-origin-of-the-chakra-system/#:~:text=The%20chakra%20system%20originated%20in

What is the soul star chakra and how to connect to it. (n.d.). Zennedout. https://zennedout.com/what-is-the-soul-star-chakra-and-how-to-connect-to-it/

Where did Buddhism originate? (n.d.). History Hit. https://www.historyhit.com/where-did-buddhism-originate/

Why Lord Shiva is the most fascinating Hindu deity. (2009). Learn Religions. https://www.learnreligions.com/lord-shiva-basics-1770459

Willis, K. K. (2016, January 18). *Grief and rage: The connection between 4th and 1st chakras.* Lucid Body. https://lucidbody.com/blog/grief-and-rage-the-connection-between-4th-and